Chinese Political Thought in the
Twentieth Century

CHESTER C. TAN is Professor of History at New York University. A native of China, he came to the United States on a State Department fellowship, and received his Ph.D. degree from Columbia University. He has published books and articles both in China and in the United States. His works include *The Boxer Catastrophe, China's Foreign Relations Under the Ming Dynasty,* and *Chinese Jurisdiction Over Aliens Before the Opium War.*

CHINESE
POLITICAL THOUGHT
IN THE
TWENTIETH CENTURY

Chester C. Tan

DOUBLEDAY & COMPANY, INC.

Garden City, New York

1971

Preface

THIS book is a study of the main currents of Chinese political thought from the Revolution of 1911 to the present. It examines the tenets and assumptions of the major doctrines, describes their origins and development, and estimates the contributions of the leading thinkers. In dealing with various theories and ideas, I have aimed at accurate presentation as a first step toward correct understanding and fair criticism.

Political thought is not created in a vacuum: it is part of a nation's political life. I have therefore tried to emphasize the relation between ideas and circumstances—the social environment in which the thinkers arise and the intellectual cross-currents that serve as a formative force in the progress of thought. In delineating major trends or assessing individual thinkers, I have paid close attention to chronological sequence. This helps not only to trace the development of thought but also to place in proper perspective its interaction with social circumstances. It also aids in explaining any inconsistencies of thought that might be caused by a change of circumstance.

While organizing my material around significant political and social movements, I have not neglected the importance of personality in intellectual developments. Prime thinkers have been dealt with separately, and special attention has been paid to their influence upon the main lines of thought. Where appropriate, I have provided a brief account of the life of the writer, emphasizing that part of his background and character that seems to explain the peculiarities of his ideas.

The twentieth century has been for China a century of revolution, in which the leading minds have gravitated toward political strategy and the means of national reconstruction. But practical discussions have also involved fundamental principles. I have given attention both to the opinions of the political leaders that have influenced the nation's thinking and to the more systematic thought that formed the foundations of the major doctrines. On the other hand, I have excluded or given only passing reference to the abstract ideas that had little connection with the main stream of political thought.

In an age of crisis in which response to situations was immediate, it was only natural that ideas often found expression in articles and tracts. But though polemic in form, some of these writings are not less systematic than formal treatises. I have therefore drawn upon material from various magazines, journals, pamphlets, and speeches, considering it an essential source of contemporary political thought.

Chinese thought in the twentieth century was dominated by the controversy over tradition. How much of old belief and philosophy should be retained and how much of Western culture adopted were the concern of all those interested in political reform. To meet the needs of some readers who are unfamiliar with traditional Chinese thought, I have devoted the first chapter of this book to its examination and appraisal, with special reference to the agitation for change from the late nineteenth century to the Revolution of 1911.

I am grateful to Columbia University for a grant which enabled me to carry out the research for this study in its early stages. My sincere thanks go to Professors C. Martin Wilbur and Howard L. Boorman for their constant interest and support. I should also like to thank Mrs. Anne Freedgood and Miss Lisa Johnson, of Doubleday, for their editorial assistance.

C. C. T.

Contents

*Chinese Political Thought in the
Twentieth Century*

Chapter I

INTRODUCTION

THE advent of the twentieth century inaugurated a new era in the history of Chinese political thought. After two thousand years during which Confucianism had been the dominant doctrine—both the principle underlying the political and social structure and the essence of Chinese morality and culture—tradition was subjected to sustained attack and Western influences penetrated deep into Chinese culture.

At the close of the feudal age, Confucius (551–479 B.C.) attempted to restore order to a world in which central authority had collapsed and feudal lords struggled among themselves to gain hegemony. As a means of achieving peace and stability, Confucius preached "rectification of names," i.e., titles connoting certain specific rights and duties. Ideally, this system, strictly adhered to, would eliminate conflict, disorder, and usurpation.

Confucius' unique contribution, however, was the moral order he endeavored to build. The crucial principle of his philosophy is *jen*. The word has been translated as "benevolence," but it means much more. Confucius defined a man of *jen* as one who is "courteous in his private life, deferential in public service, and faithful to other people."[1] He asserted that "the firm, the resolute, the simple, and the modest is near to *jen*."[2] *Jen* is therefore the manifestation of what is genuine in human nature and the doing of what is right and proper. It embraces all the moral qualities a man should exhibit in his relations with others, emphasizing sympathetic fellowship among men. It advocates unselfish assistance to others: "A man of *jen*, wishing to establish himself, seeks also to establish others; wishing to elevate himself, he seeks to elevate others."[3]

The Confucian state is founded not on a legal system but on moral principles. "If you govern men by laws and keep them in order by penalties," says Confucius, "they will avoid penalties, but lose their sense of shame. If you govern them by the principles of virtue, and keep them in order by *li*, they will retain their sense of shame, and moreover will become good."[4] *Li* signifies decorum, ritual, or rules of propriety. While law is backed by force, *li* relies on public opinion and social pressure. *Li* is the nucleus of customs that regulate men's lives gently but effectively. Although it was later to develop into tedious and cumbersome ceremony, Confucius placed *li* second to virtue. Given a virtuous rustic and a well-mannered un-virtuous man, Confucius would have preferred the former.

Government by virtue was to create a new governing class. Integrity and ability, not noble birth, were to be the qualifications for officials. To train men accordingly, Confucius revised the educational system. To reform a society in which only aristocratic families could afford tutors for their children, Confucius offered education to qualified students, regardless of birth and wealth. In doing so, he made it possible for people of humble condition to enter government service and rise in the social scale.

Although his philosophy incorporated certain democratic concepts, Confucius did not advocate government by the people. He did not wish to overthrow the hereditary prince, insisting instead on loyalty to and respect for him. He proposed that men of virtue should assume the responsibility of governing within a monarchical structure, but for the benefit of the people. This view was further developed by Mencius (c. 385–303 B.C.), the great disciple of Confucius, who held that it is the duty of the government to see that the people are well maintained, with attention to the careful inculcation of filial and fraternal duties. Mencius goes beyond Confucius in upholding the rights of men. The people, Mencius says, are the most important element in a state, the sovereign the least. If a ruler outrages humanity and justice, he may be put to death.

Another highly influential school of thought in old China was Taoism. This doctrine has traditionally been attributed to Lao Tzu, a contemporary of Confucius, although modern research suggests that the *Book of Tao*[5] was composed in a later period, at some time during the fourth century B.C. Taoism teaches that the secret of the universe is in its natural development. It preaches the wisdom of inaction and the value of quietude and calm. Inaction, however, does not mean inertia; rather, Taoism opposes action that is unnatural, strained, calculated, or self-assertive. Taoists denounce the Confucian principles of humanity and justice, the rules of propriety, and the institutions of ceremonials and rituals, all of which they regard as artificial and futile restraints on natural growth.

Taoism further scorns governmental interference, punishment, and war. An incipient anarchism, it asserts that "when the government is dull and lazy, its people are pure and happy; when the government is efficient and sharp, its people are discontented."[6] Denying the efficacy of governmental regulation and social convention, it advises curbing one's desire and opposes the quest for the knowledge that stimulates desire. "Abandon wisdom and eject knowledge," it counsels, "and the people will be benefited a hundredfold."[7]

The movement of nature, according to Taoism, consists in reversion. "All things, however flourishing they may be, return to their roots."[8] Thus weakness is preferable to strength, for things decay after reaching their prime;

tolerance is preferred to dogmatism, which provokes opposition. He who knows glory but remains humble will preserve sufficient power. These precepts not only describe the operation of nature and life, they are offered as rules for individual conduct. As revelations of the paradoxical nature of human relations they become maxims for self-preservation.

The Taoist rejection of authority, while conducive to individual freedom, of course undermines the very foundation of social life. In their reliance upon the state of nature, Taoists neglect man's social character and natural fallibility. Even so, the emphasis of Taoist thought on simplicity provides a valuable safeguard against hypocrisy and rigidity; its principle of relativity is of great significance in terms of the Chinese mentality. By discouraging aggressiveness, Taoism fosters a certain serenity in its adherents.

Legalism, the third major political philosophy in Chinese history, originated with Kuan Tzu (seventh century B.C.) and culminated in the thought of Han Fei Tzu (d. 233 B.C.). Legalism developed in the Age of Warring States (403–221 B.C.), a time of intensified struggle for power in which feudal princes either conquered or were forced to submit. To achieve hegemony over other states it was necessary for the feudal prince to make his state strong and wealthy. It is not surprising, therefore, that while the Confucianists held that cultivation of virtue was the best way to achieve good government, the Legalists believed in law and force as the only viable policy.

Legalists separate morality from politics in their refusal to entrust the maintenance of social order to virtue alone. Instead, they advocate an authoritarian government with a legalistic basis. Law is regarded as an instrument with which the ruler upholds his supremacy over the people. It regulates social relations in detail and provides for every political and administrative contingency. To ensure the primacy of the law, heterodoxy and nonconformism must be prohibited. Law is the sole standard for determining the propriety of word and deed.

It would follow, then, that laws, in order to be effective, must be enforceable. The sovereign, if he is to consolidate his position as the supreme ruler, must have absolute power.

In the last phase of feudalism, political crises often arose from attempts at usurpation. Ministerial obeisance was a major problem of statecraft. Han Fei Tzu devotes much attention to the discussion of *shu,* or methods of government. In order to sustain absolute control of his ministers, Han advises, the ruler must forestall their conspiracies, prevent their factional struggles, avoid favoritism, and refrain from relying on any single adviser. Above all, the ruler must keep his plans secret, lest his ministers anticipate them and plot to circumvent them.

The Legalist theories of law *(fa),* power *(shih),* and statecraft *(shu)* have one aim: to maintain the ruler's supremacy. The basic idea of Legalist absolutism is that the state and its components belong to the ruler and exist to further his interests. The people may benefit from the power and wealth of the state, but the increase of economic and military power essentially is intended to strengthen the position of the ruler.

Legalism was adopted by the state of Ch'in, which eventually became strong enough to subdue other feudal states. In 221 B.C. China was unified by the first emperor of Ch'in, who abolished feudalism, established a unitary government, and widely extended the influence of his empire. But Ch'in's rigid and oppressive despotism proved to be too much for his subjects to tolerate: revolt became widespread enough to topple the Ch'in dynasty in 207 B.C.

Its fourteen-year duration was to be the shortest in Chinese history.

At the beginning of the Han dynasty (206 B.C.–A.D. 219), Taoism, Legalism, and Confucianism competed to gain governmental favor. The adoption of Confucianism as the national doctrine in 136 B.C. finally ensured its dominance. Confucianism, when compared with other major philosophies, has obvious advantages. Its humanism is in accord with popular sentiment; its doctrine of the golden mean avoids extremism; its emphasis on the family as the basic social unit recognizes and exploits Chinese custom. It has great appeal for the ruler through its ethical values, which promote political and social stability. But despite the ascendancy of Confucianism, Taoism and legalism continued to exert an influence on the Chinese mind; even Confucianists had to acknowledge that government by virtue must be supplemented by law.

The Confucianist doctrine regards the state as an enlarged family and the emperor as one whose paternalistic function it is to "teach and nourish" the people, that is, to develop their moral character and take good care of them. The emperor holds his office by the mandate of Heaven, and is responsible to Heaven alone. Though Mencius maintains that "Heaven sees as the people see and hears as the people hear," there are no channels through which the people can exert their will against that of the emperor. Their sole recourse is rebellion, which—if successful—effectively deprives the emperor of his heavenly mandate. This theory may provide the justification for a successful rebellion, but it can hardly be interpreted as even a rudimentary precursor of government by the people.

Tradition requires the emperor to rule in accordance with Confucian principles, but if he chooses to rule despotically, there is no political remedy except rebellion. Even so, owing to an emphasis on moral cultivation, and the absence of an efficient administrative machinery, laissez faire prevailed in the traditional government. "Imperial power," the Chinese were fond of saying, "is as far away as the sky above."

From the standpoint of modern democracy, the Confucian state left much to be desired. Not only did it deny the people their political rights, it also disregarded the principle of equality. If its civil service examination provided an opportunity for humble men to rise in the political hierarchy, it also gave rise to a scholar-gentry class that was sharply distinguished from the common people. Rules of propriety may contribute to the moral order, but they are plainly inadequate to cope with the complexity of modern commercial and industrial relations. Moreover, the Confucian concept of grand unity, which viewed the Chinese Empire as a cultural universe embracing all of humanity, is obviously unsuitable to the modern world of sovereign, independent states committed to power politics.

The traditional institutions, which had served China for two thousand years, showed their weaknesses under the impact of the West in the nineteenth century. After sustaining two defeats by the European powers between 1839 and 1860, China undertook to strengthen itself along Western lines. Unfortunately, the reform of the 1870's was confined to military and industrial innovations. It was the Chinese conviction at this time that weapons and techniques could be changed, but not principles and institutions.

The limited reform, however, failed to save China from the disastrous defeat by Japan in 1895. As a result, some Chinese thinkers realized that a different approach was necessary if their country was to regain its strength. By this time China had been exposed, in several ways, to new ideas. There were contacts with Western commercial communities in the treaty ports and nearby foreign colonies, an intensification of missionary activity, translations of Western works on humanities and science, and teachings in the modern language schools.

In 1898, a reform movement led by K'ang Yu-wei was directed at institutional change. K'ang, who had learned about Western history and institutions through translated works, was basically a Confucian scholar. He advanced the idea that Confucius was a reformer, and he based his reform theory on the Confucian doctrine of Three Ages. Under this doctrine, according to K'ang, human civilization advances according to a fixed sequence: from the Age of Disorder through the Age of Approaching Peace to the Age of Great Peace. The more numerous the reforms, the faster will be the advance. On the other hand, if a nation that has entered upon a new age insists upon clinging to the institutions of the old, great disorder will result. K'ang considered his era to be the Age of Approaching Peace, in which the practice of self-government and the introduction of a constitution were required.[9]

In extending reform to political institutions, K'ang differed from the reformers of the 1870's. Although he himself proposed only moderate institutional reforms of an administrative nature to the emperor, his followers were outspoken in their advocacy of radical change. For example, Liang Ch'i-ch'ao (1873–1929) expounded the theory of popular rights in the context of parliamentary government, and T'an Ssu-t'ung (1865–1898) advocated the abandonment or reshaping of the traditional culture. T'an emphatically attacked the Confucian canons of moral obligations which, he felt, impaired individual liberty and were exploited by rulers in order to oppress their subjects.[10]

Not surprisingly, institutional reform was strongly opposed by the conservatives who contended, in the Confucian tradition, that good rule depends on the moral state of the people and not on the form of government. They would cultivate human virtue rather than political change. If a government is run by unworthy men, new institutions only provide new opportunities for corrupt self-interest.

The conservatives had no doubt that its moral teachings had rendered China superior to the West. Occidentals were said to value utility above all other considerations. Thus they might build wealthy and powerful countries, but were unable to achieve harmony and unity.[11] The conservatives feared that substantial institutional changes would undermine the Confucian doctrine by reducing it to a platitude.

A syncretic view, intended to strike a balance between reformism and conservatism, was offered by Chang Chih-tung (1837–1909), a brilliant scholar and a powerful Chinese official. In his *Exhortation to Study (Ch'üan-hsüeh P'ien*, 1898) Chang criticized conservatives and reformers alike for their extremism. He reduced his solution to the formula: "Chinese learning for substance, Western learning for function." Traditional principles were to remain the foundation of Chinese culture; the adoption of Western techniques and methods was to revitalize Chinese economic and military systems. Although he spoke of "institutional" reform, Chang was interested strictly in changes affecting administrative method, not the principle of government. He defended the traditional institutions vigorously and his loyalty to the Manchu monarchy was never in question.

K'ang Yu-wei's reform was doomed to failure when the empress dowager, the real power behind the throne, gave her support to the conservative factions in the fall of 1898. Acting swiftly, she imprisoned the emperor for adopting K'ang's proposals, and rescinded his decrees.

A number of reformers were executed or punished, but

K'ang Yu-wei and Liang Ch'i-ch'ao managed to escape to Japan. There both men continued to advocate the theory of enlightened government. A revolutionary movement was gathering force, however, in China itself and among Chinese expatriates.

The first Chinese revolutionary party was founded in Honolulu in 1894 by Sun Yat-sen. Known as the Hsing-chung Hui (Revive China Society), it established its headquarters a year later in Hong Kong. Its purpose was to expel the Manchus and replace them with a republican government. Uprisings, which proved to be abortive, were organized in Canton and Hui-chou, Kwangtung Province. The idea of revolution was premature, and Sun Yat-sen could recruit only a very small following. But the Boxer Rebellion (1900) turned the tide. Shocked by the utter ineptitude of the Manchu court during the crisis and the humiliating treaty imposed by the foreign powers in consequence, many Chinese intellectuals began to look in the direction of revolution.

New revolutionary organizations proliferated, among them the Patriotic Institute (Ai-kuo Hsüeh-she) in Shanghai, the China Resurgence Society (Hua-hsing Hui) in Hunan, and the Recovery Society (Kuang-fu Hui) in Chekiang. A number of revolutionary magazines were issued; many of them were smuggled into China after publication in Japan.[12] Among those that originated in China, *Supao* (*The Kiangsu Journal*) was the most notable. It was in this magazine, in 1903, that the classicist Chang Ping-lin published his pungent anti-Manchu articles. They so infuriated the regime that the journal was suppressed and the author sentenced to a term of imprisonment in the Shanghai International Settlement.

In the decade before the Chinese Revolution of 1911, the reformism of K'ang Yu-wei's group no longer dominated the trends of political thought. Instead, revolutionary ideas first challenged, then eclipsed K'ang's philosophy. The reformists, driven into exile by the empress dowager, made their headquarters in Japan. Their major publication, *The New People's Magazine (Hsin-min Ts'ung-pao*, 1902–1907), was edited by Liang Ch'i-ch'ao, a vigorous thinker and voluminous writer who was gaining a reputation equal to that of K'ang himself.

The reformists opposed revolution on the ground that it would lead to destruction and disorder and eventually to foreign intervention and perhaps even partition of China by the great powers.[13] They proposed gradual change, beginning with improving the people's ability to participate in political matters.[14] In his *A People Made New*, Liang Ch'i-ch'ao urged the transformation of the Chinese way of life, especially in the area of public morals. Applying Darwinism to social concerns, Liang maintained that there are no absolute moral principles. This was a rather progressive idea in view of the prevalent conservative belief in the inflexibility of Confucian morality.

Significantly, however, Liang did not challenge the traditional moral principles themselves, but asserted that Chinese morality was mainly concerned with personal relations. As such, it was deficient in regard to relations between the individual and society. He urged adoption of modern concepts of state, civil rights, liberty, progress, self-government, and independence.[15] While the notion of renovating the people is traceable to the Confucian classics, the idea of adopting Western public morals is original with Liang.

Moral renovation would be a long process, which might be preceded by the adoption of democratic principles only at the risk of chaos. Thus, during the period of transition, enlightened absolutism was the desirable policy. In a manner worthy of the logic of Thomas Hobbes, Liang defined the new system as a government in which absolute power is exercised by the sovereign in the interests of the people. Even so, Liang's concept of enlightened despotism quite obviously resembled the Confucian doctrine of benevolent government.

The reformists inveighed against republicanism, urging constitutional monarchy as the best form of government. They anticipated that the transition from enlightened absolutism to constitutional monarchy would take from ten to twenty years.[16] The monarchy, whether enlightened or constitutional, should be headed by the Manchu emperor, whose continued rule was regarded as crucial to the peaceful transition.[17] Partly because of their eagerness to maintain order and stability, and partly because of their personal loyalty to the emperor whose confidence they had enjoyed, the reformists fought vigorously against the revolutionary attempt to overthrow the Manchu dynasty.[18] In doing so, they ignored the intensified development of Chinese nationalist sentiment. They gallantly tried to sustain a regime that had rapidly fallen into a decline.

Liang did not think social revolution necessary in a China where there was no great concentration of landed or industrial wealth: China's need was for the formation of capital for increased production. Socialism, he predicted, would destroy individual incentive and add to bureaucratic tyranny. Liang was in agreement with such social policies as public ownership of utilities, improvement of factory conditions, and progressive income tax, but he believed that private ownership is not only the motivating factor for economic development, but the source of civilization as well. Against the background of the Confucian welfare state, it was not difficult for Liang to subscribe to a moderate social reform. He regarded socialism, however, as a noble doctrine for the future.[19]

In 1905 the T'ung-meng Hui (League of the Common Alliance) was organized in Tokyo under the leadership of

Sun Yat-sen. The organ of this revolutionary party, the *People's Journal* (*Min-pao*), was first published in Japan the same year. Among its editors were Chang Ping-lin and three of Sun Yat-sen's faithful disciples: Hu Han-min, Wang Ching-wei, and Chu Chih-hsin. The *People's Journal* lost no time in engaging Liang Ch'i-ch'ao in prolonged and fierce debate. In a series of articles, it argued that revolution was necessary to overthrow the Manchu regime, which was an obstacle to the building of a nation-state, the establishment of a democracy, and the practice of land nationalization. The writers did not think that revolution would lead to internal chaos or foreign intervention: theirs would be an orderly "civilized" revolution, not a mob disturbance. The revolutionary government would observe international law, recognize the treaties previously concluded by China, and make sincere efforts to cultivate friendly relations with other nations.[20] Imperialism was not then the specific target of the revolution.

It has been asserted in books recently published on the Chinese mainland that revolutionaries at the turn of the century were advocating a bourgeois insurgency, while paying scant attention to the lower classes.[21] While it is true that the revolutionaries, exiled to Japan, did little to arouse the Chinese masses, it is incorrect to say that they favored the bourgeoisie over the lower classes. Wang Ching-wei, for example, wrote that the humble members of society, though occupying the lowest place, carried the heaviest burden of the nation. For Chu Chih-hsin, the revolutionary force would come not from the rich and powerful, nor entirely from the secret societies, but mainly from the lowest classes.[22] In view of the ignorance of the masses, some revolutionaries did hold that the middle class should assume leadership in the revolution, but they were referring to the intellectuals. Although they thought leadership by the educated was necessary, they considered the morality of the peasants to be superior to that of the scholars, especially the Confucianists.[23]

The revolutionaries' dedication to the overthrow of the Manchus was indeed the objective that unified them notwithstanding their conflicting views on other issues. But though the anti-Manchu slogans of the revolutionaries seemed vengeful, they were not concerned primarily with persecuting the Manchus as a race. Their chief aim was to restore political power to the Chinese people. If the Manchus should choose to stay in China proper and become assimilated with the Chinese, they would be allowed to do so.[24]

The revolutionaries espoused republicanism while vigorously denouncing enlightened absolutism as a restrictive ideal only too consistent with prevailing autocratic forms. Any political system that did not permit the people to rule themselves could not serve as a proper transition to the complexities of a democracy. A constitution, if it is to be viable, must be made by the people rather than granted by the ruler.[25]

When *Min-sheng chu-i* (Principle of the People's Livelihood) was first announced in the *People's Journal* in 1905, it was intended to be the Chinese name of socialism. China was not yet industrialized; capitalism had not yet developed sufficiently to cause serious social problems, and Sun Yat-sen wished to introduce socialistic techniques in time to avoid the painful consequences he believed would otherwise inevitably follow. Moreover, socialism obviously could be more easily introduced when there were still relatively few powerful capitalists to oppose it.[26]

Sun Yat-sen favored land nationalization according to the principle of the single tax advocated by Henry George. Such a method would not constitute full socialization, but it was believed to be the easiest to effect and the one most suitable to a predominantly agricultural country. The Sunists planned to begin their socialist program at the early, or military stage of the revolution, when the revolutionary government would have full power to make the radical changes that the people would have been conditioned to expect. They feared that if socialism was not adopted during the revolution itself, later economic developments would strengthen capitalist resistance.[27] The speedy collapse of the Manchu regime in 1911, however, hardly left a military period in which the revolutionaries could launch their scheme. As a result, although they established a republic, they were forced to shelve their socialist program.

The editor of the *People's Journal*, the famous scholar Chang Ping-lin (1868–1936), also known as Chang T'ai-yen, was a brilliant writer given to archaic words, as well as a leading authority on Chinese classics, philology, and history. In 1906, immediately after his release from prison in Shanghai, he went to Japan. There he joined the T'ung-meng Hui and assumed the editorship of the *People's Journal*. In his new role, Chang took the opportunity to propound original ideas not always in accordance with Sun Yat-sen's principles.

Chang has been described as an eccentric with a quaint philosophy, but the underlying harmony of his apparent inconsistencies may be sensed once it is realized that he acknowledged two philosophical levels, the metaphysical and the social. Metaphysically, the highest ideal is to end not only the state but all forms of life and strife.[28] Socially, however, it is necessary to recognize what actually exists and make the best of it. The state is the basest of things, but it is essential to our protection. Until we are socially capable of dispensing with it, we cannot but choose to maintain it.[29]

Chang, pursuing his dualistic vision, stressed the importance of moral behavior to a revolution. He was able to condemn selfishness, cowardice, jealousy, and corruption while asserting the seemingly contradictory idea of individual freedom unrestricted by the so-called principles of justice. In fact he believed in a moral conscience shaped by a free will. He held, with the Fa Hsiang (Dharma-Character) school of Buddhism, that precepts rise from the cognition of the mind.[30] If the individual mind is the arbiter of truth, it follows logically that virtues cannot be imposed by social rules.

Chang's proto-anarchic temperament could not have appealed to revolutionists intent upon building a politically modern state through progressive social programs. Nevertheless, he made a substantial contribution to the revolutionary cause during his two-year editorship of the *People's Journal.* His reputation as a classical scholar commanded the respect of the intellectuals, whose support was crucial to the initial success of the revolution. Of all the contributors to the party magazine, Chang was the one best qualified to reply to the outstanding interpreter of Confucius, K'ang Yu-wei. Chang's influence reflected the complexity of intellectual trends at the turn of the century when the appeal of Western pragmatism was seen in varying degrees as a challenge to an equally attractive Eastern tradition.

In the decade before the Revolution of 1911, the revolutionists disagreed over the question of the relevance of Chinese tradition. One group, represented by the *Kuots'ui (National Quintessence)* magazine, believed that national identity emerges from a knowledge of national history and culture.[31] Others, realizing the close relationship between monarchism and Confucianism, could not attack the one while condoning the other. Thus Confucianism was criticized for its principle of loyalty to and support

of the monarchy, and for its perpetuation of a social hierarchy and class distinction.[32] Even Lao Tzu did not escape denunciation: his teachings were condemned for
their implicitly submissive attitude toward tyranny.[33]

Contributors to the *People's Journal* were more concerned with expounding their revolutionary theories than
with attacking the traditional faith. Even so, they generally
denounced Confucian politicians for their sycophancy, opportunism, and indifference to the popular sensibility.[34]
Neo-Confucianists of the Sung dynasty (960–1276) were
censured as well for their harsh moral teachings, which
did not allow for the natural development of human
character.[35]

The philosophy of Wang Yang-ming (1472–1529) was
generally regarded by the exiled revolutionists as a sound
basis for a revolutionary morality. Courage was required
not only to face constant physical danger but also to sustain social counterpressure. Wang Yang-ming taught that
mind is reason and that one's actions should accord with
one's intuitive knowledge, or conscience. This theory, of
course, suited the needs of a revolutionary whose success
is often in direct proportion to his degree of conviction.

Some contributors to the *People's Journal* considered
jen, as interpreted by Mencius, the motivating spirit of
revolution. It is man's compassion for humanity, his natural sympathy with those who suffer from injustice and
oppression, that moves him to join the revolution and martyr himself. Chang Ping-lin, who criticized Confucius for
his excessive subservience to the monarch, preferred
Wang Yang-ming's precept of fearless conscience. Chang,
however, would have reinforced this doctrine with the
Buddhist teachings of Fa Hsiang and Hua Yen (Flower
Garland) schools. The Fa Hsiang Buddhists, as we have
seen, believed that all precepts are in one's mind, while
the Hua Yen school advocated self-sacrifice for the salva-

tion of others. The Buddhist approach disregarded material considerations and regarded danger and death with equanimity.[36]

Virulent attacks on traditional Confucian philosophies and institutions began in earnest with the publication of *New Century* in 1907, in which Chinese radicals consciously adopted anarchistic and social Darwinist theories.[37] But it was only with the overthrow of the Manchu regime in 1911 that the new radical thought began its corrosive infiltration into traditional Chinese culture.

The twentieth century has been a deeply revolutionary age for China. Within a period of forty years, the country has known three revolutions, while cultural and social movements have shaken tradition to its foundation. During this period Chinese thinking has naturally increasingly emphasized the pragmatic. Political theories, offered to meet the needs of the times, have often been answers to particular problems rather than detached speculation. Chinese political thinkers have become more concerned with building a modern state than with analyzing the theoretical implications of its total structure, which in any case is still indeterminate. They have dealt with broad sociopolitical problems immediately relevant to national reconstruction.

One of the important questions in this regard has been that of tradition: should it be preserved or rejected? Is a synthesis possible between old and new? Disavowal of the deeply integrated ideologies and institutions of two thousand years presents difficult psychosocial problems. Nevertheless a modern state requires a modern texture.

The impact of the West on Chinese political thought in this century can hardly be exaggerated. Much of the "new" Chinese doctrine is clearly traceable to Western sources. Modern influences have become so irresistible that even traditional ideas have had to employ a new terminology. But always there has been the problem of assimilation of Western doctrine in the context of existing national conditions.

Two predominant problems have inevitably affected modern Chinese philosophy: foreign aggression and internal strife. Attention has been given not only to the justification of a strong government but to the definition of a good government as well. As the conception of good government varied, theories multiplied. Whatever one may say of modern Chinese political thought, it has not been sterile.

Notes

CHAPTER I. INTRODUCTION

1. *The Analects*, Bk. 6, ch. 19.
2. *Ibid.*, Bk. 13, ch. 27.
3. *Ibid.*, Bk. 6, ch. 28.
4. *Ibid.*, Bk. 2, ch. 3.
5. *Tao-te ching*, hereafter cited as *Lao Tzu*.
6. *Lao Tzu*, ch. 58.
7. *Ibid.*, ch. 19.
8. *Ibid.*, ch. 16.
9. See K'ang Yu-wei, *K'ung-tzu kai-chih k'ao* (Study of Confucius as a Reformer); *Lun-yü chu* (Commentary on *The Analects*); *Chung-yung chu* (Commentary on *The Doctrine of the Mean*).
10. T'an Ssu-t'ung, *Jen-hsüeh* (A Study of Benevolence).
11. See Ch'u Ch'eng-po, *Chien-cheng t'ang che-kao* (Memorials of Ch'u Ch'eng-po), II, 18–22; Su Yü, ed., *I-chiao ts'ung-pien* (A Collection of Essays in Defence of Confucianism).
12. Among the revolutionary magazines published in Japan were *Kuo-min pao* (The Citizen), *Hsin Hunan* (New Hunan), *Yu-hsüeh i-pien* (Foreign Student Translation Series), *Hupeh hsüeh-sheng chieh* (Hupeh Students), *Chekiang ch'ao* (Chekiang Tides).
13. K'ang Yu-wei, "Pien ke-ming shu" (A Letter Disputing Revolution), *Hsin-min ts'ung-pao* (The New People's Magazine, hereafter cited as *HMTP*), No. 16 (Sept. 1902).
14. Liang Ch'i-ch'ao (under pseudonym Yin-ping), "Pao-tung yü wai-kuo kan-she" (Uprisings and Intervention of Foreign Powers), *HMTP*, No. 82 (July 1906).
15. Liang Ch'i-ch'ao (under pseudonym Chung-kuo chih hsin-min), "Hsin-min shuo" (A People Made New), *HMTP*, Nos. 1–12, 14, 16, 19–20, 24.
16. Liang Ch'i-ch'ao, "K'ai-ming chuan-chih lun" (Enlightened Absolutism), *HMTP*, Nos. 1–3 (1906).
17. As late as April 1906, Liang still maintained that constitutional monarchy could not be realized until ten or twenty years later. See *HMTP*, No. 4: 60 (1960). It was only after the Manchu court proclaimed the preparation for constitutional government in 1906 that the reformists shifted from the advocacy of enlightened absolutism to that of constitutional monarchy.
18. See K'ang Yu-wei, "Pien ke-ming shu"; Liang Ch'i-ch'ao, "Li-shih shang Chung-kuo min-tsu chih kuan-ch'a" (A Historical View of the Chinese Nation), *HMTP*, No. 17: 43 f. (1905).
19. *HMTP*, No. 12: 1–52 (1905); No. 18: 1–34 (1906).
20. Wang Ching-wei, "Po ke-ming k'o-i kua-fen shuo" (Refutation of the Theory that Revolution May Lead to Partition), *Min-pao* (People's Journal, hereafter cited as *MP*), No. 6: 18 (1907); Ssu-huang (Ch'en T'ien-hua), "Chung-kuo ke-ming shih lun" (On Chinese Revolutionary History), *MP*, No. 1 (1905).
21. Chang Nan and Wang Jen-chih, eds., *Hsin-hai ke-ming ch'ien shih-nien chien shih-lun hsüan-chi* (Selected Essays on Current Affairs,

1901–1911) (Hong Kong: San-lien shu-tien, 1962), Pt. 1, Vol. 1, Preface.

22. Wang Ching-wei, "Lun ke-ming chih ch'ü-shih" (On Revolutionary Tendencies), *MP*, No. 26: 14 (1910); Hsien-chieh (Chu Chih-hsin), "Lun she-hui ke-ming tang yü cheng-chih ke-ming ping-hsing" (Social Revolution and Political Revolution Should Go Together), *MP*, No. 5: 58–59 (1906).

23. K'uei-cheng (T'ang Tseng-pi), "Ch'ung-hsieh p'ien" (Respect for Knights-errant), *MP*, No. 23 (1908); T'ai-yen (Chang Ping-lin), "Ke-ming chih tao-te" (Revolutionary Morality), *MP*, No. 8 (1906).

24. Wang Ching-wei, "Ch'ih wei man-chou pien-hu-che chih wu-ch'ih" (Shame to Those Who Defend the Manchus), *MP*, No. 12: 155–86 (1907); Wei-i (Liu Shih-p'ei), "Pien man-jen fei Chung-kuo chih ch'en-min" (Manchus Are Not Chinese Subjects), *MP*, No. 14: 40 (1907); Hsien-chieh, "Hsin-li ti kuo-chia chu-i" (Psychological Nationalism), *MP*, No. 21: 30 (1908); T'ai-yen (Chang Ping-lin), "She-hui t'ung-ch'üan shang-tui" (A Discussion of *A History of Politics*), *MP*, No. 12: 16 (1908); Wang Ching-wei, "Lun ke-ming chih ch'ü-shih"; Chi-sheng (Wang Tung), "Fu-ch'ou lun" (On Revenge), *MP*, No. 10: 33 (1906).

25. Wang Ching-wei, in *MP*, No. 4: 15 (1906); No. 12: 24 (1907); No. 5: 7 (1906); No. 8: 35 (1906).

26. Sun Yat-sen, "Fa-k'an tz'u" (Foreword), *MP*, No. 1 (1905); Feng Tzu-yu, in *MP*, No. 4: 100, 107 (1906).

27. Feng Tzu-yu, p. 108.

28. T'ai-yen, in *MP*, No. 16: 1 ff. (1907).

29. T'ai-yen, "Kuo-chia lun" (The State), *MP*, No. 17: 1, 13 (1907).

30. T'ai-yen, "Yen-shuo" (Address), *MP*, No. 6: 7 (1907).

31. Chang Nan and Wang Jen-chih, *op. cit.*, Pt. 2, Vol. I, pp. 42 ff.

32. "Chen nu-ti" (Warnings to Slaves), *ibid.*, Pt. 1, Vol. II, pp. 706–7.

33. *Ibid.*, p. 707.

34. K'uei-cheng, "Ch'ung-hsieh p'ien."

35. T'ai-yen, "Yen-shuo."

36. T'ai-yen, "Ta T'ieh-cheng" (Reply to T'ieh-cheng), *MP*, No. 14: 113–22 (1907); Wei-i, "Li-hai p'ing-teng lun" (Equalization of Benefits and Hardships), *MP*, No. 13: 2–15 (1907); Shou-yo (Wang Ching-wei), "Ke-ming chih chüeh-hsin" (Determination for Revolution), *MP*, No. 26: 2–5 (1910); K'uei-cheng, "Ch'ung-hsieh p'ien."

37. See below, ch. 4. A severe criticism of Confucianism appeared in the *T'ung-tzu shih-chieh* (Children's World), 1903, under the pen name of Chün-yen. In style and substance the article sounds very much like Wu Chih-hui, an editor of *Hsin shih-chi* (New Century). See "Fa-ku" (Imitating the Ancients), in Chang Nan and Wang Jen-chih, *op. cit.*, Pt. 1, Vol. II, pp. 529–33.

Chapter II

MORAL CONSERVATISM AND
LIBERAL DEMOCRACY

THE overthrow of the Manchu dynasty in 1911 broke the continuity of Chinese history. For two thousand years, beginning with the establishment of the Han monarchy in 206 B.C., there had been numerous dynastic changes, but always the monarchical form of government and the basic political institutions had been retained. The establishment of the Republic following the fall of the Manchu regime was therefore revolutionary in every sense.

It is true that beginning in the 1860's, after China had been twice defeated by the European powers, attempts were made to reform China; but even in the Hundred Days of Reform in the late nineteenth century, the policies were never carried to the point of republicanism. It is also true that Sun Yat-sen initiated the revolutionary movement as early as the 1890's, but his activities were pursued largely abroad. To recruit members and raise funds for his revolutionary party, he traveled extensively in Europe and the United States, but except for some propaganda agencies in Hong Kong and Shanghai, revolutionary activities in China were at best surreptitious. Revolutionary propaganda hardly penetrated China's interior, and democratic principles were practically unknown to the Chinese masses. The revolution was, in fact, a minority affair, led and advocated by Chinese intellectuals studying abroad, financed by Chinese business overseas, supported by secret societies in the Yangtze valley and southern provinces, and abetted by some army units that had been infiltrated by revolutionaries. Thus it is little wonder that the Republic, when it was finally established, did not have a popular base.

Furthermore, the abdication of the Manchu dynasty came too soon; there was no prolonged struggle that might have stimulated a popular understanding of revolutionary principles. A premature bomb explosion at Hankow on October 9, 1911, started the revolution, which immediately received support from South China, where one province after another declared its independence of the Manchu government. On December 29, 1911, Sun Yat-sen was elected provisional president. The helpless Manchu rulers called into office Yüan Shih-k'ai, the former viceroy of Chihli, whose potential power as the founder of the New Army made him the most promising man in such an emergency. He was appointed prime minister and entrusted with the mission of saving the toppling dynasty. For Yüan, however, loyalty was not a virtue. Seizing the opportunity to advance his own career, he arranged the abdication of the Manchu emperor and at the same time negotiated with the revolutionary forces to have himself elected president of the Republic. On February 12 the Manchu emperor announced his abdication. Two days later Yüan was elected provisional president by the National Council in Nanking, succeeding Sun Yat-sen, who had offered to resign in his favor.

Under the sponsorship of the revolutionary forces, a provisional constitution was proclaimed in March 1912. To curb the powers of Yüan Shih-k'ai, it adopted a simplified form of parliamentary government, giving the National Council the power to approve the appointment of cabinet members. But Yüan had no intention of observing constitutional restrictions. And as an official of the old regime, he was supported by mandarins and militarists who were equally contemptuous of democratic principles. He soon discarded the provisional constitution, outlawed the opposition party, and called a constitutional convention to pass a new constitution giving him control of the legislature. In 1915, with the support of his military lieutenants, he had himself elected emperor, amidst general consternation.

During this period, however, Yüan had been under close scrutiny. As soon as his dictatorial intentions became known, the revolutionary forces under Sun Yat-sen called for an armed uprising. Although the revolt was quickly suppressed, the opposition in southwest China forced Yüan to renounce his monarchical scheme. Frustrated and bitter, he died in 1916, leaving the country to his ambitious generals, who soon inaugurated a series of civil wars to gain domination. It was against this background of struggle and chaos that political ideas were expounded in the early years of the Republic.

K'ang Yu-wei

After Yüan's death, K'ang Yu-wei (1858–1927), who had advocated constitutional monarchy while he was a political refugee in Japan, theorized that a republican government was unsuitable for China, since neither the Chinese people nor the country's intellectual leaders had any experience or knowledge of this form of government. Like Rousseau, K'ang maintained that democracy could apply only to a small community. In order to have a parliament of manageable size in China, he argued, as many as 800,000 voters would have to elect one representative. With poor transportation, lack of contacts, and ignorance of voting procedures, the difficulties would be insurmountable. How could the voters know the candidate well enough to elect him? How could the elected representative know the wishes of the electorate well enough to represent it? The argument that a parliamentary member should represent the nation as a whole rather than his constituency was, to K'ang, begging the question.[1]

K'ang also saw special conditions that made republican government dangerous for China: the lawlessness of the militarists which threw the country into incessant war, and foreign aggression, which threatened China's very existence. The first prerequisite of good government, he argued, was to rid China of military rule. But military rule had to be ended without decreasing the military power of the state. While China was coveted by foreign powers, its existence depended upon its defensive strength. Therefore the power of the state had to be augmented so that it could control the generals on the one hand, and resist foreign aggression on the other.[2]

K'ang considered the concept of the people's rights incompatible with that of state power. "When you talk about equality, freedom, and the rights of the people, you extend the rights and privileges of individuals. When individual rights and privileges are extended, the power of the state will necessarily be weakened." The theory of equality and freedom might perhaps be adopted in time of peace and unity. In time of international struggle, the power of the state rather than the rights of individuals had to be upheld.[3]

Whether or not a republic in which people enjoy civil rights is necessarily a weak country is, of course, open to question. But K'ang was writing before 1920, at a period when the United States had yet to play a powerful role in international affairs. In fact, he cited the United States and France as militarily weak powers compared with Germany and Japan. Great Britain was admittedly a great world power, but Great Britain was a constitutional monarchy, not a republic.

K'ang saw in republicanism, furthermore, a serious

menace to China's culture and customs. He recognized that the Revolution of 1911 was more than an overthrow of the Manchu dynasty; that it was a cultural as well as a political revolution, undermining the foundations of Chinese tradition. Already the Chinese had taken to shaking hands and doffing hats without knowing the "barbaric" origins of these customs. More seriously, the Chinese language was being adulterated with Japanese elements. In a spirit worthy of Fichte, K'ang maintained that Chinese was the most elegant and dignified language in the world and insisted that its purity be preserved.[4]

To K'ang the most important thing was keeping intact the national soul, which he defined in the following terms:

A nation must have something upon which to base itself. The principle upon which the nation is built is called the national soul. Through politics, culture and custom, it penetrates deeply into the mind of the people, forms their spirit and thought, blends with their way of life, and molds their customs. No nation, be it large or small, with or without a long history, can exist without it. . . . A man losing his soul will become mad or die. A nation losing its soul will become mad or perish.[5]

The national soul, according to K'ang, manifests itself in the accumulated body of customs and social norms. Even if elements of other cultures are adopted to supplement or strengthen one's culture, national traits must not be entirely abandoned. K'ang's national spirit, unlike Hegel's, is more a historical product than a metaphysical construct. "China's national doctrines and institutions have been formed and shaped by innumerable sages and philosophers for several thousand years. They have long been practised and well adapted to the needs of the people."[6] Historical continuity demands that institutional adjustments be gradual to avoid upsetting the social equilibrium.

The national soul predicates a moral order. Human society rests ultimately on morality, without which laws will be false and politics evil. But each nation has its own moral principles, which become the foundations of its institutions. It is therefore futile to adopt foreign institutions, which are founded on different principles.

In the best Confucian tradition K'ang criticized the rule of law in modern democracies. The enforcement of law depends on power. While the government can enforce law upon the powerless, it is helpless toward the powerful. Particularly those who have military power will certainly disregard law at their convenience. Should not the militarists be controlled by law enforced by state power? K'ang ignored the question but pointed to the "peace and order" of earlier times when people cultivated their virtues and observed the Confucian rules of propriety.[7]

According to K'ang, the Confucian virtues should serve as the foundations of the Chinese moral life, and he therefore attributed the disorder after the Revolution of 1911 to the decline of Confucianism. Protesting the suspension of Confucian worship, he proposed the establishment of Confucianism as the national religion.

No nation in the world, even the most barbarous, can exist without religion. . . . A nation's religion must be compatible with the national customs and become the basis of its laws. Only then can we have the benefits of a good government. Our country has its own religious master, whose teachings blend with our customs and form the basis of our thought and behavior. The master's words have been upheld as laws, his deeds as norms. For several thousand years our beliefs and customs, as well as our moral standards of politics, have been based on Confucianism, which has welded and united them. If we abandon Confucianism, the people would have no guide. They would be lost, miserable, and perplexed.[8]

This proposal created an uproar among the intellectuals who did not consider Confucianism a religion, or a way of God, but rather, with its emphasis on ethics, a doctrine for men. K'ang's reply was that religion was not necessarily a way of God. Man must have faith in some beliefs that will guide his inner thoughts and regulate his conduct. In primitive times when the spirit was emphasized, the way of God prevailed. In modern times when humanism was stressed, the way of man took precedence. The way of man is more advanced than the way of God, but both constitute religions. Confucianism, K'ang pointed out, reveres Heaven and worships ancestors. Even if it is more concerned with human relations, it does not neglect the spirit. It is therefore an advanced modern religion.[9]

In spite of his traditionalism, K'ang's enthusiasm for religion may well have been influenced by his observations of spiritual life in the West during his tours of Europe and America. Order and peace in the West, he observed, were maintained not by legalism, but by religion, which "rules people as an unseen force."[10] His plan to organize Confucian associations in a hierarchical order followed the pattern of the Roman Catholic church. In grafting organized religion onto Confucianism, K'ang was inspired less by his belief in the supernatural than by fear of the developing political and social chaos. He tried to use Confucianism as a cure for China's moral laxity, and he thought this could be done by establishing Confucianism as the national religion and equipping it with an elaborate organization. He hoped that Confucianism as a religion would strengthen the social and moral bonds and keep the country in good order.

K'ang continued to advocate a constitutional monarchy, which he described as a "democratic government with a figurehead ruler," with true governmental power being exercised by the prime minister, who would maintain his authority through parliamentary debate and suasion. Thus bloody struggles for dominance would be avoided.[11] K'ang's attempt to justify the imperial figurehead by comparing it to the institution of idol-worship is a bit muddled, however, and his assertion that the militarists would stand in awe of the powerless symbol of royalty is not very convincing. He had the insight to recognize the value of a symbolic emperor, but he failed to see that an emperor who had been overthrown might no longer capture the imagination of the people.

K'ang was the first, and also the last, eminent conservative thinker to defend traditional Chinese institutions who had a broad view and a profound appreciation of their spirit and values. By emphasizing institutional adjustment to environment, the importance of historical continuity, the superiority of evolution over revolution, the inadequacy of government by law, the hierarchical nature of society, and the establishment of a moral order, he went beyond the solution of immediate problems to the basic issues of political philosophy. His "democracy with a figurehead" was a conservative synthesis, aiming to save the traditional monarchy by compromise with modern democratic trends.

At first glance, these conservative views seem strange for a man known as a radical reformer in the late nineteenth century. Yet in a way K'ang was quite consistent, for he never in his reform days thought of overthrowing the monarchy or supplanting Confucianism. It was his misfortune to live in an age of revolution in which rapid changes left him far behind.

It fell to K'ang to be the spokesman of the conservatives, not only because of his extraordinary loyalty to the Manchu dynasty, but also because of his long conviction that constitutional monarchy was preferable to a republic. A resolute and persistent man, he retained his ideas even though he knew they were unpopular. His hatred of Sun Yat-sen and his bitter experience with Yüan Shih-k'ai, who betrayed his reform in 1898, may have influenced his opposition to the republic they led, but beyond this, he was genuinely alarmed by the disunity and civil wars and the consequent moral and political disruptions. K'ang lived too close to the confusion of the Republic to appreciate its underlying democratic principles; he died too early to see the United States, whose military weakness he deplored, emerge as a great power.

Liang Ch'i-ch'ao

Few writers at the turn of the century exerted a greater influence on the Chinese than Liang Ch'i-ch'ao (1873–1929). He turned his breadth of view and grasp of issues to a great variety of subjects, including philosophy, literature, history, Western thought, and Oriental religions, but his main concern was with politics and economics. He wrote with eloquence and emotion, mingling brilliant images and homely examples, literary allusions and fiery arguments; and while some of his contemporaries may not have agreed with him, they all read him eagerly.

He had, with K'ang Yu-wei, fought the revolutionists and opposed their republicanism while a refugee in Japan, but he returned to China a few months after the establishment of the Republic and became a leader of the Republican (subsequently the Progressive) party, which opposed the Kuomintang. In 1913 he joined the government as minister of justice, but he found actual politics too sordid. He resigned his post the following year, but continued to support President Yüan Shih-k'ai, partly out of considerations of friendship and partly because he hoped "to lead Yüan to the right path."[12] When, however, in 1915 Yüan revealed his intention to become emperor, Liang took an active part in preventing the restoration. Although the articles he published during the early years of the Republic were mostly inspired by immediate issues, they often went beyond them to consider basic questions of state and government.

One of the problems that faced Liang upon his return to China was his position toward the new republic. In Japan he had advocated constitutional monarchy in a fierce debate with the revolutionists. But after the Republic was established, he supported it. In "The Three Basic Principles of Constitutionalism," published in 1913, he maintained that a distinction should be made between the state and the governmental system. The state could take only two forms, republican or monarchical. Government, however, could take one of several forms: it could be representative or a direct democracy; its powers could be centered in the executive or in the legislative branch; its administration could be centralized or decentralized. Political progress, he argued, depends on the form of government adopted, but has little to do with the state; any form of government can exist as well in a republic as in a monarchy. Political discussion should therefore be concerned with the form of government, to ensure the adoption of the most suitable one. Once the form of the state has been established, however, it must be accepted; change would involve violent struggle and could provoke another revolution.[13]

Unlike K'ang, Liang did not believe that a figurehead monarch would command popular loyalty or maintain national stability. "The majesty of an emperor," wrote Liang, "depends on mysterious historical concepts. Imperceptibly, it becomes a force that directly or indirectly secures political stability. That is the advantage of a monarchy. However, majesty must not be profaned. Once profaned, it will not be able to sustain itself."[14] To Liang the im-

perial majesty was profaned when the Manchu regime collapsed in 1911.

But there was a more fundamental concept in Liang's
opposition to restoration. He believed that any attempt to
change the state was revolutionary, and that revolution
was a destructive process which could do only harm to the
people. Furthermore, revolution tends to perpetuate itself;
when it succeeds, it is glorified and people are led to believe
that the highest honor is to become a revolutionary. Since
revolution aims at subverting the social order, members
of the lower classes naturally come to regard it as an effective means of improving their individual condition.
After the violent destruction caused by a revolution, however, rehabilitation is necessarily gradual. Therefore, during the immediately ensuing years national discontent continues to be a source of revolutionary disturbances.[15]

It is important, therefore, to eliminate revolutionary in-
citements by immediately improving political conditions.
Liang thought this could be accomplished by accepting the
new republic and establishing within its framework a rational governmental system suitable to the nation. He
recognized the trend toward nationalism and favored a
strong government. Historically China had been a cultural
empire rather than a sovereign state; now it was imperative
that she transform herself into a modern state with a complex governmental structure, in order to survive in an age
of power politics. Individualism, according to Liang, was
an obstacle to national reconstruction: it inspired minority demands, undermined common beliefs, championed
undisciplined freedom, and opposed national goals. Nor
was laissez faire compatible with the modern state whose
function was to promote the welfare of the people on the
one hand, and to protect infant industry on the other.
While Liang did not go so far as to suggest complete abolition of free enterprise, he held that unrestricted competi-

tion would produce privileged classes and monopolies rather than equal opportunity for all.[16]

In order to build a modern state, the people must be politically united. Liang maintained that this could be done by a strong government founded on the alignment of central and local powers. He considered federalism to be unsuitable, not only because China had a historical background and geographical position quite different from those of the United States, but also because the modern trend of nationalism stressed unification and expansion. Nor did he think that a separation of powers on the American pattern made for strong government, because the checks and balances curbed the freedom of government action and made speedy formulation and implementation of policy impossible.

A government is established not for decoration, but to administer public affairs. The people should therefore trust it rather than curb it; hold it responsible rather than become jealous and suspicious of it. It is only when the government is obeyed in every part of the country that it can be responsible for the whole nation; only when it has freedom of decision that we can criticize its policies; only when it has full power to appoint its personnel, and its internal organization constitutes a unified system, that we can expect good results from it.[17]

Liang favored the cabinet system of government in the belief that legislative and executive unity assured effective administration and flexibility of replacement. His enthusiasm led him to argue that cabinet government was infallible because its members would be party leaders whose political abilities and virtues had already been fully tested. Liang had advocated cabinet government before the formation of the Republic of 1911; it was at least consistent of him to continue to do so. Nevertheless, it required courage to champion a system based upon collective responsibility to parliament at a time when President Yüan Shih-k'ai, upon whom Liang depended for financial support to his party, had made clear his intention of maintaining absolute control of the government. Perhaps because of this delicate situation Liang was somewhat equivocal in regard to the president's position under the cabinet system. In the "Draft of the Chinese Constitution," which he wrote on behalf of the Progressive party, he assigned to the president a much more powerful role than the one taken by the French president before World War II.[18] However, the draft was too brief a document to represent his definitive position with regard to this particular matter.

In accordance with his idea of strong government, Liang favored a two-party system, believing that multiple parties would lead to confusion and instability in the event that no single party commanded a parliamentary majority. He was particularly anxious to prevent party schisms and eliminate pseudo-parties, i.e., parties composed of bureaucratic elements and parties that were, in fact, secret societies. The cabinet system could function well only with a strong and proper Opposition that believed in its own principles and that, in their defense, would not allow itself to be "coerced by might or seduced by profits." Liang urged the government to recognize the valuable role of the Opposition party, and warned that such a party would lose its usefulness if it was too weak to stand up against the power of those in office.[19]

Constitutional government for Liang was government by political parties, and he thought it natural that party leaders should come from the upper classes of society. "It accords with human nature that the good, peaceful majority should follow the lead of the distinguished minority. Throughout history and in countries all over the world, it is always the minority that controls the destiny of a nation."[20]

Liang did not think that the people were capable of governing themselves, agreeing with the ancient Legalists that the people can enjoy good results but can hardly be expected to take the initiative in a long-range plan that incurs hardships at the outset. Government by the people, he argued, is historically an illusion.[21]

Furthermore, the masses are easily swayed and exploited by the crafty and ambitious. Even in historically democratic countries, demagoguery survives and has often flourished in direct violation of the people's rights. The function of a democratic government is to protect those rights on the one hand and to promote the interests of the state on the other. Ironically, government by the people may well thwart both these aims.[22]

If government by the people is out of the question, government by the elite is the logical solution. Good government depends on the intelligence and virtues of its rulers, and Liang was confident that such rulers would be found among the upper classes. The "gentlemen-scholars" in old China had set a magnificent example; he felt that there must be enough people in the China of his day who could live up to the tradition. The rational society, declared Liang, is one in which men with unbending self-respect and incorruptible integrity form the reservoir from which political leaders are drawn. It is the natural order that the intelligent and wise should be the guardians, teachers, and patrons of the illiterate and uninformed.[23] Liang's "gentlemen-scholars" resemble Burke's "natural aristocracy," but basically the concept is derived from the Confucian model of "superior men."

Government by the elite is not only desirable, but inevitable. It was not difficult for Liang to prove that in theory democracy means rule by the majority, but in reality it is the minority that rules the majority. The question, then, is not whether majority rule is desirable, but whether it is practicable. In holding that government is inevitably a minority rule, Liang had much in common with Mosca, Michels, and Pareto. But while the notions of these European sociologists were colored by cynicism, Liang idealized the elite class, which he credited with intellectual and moral superiority in the tradition of Confucianism.

Liang was not blind, however, to the evil elements of the ruling class, especially the bureaucrats. Like Burke who found among the English nobility "flatterers, tale-bearers, parasites, pimps, and buffoons," Liang noted that the so-called superior class of post-revolutionary China was composed of some of the vilest elements. He attributed this demoralization to the revolution, which had overthrown social norms and the moral principles upon which good men live.[24]

Like K'ang Yu-wei, Liang recognized that the Revolution of 1911 was more than political in character: "It destroys the principles commonly accepted for several thousand years, thus upsetting the very basis of our social structure."[25] Liang acknowledged the need to adjust national doctrines to changing conditions, but he insisted that in a revolution the period of political transition is so short and the outbreak of social disruptions so violent that the entire social order is threatened. For him the greatest danger in post-revolutionary China lay in the centrifugal force that had been unleashed, with its overwhelming impact not only on politics but also on custom and morality—a force that, unless arrested, would dissolve all social cohesion.[26]

In Liang's view, a good government exists only in a good society based on a moral order according to which the government should be judged and political leaders appointed. The question, then, is how a moral society is to be built. Liang's answer was that it should be built on China's own character. "A nation has its character as an

individual has his. . . . To lose one's character is to lose
one's essence. The same is true of a nation. Because of
their distinctive characters, nations develop separate exist-
ences. Without its own character, a nation cannot begin to
exist. If the character of an established nation remains un-
fulfilled, that nation will be weak. When a nation loses its
character because of radical change, it perishes."[27]

Liang found it difficult to say exactly how the intangible
thing called national character is formed, but he was certain that it took a long time for a people, living in the
same geographical area and united by blood, social contacts, interests, and a common group of languages and
thoughts, to develop the doctrines and beliefs that deeply
penetrate men's minds, exercise on them a supreme authority, and weld the people together. These common doctrines and beliefs are embodied in a national language, national teachings, and national customs; and their essence
is the national character.

Because of its gradual and evolutionary nature, national
character "can be helped to grow, but cannot be created"
in accordance with certain ideals. National character must
grow continuously without interruption. If the continuity
is broken, disorder, demoralization, and disintegration follow. When common doctrines and beliefs are discredited,
all standards of personal conduct and social relations are
upset, and the basis for a common life is lost. All communities, whether families, villages, cities, or the state itself,
then lack the central force of cohesion.[28]

The fact that China continued to exist for several thousand years amidst the rise and fall of many nations was
owing, according to Liang, to the strong foundation of its
national character, which despite its shortcomings had
points of strength that were unsurpassed. In any case, it
was the force of the Chinese character that sustained

China's growth in the past; and the same force should serve as the basis for her growth in the future.[29]

The spirit of the national character is contained in the moral principles upheld by the people. Liang distinguished the ultimate moral reality, which is universal for all mankind, from its relative forms, which vary with time and place. Each nation has its own moral principles, inherited from its ancestors and enriched by later generations, which shape the collective mind in an eternal continuum.

Liang cited three basic concepts as the sources of Chinese morality: first, *repayment of kindness,* the underlying principle of Chinese rites and sacrifices. According to Liang, rites are performed in gratitude to ancestors, while sacrifices are offered to those who benefited the people. Kindness begins in the family and gratitude is first expressed to the parents. Extend these feelings to distant relatives and the clan is formed. From love of clan to love of country is a small step, merely a difference in degree. Ancient peoples gratefully pledged loyalty to the emperor as the symbol of the state that made their life possible. The old concept of gratitude should continue to serve as the basis of the moral society because, no matter how brilliant and capable one may be, it is impossible to live without depending on others. It is only proper that one should repay society with active concern for one's fellows.[30]

The second basic concept is *recognition of status.* It is a cardinal principle of Confucianism that "terms [or titles] should be set right and positions properly determined," so that each man acts the part required by his position. Confucian society is a hierarchy of ranks, but it is regarded as highly moral because it mirrors the natural order of life, which follows from "the natural inequality of men that cannot be eradicated by force."[31] In reviving the Confucian concept of status, Liang stressed its value as a stabilizing force. He admitted that social progress depends upon the individual's desire to advance himself, but he maintained that legitimate ambition is different from opportunism, which leads only to social disorder.

The third basic concept is *concern for the future*. The Chinese, declared Liang, have been historically aware of the need to perpetuate the race, a tradition traceable to Mencius, who said, "the greatest filial impiety is the failure to have descendants." For Liang this concept was the key to the continuation of the Chinese nation. It is also one of man's most noble duties to repay society for his ancestral and contemporary heritage by contributing his utmost for the welfare of future generations.[32]

It is interesting to note that these Confucian concepts, particularly the first two, had been adopted in Japan and become the foundations of its social relations. Liang had lived in Japan for a long time, and the essay setting forth these ideas was written in 1913, shortly after his return to China. In selecting these concepts as the main sources of Chinese morality, he may have been influenced by the peace and order of Japanese society.

But although Liang regarded Confucianism as the essence of Chinese culture, he did not think, as K'ang did, that it should be established as the national religion. To do so would be a violation of tradition. Ceremony and ritual would add nothing to the greatness of Confucianism and would detract from its true goodness. "Confucius never considered himself to be God," Liang declared, "nor did he attempt to convert his disciples by means of mystical power."[33]

In keeping with his secularism, Liang believed conscience to be the final sanction of morality. When the paralysis of conscience becomes general, especially among the upper classes, which are the backbone of society, the entire moral order collapses. Liang, however, did not pur-

sue the question to its logical end as did Rousseau, who
maintained that appreciation of good and evil is innate
with the individual.[34] He might have reached a similar
conclusion if he had followed the reasoning of Mencius
and Wang Yang-ming (1472–1529), who held that man's
conscience is innately good. But Liang was more concerned
with moral order than with the ultimate source of moral
enlightenment. He was content to enumerate the basic
concepts of Confucian ethics, assuming that they would be
acceptable to conscientious Chinese.

Thus Liang Ch'i-ch'ao, in the early years of the Republic, stood midway between traditionalism and the new order. An open-minded man, he noted the new trends and
was prepared to make compromises, even at the risk of
inconsistency. But partly because of his background as a
Confucian scholar and partly because of the turmoil and
disorder of the years immediately following the establishment of the Republic, he tended slightly toward the conservative side.

Liang's middle-of-the-road position characterized most
of his political ideas. As we have seen, he regarded Confucianism as the cornerstone of Chinese culture, but he
opposed its establishment as the national religion. He recognized that doctrines should be adjusted to the times, but
insisted that change should not be too radical.[35] He maintained that society is the foundation of government, but
agreed that government and society are interdependent.[36]
Indeed, his elite rule was a kind of limited democracy.

Liang was at heart an evolutionist. He believed in
change, but he abhorred the abuses that accompany radical
transformation. Living in a revolutionary age, he set himself the task of bringing in the new without a violent break
with the moral tradition essential to social stability. But
the wheel of time was turning too fast for him, even

though, unlike his teacher K'ang Yu-wei, he did in a way
try to catch up with it.

Chang Shih-chao

Among the publicists in the early years of the Republic,
Chang Shih-chao (b. 1881) was one of the few who had
precise knowledge of Western theories of government. He
had studied law in Great Britain and read widely in politics
and philosophy. His legal training inclined him toward
great discrimination in his treatment of philosophical concepts and in the use of terminology concerning the nature
of the state and government. He was the first to translate
the writings of Western political philosophers into "West-
ernized" classical Chinese, which did not so much change
the form of the Chinese language as make it more exact
and elaborate. His writings were noted for their extremely
logical exposition.

As early as 1903, at the age of twenty-two, Chang Shih-
chao had joined the Ai-kuo Hsüeh-she, a revolutionary
organization in Shanghai, and soon published his anti-
Manchu articles in the Su-pao (The Kiangsu Journal).[37]
He retained his anti-monarchism after the overthrow of
the Manchu dynasty, and though for some time he enjoyed
the patronage of Yüan Shih-k'ai, he disavowed him as soon
as the latter's imperial ambitions were revealed. In 1914
he founded the Chia-yin ("The Tiger") magazine, in which
he discussed fine points of law and political philosophy
and argued for liberal republicanism.

In the early days of the Republic, much confusion
arose from such ill-defined terms as "state's rights" and
"people's rights." Those who advocated a strong government emphasized state's rights; those opposed emphasized
people's rights. Chang, in the tradition of Bagehot and
Burgess, emphasized the sovereignty of the state as dis-

tinct from the rights of the government and the rights of
the governed. Sovereignty is absolute and unlimited, and
from it both the government and the people derive their
prerogatives. Sovereignty resides in the state, which has
the power to grant and limit the rights of both the government and the people. Chang did not fear oppression of the
people by the state, for he defined the latter as "a body of
free persons united together for common benefit." He defined government as the body that administers public affairs in accordance with the will of the state.[38]

Chang defended the republican form of government,
observing that the so-called failure of republicanism was
in fact no more than the failure to practice it. In Latin
America as well as in China, argued Chang, the break-
down of republican government was largely due to the ambitions of men who did not believe in democracy and who
from the outset did not give it a chance to prove itself.
Moreover, those who supported the republic at the beginning were too impatient to await good results and consequently withdrew their support precisely at a time when it
was most crucial.[39]

Chang rejected Frank J. Goodnow's view that Chinese
tradition is incompatible with republicanism. In a most
cogent disquisition he asserted that tradition should mean
that which has continued to exist. An old tradition can
lose its force just as a new one can be created to take its
place. When we consider the facts, we must not neglect
the fact of change. Republicanism was indeed unprecedented in China, but once it had been instituted and absorbed, it would gradually become traditional.

It is undeniable that the form of government must be suited
to the nation. But by "suited" we should mean suited to the
whole situation rather than a particular situation. History consists of the present as well as the past. To emphasize the past

and neglect the present can only attain partial suitability.[40]

For Chang, government by law is preferable to government by men, as democracy is preferable to despotism. Justice and stability are the essentials of good government, but these can be provided only by a constitution representing the various interests of the people and receiving the support of different groups. It is only when the people of the nation agree to the basic provisions of the constitution and are convinced that "their lives and property as well as the lives and property of their descendants depend on those provisions" that the stability of the constitution can be assured.[41]

Revolution breaks out when there are serious conflicts of interests and sentiments. Compromise, therefore, not only prevents revolution; it is also the cardinal principle of democracy, which, although based on the general principle of majority rule, gives the minority the opportunity to persuade the rest. Political stability is attainable only when the minority feels that it is fairly treated.[42]

Toleration is another principle of good government essential not only to freedom of thought but to national unity. Progress requires flexibility of standards. It must be realized, noted Chang, that no perfect form of government has yet been developed and that institutional improvement is directly related to experimentation.[43]

The emphasis on the rule of law leads logically to the emphasis on governmental organization. Although Chang did not minimize the need for virtuous men in government, he believed that a good governmental organization would at once benefit the virtuous and control the corrupt. Disputing Liang Ch'i-ch'ao, who believed that society shapes politics, Chang argued that Chinese politics influenced Chinese society.[44] Like Liang, however, Chang favored the cabinet system with two political parties, limitation of the size of the electorate, and the assumption by the elite class of the political leadership of the nation.

In the early years of the Republic, Chang Shih-chao represented the liberal school of thought that sought to provide a working formula for the new government. Although he was determined that China should not return to monarchism, Chang entertained no radical ideas. His inspiration was Western liberalism, and his model was Great Britain.

Chang was popular among the scholars, who admired his moderate proposals, logical exposition, and the elegant language in which he discussed complex Western institutions and theories. Unfortunately, however, his scholarly approach and pithy style did not have wide general appeal. As the tide of revolution rose in China in the early 1920's, his moderate views became increasingly unacceptable to the radicals. Chang's reaction was toward more pronounced conservatism.

He came to advocate traditional Chinese values in opposition to the new culture; he even proposed that China return to an agricultural economy, on the theory that the industrial state was frustrating and that agrarian life was intrinsically more rewarding. In an agricultural state subsisting on its own produce it would be relatively easy to realize the principle of equitable distribution. Conversely, in an industrial state that manufactures goods for financial gain rather than directly for the people's use, capital would tend to be centralized in the hands of the few. The result would be a wide barrier between rich and poor and the division of the nation into capitalist and laboring classes, and consequently, endless struggle and conflict.[45] Agricultural morality is therefore superior to industrial morality. Chang envisioned his agricultural state as a peaceful society in which affection and contentment, harmony, courtesy, simplicity, and "inaction" prevail. He offered a Taoist utopia with Confucian virtues.

Chang, of course, denied that his agricultural state would be retrograde. Instead, he maintained that it would amount to the rebirth of the old and therefore would be new.[46] He argued that reconstruction on the basis of the old constitutes progress. Evolution is the blending of the old and new.[47] As an interpretation of history, Chang's theory was not without merit; but it did not alter the fact that a return to agrarianism amid modern trends of indus- trialization would be a return to traditional ways rather than a synthesis of old and new.

Chang's radical change from modern liberalism to tra- ditionalism came about partly because, like Liang Ch'i- ch'ao, he was dismayed at the First World War, which shattered the prestige of Western culture. Parliamentary politics no longer seemed the key to social stability and national welfare. Material civilization had led to aggres- sion and conquest. His time in the cabinet might well have inclined him toward a distrust of radical ideas; but perhaps the most crucial factor in Chang's reactionism was his clas- sical background with its inordinate emphasis on spiritual values. The trouble with Chang, observed a contemporary, was that he was too fond of culling archaic words and phrases from traditional literature.[48] It is an easy transi- tion from the love of archaic words to the love of archaic ideas.

Notes

CHAPTER II. MORAL CONSERVATISM AND LIBERAL DEMOCRACY

1. K'ang Yu-wei, "Chung-kuo tien-wei wu-tsai ch'üan-fa Ou-mei erh chin-ch'i kuo-ts'ui shuo" (China's Grave Situation Is Due to the Complete Imitation of Europe and America and the Entire Abandonment of National Heritage), *Pu-jen* (We Can't Bear It!, hereafter cited as *PJ*), No. 6: 10 (July 1913).
2. K'ang, "Kung-ho p'ing-i" (Comments on Republicanism), *PJ*, Nos. 9–10: 32–34, 36 (Dec. 1917).
3. K'ang, "Wen wu-kuo ssu-wan-wan t'ung-pao te min-ch'üan p'ing-teng tzu-yu hu" (Have My 400 Million Compatriots Secured Civil Rights, Equality and Liberty?), *PJ*, No. 6: 7–8.
4. Kang, "Chung-kuo tien-wei wu-tsai ch'üan-fa Ou-mei erh chin-ch'i kuo-ts'ui shuo," *PJ*, No. 6: 33–34.
5. *Ibid.*, p. 1.
6. K'ang, "Chung-kuo huan-hun lun" (Revival of the Chinese Soul), *PJ*, No. 8: 5 (Nov. 1913).
7. K'ang, "I K'ung-chiao wei kuo-chiao p'ei-t'ien i" (A Proposal to Establish Confucianism as the National Doctrine and a Complement to Heaven), *PJ*, No. 3: 1–12 (April 1913).
8. K'ang, "Fu chiao-yü-pu shu" (Reply to the Ministry of Education), *PJ*, No. 4: 4 (May 1913).
9. K'ang, "Chung-hua chiu-kuo lun" (On the Salvation of China), *PJ*, No. 1: 55 (March 1913).
10. *Ibid.*, p. 49.
11. K'ang, "Yü Hsü t'ai-fu shu" (Letter to Assistant Grand Tutor Hsü), *PJ*, Nos. 9–10: 8 (1918).
12. Ting Wen-chiang, ed., *Liang Jen-kung hsien-sheng nien-p'u ch'ang-pien ch'u-kao* (A Chronological Biography of Liang Ch'i-ch'ao, First Draft) (Taipei: Shih-chieh, 1959), pp. 460 ff.
13. Liang Ch'i-ch'ao, "Hsien-fa chih san-ta ching-shen" (The Three Essentials of Constitution), *Yung-yen* ("The Justice," hereafter cited as *YY*), 1.3: 3–4 (Jan. 1913).
14. Liang, "I-tsai so-wei kuo-t'i wen-t'i che" (Strange, the So-Called Question of National Polity!), *Ta Chung-hua* ("The Great Chung Hua Magazine"), 1.8: 13 (Aug. 1915).
15. Liang, "Ke-ming hsiang-hsü chih yüan-yin chi ch'i o-kuo" (The Causes and Evil Effects of Continued Revolution), *YY*, 1.14: 1–10 (June 1913).
16. Liang, "Chung-kuo li-kuo ta-fang-chen" (Basic Guidelines for the State of China), *YY*, 1.1: 9–10 (Dec. 1912).
17. *Ibid.*, 1.2: 11.
18. Liang, "Chin-pu-tang i Chung-hua min-kuo hsien-fa ts'ao-an" (A Draft Constitution Proposed by the Chinpu Party), *YY*, 1.8 (Aug. 1913).
19. Liang, "Cheng-chih shang chih tui-k'ang-li" (Opposition in Politics), *YY*, 1.3: 7 (Jan. 1913).
20. Liang, "Chung-kuo li-kuo ta-fang-chen," *YY*, 1.4: 13 (Jan. 1913).

21. Liang, "Hsien-fa chih san-ta ching-shen," *YY*, 1.4: 12 (Jan. 1913).
22. *Ibid.*, pp. 13–14.
23. Liang, "Ou-chou cheng-chih ke-chin chih yüan-yin" (The Causes of Political Progress in Europe), *YY*, 1.5: 1–5 (Feb. 1913).
24. *Ibid.*, pp. 9, 11.
25. Liang, "Chung-kuo li-kuo ta-fang-chen," *YY*, 1.4: 11.
26. *Ibid.*
27. Liang, "Kuo-hsing lun" (On National Character), *YY*, 1.1: 1 (Dec. 1912).
28. *Ibid.*, pp. 2–3, 5.
29. Liang, "Chung-kuo tao-te chih ta-yüan" (Major Sources of Chinese Morality), *YY*, 1.2: 1–2 (Dec. 1912).
30. *Ibid.*, pp. 6–7.
31. *Ibid.*, pp. 1–2, 4.
32. *Ibid.*, p. 5.
33. Liang, in *Ta Chung-hua*, 1.2: 4 (Feb. 1915).
34. J. J. Rousseau, *Emile* (Everyman's Library, 1961), pp. 242–45.
35. Liang, "Chung-kuo li-kuo ta-fang-chen," *YY*, 1.4: 11.
36. Liang, "Cheng-chih chih chi-ch'u yü yen-lun-chia chih chih-chen" (The Foundations of Politics and the Advice of Publicists), *Ta Chung-hua*, 1.2: 1–2 (Feb. 1915).
37. Shen Yen-kuo, *Chi Chang T'ai-yen hsien-sheng* (Notes on Chang Ping-lin) (Shanghai: Yung-hsiang, 1946), p. 15.
38. Chang Shih-chao (under pseudonym Ch'iu-t'ung), "Kuo-ch'üan yü min-ch'üan" (State Rights and People's Rights), *Tu-li chou-pao* (The Independent Weekly), No. 10 (Nov. 1912). Cf. Walter Bagehot, *British Constitution;* John W. Burgess, *Political Science and Comparative Law.*
39. Chang, "Kung-ho p'ing-i" (Comments on Republicanism), *Chia-yin* ("The Tiger," hereafter cited as *CY*, 1.7: 16 (July 1915).
40. Chang, "Ti-cheng po-i" (Refutation of Monarchism), *CY*, 1.9: 22 (Sept. 1915).
41. Chang, "Lun hsien" (On Constitutionalism), *CY*, 1.8: 6 (Aug. 1915).
42. Chang, "T'iao-ho li-kuo lun" (Compromise in the Making of the State), *CY*, 1.4: 2–3 (Nov. 1914); "Tzu-chüeh" (Self-Awakening), *CY*, 1.3: 4–5.
43. Chang, "T'ung-hsin" (Correspondence), *CY*, 1.2: 1–3; 1.8: 2; "Cheng-pen" (Foundations of Government), *CY*, 1.1: 7 (May 1914).
44. Chang, "Cheng-chih yü she-hui" (Politics and Society), *CY*, 1.6: 4, 14, 29 (June 1915).
45. Chang (under pseudonym Ku-t'ung), "Nung-chih i" (Wings of Agricultural Politics), *Chia-yin chou-k'an* (Chia-yin Weekly), 1.5: 6 (1925?).
46. Chang, "Shuo hun," *ibid.*, 1.17: 5.
47. Chang, "Hsin chiu" (New and Old), *ibid.*, 1.7: 9.
48. Wu Chih-hui, *Wu Chih-hui ch'üan-chi* (Complete Works of Wu Chih-hui) (Shanghai: Ch'un-i, 1927), Vol. III, Bk. 6, p. 62.

Chapter III

THE NEW TIDE

Anti-Confucianism

WHEN K'ang Yu-wei and the conservatives advocated the establishment of Confucianism as the national religion, they incurred a violent reaction among the intellectuals. Classical scholars like Chang Ping-lin pointed out that Confucius never intended to found a religion and that the strong point of Confucianism was not a religious system. Confucius' greatest contribution lay in compiling history, publishing the classics, promoting learning, and democratizing education.[1] The new thinkers, however, wanted not only to deny Confucianism the sacredness of a religion, but to demolish it as a national doctrine. They found the traditional ideology an obstacle to the construction of a modern China, because its principles and concepts were incompatible with republicanism and the democratic way of life. A successful democracy, they reasoned, requires not only a republican constitution but also a democratic mentality. So long as the Chinese people believed in feudalistic ideas, no democratic institutions could be successfully established.

Thus began the New Culture Movement, which during the years 1916–1922 revolutionized the mental outlook of the Chinese people. While anti-traditionalism is traceable to the *New Century* (*Hsin Shih-chi*), published in 1907, it was the New Culture Movement that launched the most devastating attack on Confucianism. At no time in Chinese history had Confucianism been subject to such systematic criticism, nor had it ever received a blow with such far-reaching consequences.

Among the leaders of the New Culture Movement, Ch'en Tu-hsiu (1879–1942) was the most influential. Bereft of his father a few months after he was born, he was taught Chinese classics by a stern grandfather who did not hesitate to subject him to corporal punishment if he failed to recite the texts. He was a very bright boy, but he was also sensitive and stubborn, showing his rebellious spirit in these early years in sullen acceptance of his punishments. "No matter how hard I was whipped, I never uttered a single cry."[2] He stood first in one of the district examinations, but the sordid conduct of the examinees at the provincial examination disgusted him so that he decided not to pursue an official career through these channels. Instead he went to study in Japan, and for some time was attracted by the reform ideas of K'ang Yu-wei and Liang Ch'i-ch'ao. Returning to China in 1915, he published and edited *New Youth* (*Hsin Ch'ing-nien*), which was to become the most influential journal among students. It was there that he advocated, with Hu Shih, the new vernacular style of writing. Under the slogan of "Down with Confucianism" he called for the supplanting of traditional culture by new goals of "democracy and science." His incisive, cogent arguments, written in a lucid and eloquent style, soon gained him a reputation as a radical leader among the iconoclasts.

Another powerful anti-Confucian writer was Wu Yü (1872–1949), who as early as 1906, while studying in Tokyo, had written poems criticizing the traditional doctrine. A student of comparative law, he had studied Montesquieu and John Stuart Mill as well as Western legal systems,[3] and thus had a basis upon which to evaluate Chinese political and social institutions. He was the first to trace the development of Confucianism from a set of ethical principles to the foundation of a network of institutions and thereby examine its effects upon Chinese

life. This institutional approach, with special attention
to effects, helped to pinpoint the essence and significance
of Confucianism while avoiding the endless controversy
surrounding the origin of certain Confucian dictates. Like
Ch'en Tu-hsiu, he held that Confucianism was unsuitable
to republican China. Under Wu Yü's systematic, scholarly exposition, often colored by Taoist thinking, the very
foundations of the traditional doctrine of Confucianism
were undermined.[4]

Hu Shih (1891–1962) will go down in the history of
the New Culture Movement as "the father of the Chinese
literary renaissance." American-educated but well versed
in Chinese classics, he achieved immense success in applying modern analytical methods to the study of Chinese
philosophy and literature. He believed in modernization
and firmly opposed the supremacy of Confucianism,
whether original or corrupted. A pragmatist, he was more
interested in actual problems than in ideological systems. He adopted a critical attitude toward traditional institutions and recommended a government of "good men"
for turbulent China. His modest, piecemeal notions of
reform represented liberal thinking in this period, and he
remained a liberal while his colleagues in the New Culture
Movement turned toward the left.

A famous writer who contributed greatly to the overthrow of Confucianism was Lu Hsün (Chou Shu-jen,
1881–1936), "the Gorki of China." His writings—
whether novels, short stories, or short essays—were noted
for their iconoclastic spirit and use of ridicule and biting
sarcasm. He believed it was impossible to reconcile the
new with the old, and he expressed his uncompromising
attitude toward Confucian tradition by quoting one of
Ibsen's plays: "All or nothing."[5]

These key figures in the New Culture Movement sought
to undermine Confucianism largely because they were

convinced it was incompatible with the new age. According to Ch'en Tu-hsiu, "Doctrines rise and fall in accordance with the changes in the social structure and living conditions. While a theory may give rise to a certain society, societies also produce certain theories." The more complex the nature of social change and the quicker its tempo, the faster a particular teaching will become obsolete. It is impossible that a doctrine can be universally applied.[6] The fact that Confucianism had been held viable in China for centuries was due primarily to the stagnant nature of Chinese society before the establishment of the Republic. Confucianism, a product of the feudal age, aimed at maintaining the privileges of the nobility. It was directly opposed to the republican principles of liberty and equality.[7]

According to the Confucian doctrine of the Three Bonds, the minister owes loyalty and obedience to the prince, the son to the father, and the wife to the husband. To Ch'en Tu-hsiu, this doctrine was the very foundation of monarchical despotism and social inequality, dividing the people into rigid status groups with different rights and duties not only in social matters but even in the realm of law.[8] The whole idea was, he held, contrary to the concept of individual independence, for it meant that the minister, the son, and the wife could not escape the position of subjects and dependents.[9]

But was the doctrine of the Three Bonds originally the teaching of Confucius? Was it not first mentioned in the apocrypha (*wei shu*) of the Han dynasty (206 B.C.– A.D. 219) and later developed by the Confucianists of the Sung dynasty (960–1276)? Ch'en Tu-hsiu believed that although the term "Three Bonds" was not found in the Confucian classics, the doctrine originated in their era. There was no doubt, he felt, that Confucius favored loyalty to the sovereign, filial piety, and wifely obedience,

all relationships basic to the one-sided obligations, unequal moral responsibilities, and the distinction between
superior and inferior in which Ch'en saw the origin of the
class system of China.[10]

Wu Yü, directing his criticism to the effects of Confucianism, maintained that the chief precept of Confucian ethics was filial piety, the basis of the absolute monarchy as well as the family system.[11] Filial piety and
ministerial loyalty to the prince are twin concepts in Confucianism, for the prince is regarded as the father of the
people, and a man's filial obligations are fulfilled only
when he extends his loyalty to the prince without reservation.[12]

Li, the rules of propriety, are supposed to be based on
the principles of benevolence and righteousness. Actually,
Wu Yü claimed, they are the means by which an absolute
ruler enforces conformity without the people's being aware
of it. They define privileges and obligations in accordance with the individual's status, and they are sanctioned
by law, which in traditional China was based on the same
principles as the rules of propriety—principles that were
directly contrary to modern concepts of liberty and
equality.[13]

In the treatment of women as prescribed by the rules
of propriety the new thinkers found the worst abuse of
the principle of equality. According to the Confucian concept of chastity, a woman whose husband died was supposed to remain a widow throughout her life and a girl
was expected to commit suicide if she should have the
misfortune to be raped. Further, the requirement of chastity applied only to women. It was this "inhuman" virtue
that called forth the strongest protest from Hu Shih and
Lu Hsün.[14]

But did not Confucianism also have democratic concepts? K'ang Yu-wei talked persistently of the Great Com-

monwealth as the ultimate goal of Confucianism, and the new thinkers had to answer him. The passage concerning the Great Commonwealth in the *Book of Rites* reads:

When the Great Principle is realized, the world is common to all. Men of virtue and ability are selected; sincerity is emphasized and harmony is cultivated. Thus men do not love only their parents nor treat as their children only their own sons. The aged are taken care of, the able-bodied are given work, the young are properly brought up, and widows, widowers, orphans, childless men, and those who are disabled and sick are adequately maintained. Men have their proper work, and women their homes. They dislike to have wealth wasted, but they do not like to hoard it for themselves. They hate not to exert themselves, but they do not work solely for their own gain. . . . This is called the Great Commonwealth.

In the past, Confucianists such as Chu Hsi (1130–1200) and Lü Tsu-ch'ien (1137–1181) had cast doubts on the authenticity of this passage. According to Wu Yü, who agreed with them, the idea of treating others' parents and sons as one's own was contrary to the Confucian principle of "determination of status," the basis of the rules of propriety, which define privileges and obligations in the family and society. The ideal of Great Commonwealth was, therefore, not a Confucian doctrine, but rather an idea of Lao Tzu's that had somehow found its way into the Confucian classics.[15]

Confucianism did approve the exile or even execution of bad kings and Mencius had said that "the people are the most important, the sovereign the least." But as long as Confucianism upheld class distinction, said Wu Yü, the august, sacred position of the prince was beyond the challenge of the common people.[16] The new thinkers had no doubt that Confucianism supported monarchism; the fact that various emperors had adopted Confucianism as

the national doctrine was clear evidence of its conge-
niality to monarchy. Furthermore, history is full of cases
of Confucianists collaborating with despots to rule the
people.[17] The close relations between the two were determined by the fact that the Confucianists, devoted solely
to the principle and art of governing, could find employ-
ment only within the government. It was only natural
that they should uphold the prince, their employer.[18]

The supremacy of Confucianism as the national doctrine incurred the new thinkers' most vehement opposition. For more than two thousand years, Confucianism
had been the underlying principle of China's political
and social institutions, the absolute standard of right and
wrong, overruling all other philosophies and admitting no
differing ideas. Both Ch'en Tu-hsiu and Wu Yü acknowledged Confucius as a great man of his age, but they held
that the times had changed and that Confucianism was
clearly a barrier to freedom of thought and an obstacle
to progress. Its supremacy must be overthrown so that
new ideas could develop and new institutions arise to
meet the requirements of the new age.[19]

Inability to serve China's urgent needs was considered
a serious shortcoming of Confucianism. To the leaders of
the New Culture Movement, modernization of China was
the only way to strengthen the country to resist foreign
aggression, and Confucianism was blamed for China's
failure to meet the challenge of the West. As Lu Hsün
puts it, "It is not so much the question of whether we
should preserve the tradition as the question of whether
tradition can preserve us."[20]

If Confucianism were to be overthrown, what moral
principles would take its place? The new thinkers seemed
to content themselves with the general suggestion that
ethics must meet the demands of the times. Hu Shih
recommended a critical attitude, maintaining that any

morals, institutions, or customs must be continually re-
viewed in the light of their suitability to present circumstances.[21] Others held that new morality must be created
freely by the people in accordance with their conscience.
People of learning and vision would play a leading role
in developing new morals on the basis of knowledge,
rather than old customs. Governmental officials should
not concern themselves with moral teaching: the Confucian principle that the prince should also be the people's
teacher was incompatible with the modern separation of
politics from morality. In a republic the president is the
servant of the people, not their father, and he should not
assume the function of rectifying the people's conduct
when it is they who are the masters of the state.[22]

But if the new thinkers offered no moral system to
replace Confucianism, they did indicate their attitudes
toward certain aspects of morality. Chou Tso-jen (b.
1885), an eminent essayist, suggested that the new morality be founded on liberty and happiness, and aim to benefit both oneself and others, for the welfare of others is
necessary to one's own.[23] The good of mankind was his
primary concern, although, in reaction to the restrictive
traditional rules of propriety, he called attention to the
importance of individual dignity and happiness. The new
thinkers demonstrated a particular interest in responsibility for future generations. Ch'en Tu-hsiu emphasized
the continuity of society, where "material is transmitted
to the descendants and the spirit is continued in history,"[24] while Lu Hsün saw in the continuity of life the
course of progress and evolution: "As new lives are more
significant than the old, nearer to perfection and therefore more valuable and precious, the old should sacrifice for the new." The new morality, he maintained,
should be built in the interest of the young rather than
the aged.[25] Hu Shih made it clear that in spite of the

emphasis on individual rights and independence, individual self-interest was not to be the basis of the new philosophy of life; rather, independent thinking and individual responsibility should be promoted so that all could contribute to the reconstruction of society.[26]

These attacks launched by the new thinkers were so potent that Confucianism rapidly lost the confidence of the rising generation; while it was not completely swept away, it was shaken to its very foundations. During the New Life Movement in the 1930's, Nationalist leaders made strenuous efforts to restore belief in the Confucian virtues, but nothing significant was achieved, and Confucianism has now been declining in China for fifty years —a period long enough to destroy its potency as a weapon against Communism.

Democracy

While he was editor of *New Youth*, Ch'en Tu-hsiu offered the slogan "Democracy and Science" as the solution to China's problems. In replying to K'ang Yu-wei's criticism of republican government Ch'en argued, as did Chang Shih-chao, that republicanism failed in China not because of its inherent defects, but because the government did not carry it out. He particularly blamed the militarists whose attempts to restore despotism led to strife and divisions. Refusing to believe that republican democracy would necessarily weaken the country, he pointed to numerous monarchies in history that had been so weak they failed to maintain their independence. Ch'en also reacted strongly against the charge that the Chinese people's lack of democratic experience made a republican government impossible.[27]

Ch'en Tu-hsiu favored representative and constitutional government, under which the people would vote directly on a constitution that would limit governmental powers. He did not believe that democracy would be achieved by the establishment of a strong central government; rather, he was interested in the development of local government at the most basic level where direct participation by the people would be practicable. He had in mind a combination of small political units and trade associations, the latter performing the functions of both trade unions and chambers of commerce within their small areas, which were to be no larger than a city precinct or a village.[28] He offered no formula for combining these local units into a national force.

Like Chang Shih-chao, Ch'en preferred government by law to government by men, but for different and quite practical reasons. He saw in the rule of law an effective antidote to clan society in which inequality prevailed.[29] Government by law was also necessary to overcome the power of the warlords, whose struggle for national domination had been the source of some of China's gravest problems. As late as 1917, Ch'en opposed unification by force, as he knew of no party that was strong enough to carry out the task, and any attempt to do so that ended in failure would only prolong the disunity and chaos. Rather, he wanted a coalition government formed by the major political parties.[30]

He believed, however, that government by law should protect and not interfere with freedom of speech. "Law," wrote Ch'en Tu-hsiu, "preserves the civilization of the present; freedom of speech creates the civilization of the future. The existing civilization and its laws are the results of freedom of speech in the past: they were created through criticism and protest against the preceding civilization and its laws." Therefore, while laws may restrict the activities of the people, they must not interfere with their opinions and thoughts.[31]

Like other thinkers in the early years of the New Culture Movement, Ch'en emphasized human rights and individual freedom and happiness. As we have seen, the anti-Confucian movement was directed toward individual liberty, equality, and independence. But Ch'en held, with Lu Hsün and Hu Shih, that man should strive not only for his own happiness but for the public welfare and the benefit of future generations.[32] He considered, moreover, that in order to contribute to the well-being of society, the Chinese people had to change their submissive attitude and assume the role of conqueror. A fighting spirit, said Ch'en, is essential to a social revolution that aims at breaking the chain of tradition. A conquering spirit is necessary to improve any environment, whether natural or political. Nature is unkind; in order to survive man must conquer nature with his technology, bend it for purposes of progress, and resist its destructive force. It is the principle of evolution that survival and progress depend on the power of resistance.

All this applies in politics as well. Externally, a nation without the power of resistance will be conquered by other nations. Internally, a people without the power of resistance will be oppressed by a despot. Whether or not a ruler turns despot often depends upon the people's will to resist. In a community where the people conform through inertia to outdated social norms, it is necessary that men of vision and courage protest the traditional shortcomings and fight for social progress. Life, said Ch'en, is a constant struggle; once the power of resistance is lost, the result will be either submission or extinction. The Chinese people, long exposed to the Taoist philosophy of inaction and the Confucian virtue of modesty, are noted for the lack of a fighting spirit. Ch'en called on his people to assume an aggressive attitude commensurate with the demands of the modern world.[33]

In advocating a fighting spirit for the Chinese people, Ch'en revealed his rebellious nature. Given his temperament and convictions, it is not surprising that he later became the leader of the nascent Communist movement.

"Problems and Isms"

Among the leaders of the New Culture Movement, Hu Shih was one of the few who consistently upheld the principles of democracy. A pragmatist, he was a liberal thinker tending toward the moderate side. He was keenly interested in politics, but his scholarly temperament prevented him from active participation, although his influence among the intellectuals was immense.

In July 1919, when socialism and anarchism came into vogue in China, Hu Shih published his article "Problems and Isms," which immediately attracted wide attention. In it he advised that the Chinese give more attention to specific problems and talk less about isms. It is highly important, Hu wrote, that we should study the actual situation of society and devise concrete ways to solve its problems. All theories and isms are merely "tools of reference," which can help us understand the actual situation so that remedies can be offered, but which must not be regarded as universal truths. Doctrines arise to meet the concrete demands of a particular time. An ism comes into being when a concrete method is turned into an abstract term and therein lies its weakness and danger, for no abstract term can comprehend the concrete policy originally proposed. The result is misrepresentation and distortion.[34]

According to Hu Shih, what China urgently needed were concrete methods to solve its serious problems. "Instead of studying how to raise the standard of living of the rickshaw men, we talk about socialism . . . ; instead of studying how to resolve the conflicts between the North and the South, we talk about anarchism. And we exultantly boast that what we discuss is the fundamental solution. This is sheer deception and humbug. . . . It will kill all chances of social reform in China."[35]

Hu Shih did not oppose the importation of foreign theories, but he insisted that any such importation must be directly related to the problems under study. Theories may be used to explain the significance of the problems; they may even be studied to see if they provide any solution. But a critical attitude must be maintained toward all theories, and they must be regarded as merely hypotheses rather than absolute rules.[36] No truth is permanently applicable; it must be tested for effects under particular circumstances.[37]

Hu Shih's rejection of "isms" elicited vehement protest. One objection was offered by Lan Chih-hsien (Lan Kung-wu), a member of Liang Ch'i-ch'ao's Study Clique* who had interested himself in guild socialism. He did not believe that all problems were concrete in nature. To him the essence of a problem was often abstract, involving a question of right or wrong. He thought, therefore, that while emphasis on concrete methods might be applicable to particular, localized problems, it was insufficient for general, far-reaching ones. An ism is valuable, said Lan, because of the ideals it provides for the future. It may not indicate the concrete methods through which they can be achieved, but it sets the standard for action and points the direction of movement. The more abstract its ideals, the more embracing its power will be, and the more numerous its adherents. Hence the power of great religious and political doctrines.[38]

Another objection was made by Li Ta-chao, who at

---

* A political group organized from the former Progressive party, the Study Clique was active in the northern government.

the time was keenly interested in Marxism. To a greater extent than Lan Chih-hsien, he stressed the practical effects of a political doctrine on the masses of the people. Problems and isms are inseparable, Li maintained. In order to solve a fundamental social problem, the united efforts of the masses are necessary, and to bring home the urgency of a social problem to sufficient numbers of people, a doctrine must offer an ideal to which they can aspire in common. Those who participate in social movements should therefore study practical problems on the one hand and propagate a chosen doctrine on the other. More specifically, while socialist ideals should serve as the basis of all social movements, practical methods should vary according to time, place, and circumstances.[39]

In calling attention to the danger of isms or doctrines, Hu Shih had in mind Marxism and anarchism, both of which had become fashionable in China. He warned that being the ideological slave of Marx or Kropotkin was just as bad as being the blind follower of Confucius or Chu Hsi (a leader of Neo-Confucianism). Since he offered no detailed criticism of socialist doctrines, his article was hardly convincing to those who were interested in them.[40] Nor did his advice to study concrete problems appeal to the revolutionary zealots who found Chinese political and social systems wholly wrong and fundamental changes absolutely necessary. The young, the ardent, and the radical were too impatient to study concrete methods for solving localized problems.

In May 1922, when the Fengtien militarists† were defeated by the Chihli group, there seemed to be some hope that the political situation would improve. At that time Hu Shih, together with other intellectuals in the north,

† The Fengtien militarists were headed by Chang Tso-lin with their base in Manchuria. The Chihli group was led by generals Ts'ao K'un and Wu P'ei-fu, who for some time controlled the province of Chihli.

published "Our Political Opinion" in the *Endeavor Weekly* (*Nu-li Chou-pao*), of which he was the editor. In it he stated that it should be obvious to all that "good government" was the primary necessity for China at the time, regardless of what political doctrine one might adhere to. He laid down two positive objectives for a good government: it should work for the welfare of the people and it should respect individual freedom and safeguard "the development of individuality." He advocated a constitutional regime that would publicize its financial operations, recruit its personnel by open examination, and, above all, plan its political programs. It would also be desirable, he wrote, to reduce the size of the national and provincial legislatures, both of which should be elected directly by the people.[41] Hu's proposals clearly outlined some concrete methods for the solution of immediate problems. He wanted to avoid discussion of political doctrines, hoping that people of all political faiths could join in supporting his practical proposals. He was willing to accept the existing government and try to improve it. While he was not in principle opposed to revolution and believed that reform and revolution could proceed together, he considered revolution a necessary evil to be resorted to only when gradual reform had proved impossible. Consistently, he had been for some time opposed to the revolutionary methods of Sun Yat-sen, who attempted to subdue the warlords by military force.[42]

Hu's hopes for a better government under the Chihli group were soon dashed. Toward the autumn of 1923 the political situation deteriorated badly as members of parliament were openly bribed to elect Ts'ao K'un, chief of the Chihli group, president of China. This was followed by a period in which the militarists utterly disregarded all laws and brazenly trampled upon the principles of democracy. Under these circumstances it was apparent that any proposal for better government was futile, and Hu Shih suspended publication of the *Endeavor Weekly*, announcing that he would devote his time to the renovation of national attitudes, for unless the "ghosts"—an Ibsenian allusion—were driven out of the Chinese mind, no democracy would ever be possible.[43]

Notes

CHAPTER III. THE NEW TIDE

1. T'ai-yen (Chang Ping-lin), "Po chien-li K'ung-chiao i" (A Criticism of the Proposal to Establish a Confucian Religion), *Chia-yin* ("The Tiger"), 1.1: 16–18 (1914).
2. Ch'en Tu-hsiu, "Shih-an tzu-chuan" (My Autobiography), in T'ao Yüan-te, ed., *Tzu-chuan chih i-chang* (Chapters from Autobiographies) (Canton, 1927), I, 1–8.
3. Wu Yü, "Chih Ch'en Tu-hsiu shu" (Letter to Ch'en Tu-hsiu), *Hsin ch'ing-nien* (New Youth, hereafter cited as *HCN*), 2.5: 3–4 (Jan. 1917).
4. See Wu Yü, *Wu Yü wen-lu* (Collected Writings of Wu Yü) (Chengtu: Ai-chih lu, 1936), I, 1–8.
5. Lu Hsün, *Je feng* (Hot Wind) (Shanghai: Pei-hsin, 1925?), pp. 44–45.
6. Ch'en Tu-hsiu, "K'ung-tzu chih tao yü hsien-tai sheng-huo" (Confucian Principles and Modern Life), *HCN*, 2.4: 2 (Dec. 1916).
7. Ch'en, "Fu-p'i yü tsun-K'ung" (Monarchical Restoration and Reverence for Confucius), *HCN*, 3.6: 4 (Aug. 1917).
8. Ch'en, "Wu-jen chih tsui-hou chüeh-wu" (Our Final Awakening), *HCN*, 1.6: 4 (Feb. 1916).
9. Ch'en, "I-chiu i-liu nien" (The Year 1916), *HCN*, 1.5: 3 (Jan. 1916).
10. Ch'en, "Hsien-fa yü K'ung-chiao" (The Constitution and Confucianism), *HCN*, 2.3: 5 (Nov. 1916).
11. Wu Yü, "Chia-tsu chih-tu wei chuan-chih chu-i chih ken-chü lun" (The Family and Clan System Is the Basis of Despotism), *HCN*, 2.6: 1–2 (Feb. 1917).
12. Wu Yü, "Tu Hsün-tzu shu hou" (After Reading *Hsün Tzu*), *HCN*, 3.1: 1–2 (March 1917).
13. Wu Yü, "Lun li" (On Rites), *HCN*, 3.3: 5–7 (May 1917).
14. Wu Yü, "Tui-yü li-chi wen-t'i chih wo-chien" (My Views on the *Book of Rites*), in *Wu Yü wen-lu*, I, 9; Hu Shih, "Chen-ts'ao wen-t'i" (The Problem of Chastity), *HCN*, 5.1: 71 (July 1918); T'ang-ssu (Lu Hsün), "Wo chih chieh-lieh kuan" (My Views on Rigid Chastity), *HCN*, 5.2: 92–95 (Aug. 1918).
15. Wu Yü, "Ju-chia ta-t'ung pen-yü Lao-tzu shuo" (The Confucian Concept of Grand Unity is Derived from *Lao Tzu*), *HCN*, 3.5: 1 (July 1917).
16. Wu Yü, "Hsün-tzu cheng-chih lun" (The Political Theory of Hsün Tzu), in *Wu Yü wen hsü-lu* (Collected Writings of Wu Yü, Supplement) (Chengtu, 1937), II, 4–5.
17. *Wu Yü wen-lu*, II, 5.
18. I Pai-sha, "K'ung-tzu p'ing-i" (A Discussion of Confucius), *HCN*, 1.6: 6 (Feb. 1916).
19. Ch'en, *Tu-hsiu wen-ts'un* (Collected Writings of Ch'en Tu-hsiu) (Shanghai: Ya-tung, 1927), Vol. 4, Bk. 3, p. 30.
20. T'ang-ssu (Lu Hsün), "Sui-kan lu" (Random Thoughts), *HCN*, 5.5: 513 (Nov. 1918).

21. T'ao Li-kung (T'ao Meng-ho), "Hsin ch'ing-nien chih tao-te" (Morality of the New Youth), *HCN*, 4.2: 97 (Feb. 1918).
22. Kao I-han, "Fei chün-shih chu-i" (A Criticism of Ruler-ism and Teacher-ism), *HCN*, 5.6: 549–54 (Dec. 1918).
23. Chou Tso-jen, "Jen ti wen-hsüeh" (Human Literature), *HCN*, 5.6: 575–80.
24. Ch'en Tu-hsiu, "Chin-jih chih chiao-yü fang-chen" (Guidelines for Education Today), *HCN*, 1.2: 3 (Oct. 1915).
25. T'ang-ssu, "Wo-men hsien-tsai tsen-yang tso fu-ch'in" (How Should We Behave as Fathers Today?), *HCN*, 6.6: 556–57 (Nov. 1919).
26. Hu Shih, "Fei ko-jen chu-i ti hsin sheng-huo" (A New Life of Non-Individualism), in *Hu Shih wen-ts'un* (Collected Writings of Hu Shih) (Shanghai: Ya-tung, 1925), Collection 1, Bk. 4, pp. 174, 185.
27. Ch'en Tu-hsiu, "Po K'ang Yu-wei kung-wo p'ing-i" (A Criticism of K'ang Yu-wei, "Comments on Republicanism"), *HCN*, 4.3: 200–6 (March 1918).
28. Ch'en, "Shih-hsing min-chih ti chi-ch'u" (The Basis for the Realization of Democracy), *HCN*, 7.1: 18 (Dec. 1919).
29. Ch'en, "Tung Hsi min-tsu ken-pen ssu-hsiang chih ch'a-i" (Differences of Basic Thought between Eastern and Western Peoples), *HCN*, 1.4: 3 (Dec. 1915).
30. Ch'en, "Chin-jih Chung-kuo chih cheng-chih wen-t'i" (The Political Problem of China Today), *HCN*, 5.1: 2 (July 1918).
31. Ch'en, "Fa-lü yü yen-lun tzu-yu" (Law and Freedom of Speech), *HCN*, 7.1: 115 (Dec. 1919).
32. Ch'en, "Jen-sheng chen i" (The True Meaning of Life), *HCN*, 4.2: 90–93 (Feb. 1918).
33. Ch'en, "Ti-k'ang li" (Force of Resistance), *Ch'ing-nien tsa-chih* (The Youth Magazine), 1.3: 4–5 (Nov. 1915).
34. Hu Shih, "Wen-t'i yü chu-i" (Problems and Isms), *Hu Shih wen-ts'un*, Collection 1, Bk. 2, pp. 147 ff.
35. *Ibid.*, p. 151.
36. Hu Shih, "Hsin ssu-ch'ao ti i-i" (The Significance of the New Currents of Thought), *HCN*, 7.1: 9–10 (Dec. 1919).
37. Hu Shih, "Shih-yen chu-i" (Pragmatism), *Hu Shih wen-ts'un*, Collection 1, Bk. 2, p. 80.
38. Lan Chih-hsien, "Wen-t'i yü chu-i" (Problems and Isms), *ibid.*, Collection 1, Bk. 2, p. 80.
39. Li Ta-chao, "Tsai-lun wen-t'i yü chu-i" (Further Discussion of Problems and Isms), *ibid.*, Bk. 2, p. 171.
40. *Hu Shih wen-ts'un*, Collection 1, Bk. 3, pp. 98, 102.
41. Hu Shih and associates, "Wo-men ti cheng-chih chu-chang" (Our Political Proposals), *ibid.*, Collection 2, Bk. 3, pp. 27–34.
42. *Hu Shih wen-ts'un*, Collection 2, pp. 35–40.
43. *Ibid.* pp. 141–51.

Chapter IV

THE RISE OF RADICALISM

Socialism

AROUND the turn of the century, socialism caught the attention of Chinese thinkers. As early as 1902 Liang Ch'i-ch'ao discussed Karl Marx in his *New People's Magazine* (*Hsin-min Ts'ung-pao*) published in Japan, and Sun Yat-sen's "Principle of the People's Livelihood," which he introduced in 1905, was a modified version of socialism. Sun's followers began to propagate the party line, and Chu Chih-hsin in particular published articles on socialism in the *People's Journal* (*Min-pao*), the organ of Sun's party in Tokyo.[1] About the same time, in 1907, Chinese anarchist journals were being published in Paris and Tokyo and smuggled to the Chinese mainland where they were read surreptitiously. It was not, however, until after the Revolution of 1911 that socialism was openly advocated in China. The first Chinese Socialist party in China was organized by Chiang K'ang-hu (Kiang Kang-hu) about a month after the outbreak of the revolution.

Chiang had gone to Japan to study some ten years before and had quickly become interested in socialism. During his second visit to Japan, in 1903, he took up the anarchist idea of "no state, no family, no religion," and upon his return to China he began to advocate equal education for women. In 1905 he established in Peking the first Chinese-supported girls' school. Four years later he went to Europe "to get in touch with the Western socialists." He did not return until 1911, when he made a number of speeches on socialism that nearly got him arrested by the Manchu regime. He was saved by the outbreak of the revolution, and lost no time in organizing the Chinese Socialist party. His ideas were tolerated at first, but the Peking government later came to consider them dangerous and in 1913 ordered the dissolution of the party. Chiang went to the United States, where for several years he taught Chinese language and civilization at the University of California at Berkeley and subsequently became head of the Chinese section in the Library of Congress.[2] In 1921 he visited Russia, but the trip did not convert him to Communism. He had conceived the idea of making Outer Mongolia an experimental district of socialism, and his failure to win Russian support for his plan may have contributed to his displeasure with the Russian Communists.[3] At any rate, when he returned to China the following year he spoke disparagingly of Russia.

Chiang might well be called a social democrat, although he himself considered general socialism preferable to any specific kind, and was more inclined by both temperament and philosophy to conciliation and compromise than to the logical extreme. He laid down four objectives for socialism:

1. Public ownership of natural resources. Land, mines, and forest, as well as sunlight, air, and water, should belong to the public, but property that is accumulated by labor should not be confiscated if it is not used for capitalist purposes. Referring to the ancient "well-field" system of equal land ownership, Chiang maintained that public ownership of land was not only desirable but feasible; but he had no particular preference as to which method was used to divest the landlord of his lands. He listed the revolutionary method of confiscation in Bolshevik Russia, the single tax of Henry George, and Sun Yat-sen's peaceful, equitable distribution of land, noting that each method was permissible according to circumstances.

2. Free education and social welfare. The state should

provide free education from kindergarten to the university, with full allowances for necessary maintenance, to all children, girls and boys. Child-care institutions, homes for the aged, and infirmaries for the disabled should be public social services, not charity enterprises.

3. Vocational representation. To counteract the influence of the intellectuals who traditionally dominated the political scene, Chiang recommended representation by vocation, which would gradually eliminate from power those who did not work. There would, however, be minimum educational qualifications to make sure that those who participated in politics were not entirely ignorant. Since education would be free, this would not be unequal treatment; on the contrary, it would encourage people to get the basic education necessary for good citizenship.

4. Direct democracy. Like Sun Yat-sen, Chiang favored initiative, referendum, and recall in addition to popular election. The government he envisaged would be a "single power system" with the parliament exercising supreme authority. The parliament, to be elected by vocational groups, would choose an executive committee and a judicial committee. Chiang felt that the modern trend was against the separation of powers, and he pointed to the council government of Switzerland, the parliamentary government of Britain, and the soviet government of Russia as examples.[4]

Chiang opposed the Communist formula "From each according to his abilities, to each according to his needs." He wanted to eliminate the artificial inequality set up by class, wealth, and power, but recognized that innate differences in intelligence and ability created an inevitable inequality that could not be eliminated. The contributions of the elite to social progress had to be recognized, and therefore work had to be paid for according to its value. Different rates of compensation would not, however, lead to capitalism, for whatever one received would be used for consumption, not for profit; they would lead only to different kinds of enjoyment, which Chiang considered an individual matter that should not be regulated by the state.[5]

Chiang believed that capitalism should be abolished, but he favored a gradual abolition rather than an outright overthrow. He did not consider it necessary to uproot the "capitalistic civilization." Since Marx had said that socialism was the ultimate development of capitalism, the only change necessary was to convert private into public ownership, while maintaining the efficiency and comfort of capitalism. Chiang deplored the naïvety of the Russian Communists who had destroyed everything connected with capitalism during the early days of the Bolshevik Revolution. He maintained that non-profit-making property could be privately owned, and he favored compensating the owner whose property was confiscated by the public and allowing former capitalists to vote if they had an occupation.[6]

How was socialism to be realized? Chiang had a low opinion of the "model establishments" of the New Village Movement begun in 1919 by the radical intellectuals in Peking, in which groups of people set themselves apart to build a new community on socialist principles. Such attempts to seek a better life outside of society were, he considered, selfishly motivated and had little to do with the welfare of the masses. Furthermore, social pressure predestined the failure of any small community within a society that was opposed to its principles. Socialism could succeed only as a fundamental solution to the whole social problem.[7]

Neither was revolution, which leads to fanaticism and results in bloodshed, the proper means to achieve socialism in Chiang's opinion. Revolution destroys too much and plays too easily into the hands of those who seek personal power. Chiang therefore refused to advocate class struggle or any form of violence. He was, however, aware that revolution is often caused by official oppression, which may not be stopped by admonitions. Therefore, he believed that if revolution came the socialist should be prepared to step forward and lead the destructive forces to socialist ends.

He considered guild socialism and syndicalism impractical because their national organization could be no more than an association of economic groups without a government's powers to deal with political problems. A socialist state must have a government, but the government must not be so powerful that it can become tyrannical. A devolution of powers to the local levels would not only provide a safeguard against bureaucratic despotism, but also ensure the protection of group or local interests. The theory of dictatorship by the proletariat was objectionable, since it would exclude from the government the intellectuals, who were indispensable to a successful social reconstruction.[8]

Thus Chiang believed the only way to attain socialism was through political participation. His own experience and observation of the socialist parties of the world led him to be cautious even in holding this view. Since past failure did not necessarily preclude future success, Chiang was willing to give the Socialist party another chance, and in 1925 he reorganized it into the New Socialist Democratic party. Before the reformed party became active, however, it was discovered that he had offered his services to P'u-i, the abdicated Manchu emperor. Public reaction to the move was so hostile that he found it necessary to leave for Canada.[9]

An analysis of Chiang's socialist ideas based on his writings in the 1920's shows that he became more consistent than he had been in the early days of the Republic, when his views were ambiguous and equivocal. In the early days, Chiang was opposed to property, family, religion, and state, and at the same time espoused freedom of business and the single tax. He had flirted with the anarchists and tried to include all kinds of socialists in a single party. Although his Socialist party had claimed over 400,-000 members, many of them had had practically no understanding of socialism. By attempting to conciliate all factions Chiang had succeeded only in antagonizing them all, and the anarchists, for one, accused him of muddle and inconsistency. Although he had become more lucid by the time he returned from Russia in 1922, his moderate views did not appeal to the new generation, which had turned radical after the May Fourth Movement (1919). He was daring enough to be the first Chinese to organize a Socialist party, but his classical background and early connection with the Manchu regime prevented him from carrying his arguments to their logical conclusion. Thus, while he had advocated freedom of love on the one hand, he had stressed the virtue of filial piety on the other. "Wherever there are human relations, there must be ethics." In his writings of the 1920's Chiang became more and more concerned with what was practicable. "Attack on filial piety may be justified in the future; for the present it is neither practicable nor desirable."[10]

It was Chiang's belief that nations should have their individual cultures and that Chinese culture would have to "marry" the West to give birth to a culture that was distinctly Chinese. Wholesale transplantation was not feasible, but a synthesis of West and East was. It is significant that while he claimed a Marxist background, Chiang was interested in developing a "great agricultural civilization" that would avoid the periodic economic depressions of industrial capitalism, international conflicts caused by commercial expansion, and all other evils associated with urban civilization. He was greatly impressed by the peaceful, healthy conditions prevalent in rural areas of the United States and thought that China's agricultural tradition could serve as the convenient basis for rural development in a similar direction.[11]

After the establishment of the Chinese Communist party in 1921, Chiang K'ang-hu's socialism soon became out of step with the developing radical trends. His lack of force in matters of organization also limited his influence. Chiang had never been much of an original thinker. His moderate syncretism was more a conglomeration of other men's views than a true synthesis. His contribution lay rather in spreading the general ideas of socialism at a time when the doctrine was regarded as a dangerous heresy in China.

Anarchism

In 1907 a number of Chinese scholars founded in Paris the *New Century* (*Hsin Shih-chi*), which immediately became an important organ of the Chinese anarchist movement. Its editors were Wu Chih-hui, Li Shih-tseng, and Ch'u Min-i. All three were well trained in Chinese classics, but were disenchanted with the traditional institutions and the old way of life.

Wu Chih-hui (1864–1953) had participated in revolutionary activities before coming to France. A learned man with an incisive mind, he believed in science and materialism, reason and progress. His influence as a writer was due to the humorous yet poignant way in which he presented his serious ideas. Among modern Chinese writers he was perhaps the only one truly able to turn vulgarism into humor and vilification into literature.

Of the early background of Ch'u Min-i (1884–1946) little is known except that he studied medicine in

France.[12] Li Shih-tseng (1881–) was the son of a top-ranking minister of the Manchu monarchy. Although it was a rarity that a scion of such aristocratic standing should turn radical revolutionist, the change may be explained partly by the fact that his study of biology led him to a strong belief in science, and traditional Chinese ideas seemed the more unacceptable to him because they were unscientific. The radical influences of France, where anarchism was embraced with passion, may have had an impact on the thinking of these Chinese students. Traditional institutions having so utterly failed to meet the challenge of the times, the radicals were eager to seek a new doctrine that could provide a fundamental solution to China's social problems.

Like Bakunin and Kropotkin from whom they drew their inspiration, the Paris group advocated anarchism of the communistic rather than individualistic type. Holding rigorous rules of personal conduct, they considered it a moral responsibility for all to participate in building an ideal society for the future. They attacked authority, government, and state as barriers to freedom, equality, and progress,[13] and they believed in evolution and infinite progress, but in the sense of Kropotkinian mutual aid rather than Darwinian survival of the fittest.

The Paris group stood for permanent revolution which, however, should not be confused with what Lenin or Trotsky meant by the term. To these Chinese anarchists revolution meant change through education. It was to be as endless a process as social progress itself. To Wu Chih-hui, there was no such thing as completion of the revolution. Just as education would not one day cease, so too revolution would be carried on forever.[14]

In this light revolution was no more than evolution or reform. But despite this fact, the Paris group agreed that reform could be supplemented by violent revolution. According to Ch'u Min-i, if education was positive evolution, revolution was negative evolution—the destructive force necessary to the building of a new society. He made it clear, however, that the more constructive process of education was to follow.[15]

The anarchist revolution was a social one, aimed at overthrowing the whole social system with its selfish, corrupt, and unjust institutions and practices. It sought to build a new society based on justice and truth, and on a new morality that would follow the laws of nature and develop with the growth of knowledge. This morality would be free, humane, genuine, and universal. Having all of humanity as its scope, it would know of no state boundaries and would not be distorted by the selfishness that arises from family and class distinctions. There would be no marriage, no property, no class, no government, and no state in the new society. Universal love and humanitarianism would prevail.[16]

Although the *New Century* writers upheld morality, they condemned religion, which, Wu Chih-hui contended, made use of morality to obstruct progress. Anarchist socialism, while it had all the moral elements of religion, had none of its superstitions and corrupt practices. Wu saw religion as being antiscience and antievolution and as having come into existence at a time when human knowledge was limited. He felt that with the inevitable expansion of knowledge, religion would recede as socialism advanced.[17]

In advocating a new society, the Paris group had to make a vehement attack upon China's traditional institutions. The concept of the Three Bonds, which served as the pillars of Chinese society, became their first target. The Three Bonds, wrote Li Shih-tseng, were based on a threefold power: that of the ruler over his subjects, that of the father over his sons, and that of the husband over his wife. According to Li, this system acted in direct violation of the principles of equality, was inhuman, and obstructed progress. To destroy it, he proposed the abolition of the family system altogether. He further wanted to eliminate ancestor worship, which he considered a "religious superstition" set up to lure the people into contentment with their fate, which shielded from them the inequity and injustice of their social system.[18]

From this attack on China's institutions, it was but a logical step to the condemnation of the traditional philosophies. These the anarchists considered to be the instruments of monarchical powers and the cause of China's decline and stratification.[19] The classical tradition was held accountable for the lack of modern knowledge, for the obstruction of social progress, and for the national arrogance and complacency that led to discrimination against all things foreign. Confucius was ridiculed as a crafty man who took advantage of the people's ignorance to make himself a sage. Taoism also came under attack, and Wu Chih-hui emphasized that anarchism, based on the concepts of evolution and progress, had nothing to do with the Taoist philosophy of inaction.[20] In their attack upon ancient ideologies, the Paris group anticipated by a decade the New Culture Movement.[21]

The *New Century* publishers maintained good relations with Sun Yat-sen. In 1905 and 1907 respectively, Wu Chih-hui and Chang Ching-chiang, the financial supporter of the journal, joined the T'ung-meng Hui, Sun's revolutionary party. But the chasm between anarchism and Sun's principles was unmistakable. Disagreement arose when Chang Ping-lin, editor of the *People's Journal,* began to expound anti-Manchuism. To the Chinese anarchists, this act smacked of revenge, contrary to the anarchist view of justice. A close comparison of the arguments of the two sides, however, reveals that their differences were of a verbal nature. The Paris group had no objection to the policy of overthrowing the Manchu authority per se, but they felt that the Manchu people as a whole should not have been made a target of revenge, but rather judged on an individual basis. A person could be punished if he had violated "universal reason," but should not be held responsible for the crimes committed by his ancestors against the Chinese people.[22] Here the anarchist position was in reality not much different from that of the *People's Journal.* Chang Ping-lin made it clear that it was the Manchu monarchy and its officials and troops that should be driven out, while the Manchu people were to be permitted to live in China and make their living if they were willing to become Chinese citizens. The *People's Journal* did insist, however, upon using the slogan of revenge— not only because revenge was proper where law was not applicable, but because the slogan would raise the morale of the Chinese rebels.[23]

It is interesting to note that Chang Ping-lin, in spite of nationalistic avowals, was at heart a nihilist of the Buddhist variety. Chang believed that anarchism was unsuitable for China at this particular time, when internally she was subject to the oppressive rule of a minority race and externally suffering from foreign aggression. But mostly he criticized the Paris group for not being radical enough in its philosophy to carry its theory to the logical conclusion. According to Chang, the highest state of enlightenment was the extinction not only of government, but also of society, of humanity, of living things, and of the world. Evolution was an illusion, since the course of nature did not advance in a straight line but revolved in a circle. The "universal reason" of anarchism, absolutely applied and unconditionally imposed on people, was, he felt, merely a dogma, as harmful to individual freedom as religion was.[24]

But Chang was known for his eccentricity. Other leaders of the T'ung-meng Hui did not necessarily subscribe to his classical nationalism or to his Buddhist nihilism. And Sun's eclecticism was purposely flexible to embrace all revolutionaries. His principle of the People's Livelihood, a modest brand of socialism, helped to soften the anarchist opposition. The leaders of the Paris group, too, were far from dogmatic in their advocacy of principles. They realized that it would take a long time—perhaps centuries—before anarchism could be achieved, and in the meantime it was desirable to support a revolution that aimed at overthrowing an oppressive authority. Thus Wu Chih-hui conceded that, when necessary, military force could be used for revolutionary purposes. He even admitted that, although they should assail those who used the state to harm people, the anarchists should forgive those who used it for self-preservation.[25] Ch'u Min-i, after pointing out the differences between anarchism on the one hand and nationalism and democracy on the other, went on to say that the two do not in fact go in opposite directions, but differ only in scope and degree. "Socialism [i.e., anarchism] aims at freedom, equality, and welfare for entire humanity, while nationalism and democracy aim at freedom, equality and welfare for a state, a nation, or a minority."[26] Partly because of this ideological proximity and partly because of personal friendship with Sun Yat-sen, the Paris group was eventually absorbed into the fold of Sun's T'ung-meng Hui.

In 1907, the same year that the *New Century* appeared in Paris, a group of Chinese revolutionaries in Tokyo organized a Socialist Discussion Society to propagate anarchism. Its leaders were Chang Chi, Liu Shih-p'ei (also known as Liu Kuang-han), and his wife Ho Chen. Chang Chi (1882–1947) was an activist rather than a theoretician. Except for the translation of two books on anarchism, he does not seem to have published much on the subject.[27] It was therefore the Lius who were mainly responsible for the publication of the *T'ien-i Pao* (*The Universal Principle*), which served as anarchism's organ in Tokyo as the *New Century* did in Paris. Since Ho Chen largely confined herself to the theme of the emancipation of women, it fell to Liu Shih-p'ei (1884–1919) to expound anarchism's general principles. A scholar with a classical education, Liu had written for the revolutionary journals in China. In Japan he had joined the T'ung-meng Hui, but he had soon made the acquaintance of the Japanese anarchists and was converted by them. His writings, citing Western anarchists but at the same time well-grounded in classical Chinese history and philosophy, attracted wide attention among the Chinese students studying in Japan.[28]

Like other anarchists, Liu Shih-p'ei analyzed the rise of authority. He traced the formation of classes to war and found the cause of war in the desire for wealth. War, he maintained, required a commander, and the successful commander eventually became the ruler. Authority was thus established, and society divided into ruler and ruled. The rulers represented military and economic power: the nobles, the rich, and the educated. The ruled were the inferior, the poor, and those having no opportunity for study, the ignorant. The key to equality lay therefore in the abolition of the army and of property.[29]

Liu devoted much of his attention to equality. Like Rousseau, he believed that men are born equal and that equality prevails in the state of nature. He had high hopes that equality could again be attained, for although it was in human nature to be jealous as well as compassionate, he believed that the good in man could be developed to overcome the evil. Not only equality, but absolute equality, was feasible in human society. One of the criticisms of communism was that while people would always be glad to take what they need, it was doubtful that they would at all times work to their capacity. And since they would not, inequality, conflicts, and disorder would ensue.

In a most daring and ingenious manner, Liu worked out a plan of "equal work" that assigned definite work to all from birth to death. His plan called for the abolition of boundaries and the division of the entire world into small districts with no more than a thousand people each. Under it rest homes would be established for children and old people, where the aged would nurse and teach the young from birth until the age of ten. Between ten and twenty years of age every one would devote half of the day to the study of liberal arts and the other half to learning how to make machinery and daily necessities. The teachers would be those who had reached the age of fifty. Between the ages of twenty-one and fifty everyone of the same age would have the same function to perform. Thus a man at the age of twenty-one would participate in the construction of roads; at twenty-two he would work in the mines and forests; from twenty-three to twenty-six he would build houses; from twenty-seven to thirty, he would manufacture metal vessels and ceramics; from thirty-one to thirty-six, he would produce textiles and clothes; from thirty-seven to forty, he would work in the kitchens; from forty-one to forty-five, he would engage in transportation; and from forty-six to fifty, he would serve as engineer or as physician. During the farming seasons everyone between twenty-one and thirty-six would devote himself entirely to agricultural work and suspend other productive activities. Except when engaged in this last occupation, everyone would be required to work only two hours a day. For the rest of the time one could study or do some other work that pleased him. In this way, said Liu, absolute equality could be attained, and there would be no jealousy and conflict. It was Liu's belief that his system would require no supervision and therefore no authority, although it is not clear to whom would be given the responsibility of assigning a specific job to an individual within the same work category.

The difficulties of this scheme are obvious. Could a person be so versatile as to be able to do, in the course of his life, almost everything in the world? Would such technical persons as doctors and engineers have enough time for learning and practicing to advance their skills and extend their knowledge? Would it not be too great a strain to live under such uniformity and systematization? But Liu was more concerned with equality than with freedom, and he saw no problem of pleasure and pain, because, he felt, the contrast between the two would disappear when all people did the same work and shared the same feelings.[30]

In contrast to the Paris group, which viewed anarchism as an ideal to be attained over the centuries through human progress and social revolution (or evolution), Liu advocated its immediate realization. He believed that anarchism could be practiced more easily in China than in the West, for the traditional philosophies of China—Confucianism and Taoism—favored a system of laissez faire and noninterference. Since the Han dynasty (206 B.C.–A.D. 219), Liu pointed out, the Confucianists had emphasized a state governed by decorum and rites over one governed by law and punishment. They held that one could influence and transform people by cultivating their virtues, and believed that as morality advanced, government interference diminished. The Confucian ideal of state was one in which government and law were no longer necessary.[31] Liu dealt with the problem of the military and economic power upon which government authority is based by pointing out that it had been Chinese tradition

to oppose militarism and to look down upon the merchants.[32]

In Liu's view the only obstacle to anarchism in China
was the traditional belief in the distinction between superior and inferior, high and low. But there would be no
great difficulty in abolishing this superstition.[33] Liu went
so far as to declare that "today, as all come to know the
fallacy of the teachings of propriety, the traditional theory
of ethical relations has collapsed."[34] The assertion was
undoubtedly premature, for in 1907 Confucian ethics remained predominant, while radical ideas were just beginning to trickle into some of the large cities. In this respect
Liu was utterly unrealistic compared with the New Century writers, who at that time recognized the strength of
traditional institutions and therefore were at greater pains
to discredit them.

Liu, too, was a member of the T'ung-meng Hui, but
his anarchist enthusiasm soon led him to criticize Sun
Yat-sen's authority as president. Liu was opposed to the
idea of any new government's being set up after the revolution, and particularly he was against the establishment
of a well-organized modern democracy with its powerful
army and advanced industry, for in the long run it would
be much more difficult to abolish. The higher the degree
of industrialization and the more advanced the civilization, Liu felt, the more poverty-stricken and the less free
the people would be. "True happiness lies not in the
false civilization but in peace, contentment, harmony and
ease."[35] Liu's ideal was very nearly the Taoist utopia
in which "people have nothing to seek and nothing to
fight for."[36] Differing from his Paris comrades, Liu constantly looked back to classical China for his inspiration,
and his plan of "equal work" can be traced to Hsü
Hsing, an ancient Chinese agronomist who advocated that

princes cultivate the land on an equal basis with their people.

Liu's career as an anarchist was cut short in 1908 when he returned to China with his wife and entered the service of the Manchu viceroy Tuan Fang as an informer. The move has been attributed to his personal quarrels with some of the T'ung-meng Hui leaders and to his inability to control the party by staffing it with Japanese anarchists.[37] Since in his view traditional Chinese government was "in a way similar to anarchism," and a new form of government would not be as good as the old,[38] his treacherous about-face involved less ideological duplicity than first appears.

Eventually anarchism took roots in China itself. During the Socialist party congress in October 1912, the leftist wing, dissatisfied with Chiang K'ang-hu's modest brand of socialism, announced its withdrawal and organized a new, more anarchistic Socialist party, which proclaimed as its platform six points: 1. the practice of communism; 2. respect for individuals; 3. the establishment of equal education; 4. the abolition of national boundaries; 5. the elimination of clans; and 6. the overthrow of religion. Within a month after its formation, however, the new party was suppressed by President Yüan Shih-k'ai, who was in no mood to tolerate an anarchist-inclined organization.

But anarchism continued to be energetically promoted in another part of the country. In May 1912 the Hui-ming She (Cockcrow Society), the first anarchist group to set itself the task of spreading anarchism to the interior, was organized in Canton. In a sense it was a continuation of the work of the *New Century,* whose seeds were now "watered and cultivated" in China itself.[39]

The leader of the Hui-ming She was Liu Shih-fu, who was born in 1884 in Hsiangshan (now Chungshan) district, Kwangtung. In 1899, at the age of fifteen, he passed the district examination with the degree of Hsiu-ts'ai (Cultivated Talent). In 1904 he went to Japan, where he joined the T'ung-meng Hui. He returned to China in 1906 and immediately engaged himself in a plot to assassinate the admiral of Canton. As he was taking out the home-made bomb, it exploded and wounded his left hand. He was imprisoned for more than two years on suspicion of intending to commit an act of violence, but the government never succeeded in getting definite evidence for his conviction and he was released. He then went to Hong Kong, where he came across some issues of the *New Century* and became interested in anarchistic theories. When the revolution finally overthrew the Manchu regime, he was so disappointed with the former revolutionaries' position-seeking and profit-making that he decided to become an active supporter of anarchism.[40]

In 1912 he organized in Canton the Hsin She (Heart Club) for the practice of individual morality. Its twelve rules were: 1. not to eat meat; 2. not to drink liquor; 3. not to smoke; 4. not to ride in sedan chairs and rickshaws; 5. not to employ servants; 6. not to marry; 7. not to carry family names; 8. not to become government officials; 9. not to become legislators; 10. not to join any political party; 11. not to enlist in any military service; 12. not to believe in any religion.[41] Although Shih-fu observed the rules strictly himself, he never interfered with the conduct of others.

In August 1913, the Hui-ming She began to publish *The Voice of the People* (*Min-sheng*). But after two issues it was suppressed by the government and the Society dispersed. In 1914 the Anarchist-Communism Comrades Club was organized in Shanghai as a headquarters for the encouragement of anarchist activities in various localities of China and for cooperation with the anarchists

of other countries. The anarchists even extended their activities to the Chinese workers in Southeast Asia, where
they published *The Voice of Justice* (*Cheng-sheng*), a
counterpart of *The Voice of the People,* which they continued to issue clandestinely in China.[42]

In general Shih-fu followed the principles of Kropotkin,
whom he regarded as anarchism's greatest exponent, and,
like other anarchists, he was noted for his clear thinking
and logical arguments. Since he rejected all kinds of authority, he did not have to bother with compromise and
reconciliation, which he felt could become the sources of
confusion and inconsistency. His severe criticism of
Chiang K'ang-hu helped to clarify the issues confronting
anarchism. In pointing out that Chiang's acceptance of
free enterprise was in direct contrast to the basic socialist
principle of abolishing private ownership, Shih-fu made it
impossible for anarchists to cooperate with him; while
in censuring the new Socialist party's political activities,
Shih-fu practically laid down the rule that all political
parties, including revolutionary ones, should henceforth
be eschewed.[43]

It was Shih-fu's belief that anarchists should reject all
authority, whether governmental, familial, or religious.
It was authority that sustained an unequal, oppressive social system whose basis was private ownership. Laws, he
held, should be abolished and the government overthrown
so that everyone would be free to do the work he liked,
to live with the woman he loved, and to take what he
needed. Shih-fu believed in man's good nature and conscience, which together would guide him to assist and
be fair and just to others, to do what social good required,
and to exert himself to make progress. He admitted that
there might be some perverse men who would work
against the good of the community, but these people were
few and could be easily expelled.[44]

Shih-fu was an exponent of communist anarchism. It was his belief that once the abolition of private ownership had taken place, all productive means would belong to the public, and that as men all work according to their capacities, they should receive according to their need. Like Kropotkin, he regarded assassination as a justified protest against repression and as a forceful means of stirring up the people. He would not eat meat, considering it cruel to kill animals that do mankind no harm; on the other hand, the elimination of a public enemy in the interests of humanitarianism he considered to be no violation of the ideals of universal love. Writing in 1914, he counseled, however, that as far as China was concerned it was not yet opportune to resort to violent measures and for the time being at least, efforts at conversion should be confined to the written and spoken word.[45]

Never in good health, Shih-fu suffered further from malnutrition and lack of medical care. But he did not give up his work, which in the later years of his life consisted mainly of publishing *The Voice of the People* and corresponding with his comrades in China and abroad. Assisted by only a few persons and always worried about funds, he not only wrote and edited, but in order to keep the journal going also performed domestic tasks in his apartment, which doubled as his workshop. The dismal struggle continued until tuberculosis and hard work finally exhausted him. He died on March 27, 1915, at the age of thirty-one. His death deprived anarchism of a vigorous leader; but if the anarchist force was scattered because of the loss of a central figure, it had yet to disappear from the Chinese scene.

In 1919, anarchist influences began to show among the radical intellectuals in Peking, who started the New Village Movement with the purpose of experimenting with socialist principles. A group of students would rent in the "New Village" a house where they would assist one another in their studies and do all the housework themselves so as to appreciate better the sanctity of manual labor. As already pointed out, the movement incurred criticism from both Hu Shih and Chiang K'ang-hu.

Also inspired by the anarchists, although they did not directly take part in it, was the Society for Mass Education, organized about this time by Chang Kuo-t'ao, later a leader of the Chinese Communist party. The Society believed in social reform through mass education and took its rationale from the anarchist slogan "Go to the masses."[46]

The anarchists were also active at this time in the Society for the Study of Socialism, organized at Peking University in December 1919. Later the group split, and an Anarchist Study Society was formed under the leadership of Chu Ch'ien-chih, an anarchist with individualistic proclivities.[47] It appears that there were more followers of anarchism than of Communism among the Peking University students at this time; for when Li Ta-chao undertook to organize a Communist party nucleus in Peking in September 1920, of the nine founding members five were anarchists. These, in accordance with their doctrine, insisted that the nucleus should have no officers. In deference to their position, it was decided at the founding meeting that Li should act as the party's coordinator rather than its secretary. This strange cooperation between the anarchists and the Communists did not last long, however.

As the Communists strengthened their organizations and increased their activities, their split with the anarchists was carried into the open. In 1920 criticism of anarchism began to appear in the pages of *New Youth*. But it was Ch'en Tu-hsiu's speech in Canton that finally roused anarchist ire and led to the debate between Communism and anarchism, in the persons of Ch'en and Ou Sheng-pai. In his speech Ch'en charged that the anarchists believed in absolute individual freedom, which, while feasible in the arts and morality, was not so in political and economic matters. A free association could never succeed if its members had absolute freedom to do what they wanted. Without a central organization to coordinate, plan, and intervene, a free association could never handle the complicated economic problems of the modern age, especially the pressing one of the socialization of China's agriculture and industry. Free contract, Ch'en added, could never take the place of law, which was necessary to the maintenance of order and peace, including the enforcement of contracts. What would happen if some people did not want to work, did not want to be educated, did not want to observe the free contracts or be persuaded and convinced? Human nature was not all good, contended Ch'en. Force was required not only to suppress evil men but to overthrow the evil political and economic system.[48]

In his reply, Ou pointed out that communist anarchism was not individualistic, because it worked through voluntary associations, which individuals could join and leave at will. It was not the communist anarchists' belief that individuals should disregard public interest and social welfare; their belief was not in absolute individual freedom, but in relative freedom and a better social life. While the majority could not force the minority to comply, the minority nevertheless should not sabotage the decisions of the majority. It could withdraw from the association if it disagreed with the decisions of the majority, but it must not obstruct the association. While an obstructor would be reasoned with, Ou added, he would be expelled if he refused either to be persuaded or to withdraw. Nor did the communist anarchists necessarily advocate nonresistance: force would be used to remove an obstructor—indeed, to eliminate the bureaucrats and the capitalists—if necessary. There was a difference between resistance and repression, Ou insisted. Force should be used for the former purpose but not the latter, that is, for self-defense but not for ruling others.[49]

The central point at issue in the debate was whether social order and peace could be maintained without government and law. According to Ou, "common will" could be substituted for law. If there was a recalcitrant member obstructing an association and refusing to withdraw, a public meeting of all the members would be held, in which it would be decided what should be done with the obstructive party. Force would be applied if common will deemed it necessary. Common will was preferable to law, argued Ou, in that it could decide in individual cases, whereas law was rigidly fixed, regardless of special situations. To Ch'en's accusation that this would lead to mob rule, Ou countered with an optimistic view of human nature. In the first place, a public meeting was necessary only on rare occasions when a recalcitrant party refused to listen to reason. A member who freely joined an association would not normally obstruct it. He had, moreover, the freedom to withdraw. A person with a sense of what is right could hardly insist on remaining a member if he was no longer wanted. Secondly, there would be no reason to fear mob rule, for with the spread of education and the advance of scientific training, men would be governed by reason. In an anarchistic society there were "very few die-hards." A public meeting to force the expulsion of a member would occur only on rare occasions.[50]

In Ou's view, free contract could take the place of law not only in solving economic problems, but also in rendering central control unnecessary. Pursuing Kropotkin's line of thought, he maintained that there would be hardly any breaches of contracts and thus no need of law to stand behind them. On the rare occasions that contracts were violated, a public meeting could be convoked to solve the problem.[51] In his debate with Ch'en Tu-hsiu, Ou attempted to steer a middle course between individualism and Communism. His Kropotkinian approach, however, gave rise to some inconsistency and confusion, forcing him to retreat from a position of absolute freedom to relative freedom, and from nonviolence to resistance.

Ch'en criticized Ou's group of communist anarchists, but at the same time tried to win them over.[52] It was for the individualist anarchists, whom he called nihilist and corrupt, that Ch'en reserved his most virulent attacks, however.[53] The individualist anarchists, for their part, were outraged by Ch'en's use of the term "enlightened despotism" for the necessity of strict interference in political and educational matters in order to sweep away the corruption and lethargy of the Chinese people. Ch'en, charged Chu Ch'ien-chih, would turn out to be an archdespot; and Chu vowed that for the freedom of man he would fight him to the bitter end.[54]

In 1924–1925, in response to Sun Yat-sen's cooperation with Soviet Russia and the Chinese Communists, the anarchists launched a vigorous attack on Bolshevism. A number of articles exposing the oppression, tyranny, terror, and destruction in Soviet Russia were published in *The People's Bell* (*Min-chung*) and *Freeman* (*Tzu-yu Jen*) and were later reprinted in book form under the title *The Tragedy of the Soviet Russian Revolution*.[55] Appended to the book was a document called "Protest of the League of South-China Anarchists to the Russian Government," which succinctly set forth the Chinese anarchists' views on Soviet Russia. In this document recognition was given to the use of force, which the Chinese anarchists thought might be employed during the process of revolution in cases of dire necessity. But their stress was upon evolution, whose function they believed to be the elimination, as far as possible, of the remnants of bestiality, and the promotion of the development of genuine human nature, that is, qualities of freedom and equality, universal love, and mutual aid. The Soviet government, in suppressing mass uprisings and eliminating socialist opponents, was using the name of revolution to camouflage bestial behavior. It was obstructing the progress of humanitarianism and had to be recognized as counterrevolutionary.[56] Thus the main ground upon which the Bolshevik Revolution was condemned was again humanitarianism, which had had a strong hold upon the Chinese anarchists since its first exposition in the *New Century*. The Chinese anarchists persistently put their faith in rational man and built their hopes on a rational world.

Among the Chinese anarchists of the 1920's who played an important part in the ideology's propagation was Li Fei-kan (1904–), also known as Pa Chin. A popular novelist, he had studied in France and had much contact with Western anarchists. He had translated a number of volumes of Kropotkin, including *Memoirs of a Revolutionist, In Russian and French Prisons, Conquest of Bread,* and *Ethics,* had contributed to the anarchist magazines, and had assumed a leading role in planning and editing the translations of anarchist literature. His major writings on anarchism include *On the Scaffold,* 1929, a eulogy of the anarchist martyrs abroad, especially those involved in the Chicago riots of May 3–4, 1886,[57] and *From Capitalism to Anarchism,* 1930, in which he set forth the principles of anarchism in simple terms for Chinese readers. In this second work, Fei-kan tackled the timely problems of class struggle, revolution, and war, ridiculing the idea that war is a courageous act. On the contrary, he said, it paralyzes the courage of man and destroys the real human spirit. War makes people irresponsible, said Fei-kan, turning them into obedient automatons or causing them to lose all rationality and become mad. Man therefore should have the courage to refuse to take part in war.[58]

Fei-kan agreed that history was but a series of class struggles. He held, however, that class struggle should not be used for purposes of revenge, but rather should aim at establishing "free communism" under which the proletariat manages its own economy. He supported the formula "From each according to his abilities, to each according to his needs," but he warned that this goal would take a long time to realize.[59]

Thus anarchism, according to Fei-kan, was long-term social revolution. It would require severe struggle to overcome the forces of social darkness, since no government would voluntarily give up its ruling power. On the other hand, revolution, which must occur as a result of social development, would fail if it broke out before the time for it was ripe. It could, however, be accelerated by political and economic oppression from above, and by propaganda and agitation from below. In short, the social revolution could be prepared by informing the masses of social evils on the one hand and effectively organizing them on the other.[60]

Fei-kan realized that it would take a long time to win the sympathy of the masses, but he did not think it necessary to be overly hasty in carrying out this educational process. He recognized the importance of cooperation among the various working groups: if the urban proletariat was to be the vanguard of the revolution, the rural workers had to be its supporting force, and the intellectuals its experts and technicians in the work of reconstruction.[61]

Social revolution could be realized through general strikes, and even through troops for defensive purposes. Such use, in Fei-kan's view, would not constitute a breach of anarchist principles. For while the use of organized force to attack others was to be condemned, use of it to defend oneself was permissible. To Fei-kan, the arming of the workers and peasants was the only effective way of achieving defense, and the workers and peasants would have to make use of their own organizations—trade unions and peasant associations—to prevent counterrevolutionary attacks. In thus advocating the turning of workers and peasants into revolutionary armies, Fei-kan went beyond the standard methods of syndicalism and came closer to advocating armed revolution.[62]

But while he subscribed to military methods, Fei-kan made it clear that he was opposed to methods of terror such as assassination. He considered it a waste of time to engage in assassination plots, which, even if they succeeded in killing a few persons, could have very little effect on overthrowing a government. On the contrary, an assassination, by arousing the ill feeling of the people, would have adverse effects on propaganda. While expressing sympathy for those anarchists who resorted to violent means, Fei-kan held that anarchism was not terrorism. Terrorism, which was based on revenge, acted in direct opposition to love, which was the foundation of anarchism.[63]

In spite of all Li Fei-kan's energetic propaganda and that of his colleagues, Chinese anarchism was soon relegated to oblivion. Its basic cause of decline was, of course, the same as in other countries: anarchism was simply impracticable in the modern age. But in China there were additional reasons for its failure. As Shih-fu pointed out, the Chinese workers were not educated, and government suppression was severe.[64] Furthermore, the negative philosophy of Taoism had adverse effects on its growth. Although the active anarchists drew their inspiration from abroad, the passive Taoist tradition contributed to the confusion of anarchism with nihilism, thus rendering it ineffective. But the most important reason for its failure lay in its incompatibility with the particular needs of China in the 1930's. At the same time that Fei-kan and his colleagues were marshaling their efforts to spread their doctrine, Japanese aggression had begun in earnest. Manchuria was invaded by Japan in 1931, and in 1937, after a period of armed truce during which Japanese aggression continued unabated, full-scale war between China and Japan broke out. With the whole of China engulfed in war, with a foreign enemy threatening her very existence, any talk of anarchism seemed remote from the urgent needs of the times, when strong government, discipline, and force were thought to be the only way of saving the nation.

From Democracy to Marxism

The success of the Bolshevik Revolution aroused a keen interest among Chinese radicals. The Bolsheviks' belief in assisting weak nations against the imperialist powers was particularly appealing to a nation that for more than half a century had been in search of a formula that would strengthen China on the one hand while modernizing her on the other. At a rally in Peking, in 1918, Ts'ai Yüan-p'ei, an eminent educator, chose "Sanctity of Labor" as the theme of his address; Li Ta-chao, also an intellectual and one of Chinese Communism's early leaders, spoke on "Victory of the Common Man." The May Fourth Movement of 1919,* by stirring up the Chinese

* The movement was launched by the students to oppose the government's pro-Japanese policies.

people to face the nation's political problems, created a
new surge of interest in socialism. For a time, however,
socialist studies remained diffuse and varied, and included
anarchistic, guild socialistic, syndicalistic, and other tendencies. But beginning in the spring of 1920, Marxism
gained increasing attention, and by the end of the year
Communist nuclei had been formed in various large cities, including Shanghai, Peking, Hankow, Canton, Changsha, and Chungking. It was also in May or June of 1920
that the Russian Communist Grigorii Voitinsky came to
China, and his contact with Li Ta-chao and Ch'en Tu-
hsiu was to contribute greatly to the promotion of Communism in China.[65]

The early development of Chinese Marxism is well reflected in *New Youth*, where one can see the gradual
conversion to Communism of its editor, Ch'en Tu-hsiu,
who later became the first head of the Chinese Communist party. It has already been pointed out that in the
New Culture Movement Ch'en attacked Confucianism
and stood for democracy and science. Although not
advocating socialism, he had in an article published in
1915 maintained that it was one of the three new developments of modern times. "The change from political
inequality to social inequality, from oppression by the
monarch and the nobility to oppression by the capitalists,
is an undeniable shortcoming of modern civilization. Socialism aims at eliminating inequality and oppression and
looks forward to social transformation after the political
revolution."[66] Ch'en traced socialism's origins to Babeuf,
Saint-Simon, and Fourier, regarding Marx as a successor
who had extended the French theories. He seemed to
recognize the difficulties inherent in the immediate abolition of private property, while he considered the prevailing European trends to be social policies that aimed at
improving the lot of the poor.

When revolution broke out in Russia in March 1917, Ch'en wrote to wish it success. In his view, the Russian Revolution represented the fight for democracy and humanitarianism against monarchism and world aggression.[67] And in the May 1919 issue of *New Youth,* there appeared a number of articles on Marxism; but while some authors were more radical than others, they were not all Marxists, as evidenced by a number of articles freely offering criticism.

Reacting to Ch'en's sympathy with the Russian Revolution and the increasing number of articles on Marxism in *New Youth,* some liberal sponsors of the magazine became apprehensive. It was apparently under their pressure that a *Manifesto of the New Youth Magazine* was published in December 1919. The document, purporting to represent the opinion of all the magazine's members and drafted by Ch'en Tu-hsiu, condemned warlordism and mammonism and held that in order to realize "social revolution," the prejudices traditionally held to be unalterable had to be overthrown. But while the antiquated ideas were to be jettisoned, it stated, new ideas would be created through a synthesis of the teachings of the ancient and modern thinkers. The authors of the document proposed an ideal society in which youth respected labor and all people were happy, a society that was to be free and equal, peaceful, full of universal love and mutual assistance.

The *Manifesto*'s authors emphasized mass movement as the means to this social reconstruction. While not considering politics all-important, they believed politics to be a significant part of public life. In a true democracy the political power should be distributed among all the people, and the only qualification for voting should be occupation, not property. While recognizing the utility of political parties, the *Manifesto*'s authors declared that it was desirable to boycott those who worked in the interests of the few or of a single class. The welfare of the whole society should be sought. The needs of progress in present and future society should be met in the political, ethical, scientific, and artistic, as well as in the religious and educational spheres.[68]

The *Manifesto* was obviously a mixture of socialism and liberalism. While it condemned mammonism and called for respect of labor and mass movements, it upheld democracy and did not condemn religion or capitalism. Its emphasis on universal love and happiness was, moreover, different from the Marxists' emphasis upon class struggle and the dictatorship of the proletariat. While it is true that Ch'en Tu-hsiu as drafter of the *Manifesto* could not entirely ignore the opinions of the other members, the articles he published in his own name at about the same time indicate that at this early stage he himself was far from being a convinced Marxist. In an article entitled "Radicals and World Peace," published in the same issue of the *New Youth* as the *Manifesto,* Ch'en maintained that those who opposed Bolshevism were the disturbers of world peace. But he added that it was too early to tell whether the Bolsheviks, if successful, would hold to their principles or if they could indeed bring peace to the world.[69] And in another article, in which he called himself one of those who desired "social reform," he departed from his former stand that Western civilization, including its ethics and politics, should be adopted by China, and instead condemned its moral corruption, which he held to be the result of its system of private ownership. However, he urged that mutual assistance, sympathy, and altruism, rather than class war, be the foundation of a new morality.[70]

Beginning in 1920, Ch'en came out more outspokenly for Soviet Russia, calling attention to its progressive and nonaggressive nature.[71] Although he criticized the Malthusian theory of population and insisted that the growth of the poor classes must not be impaired, he declared that no theory, including Marxism, was applicable in all places and at all times.[72] But in the May 1920 issue of *New Youth,* he began to discuss surplus value, maintaining that it should not be expropriated by the capitalists; and he suggested that Chinese workers should not merely ask for better treatment but should demand participation in the administration of industrial, political, and military affairs.[73] He conceded, however, that this was a goal not immediately realizable.

September 1920 marked a definite turning point in Ch'en's writings on Communism. In answer to a reader, Ch'en wrote that the only way to solve China's social problems was to change the social system through class struggle and war.[74] He was to discuss the problem in more detail in his article "Speaking of Politics." In order to sweep away the inequality and the hardships imposed on the workers by the capitalists, Ch'en wrote, "it is necessary for the proletariat to create a new power for itself, and to completely conquer the capitalists."[75] To Ch'en, force and class war were now the indispensable means not only of conquering the capitalists but of making sure they would not rise again. He criticized the Marxist revisionists and social democrats for their failure to adopt revolutionary methods: their participation in parliamentary politics would result only in their assimilation by the capitalists. The establishment of a proletarian state called for the adoption of the Russians' revolutionary spirit.[76]

The decision to launch a Communist revolution on the Russian model in China set the stage for clearing away the confused thought and hostile criticism that had proved obstacles to the Chinese Communist movement. The de-

bate on anarchism between Ch'en Tu-hsiu and Ou Sheng-
pai has been described above; toward the end of 1920
the Communists were engaged in another battle, between
Ch'en on the one hand and Chang Tung-sun and Liang
Ch'i-ch'ao on the other, on the desirability of practicing
Marxism in China.

The debate began with an article by Chang Tung-sun,
a noted philosopher, stating that a tour of the country
had shown that the people were so poor that obviously
what was needed in China was not socialism but the development of industry and the manufacture of goods.
Poverty had to be cured first; before that was done no
doctrine could be of any use. He did not condemn Communism, but he maintained that it should not be adopted
too early; the urgent task was to give people a decent
living. The lack of industrial development, which Chang
thought to be at the root of poverty, was in turn due to
two causes: the lack of and the failure to accumulate
capital, and the pressure of foreign goods, whose importation was backed by foreign regimes. To Chang, Chinese
capitalists were as few as morning stars, a fact he ascribed
to foreign oppression; their pitiable position warranted
no attacks from their countrymen. Even if they were to
be overthrown, it would be like snuffing out two or three
lamps under a bright sun. It would not, moreover, help
to do so; on the contrary, it would facilitate the further
penetration of foreign capital. The solution of the problem
of poverty, Chang felt, depended upon industrial development, which in turn depended upon the formation of capital. The overthrow of imperialism, which was impeding
China's industrial development, was of course the best
policy, but this was more easily said than done. The more
practical method, Chang said, was to develop Chinese capital wherever there was an opening in the net of foreign
capital. He did not oppose socialism; he was, in fact, in

favor of guild socialism. But he held that socialism could
be achieved only after there was a strong working class,
which could be developed only under capitalism. Suggest-
ing that socialists be patient and wait until Chinese society
was polarized into capitalist and proletarian camps, Chang
counseled that for the time being private enterprise should
be encouraged and cooperative societies established—not
in conformity with a particular theory, but in accordance
with local needs.[77]

Writing in 1920, Chang Tung-sun did not consider Soviet Communism practical for China. For one thing,
China's huge size and difficult transportation made it impossible to practice any totalitarian doctrine; China
needed self-determination at the local level, which was
definitely not a Soviet principle. Secondly, the tradition
of laissez faire in China made it impossible for the government to force its doctrine upon the people. When a
government was forced to leave everything to its people,
it could no longer claim Soviet tendencies. Furthermore,
a Communist dictatorship had to depend on the support
of the people in the absence of a proletariat, but in China
the common people hardly knew the meaning of support.
Of course, said Chang, a dictatorship could be upheld
by military force, but then it became something else.[78]

Ch'en Tu-hsiu answered Chang in the debate. Ch'en's
thesis was that capitalism, not lack of material resources,
was the cause of general poverty in China. The rich who
made money in the cities bought land in the countryside,
Ch'en maintained, thus depriving the peasants of a livelihood. Capitalist manufactured goods were responsible
for driving handicraft goods from the market, which led
to the bankruptcy of the handicraft industries. The high
prices of manufactured goods, Ch'en held, made life difficult for the middle class, rendering them poorer and
poorer. In his opinion, since capitalism was at the root

of general poverty, it made no difference whether the capital was foreign or domestic. Even were foreign capital to be replaced, the situation would be the same. To Ch'en, socialism arrived at through economic development and better treatment of the workers was not feasible for China; for a nation that was backward in modern knowledge, weak in organization, and subject to foreign political and economic oppression, which every day became more critical, there was not time for slow methods such as gradual evolution. Ch'en thought it hopeless to expect the domestic capitalists, directly or indirectly associated with foreign capital as they were, to rise against the imperialists. He pointed to Soviet Russia as an example of a large country where Communism was possible; and he insisted that localism had to give way to central control before industrialization could be achieved. Making a distinction between capital and capitalists, Ch'en maintained that while capital was necessary for industrial development, capitalists were not. He rejected the argument that China had no working class, saying that the rice-growers were members of the Chinese working class.[79]

Chang Tung-sun's views were seconded by Liang Ch'i-ch'ao, who agreed that the urgent problem of China was to provide work for the poor. Like Chang, he attributed widespread unemployment to foreign economic exploitation and suggested that domestic capitalists be "welcomed" so that industry could be developed and more jobs created. Only then, he felt, would a laboring class, the prerequisite for a socialist movement, come into existence. For the amelioration of capitalism's evils, Liang suggested first, that the capitalists be made to understand and promote the welfare of the working people; and second, that public operations in industry gradually be expanded and cooperative societies set up. At the same time, Liang thought, the workers should be educated to prepare them for their central role in future social reconstruction.[80]

In this debate on Marxism several points emerged. Both the Communists and their critics regarded foreign exploitation in the form of imperialism as the cause of China's economic difficulties. But while both agreed it must be overthrown, they disagreed on methods. The Communists believed that foreign exploitation could be used to foster class struggle and that for any social revolution China would need the support of the international socialist movement.[81] Their critics, however, placed their hopes in domestic capitalism, whose immediate development they felt would help to contain the penetration of foreign capital, and in the working class, whose new position in the coming industrial society would ultimately lead to China's social transformation.[82]

It is notable that neither Liang Ch'i-ch'ao nor Chang Tung-sun, leaders of the Study Clique connected with the northern warlords, opposed socialism; indeed, they believed that it would in the future, though perhaps in the remote future, prevail.[83] What they opposed, rather, was an immediate social revolution on the Bolshevik model. The idea of a welfare state goes back to the Chinese classics, and it was thus not surprising that thinkers having a Confucian background like Liang and Chang were not hostile to socialism of the moderate sort. Even the early leaders of the Chinese Communist movement, though believing that something should be done to start the social revolution, did not seem to think immediate seizure of power feasible; Li Ta, for instance, referred to the movement as "the beginning of the preparation for the practice of socialism."[84]

One of the questions that came up most frequently in these debates was whether the attainment of Marxism necessarily entailed a revolution. Had not Marx said that when capitalism had developed to the utmost it would fall, and socialism would take its place? There was no doubt that capitalism in China, if it existed at all, was not highly developed. Should there be a social revolution before capitalism had had a chance to develop? There was no single line of interpretation. Those wanting an immediate revolution felt that the fact that China as an agricultural country was different from the industrial states of the West negated the experience upon which Marx had formulated his theory. But even in the industrial West Marx's theory was not always applicable, for socialism had not evolved in highly industrialized countries like Britain and the United States but in a somewhat underdeveloped state like Russia. Further, although Marx had said socialism would be realized as a result of the ultimate development of capitalism, he had nowhere said that it could not be realized before capitalism's ultimate development.[85]

It was Chou Fu-hai (1897–1948), one of the founders of the Chinese Communist party, who formulated one of the more sophisticated solutions to the problem. To Chou, Marx's dialectical interpretation of history consisted of two phases: evolution and revolution. Waiting until capitalism developed to the ultimate state and toppled by itself was to rely too much on evolution and to forget revolution's role. True, revolution was futile until economic development had reached a certain level. But having reached that stage, social development could be speeded by human efforts—which was the reason that Marx had dwelled on class struggle. Therefore, said Chou, to hasten the fall of capitalism, evolution had to be supplemented by revolution; and it was necessary for the people in a given society to shape that society's development.[86] Chou favored a Communist revolution; however, his belief that the people had the power to control the direction of historical development differentiated him at that time from

the more strict Marxists, who adhered without qualification to the doctrine of the inevitable end of capitalism.
Perhaps it was this faith in human efforts that caused
Chou to withdraw from the Chinese Communist party
soon after its formation.[87]

Li Ta-chao

Li Ta-chao (1889–1927) was one of the earliest intellectual leaders of the New Culture Movement, if not the
very first, to make the transition from liberalism to Communism. The Marxist study group in Peking was organized under his direction, and it was he who introduced
Grigorii Voitinsky, the Russian Comintern representative,
to Ch'en Tu-hsiu—a significant step in the establishment
of the Chinese Communist party. His interest in Communism seems to have antedated that of Ch'en Tu-hsiu. In
August 1919 he publicly acknowledged his inclination
toward Communism and declared that it was he, rather
than Ch'en, who had edited the special issue of *New
Youth* on Marxism that had appeared in May.

Born of a poor family in Hopei province, Li Ta-chao
studied in the Peiyang Institute of Law and Politics and
at Waseda University in Japan. Some Chinese Communist
writers have recently asserted that he became interested in
Marxism while in Japan, but in view of his own statement in 1919 that he had not made any serious study of
Marxism before, this is doubtful.[88] In fact, the few articles he published during the period 1913–1916 were
largely confined to the problems of national independence
and democracy. Returning to China in 1916, Li had participated in the New Culture Movement spearheaded by
New Youth. He became more active in 1918 when he
was appointed professor of history and librarian at Peking
University, where he was in close contact with student

leaders and was highly regarded by young men who were interested in new ideas for China's modernization.

Li is reputed to have been a kind, modest man, willing to listen to others and ready to help. It was perhaps his conciliatory, compromising temperament that led him at the beginning of the Communist movement to include anarchists in his nucleus, to endorse the pragmatic "Good Government" proposed by Hu Shih, and to support as well as play an important part in bringing about the cooperation between the Communists and the Kuomintang. His writings were marked by their poetic style, their tone of philosophical inquiry, and their emotional appeal; and his keen interest in historical philosophy seems to have contributed to a broad-mindedness unique in a Marxist.

An early article in *New Youth,* entitled "Youth," first revealed these qualities in Li. In it, he sought to explain the value of individual life. An individual in the universe, said Li, was but a mere grain in a vast barn. Whether he could forever enjoy youth's happiness depended upon whether he viewed the universe as infinite. If for a youth the universe was limited, his enjoyment of that youth would necessarily be limited. If, on the other hand, the universe was infinite, and if he exerted himself resolutely to advance with it, he would have a limitless future. For Li the universe had neither beginning nor end; it was limitless in space and in time. In the absolute sense it was "not anything" (*wu*).

In a relative sense, however, Li thought the universe to have progressed and retrogressed, and it was from this movement that all phenomena had arisen. But these were only parts of the whole. No matter how big they were, they were limited in size; no matter how long they lasted, they would have their end. Thus while there was life, there was death; while there was growth, there was decline. It was the same with negative and positive, fortune and misfortune, youth and old age, rising vigor and drooping frailty. Those were the circumstances of "being" (*yu*).[89] The Chinese Communists have read dialectical materialism into Li's discussion. Actually, the ideas are more reminiscent of Lao Tzu, who used *wu* (nonbeing) to describe the origin of the universe, and *yu* (being) to describe its various manifestations. The relativity of things in this world, particularly the contrast between strength and weakness, between fortune and disaster, is a fundamental principle of Taoism. Indeed, in his article Li cited Buddhism, the *Book of Changes,* and the sayings of Su Tung-p'o (1036–1101), a poet with Taoist and Buddhist sentiments; nowhere did he make reference to dialectic materialism.

But while Taoism taught the eternal revolving of life, as indicated in its principle of reversion, Li Ta-chao believed in the eternal evolution of the universe. Individual life, which faced growth and decline, was changeable; but the universe, eternally young and infinitely evolving, remained unchanged. He counseled the Chinese youth to unite his life with that of the universe and find everlasting significance in its eternal youth. While all this is traceable to classical Chinese thought, Li's philosophy seems also to have been influenced by Henri Bergson's *Creative Evolution.*[90]

Li Ta-chao, in stressing the eternal youth of the universe, aimed at giving a new meaning to the life of Chinese youth, so that they would in turn be moved to bury the China of the ancients and bring about the nation's rebirth. To Li, it was necessary for Chinese youth to strive unceasingly and fearlessly to break all historical fetters, shatter all antiquated conventions, kill all of the old thoughts that they might have had today to make sure they would be reborn as new persons tomorrow—in this way they would build a new China that, like the infinite universe, would be forever youthful.

In urging Chinese youth to build a youthful China, Li Ta-chao was concerned with Chinese decay and dilapidation in face of the vigorous challenge presented by the modern West. He was aware there were still die-hards in China who looked to the past as to a golden age, and pessimists who were so disappointed with the present that they could only dream of the future. Li's advice to seize the present, for only in using the present wisely could a bright future be created,[91] helped to rouse Chinese youth from the pessimism that prevailed at a time when their country was subject to foreign aggression and internal strife.[92] His plea for burying the old and reconstructing the new not only aimed at relieving the strain arising from the conflict between the two, but also at preparing the way for the new's arrival.[93] It was this unswerving pursuit of the new that eventually led Li to Communism.

It was not until 1918, after the success of the Bolshevik Revolution in Russia, that Li actually showed signs of turning to Communism. In that November's issue of *New Youth* he declared the victory over Germany in the First World War to be a victory of Bolshevism, a victory for the world proletariat and for the new trend of the twentieth century. It was a victory not of Wilson, but of Lenin and Marx.[94] In a public speech about the same time he spoke of the end of the war as the defeat of capitalism, and urged that the new trend represented by Bolshevism, though full of difficulty and pain, be accepted, for any resistance would be futile.[95] As late as the May 1919 special number on Marxism in *New Youth,* however, Li viewed Marxism critically and tended toward revisionism rather than Bolshevism. While recognizing Marx as the father of "socialist economics," which had opened up a new era in world reform, he pointed out that Marx had frequently ignored the function of ethics, and that his concept of class struggle was indeed disturbing. Li tried to exonerate Marx by saying that Marx had not rejected the individual's capacity for noble aspiration, but had only thought the average moral attitudes reflected in the community as a whole incapable of influencing that group's actions, which were based instead upon its common economic interest. Li felt the ethical principle behind socialism to be the ideal of mutual assistance and universal love; and while during the period of class struggle this ideal would have to remain submerged, as soon as class struggle ended, the history of mutual assistance could begin.

Apparently, however, Li was not willing to wait for the state to wither away, for he looked to revisionism as the immediate reinstatement of ethics. "Recently," he wrote, "there has appeared in philosophy a new idealism which can revise Marx's materialism and remedy its defects. There are socialists in various countries who stress the role of ethical and humanitarian movements. This may well be the dawn of social reform and the harbinger of mankind's true history." In the transitional period before the final extinction of the old social structure, Li maintained, men had to redouble their efforts at ethical behavior and humanitarian movements to wipe out the evil habits and traits that had arisen under the class system.

We must not depend alone upon material changes; and this is the place where we should rectify Marxism. It is our aim to reform the spirit of mankind by humanitarianism, and at the same time to reconstruct the economic system by socialism. It is futile to reform the human spirit without reconstructing the economic system, but I am afraid we shall be equally unsuccessful if we try to reconstruct the economic system without reforming the human spirit. We believe in reconstruction of both matter and mind, in the simultaneous reconstruction of soul and flesh.[96]

Li wrote this passage when the study of Marxism was just becoming organized; he, however, did not abandon his scholarly, broad-minded attitude. Seven months later, after the May Fourth Movement had ushered in an era of radicalism, he wrote an article on "Material Change and Spiritual Change," in which his adoption of the Marxist interpretation of history became more clear. Tracing the origin of morality in terms of Darwinism to man's instinct to meet the demands of his social life, Li used Marxism to explain the evolution of morals, adhering now to Marx's theory that the spiritual superstructure was founded on an economic basis and the thoughts and morals determined by material changes. Still his espousal of Marxism was not total; in tracing the origins of the social instinct to mutual aid, he leaned more toward Kropotkin, and in emphasizing the need for a new morality that would fit the "one-world society,"[97] he had something very different from class struggle in mind.

In 1923, after the founding of the Chinese Communist party, Li Ta-chao published a pamphlet on "Democracy," in which he asserted that true democracy must not include the idea of ruling, for any such idea would mean the division of the people into rulers and ruled. A true democracy, he wrote, was based on the free consent of the people, without any compulsion or threat of compulsion. Democracy should consist in the administration of public affairs rather than in government over the people. Citing Woodrow Wilson and John Stuart Mill, he opined that a true democracy was a "free government" in which the minority must not be forced into conformity by the majority. He admitted the necessity of "ergatocracy," or government by the working class, during the period of revolution, but he hastened to add that with the extinction of social classes and private ownership, all people would be workers and the relationship between rulers and ruled would disappear. In all his discussion the theme of the utopia of "free association" stands out as central. A free association was one in which "any unit with an individuality, whether it be a group, an area, a nationality, or an individual, will have its province of freedom, subject to no outside interference."[98] Although this discourse on democracy was to signify Li's clear acceptance of Communism, there lurked in the background the influence of liberalism which he somehow could not entirely abandon. This liberal background was to distinguish Li Ta-chao from his later comrades, whose unqualified adherence to Marxism-Leninism contrasted unmistakably with his own scholarly approach.

Li's continuing interest in the philosophy of history led him to the study of Saint-Simon, and he warned against ridiculing utopian socialist thought, not only because utopian socialism and scientific socialism occupied an equally important place in the history of socialism, but because the latter was in fact the child of the former. Saint-Simon Li considered to be the "pioneer of the materialistic interpretation of history," and Marx the successor, "picking up the loose threads."[99] In his *Essentials of the Science of History,* published in 1924, he favored the Marxist conception of history, but his description of history as a living thing that was constantly changing and growing is very reminiscent both of the vitalism he expressed in his "Youth" and of Condorcet's theory of human progress.[100] Furthermore, if history was continually changing, Li felt, so was the philosophy of history. Each age made its own contribution to the conception and knowledge of history. As a result, what was thought of as truth the year before might not be the next year, and history had yet to develop into a well-integrated science. Compared with the Communist view that Marxism was universally applicable regardless of time and place, Li's concept of history was singularly undogmatic. Li even went so far as to maintain that each historian should have his own subjective standards for evaluating facts and interpreting their interrelationships, and that historical philosophy was to be formed on the basis of an individual's temperament, tastes, environment, the time in which he lived, and the schools of thought to whose influence he might have been subject.[101] Such views as these differ markedly from dogmatic Marxism and could have come only from someone with Li's strong liberal background. It is significant that at a time when his Communist colleagues were busy spouting the Marxist-Leninist jargon, Li was citing Bodin, Bacon, Tassoni, and Descartes.

In recent years the Chinese Communists have published Li Ta-chao's writings and paid him tribute as a beloved founder of the Chinese Communist party. But despite their labored attempts to read Marxism into his writings, they have found it necessary to state that "some of his views are certainly not correct."[102] That Li, unlike some other early Communist leaders, should have received tributes from the Communist regime under Mao Tse-tung is partly attributable to his early death.[103] Had he lived long enough to become involved in the later bitter controversies over party strategy, his liberal views could easily have been condemned as heretical.

Notes

CHAPTER IV. THE RISE OF RADICALISM

1. *Hsin-min ts'ung-pao* (The New People's Magazine), No. 18 (1902), Nos. 42–43 (1903); Sun Yat-sen, "Fa-k'an tz'u" (Foreword), *Min-pao* (People's Journal, hereafter cited as *MP*), No. 1: 1–4 (1905). See also Chu Chih-hs'in's articles (under the pen name of Chih-shen or Hsien-chieh) in *MP*, Nos. 2, 4 (1906); Hu Han-min, "Min-pao chih liu-tai chu-i" (The Six Major Principles of *Min-pao*), *MP*, No. 3 (1906).
2. Chiang K'ang-hu, *Chiang K'ang-hu po-shih yen-chiang chi* (Collected Speeches of Dr. Chiang K'ang-hu) (Shanghai: Nanfang University Press, 1923), I, 1; *Chiang K'ang-hu hsin-O yu-chi* (My Journey to the New Russia) (Shanghai: Commercial Press, 1924), Appendix, p. 21.
3. *Chiang K'ang-hu yen-chiang chi*, I, 18–19, 68–75.
4. *Ibid.*, I, 120.
5. *Ibid.*, II, 42.
6. *Ibid.*, II, 8–9, 23–24, 26.
7. *Ibid.*, I, 77–79, 81.
8. *Ibid.*, I, 59, 80; II, 177.
9. Nan-lou sui-pi, "Jan-i lu," *Hua-mi jih-pao* ("The China Tribune," New York), Sept. 7, 1961, p. 4.
10. *Chiang K'ang-hu yen-chiang chi*, II, 105, 120, 135.
11. *Ibid.*, I, 104, 164, 175–76.
12. Ch'u Min-i later married a sister of Wang Ching-hui's wife and thereafter became a faithful follower of Wang. He joined Wang's puppet regime at Nanking in 1940, and was executed as a traitor by the Nationalist government in 1946.
13. Ch'u Min-i (Min), "Wu-cheng-fu shuo" (On Anarchism), *Hsin shih-chi* (New Century, hereafter cited as *HSC*), No. 31: 2 (Jan. 1908).
14. Wu Chih-hui (Jan), "Wu cheng-fu chu-i i chiao-yü wei ke-ming shuo" (Anarchist Revolution through Education), *HSC*, No. 65: 11 (Sept. 1908).
15. Ch'u Min-i, "Wen ke-ming" (Questions on Revolution), *HSC*, No. 20: 4 (Nov. 1907).
16. Ch'u Min-i, "Hsü wu-cheng-fu shuo" (On Anarchism, II), *HSC*, No. 34: 4 (Feb. 1908).
17. Wu Chih-hui, "Tsung-chiao wen-t'i" (The Problem of Religion), *HSC*, No. 54: 3–7 (July 1908).
18. Li Shih-tseng (Chen), "San-kang ke-ming" (Revolution against the Three Bonds), *HSC*, No. 11: 1–2 (Aug. 1907); "Nan-nu ke-ming" (Revolution of the Relationships between Men and Women), *HSC*, No. 7: 3–4 (Aug. 1907); "Tsu-tsung ke-ming" (Revolution against Ancestors), *HSC*, No. 2: 3–4 (June 1907).
19. Wu Chih-hui, "Chen pu na-jen tang-jen" (They Really Don't Treat Man as Man), *HSC*, No. 16: 4 (Oct. 1907).
20. Wu Chih-hui (X yü X), "T'an wu-cheng-fu chih hsien-t'ien" (Rambling Talks on Anarchism), *HSC*, No. 49: 51 (May 1908).

21. See *HSC*, No. 37: 4 (1908).
22. Ch'u Min-i, "Shen-lun min-tsu min-ch'üan min-sheng san chu-i chih i-t'ung" (On the Differences and Similarities between Nationalism, Democracy and Socialism), *HSC*, No. 6: 3 (July 1907).
23. T'ai-yen (Chang Ping-lin), "P'ai-Man p'ing-i" (On the Exclusion of the Manchus), *MP*, No. 21: 11 (1908); "Ting fu-ch'ou chih shih-fei" (Determining the Right and Wrong of Revenge), *MP*, No. 16: 25 (1907); Wang K'an (Yün-pi), "Chuan-i chih ch'ü-Man chu-i" (The Single Purpose of Expelling the Manchus), *MP*, No. 17: 21.
24. T'ai-yen, "Shih-huo lun" (Four Delusions), *MP*, No. 22: 2–3 (1908).
25. Wu Chih-hui, "Wen-ming chih Hsien-lo" (The Civilized Siam), *HSC*, No. 81: 9 (Jan. 1909).
26. Ch'u Min-i, "Shen-lun min-tsu min-ch'üan min-sheng san chu-i chih i-t'ung."
27. See Chang Chi, *Chang P'u-ch'üan hsien-sheng ch'üan-chi* (Complete Works of Chang Chi) (Taipei, 1951), pp. 236 ff.
28. Feng Tzu-yu, *Ke-ming i-shih* (Reminiscences of the Revolution) (Taiwan: Commercial Press, 1953), II, 231, 233.
29. Shen-shu (Liu Shih-p'ei), "Fei-ping fei-ts'ai lun" (Abolition of the Army and Property), in Chang Nan and Wang Jen-chih, eds., *Hsin-hai ke-ming ch'ien shih-nien chien shih-lun hsüan-chi* (Selected Essays on Current Affairs, 1901–1911) (Peking: San-lien shu-tien, 1963), Pt. 2, Vol. 2, pp. 900–4.
30. Shen-shu, "Jen-lei chün-li shuo" (Equalization of Human Energy), *ibid.*, p. 907.
31. Ho Chen and Liu Shih-p'ei, "Lun chung-tsu ke-ming yü wu-cheng-fu ke-ming chih te-shih" (Advantages and Disadvantages of Nationalist Revolution and Anarchist Revolution), *ibid.*, p. 958.
32. Shen-shu, "Fei-ping fei-ts'ai lun," p. 904.
33. Kung-ch'üan, "She-hui chu-i chiang-hsi hui ti-i-tz'u k'ai-hui chi-shih" (Records of the First Meeting of the Socialist Discussion Society), *ibid.*, p. 945.
34. Ho Chen and Liu Shih-p'ei, *op. cit.*, pp. 949–50.
35. *Ibid.*, p. 954.
36. Shen-shu, "Fei-ping fei-ts'ai lun," p. 904.
37. Feng Tzu-yu, *Ke-ming i-shih*, II, 232–33.
38. Ho Chen and Liu Shih-p'ei, *op. cit.*, p. 947.
39. Liu Shih-fu, *Shih-fu wen-ts'un* (Collected Writings of Liu Shih-fu) (Canton: Ke-hsin, 1928), p. 226.
40. Feng Tzu-yu, *Ke-ming i-shih*, II, 207–11.
41. *Shih-fu wen-ts'un*, p. 144.
42. *Ibid.*, pp. 2–8, 257–65.
43. *Ibid.*, p. 36.
44. *Ibid.*, pp. 1–12, 183.
45. *Ibid.*, pp. 45–47, 89, 290–91.
46. Chang Kuo-t'ao, [*Autobiography*] (manuscript, 1958), p. 135.
47. *Ibid.*, pp. 258, 262.
48. Ch'en Tu-hsiu, "She-hui chu-i p'i-p'ing" (A Criticism of Socialism), *Hsien ch'ing-nien* (New Youth, hereafter cited as *HCN*), 9.3: 314 (1921).
49. Ou Sheng-pai and Ch'en Tu-hsiu, "T'ao-lun wu-cheng-fu chu-i" (A Discussion of Anarchism), *HCN*, 9.4: 449–51, 468 (1921).

50. *Ibid.*, pp. 456, 460–61.
51. *Ibid.*, pp. 459, 470.
52. Ch'en Tu-hsiu, "Ta Ling-shuang" (Reply to Ling-shuang), *HCN*, 9.6: 802–3 (1922); Shih Ts'un-t'ung, "Tu Hsin-k'ai hsien-sheng ti 'Kung-ch'an chu-i yü chih-erh-te chu-i'" (On Reading Mr. Hsin-k'ai's "Communism and Guild Socialism"), *HCN*, 9.6: 745 (1922).
53. See Ch'en Tu-hsiu, *Tu-hsiu wen-ts'un* (Collected Writings of Ch'en Tu-hsiu) (Shanghai: Ya-tung, 1927), Vol. III, Bk. 1, pp. 541–56; Bk. 2, p. 118; Vol. 4, Bk. 3, pp. 258–62.
54. Chu Ch'ien-chih, "Chih Ch'en Tu-hsiu shu" (Letter to Ch'en Tu-hsiu), in *Tu-hsiu wen-ts'un*, Vol. 4, Bk. 3, p. 281.
55. See *Su-o ke-ming ts'an-shih* (The Tragedy of the Soviet Russian Revolution) (Shanghai: Tzu-yu, 1928).
56. "Nan Chih-na wu-cheng-fu chu-i-che tui O-cheng-fu k'ang-i shu" (Letter of Protest from the South China League of Anarchists to the Soviet Government), *ibid.*, pp. 164–71.
57. *Tuan-t'ou-t'ai shang* (On the Scaffold) (Shanghai, 1929) is an enlarged edition of *Ke-ming hsien-ch'ü* (Revolutionary Forerunners).
58. Li Fei-kan (Pei-kan), *Ts'ung tzu-pen chu-i tao an-na-ch'i chu-i* (From Capitalism to Anarchism) (San Francisco: The Equality Society, 1930), p. 63.
59. *Ibid.*, pp. 222–23.
60. *Ibid.*, p. 235.
61. *Ibid.*, pp. 248, 253.
62. *Ibid.*, 258.
63. *Tuan-t'ou-t'ai shang*, Appendix, pp. 301–14.
64. Liu Shih-fu, *Shih-fu wen-ts'un*, pp. 264–65.
65. Chang Kuo-t'ao, *op. cit.*, p. 222.
66. Ch'en Tu-hsiu, "Fa-lan-hsi-jen yü chin-tai wen-ming" (The French People and Modern Civilization), *Ch'ing-nien tsa-chih* (The Youth Magazine), 1.1: 3 (1915).
67. Ch'en, "O-lo-ssu ke-ming yü wo-kuo-jen chih chüeh-wu" (The Russian Revolution and the Awakening of Our People), in *Tu-hsiu wen-ts'un*, Vol. 1, Bk. 1, pp. 141–45.
68. *HCN*, 7.1: 1–4 (Dec. 1919).
69. Ch'en, "Kuo-chi-p'ai yü shih-chieh ke-ming" (The Radicals and the World Revolution), *HCN*, 7.1: 116.
70. Ch'en, "T'iao-ho lun yü chiu tao-te" (Compromise and Old Morality), *HCN*, 7.1: 117–18 (Dec. 1919).
71. Ch'en, "Pao-shou chu-i yü ch'in-lüeh chu-i" (Conservatism and Aggression), *HCN*, 7.2: 155 (Jan. 1920).
72. Ch'en, "Ma-erh-se-ssu jen-k'ou lun yü Chung-kuo jen-k'ou wen-t'i" (The Malthusian Theory of Population and the Problem of Chinese Population), *HCN*, 7.4: 1 (March 1920).
73. Ch'en, "Lao-tung-che ti chüeh-wu" (The Awakening of the Laborers), *HCN*, 7.6: 1–2 (May 1920).
74. Ch'en, *Tu-hsiu wen-ts'un*, Vol. 4, Bk. 3, pp. 217, 224.
75. Ch'en, "T'an cheng-chih" (Speaking of Politics), *HCN*, 8.1: 3–11 (1920).
76. Ch'en, *Tu-hsiu wen-ts'un*, Vol. 3, Bk. 2, p. 93.
77. Ch'en and others, "Kuan-yü she-hui chu-i ti t'ao-lun" (Discussions concerning Socialism), *HCN*, 8.4: 498–500 (1920).

78. *Ibid.*, p. 502.
79. *Ibid.*, pp. 508–14.
80. Liang Ch'i-ch'ao, "Fu Chang Tung-sun t'ao-lun she-hui chu-i yün-tung" (A Reply to Chang Tung-sun Discussing the Socialist Movement), *Kai-tsao* (Reconstruction), 3.6 (1921).
81. Li Ta, "T'ao-lun she-hui chu-i ping chih Liang Jen-kung" (Discussions on Socialism and Questions for Liang Ch'i-ch'ao), *HCN*, 9.1: 14–24 (1921).
82. Ch'en Tu-hsiu, "She-hui chu-i ti p'i-p'ing" (A Criticism of Socialism), *HCN*, 9.3: 511 (July 1921).
83. *Ibid.*, p. 500.
84. Li Ta, *op. cit.*, p. 17.
85. Li Chi, "She-hui chu-i yü Chung-kuo" (Socialism and China), *HCN*, 8.6: 803 (1921).
86. Chou Fu-hai, "Ts'ung tzu-pen chu-i tsu-chih tao she-hui chu-i tsu-chih ti liang-t'iao lu—chin-hua yü ke-ming" (Two Paths from Capitalist Organization to Socialist Organization: Evolution and Revolution), *HCN*, 9.2: 151–59 (1921).
87. Chou Fu-hai joined the Kuomintang not long after the formation of the Chinese Communist party. In 1940 he helped Wang Ching-wei set up the puppet government at Nanking and soon became one of its most powerful leaders. He died in prison in 1948, having been found guilty of treason by the Nationalist court.
88. Shih Chün, "Li Ta-chao yü Ch'en Tu-hsiu ssu-hsiang" (The Thoughts of Li Ta-chao and Ch'en Tu-hsiu), in *Chung-kuo chin-tai ssu-hsiang shih lun-wen chi* (Collected Essays on Modern Chinese Thought) (Shanghai: Jen-min ch'u-pan she, 1958), p. 177.
89. Li Ta-chao, "Ch'ing-ch'un" (Youth), *HCN*, 3.1 (Sept. 1916).
90. Li Ta-chao, *Li Ta-chao hsüan-chi* (Selected Essays of Li Ta-chao) (Peking: Jen-min ch'u-pan she, 1962), p. 31.
91. Li Ta-chao, "Chin" (Now), *HCN*, 4.4: 307 ff. (April 1918).
92. Li Ta-chao, "Yen-shih-hsin yü tzu-chüeh-hsin" (Pessimism and Self-Consciousness), *Chia-yin* ("The Tiger"), 1.8: 7–14 (Aug. 1915).
93. Li Ta-chao, "Hsin-ti, chiu-ti" (The New and the Old), *HCN*, 4.5: 446–49 (May 1918).
94. Li Ta-chao, "Bolshevism ti sheng-li" (The Victory of Bolshevism), *HCN*, 5.5: 442–48 (Nov. 1918).
95. Li Ta-chao, "Shu-min ti sheng-li" (The Victory of the Masses), *HCN*, 5.5: 436–38.
96. Li Ta-chao, "Wo-ti Ma-k'e-ssu chu-i kuan" (My Views on Marxism), *HCN*, 6.5: 536 (May 1919).
97. Li Ta-chao, "Wu-chih pien-tung yü ching-shen pien-tung" (Material Change and Spiritual Change), *Hsin-ch'ao* (The New Tide), 2.2: 208–23 (Dec. 1919).
98. Li Ta-chao, *P'ing-min chu-i* (Democracy) (Shanghai: Commercial Press, 1923), pp. 10, 13, 30.
99. Li Ta-chao, "Sheng-hsi-men ti li-shih kuan" ("St. Simon and His Conception of History"), *She-hui k'o-hsüeh chi-k'an* (Social Science Quarterly), 1.4: 637–45 (Aug. 1923).
100. Li Ta-chao, "K'ung-te-hsi ti li-shih kuan" ("Condorcet and His Conception of History"), *ibid.*, 2.1: 59–66 (Nov. 1923).

101. Li Ta-chao (Li Shou-ch'ang), *Shih-hsüeh yao-lun* (Essentials of the Science of History) (Shanghai: Commercial Press, 1924), p. 10.
102. *Li Ta-chao hsüan-chi*, p. xii; Shih Chün, *op. cit.*, p. 187.
103. Li Ta-chao was executed by a warlord in Peking in 1927.

Chapter V

SUN YAT-SEN

LIKE all other influential political doctrines, Sun Yat-sen's has been controversial. That it at one time held tremendous sway over the minds of the Chinese and played an important role in the shaping of modern China's development is indisputable. Under the Kuomintang, it became the guiding principle of China, and during the years when winning the support of Sun's followers was essential to their victory, even the Chinese Communists were compelled to pay it lip service. It is in the interpretation of Sun's doctrine that opinion differs. While some saw in him a continuation of traditional Chinese philosophy, others have pointed to the influence on him of such foreign doctrines as Communism, and it has become popular among his Western critics to expose his "inconsistencies" or "incongruous borrowings."

It was as a revolutionist that Sun distinguished himself, and to revolutionary change that he dedicated his political teachings. In Chinese history there had frequently been rebellions, some of them resulting in the overthrow of a dynasty; but appropriately they had not been called revolutions, for they had never attempted a thorough change of the political and social systems. Sun, in advocating democracy and socialism, was the first to go beyond these merely dynastic changes. Centered around the theme of political revolution, Sun's political thought also included plans for reconstruction, which he believed to be essential to the revolution's completion.

Program of Revolution

Sun proclaimed his revolutionary strategy as early as 1905. The revolutionary process, he stated, consisted of three stages: military rule, provisional constitution, and constitutional government. In the first stage, the Manchu regime and all its undesirable political and social practices—such as bureaucratic extortion, exorbitant taxation, cruel punishment, foot-binding, opium-smoking, and the superstition of geomancy—would be overthrown. In the second stage, the people would be granted self-government and would elect local legislators and administrators. Their rights and duties, as well as the powers and functions of the local governments, would be provided for in the provisional constitution. This stage would last for six years, when the final stage would be proclaimed, and all the powers of the military government would surrender to the new constitutional government, elected by the people.[1]

Sun's revolutionary strategy pivoted upon the second of these stages, the period of political tutelage, to which he was to assign increasing importance toward the latter part of his political career. The failure of the Republic in its early years convinced Sun of the tremendous difficulties inherent in establishing democracy in a nation that had neither tradition nor experience. Therefore, in 1918, when he wrote his *Program of National Reconstruction,* Sun placed new emphasis on the transitional period. In this work, Sun held that because they had been "soaked in the poison of absolute monarchy for several thousand years," the Chinese were deficient in democratic knowledge. But, he firmly believed, they were capable of being trained for democracy. In Sun's view, just as a schoolboy must have good teachers and good friends, so the Chinese must be trained by a farsighted revolutionary government. But there was to be no question about the ability of the people eventually to learn the democratic way of life. His optimism led him to maintain, as he did in 1905, that six years would be sufficient for this transitional period.[2]

In his *Fundamentals of National Reconstruction,* however, written in 1924, Sun neglected to mention a definite time schedule, and it was this omission that later enabled the Kuomintang under the leadership of Chiang Kai-shek to extend the period of political tutelage to twenty years. Much controversy has arisen concerning the intention of the *Fundamentals,* involving the question of possible Communist influence on Sun, and it is worthwhile to examine the work's background and meaning.

The *Fundamentals* was written shortly after the reorganization of the Kuomintang, when it had begun cooperating with the Soviet Union and the Chinese Communists. In this document, Sun omitted any reference not only to a time schedule, but also to his concept of a provisional constitution. The latter omission was not inadvertent, for, in Sun's view, the root of the trouble accompanying the early period of the Republic lay not in the inadequacy of the provisional constitution, but in "precipitating the people into constitutional government without passing through the stages of military rule and political tutelage."[3] Believing that the provisional constitution could never achieve what was expected of it without the help of military rule and political tutelage, Sun abandoned it as the fundamental tenet of the transitional stage.

This omission signified an important change in Sun's revolutionary program. From 1905 to 1923, he constantly advocated a provisional constitution for the transitional period, which was to be of six years' duration. As late as January 1923, in his *History of Revolution,* Sun held to this view, and to his notion of the practice of self-government as a first step toward full-scale democracy.[4] What made him change his mind in 1924? Was it because he had lost faith in the capacity of the Chinese people for democracy,[5] or was it because he had come under the influence of Communism, whose ideology called for a transitional period of dictatorship?[6]

Sun's disappointment with his countrymen after the establishment of the Republic, especially with the behavior of some members of his party who had failed to support him in his struggle against the arbitrary rule of Yüan Shih-k'ai, was first reflected in his reorganization of the party in 1914 into the Chunghua Keming Tang (The Chinese Revolutionary Party, later the Kuomintang) whose members, he stipulated, were to obey the party chief and were to be responsible for all political and military affairs during the revolutionary period.[7] But the idea behind the party was still that of unifying its command, so that its efforts could be efficiently directed toward the overthrow of the warlords and the people's preparation for democracy. In 1920 Sun was still stressing the distinction between the state, which he held should be governed by law, and the party, which should be ruled by men. Obedience to him as its chief, he added, would be no more than observance of the principles of the party. It was not his intention, he emphasized, to be an autocrat whose every word must be obeyed.[8]

It was not until the reorganization of the Kuomintang toward the end of 1923 that the concept of monolithic rule by one party appeared in Kuomintang literature. In a lecture in October of that year Sun for the first time revealed his intention of following the Soviet example of one-party rule.[9] His position was further clarified in January 1924, when he proposed to place the Kuomintang above the state: "There is one thing more which we may take as our model. Russia is governed entirely by

one party, which wields greater power than parties in
Great Britain, the United States and France. . . . [The
success of the Russian Revolution] was due to the fact
that the party has been placed above the state."[10] With
the party above the state, a provisional constitution during the revolutionary period was apparently unnecessary,
which should explain why in the *Fundamentals* Sun
omitted reference to one. But while, in accordance with
Soviet principles, he adopted a one-party rule, it is notable
that his notion of political tutelage was quite different
from the Communist belief in dictatorship of the proletariat. In the first place, the Communist party exercised
its dictatorial rule in behalf of the proletariat only. The
Kuomintang was to carry out its political tutelage on all
class levels. Thus while the Soviet precept aimed at eliminating opponents, in particular the bourgeoisie, the Kuomintang was to represent the entire Chinese people. To
the Marxists, dictatorship of the proletariat was to lead
to a classless society in which the state had withered away;
but to Sun Yat-sen, the period of party rule by the Kuomintang was an interval in the creation of a fully independent, sovereign state, in which people exercised their
democratic rights and enjoyed a comfortable livelihood.
Sun placed particular emphasis upon local self-government as democracy's foundation.[11]

The Three Principles of the People

To Sun, then, government by a single party was to form
the basis of the Chinese state. "At present we have no
state to govern, and we can only say that we should use
the party to build a state."[12] But what kind of state? Sun
felt that the objectives of the revolution and the blue-
print for a new China should be the Three Principles of

the People, whose development was, as we shall see, directly related to political events.

The first of these, the Principle of Nationalism, was adopted as early as 1894, when the Hsing-chung Hui (Revive China Society) was organized in Hong Kong. From 1894 to the establishment of the T'ung-meng Hui (League of the Common Alliance) in 1905, the sole nationalistic aim of Sun's revolutionary party was to overthrow the Manchus, who were regarded as aliens imposing their rule upon the Chinese, a fact that the T'ung-meng Hui revolutionaries ransacked Chinese classics and historical works to prove in their debate with the constitutional monarchists.[13] Their arguments were not based entirely on racism; cultural and political aspects of minority rule, with due emphasis on its despotism, were also aired. Still, Sun Yat-sen's early nationalism was aimed internally at the overthrow of the Manchus rather than externally at the expulsion of Western dominance. Thus, in 1912, upon the abdication of the Manchu emperor, Sun was able to declare that the principle of nationalism had been achieved; and when the Chinese Revolutionary party was organized in 1914, Sun defined its objectives to be the realization of the principles of democracy and the people's livelihood, without mentioning nationalism. Toward the end of the First World War, when Woodrow Wilson introduced the principle of self-determination into world affairs, Sun's concern was how to weld the five races of China into a great Chinese nation, and he suggested that the Han Chinese give up the superior feelings they had derived from history and humbly and sincerely take the initiative in mixing with other races.[14]

With such concentration on internal affairs, Sun's nationalism had practically no application to the sphere of foreign relations before the end of World War I. His long residence abroad and prolonged contact with foreigners had led him to a sympathetic understanding of Western cultures and a yearning for international cooperation. Thus, during the early years of the Republic, Sun consistently advocated world peace and friendly relations between nations. While he recognized the difficulty of getting all men to belong to the same World Commonwealth, he voiced optimism that this could be achieved, and he called on the Chinese people to contribute their part to the worthy cause.[15] He spoke of recovering foreign settlements in China, revising the tariff, and abolishing extraterritoriality, but made it plain that he thought negotiations toward these ends would not begin for quite a while.[16] His goal in this period was to strengthen China through modernization, to promote mutual benefits through expansion of foreign trade, and to industrialize the country with the help of foreign capital. It was his belief that as soon as China had become modernized and prosperous, and hence a strong nation, humiliating treaties with foreign powers would be revised, and China, as a fully sovereign state, could contribute her share to the promotion of world peace and fraternal relations.

Sun persisted in these beliefs until 1920, when he announced that nationalism had yet to be attained,[17] abandoning his earlier stand that the principle of nationalism had been realized in the downfall of the Manchu regime. Japanese aggression in China during the First World War and China's disappointment with the Paris Peace Conference, which failed to rectify her humiliating situation, might well have been the cause of his reversal. Still, as late as May 1921, Sun held that China would recognize legitimate foreign rights based on treaties, contracts and precedents, and he did not as yet associate warlords with foreign imperialists, as he would three years later.[18]

Sun first attacked imperialism in his lectures on *The Three Principles of the People* in 1924, when he had begun to cooperate with the Communists. It has therefore been debated whether his views on imperialism were Communist-inspired. Sun had discussed "imperialism" as early as 1904, and had mentioned it again in 1912 in connection with American policies. But in both instances he had seemed to regard it as a kind of territorial expansion and did not consider it an immediate threat to China's unity or political stability.[19]

In January 1923, the Sun-Joffe Agreement, which provided Russian assistance to the Kuomintang, was concluded. But in October of that year, Sun still maintained that it was not necessary to couple "overthrow of the warlords with resistance against the foreign powers."[20]

In 1924, when the Kuomintang was reorganized and Chinese Communists were admitted, a new chapter began. The Manifesto of the First Congress of the Kuomintang, issued in January, declared that "unequal treaties" which provided leased territories, extraterritoriality, foreign control of the Chinese customs, should all be abrogated, clearly reflecting the party's new Communist bias. For the first time, collaboration between warlords and imperialists was stressed in Kuomintang literature, and China's recurrent civil wars were attributed to conflicts of interest between the foreign powers. Hitherto Sun had regarded foreign capital as a key element in Chinese industrialization; now he condemned it as a form of economic exploitation and regarded it as the curse of Chinese industry and economy. Since it was imperialism, he now felt, that had reduced China to the status of a semi-colony, any struggle for national liberation had to be directed against these extraneous forces.[21]

Sun further clarified his attitude toward imperialism in his lectures on nationalism in 1924. Against Lenin's view of it as the ultimate phase of capitalism, Sun saw it as a "policy of aggression upon other countries by means of political force,"[22] and attributed the First World War to the rivalry between Britain and Germany for control of the sea, and to the great powers' ambition to secure more territory. Imperialism was, in short, political expansion based upon military power. Sun further condemned economic penetration of China by foreign powers, and its ruinous effects on the nation's economic life. But he made a distinction between economic oppression and imperialism, which he felt to be "political oppression."[23] If Sun had been led into anti-imperialism by the Communists, his interpretation differed markedly from theirs.

There has been some question whether Sun's view of war in these lectures was derived from the Communist concept of class struggle, centering around his statement: "Since the occurrence of the new events in Russia, as I study developments of the past and foresee tendencies of the future, I believe great international wars will be inevitable. But these wars will not arise between different races; they will arise within races, white against white, yellow against yellow. These wars will be wars of classes, wars of the oppressed against the tyrants, wars of right against might."[24] Throughout the lectures, class war is mentioned only in this sentence; in other places the examples of war he gave were of wars between nations. Taking the statement at face value, one can hardly say that Sun tended toward Marxist thinking. "Wars of classes" may not necessarily mean wars between the proletariat and capitalists. But even granted that Sun had in mind wars of social classes, he also mentioned other kinds of wars—wars of the oppressed against the tyrants and of right against might. When he spoke of the latter kind, he often made it clear that he meant wars of oppressed nations against aggressor nations. Thus, in his statement Sun was most likely describing only one possible type of future war and not advocating class struggle.

Returning now to the basic precepts of the Principle of Nationalism, Sun's nationalism was, during its later years, directed against foreign aggressors. Sun thought that to attain independence and equality, China now had to free herself from the imperialist yoke, to recover all her lost territory and sovereignty, and to unify herself by the elimination of all separatist elements and the creation of a sense of solidarity in her people. Sun saw a day when the Chinese nation would represent the whole people rather than certain classes, and China would be a melting pot for all races, all equal. He believed the lack of any spirit of nationalism was due to long periods of subjection to alien rule, such as the Manchu regime, and to the traditional Chinese belief in universalism. The Chinese people needed a new surge of patriotism, which would lead to a transfer of loyalty from the family to the state and a sacrifice of individual freedom for national freedom.

Sun was not advocating the arrogant and narrow outlook some modern ultranationalists have been guilty of, for he held that China, while fighting for its own equality with the powers, should also help smaller nations to attain equality. Rescuing the weak and lifting up the downtrodden was a traditional virtue that China could, Sun felt, apply to international relations. In his *Great Asianism,* he called on Japan to become China's partner in the defense of Oriental virtues. The Oriental "kingly way" of persuasion and peace, he said, could successfully challenge the "tyrannical way" of force and aggression the Western powers had adopted in dealing with weak nations.[25] Great Asianism had none of the exclusiveness that characterized the so-called Asian Monroe Doctrine advocated by the Japanese militarists before the Pacific war. It was a sort of regionalism aimed at the defense of the Asian continent against Western aggression, but secondarily it would promote peaceful relations with all countries. Sun's ideal was of a great commonwealth of nations, founded on equality and fraternity.[26] But before China could become cosmopolitan, he felt, it had first to become an independent state.

Sun's second principle concerned the basic tenets of democracy. Sun thought Lincoln's phrase, "government of the people, by the people, and for the people," adequately described his own goal. By "people," however, Sun meant a unified and organized body of men rather than individuals. He was opposed to individualism and rejected the contract theory of the state. To him the state was an organized body for mutual assistance rather than a conglomeration of individuals for the protection of each one's rights. Against Rousseau's theory of natural rights, Sun held that all political rights were to be won through revolution. According to this view, political rights would be conferred only on citizens who were loyal to the republic, and would be denied to those opposed to it, especially those engaged in attempting its destruction.[27]

In like manner Sun viewed liberty as the fruit of mankind's long struggle. To the Chinese, who had experienced no such struggle, liberty was often synonymous with "running wild without bridle."[28] It was this excessive individual liberty that made it difficult for the Chinese people to subject themselves to organizational discipline. So long as they remained a sheet of loose sand, all revolutionary struggle would be impossible, and the hope for a well-organized state could never be fulfilled.

It is because of this position that Sun has been charged with opposing liberty.[29] As a political philosopher, he took up the question of liberty, but as chief of a revolutionary party, he was naturally more concerned with authority and discipline. One may challenge his premise that historically the Chinese had enjoyed ample liberty, but one can hardly question his assertion that after the establishment of the Republic a wild libertarianism, destructive to corporate discipline and unified action, prevailed. It is true that in 1924 Sun came out quite vehemently against unbridled individualism, but it is hardly correct to suggest that he owed this view to the Communists. He had stated as early as 1904 that the Chinese people were "traditionally free from government interference."[30] In 1912 he warned against thinking that after the overthrow of the absolute monarchy one could do whatever one liked without the least regard for authority.[31] He emphasized in particular that liberty was for the common people, but not for soldiers and government officials, who should be subject to strict discipline.[32] He cautioned students who were eagerly involved in all agitations to restrain themselves, adding that students did not have the qualifications to choose their teachers. If they did, they were no longer students.[33]

Thus, to Sun, it was the duty of members of revolutionary parties to sacrifice their individual liberty for the freedom of the nation. Sun had been greatly disappointed by his own party members' failure in 1913 to answer his call for war against President Yüan Shih-K'ai. In any revolution, unity of command was indispensable to success. All this, however, did not mean that Sun was opposed to liberty in general. Although he agreed with John Stuart Mill that there should be limits on freedom, and was definitely opposed to unbridled libertarianism, he vowed in September 1924, on the eve of his leaving for Peking to confer with the northern leaders on national unification, that his party would "protect the liberty of the people with all its powers."[34]

In Sun's view, "nature originally did not make man equal."[35] It was his belief that since there was no natural equality, any attempt to force quality upon human society would result only in a false equality. Men were endowed with varying intelligence and ability. If one disregarded these differences and pushed down those who rose to a high position in order to make all men equal, there would be no progress, and organizations would be deprived of essential leadership. What men needed, Sun felt, was an equal position to start with, and an equal opportunity for each to develop his career according to his intellectual endowments and capacities.

The first important step in ensuring equal opportunity was to give men equal political status. "Only when people have won political rights can liberty and equality prevail."[36] But Sun realized that the mere exercise of political rights, as in an election, did not in itself create equal opportunities. He therefore stressed the importance of free education for developing men's native intelligence and talents.[37] In the final analysis, no government action could ever hope to level the abilities of the people. To reduce the evil consequences of this natural disparity, Sun could only appeal to man's conscience:

Although nature produces men with varying intelligence and ability, yet the human heart has continued to hope that all men might be equal. This is the highest of moral ideals and mankind should earnestly strive towards it. . . . Everyone should make service, not exploitation, his aim. Those with greater intelligence and ability should serve thousands and ten thousands to the limit of their power and make thousands and ten thousands happy. Those with less intelligence and ability should serve tens and hundreds to the limit of their power and make tens and hundreds happy. . . . In this way, although men now may vary in natural intelligence and ability, yet as moral ideals and spirit of service prevail, they will certainly become more equal. This is the essence of equality.[38]

Sun held that ability and sovereignty were distinct from

one another. Compared with his other concepts, this idea
—first discussed in 1924 in his lectures on democracy[39]—
seems to have been conceived by him somewhat late. An
attempt to solve one of the great difficulties in modern
democracy, it is based on an analysis of Western experience. Sun recognized that in modern democracies the
government was usually very weak, owing to people's
dread of an all-powerful government they could not control. But at the same time modern civilization required
that the multifarious affairs of the state be dealt with by
powerful governments. The solution, Sun felt, lay in the
distinction between administrative power, which should
be exercised by the government, and sovereign rights,
which should be retained by the people. The great majority of people are incapable of government work. The
operation of the government must be given to the qualified, who must not be hampered by constant interference
by the people or representatives of the people. On the
other hand, it is essential to a democracy that the government be subject to the control of the people and that its
policies and actions be responsive to popular will. Sun
compared government to modern industries, and the president and his staff to experts who know how to manage
the company, while the people were like shareholders,
retaining control over the president but in general not
interfering with the management.[40]

To implement this idea, Sun proposed a five-power constitution that would provide China with an all-powerful
government, and a "direct democracy" that would ensure
popular control. One of the weaknesses of Western government, he said, was its domination by the legislature,
which controlled it and interfered with its work. Parliamentary government, especially along the French model
of that particular time, was a clear example. But even in
a presidential form of government, Sun held, the inter-

ference of Congress weakened the executive. He proposed the division of government into five powers: executive, legislative, judicial, examinatorial, and censorial. The latter two powers were traditional Chinese institutions, which Sun included in the hope that they would be independent of the others and therefore more judiciously and efficiently exercised. But the chief purpose of the scheme was to create a powerful government without domination by any one branch. Under Sun's system, the Chinese legislature, unlike Western parliaments, would not control the executive or exercise powers of impeachment and investigation to the embarrassment of the executive. These functions would be given to the control *yüan* (council). Similarly, the power to appoint a civil service would be taken away from the executive and assigned to an independent *yüan*. A government so constituted would exercise administrative power, or ability, as distinguished from sovereign power. Sovereignty would reside in the people, who would retain the four powers of direct democracy: suffrage, recall, initiative, and referendum. With these four powers the people would be able to control the government directly and not have to fear its becoming too strong.[41]

However, Sun's theory, in spite of its commendable intention of providing a powerful government on the one hand and effective popular control on the other, had its difficulties. In the first place, one must ask whether all the powers of the government could be of an administrative nature without also involving the exercise of sovereign power. Was the legislature merely a body of technical "ability," exercising nothing other than administrative power? If so it would be no more than a drafting bureau, and yet there would have to be some agency to determine the principles and purposes of legislation, and this necessarily involved the sovereign will of the people.

Sun's distinction between ability and sovereign power, in so far as the whole government with its legislative branch was considered to be no more than an administrative body, had, therefore, its theoretical limitations.

There is also the question of whether the five-power constitution could really provide a powerful government as intended. To ensure that the legislative body would not dominate the executive, Sun insisted that the five powers of government be independent of each other.[42] In the West, the separation of powers into three branches to provide the government with a system of checks and balances has often obstructed its exercise of power and rendered it weak and inefficient. The division of power into five branches would necessarily further complicate the governmental process; and if each insisted on its independent power, the purpose of powerful government could well be undermined.

Granted that Sun's idea of a direct democracy had its merits, whether it was practicable for a country as large as China is questionable. In 1916 Sun stated that direct democracy should not be practiced in such large areas as provinces, but should be confined to districts.[43] He maintained the same opinion in his lecture on the "Five-Power Constitution" in 1921.[44] The lecture was given, however, before Sun had formulated his theory of the distinction between ability and sovereignty. In his sixth lecture on democracy, on April 26, 1924, Sun declared that the people should exercise the four powers of election, recall, initiative, and referendum so as to have direct control over the five-power government. "When the four political powers of the people control the five governing powers of the government, then we will have a completely democratic government organ, and the strength of the people and of the government will be well balanced."[45] In this lecture he did not mention the districts as possible units of direct democracy, nor did his diagram of the relation between the political power of the people and the administrative power of the government show any national congress that might exercise the sovereign rights for the people. However, in Article 9 of his *Fundamentals of National Reconstruction,* written on April 12, 1924, he declared that "citizens in a completely self-governing district shall have the powers of suffrage, recall, initiative, and referendum."

It was further provided in Article 24 that "after the promulgation of the Constitution, the governing power of the central government shall be vested in the People's Congress. That is, the People's Congress shall exercise the powers of election and recall in reference to officials of the central government, as well as the powers of initiative and referendum in reference to laws enacted by the central government."[46] On the basis of the *Fundamentals,* the Kuomintang was later able to maintain that the People's Congress, composed of representatives of the people, was an organ of sovereign rather than of administrative power.[47] This interpretation was incorporated into the 1936 Draft of the Constitution, which delegated the four powers of democracy to the People's Congress. In this way the original scheme to avoid parliamentary exercise of sovereign power was thwarted, and the four rights of direct democracy, considered to be essential to the control of the five-power government, were no longer exercised by the people.

Sun's third principle was that of the People's Livelihood. "The Principle of the People's Livelihood," declared Sun Yat-sen, "is socialism, it is communism, it is Utopianism." Sun's use of the term "communism" here has given rise to serious controversy. Some have regarded the statement as a political tactic for relaxing tension between the Communists and the right wing of the Kuomin-

tang; others have considered it to be evidence of Sun's
pro-Communism.[48] Actually it was neither. In Sun's
mind communism was a term interchangeable with socialism and in its ideals not different from the traditional
Chinese concept of utopia. His Principle of Livelihood
was intended to be broader than all of these, including
something of communism and something of collectivism,
a term he often used to mean state communism.[49] To
Sun, communism was not necessarily the Marxist brand
or the Soviet brand. In February 1924, he stated that
Marxism was not communism; what Proudhon and
Bakunin had advocated was really communism.[50] Until
August 1924, when he delivered his first lecture on the
Principle of Livelihood, Sun had never equated his principle with communism; on the contrary, he had often
stated that the People's Livelihood was socialism, especially the state socialism that had appeared in Germany
and other European countries.[51] As will be seen later,
the People's Livelihood, both in principle and in method,
was indeed closer to state socialism than to anything
else. But it was characteristic of Sun not to adhere
to any one person's doctrine; his People's Livelihood was
broader than state socialism. Its ultimate ideal was
"communism" in the sense that all people should share
the natural resources and national wealth. Thus, said
Sun, "Communism is the ideal of People's Livelihood,
and People's Livelihood is practical communism."[52] But
the Principle of People's Livelihood aimed at communiz-
ing future property, rather than existing property, so that
no one who had property would suffer.[53]

To Sun, communism could not be realized for several
thousand years, since the morality of the present world
had not reached the stage where the formula "From each
according to his abilities, to each according to his needs"
was practicable.[54] Particularly in China the conditions

were not suitable for communism, for China had been suffering from poverty, not from unequal distribution of wealth. The urgent need, therefore, was to create wealth through industrialization. "In seeking a solution for our livelihood problem, we are not going to propose some impracticable and radical method and then wait until industry is developed. We want a plan which will anticipate dangers and forearm us against emergencies, which will check the growth of large private capital and prevent the social disease of extreme inequality between the rich and the poor."[55] To Sun the methods of the Russians were ones that would "burn the head and mar the forehead."[56]

Communism was not only impracticable, it was also theoretically unsound. Sun criticized the Marxian materialistic conception of history and agreed with Maurice William that the struggle for subsistence, not the struggle between classes, was the central force in history.[57] For Sun, cooperation rather than war was the law of social progress. In the struggle for subsistence, mutual trust and cooperation were essential to success; in class war the destructive effects might well obstruct social progress and make living difficult.[58]

Thus, the Principle of Livelihood was based on mutual dependence and cooperation between the classes. "Society progresses through the adjustment of major economic interests rather than through the clash of interests. If most of the economic interests of society can be harmonized, the great majority of people will benefit and society will progress."[59] Sun did not deny the existence of class struggle, but he considered it to be an abnormal phenomenon in social development.[60] He distinguished between the human world and the animal world. The latter was characterized by natural selection and survival of the fittest; the former was founded on conscience and justice. Mankind has attained the level of morality; it seeks progress through mutual assistance. Society and state function on ethical principles. Men have not always been able to follow these principles because of the remnant barbaric nature they inherited from the animal world. Hence the ugly side of society, characterized by struggle, defeat, and elimination. But, in Sun's view, the more civilized we become, the less natural selection will apply. And it is the duty of man to develop his human nature, to eliminate the animal instinct, to promote morality—in short, to replace natural selection with mutual assistance.[61]

Sun's adoption of Maurice William's arguments to refute Marx's materialistic conception of history has led to the speculation that it was William who saved Sun from the influence of Communism. Thus Jeremiah W. Jenks, in a lecture at New York University in 1929, stated that "in the early part of his great book *The Three Principles of the People* Sun has apparently adopted the doctrines of Karl Marx and believes in the class struggle. . . . Later on, in the latter part of his book he changed his views quite decidedly and that change was apparently brought about by the falling into his hands of Maurice William's *The Social Interpretation of History*."[62] Prompted by this assertion, William published in 1932 his *Sun Yat-sen versus Communism*, in which he attempted to establish: that Sun's lectures on nationalism and democracy delivered between January 27 and April 26, 1924, were thoroughly Marxian in tone (he "endorses the class struggle" and "repudiates Western democracy"); that Sun at that time was unfamiliar with *The Social Interpretation of History*, which must have fallen into his hands immediately thereafter; that Sun must have devoted the next few months to an intensive study of it; and that in the first lecture on livelihood delivered on August 3, Sun boldly proclaimed that he had completely reversed his views on Marxism and Bolshevism.[63] We have discussed Sun's views on imperialism above, and we may say here that a careful reading of his lectures on democracy will show that in them Sun adopted the ideas of Western democracy, the separation of powers, and even direct democracy on the Swiss model. The lapse of three months between the last lecture on democracy and the first lecture on livelihood was not due to Sun's coming upon William's book "almost immediately" after the last lecture on democracy nor his need for a period of intensive study, but in reality to an illness of two months. Also, Sun had already mentioned *The Social Interpretation of History* once before, on January 21, 1924, at a meeting of the First National Convention of the Kuomintang.[64] He made use of William's arguments against Marxism because they fit in with his Principle of Livelihood. Maurice William did not save him from Communism, since he had never abandoned his own principles, which were quite different from Marxism.

Sun proposed two methods as a solution to the problem of livelihood: equalization of land ownership and regulation of capital. The first, sometimes called land nationalization, was derived from the theory of Henry George.[65] Sun adopted George's socialism because in China the land problem was so much more conspicuous than the problem of capitalism. Thus from 1904 to 1924, Sun spoke of equalization of land ownership as if it were the only solution to all economic inequities.[66] He proposed that all unearned increment in the rise of land prices go to the state and that private ownership of land be gradually abolished through taxation, which would make it unprofitable for an individual to own land. A landlord would be required to report the value of his land to the government, and it would be taxed accordingly. If the landlord reported a value lower than the market price, the government would have the option of buying it at the reported price. Any increase in land value after the date of the reported price would go to the state. The landlord, finding it unprofitable to own land, would gradually sell it to the government, which alone could handle land transactions. Nationalization would thus be eventually realized.[67]

It is this gradualism that stands foremost in Sun's socialist thought. Believing that capitalism had not yet developed in China and that even the land problem was not very serious for the moment, he regarded his plan as a precautionary measure against future crises.[68] Thus all of China's land did not have to be nationalized at once; the government would not have enough funds for the purpose, nor was it necessary to do so. But although he would let private ownership exist for the time being, he envisaged its eventual abolition. George's theory, in so far as it advocated that land be common property, persisted in Sun's mind. But he thought it necessary to make some modifications. Thus, in 1922 he declared that with modern life becoming daily more complex and political functions undergoing vast changes, it was no longer possible to place all taxes on land alone.[69] Another significant revision of George's theory occurred when, in 1924, Sun proposed "regulation of capital" as a second method of solving the problem of livelihood.

In 1924, during his cooperation with the Communists, Sun gave an address on "Land to the Tillers" at the Institute of Agrarian Movement. The slogan was immediately used by the Communists to stir up the peasants, and it was later interpreted to mean that Sun endorsed seizure of land from the landlords. Is it true that the slogan signified Sun's adoption of a new position toward the problem of land? A study of his statements on the subject indicates that until 1924 his major attention was focused on nationalization of land rights in the cities. He

always spoke of the tremendous increase in land value
in the urban centers, and the injustice that this unearned
increment should be pocketed by private owners. He did
not seem to think that the rural problem was a serious
one, and in 1919 maintained that there were few great
landlords in China. He declared that "the peasants,
though their hardships might perhaps have increased
since the well-field system of ancient times, could still be
small landowners, . . . and are therefore not entirely cut
off from the path of making a living."[70] On the other
hand, it is untrue to say that Sun ignored the rural problem in those early years. In 1905 when nationalization of
land was proposed in the *People's Journal* (*Min-pao*),
it was pointed out that the landlords' monopolization of
profits would drive the peasants out of work. The revolutionary journal considered it desirable that "those who
do not till the land themselves should not receive land
from the state."[71] Again, in 1919, Sun stated that as the
capitalists began purchasing land in the rural areas, the
peasants would have no land to till, and if they became
tenants they would be unable to pay the rent.[72]

These views are similar to those of George, who maintained that as the burden of taxation is shifted from production and exchange to the value or rent of land, no
one would care any longer to hold land unless he cultivated it himself. As land monopolization would no longer
pay, "millions and millions of acres from which settlers
are now shut out by high prices would be abandoned by
their present owners or sold to settlers upon nominal
terms."[73] According to the account of a contemporary,
Sun discussed the problem of "land to the tillers" with
Yüan Shih-k'ai as early as 1912;[74] not a very surprising
fact, since the nationalization of land along lines set down
by George leads logically to the conclusion of land for
the tillers.

The question arises whether in 1924 when Sun spoke again on "land to the tillers," he had abandoned his former position and adopted Communist principles.[75] A study of the speech will reveal that Sun had no intention of following the Communist policy of confiscating land for redistribution to the peasants, for he believed that, except for the peasants, members of other social classes were in a way small landowners. Any confiscation of land would arouse strong opposition too powerful for the peasants, unorganized and ignorant as they were, to resist. He advised that the peasants be organized first, and a program of propaganda developed to help them understand their situation. Only when the government could count on the organized support of the peasants could it proceed to solve the problem. Still, the methods he proposed were the same that he had advocated previously. The landlords should be taxed according to the value of their land. If they refused to pay, then their land would be confiscated by the state and redistributed among the tillers. The latter would then pay taxes to the state, presumably just as the landlords had done. Sun insisted that the peasant problem had to be solved slowly and peacefully so that on the one hand the peasants would be benefited, while on the other the landowners would not suffer losses.[76] In 1924, Sun did not turn to the revolutionary method of the Communists to solve the peasant problem; what he proposed was in fact based on the same old concept of land nationalization derived from Henry George.

Sun first mentioned regulation of capital, the second method of solving the problem of livelihood, in 1912.[77] But he did not refer to it again until 1924, and throughout this period his emphasis was on economic development by the state, which was to own and operate essential industries. Although it was his belief that private capitalism was not well-developed in China and that there was therefore no urgent need to regulate it, he recognized the necessity of taking precautions to prevent its development. Sun saw in the Principle of Livelihood a means to achieve industrialization and socialism simultaneously by skipping the stage of private capitalism. He again maintained this position in 1924, when the Kuomintang declared that enterprises of a monopolistic nature or of a scale beyond the capacities of private individuals should be operated by the state.[78] In spite of his cooperation with the Communists, Sun in general succeeded in holding to the principles he had conceived at the end of the nineteenth century.

Knowledge and Action

Sun's political doctrine, as we have seen, was mainly concerned with revolution and national reconstruction. To carry out these tasks, he believed that plans and action, as well as leaders and followers, were necessary. He felt that the followers must have faith in the leaders, whose instructions they should carry out without hesitation or doubts. The bitter experience of the Revolution of 1911 convinced Sun that the great obstacle in his work was the Chinese aversion to action, which was part of the general attitude, traceable to the teachings of ancient times, that "to know is easy and to act is difficult." The psychological effects of this teaching are obvious. It creates hesitation in the minds of the people, who will not take action, even though they know the way to do it, for fear of failure.

To replace the old precept, Sun advanced the theory that "to act is easy but to know is difficult." This conception was based upon his belief that the evolution of mankind is divided into three stages. In the first, when man evolves from primitivism to civilization, it is characteristic of him to act without knowing. In the second, when civilization advances to a higher level, man derives knowledge from action. In the third, characterized by the predomination of science, man acts after he knows, or in accordance with the scientific knowledge he has discovered.[79] It is because man in the first stage takes action without knowing that he makes progress without waiting. It is because man in the later stages continues to take action without previous knowledge, and initiates even more acts after he knows for sure, that he achieves the tremendous progress in modern times. The key to progress, therefore, is action, and to act is easier than to know.

"The advance of civilization," said Sun, "is achieved by three groups of persons: first, those who see and perceive ahead, the discoverers; second, those who see and perceive afterward, the promoters; and third, those who do not see or perceive, the practical workers."[80] There are only a few who can see ahead and have knowledge of the future. It is not possible for all people to have complete knowledge of the revolution and national reconstruction before joining in a movement; rather they must have implicit faith in the leaders and confidently carry out their plans. Nothing can be done if the followers should think their leaders' program impractical, or that it is easy to plan but difficult to put anything into practice. They will then fail to act and thereby hinder the revolutionary movement.

Sun's theory reactivated in China the time-honored controversy over the problem of knowledge and action.[81] A strong criticism was raised by Hu Shih, who considered it erroneous to distinguish knowledge from action. Much of our knowledge, declared Hu, is inseparable from action, especially knowledge of social science, which is derived pragmatically from experience—the result of action.[82] To be fair to Sun, he, too, acknowledged the

value of experiment. "Theories may be true or false, and
they must be verified by experiment."[83] Nor did he
mechanically separate knowledge from action. "Those who
can act will be able to know."[84] But he insisted that
while it was no longer advisable to act without knowledge
in the age of science, it was impossible for every one who
did practical work to have expert knowledge.

The second error in Sun's theory, according to Hu
Shih, was the belief that knowledge is more difficult than
action. To Hu practicing medicine, for instance, was just
as difficult as learning medicine. Here again, his criticism
was a bit too sweeping. Sun's "knowledge" was not necessarily that gained from books, and might well include skill
attained through practice. Sun was not unaware that action
is difficult, but he maintained that knowledge is more difficult. Whether knowledge is more difficult than action
depends very much on the kinds of knowledge and action
involved. Where technical matters are concerned, it would
seem reasonable to say that to know is difficult and to
act is easy. When it comes to the question of morality,
however, the situation may be different. As Feng Yu-lan,
a Chinese philosopher, pointed out, knowledge in the
sense of cognition is easy, but knowledge in the sense of
understanding is difficult. Granted that a person under-
stands that he ought to do a certain thing, still that does
not mean that he can do it, for he may be deterred by
other desires.[85] When it comes to moral actions, there
is no doubt that will or determination plays an important
part.

In creating his theory of knowledge and action, Sun
certainly recognized the importance of determination in
the carrying out of revolutionary programs. His theory
was, in fact, designed to restore the Chinese people's
faith in the revolution by convincing them of his plans'
easy implementation. His hope was to strengthen the de-

termination of those followers who hesitated because they thought his program for revolution impracticable. To Sun the first step in fostering faith in the revolution was to convince the Chinese people that it is difficult to know, but easy to act. The belief that action is easy, while not necessarily leading people to act, would certainly encourage them to look in that direction.

Origins and Foundations

Western writers have often held that Sun's doctrine is a mixture of Western sources and traditional Chinese ideas. The conclusion that Sun was eclectic, though appearing fair and safe, is not the product of careful study, but of too easy generalization. Chinese scholars, on the other hand, have for the most part concentrated on tracing Sun's thought to traditional ideas. Among Sun Yat-sen's traditionalist interpreters, Tai Chi-t'ao was probably the most influential. His *Philosophical Foundation of Sun Yat-senism* was published in May 1925, when the Chinese Communists were active inside and outside the Kuomintang and the Marxist interpretation of history was rampant among the Chinese intellectuals. It was to counteract this wave of materialistic orientation that Tai wrote his pamphlet, whose theme is that Sun was the successor to the ancient sages and had continued their line of thought. While Sun had attempted to modernize political institutions, he made the ethical basis of this reconstruction the traditional Chinese virtues, which he wanted to revive and did not hesitate to praise. In Tai's view, the cornerstone of Sun's revolutionary ideology was *jen* (benevolence), which Sun felt to be the force behind man's will to knowledge and action, and the central force of historical development.[86]

The traditionalists based their interpretation of Sun on

the following passage from his sixth lecture on the Principle of Nationalism:

Because of the high moral standards of our race, we have been able not only to survive in spite of the downfall of the state, but we have had power to assimilate these outside races. So coming to the root of the matter, if we want to restore our race's standing, besides uniting all into a great national body, we must first recover our ancient morality—then, and only then, can we plan how to attain again to the national position we have held.[87]

and on this passage on the New Culture Movement:

Since our domination by alien races and since the invasion of foreign culture which has spread its influence all over China, a group intoxicated with the new culture have begun to reject the old morality, saying that the former makes the latter unnecessary. They do not understand that we ought to preserve what is good in our past and throw away only the bad.[88]

These statements seem syncretistic, and reminiscent of Chang Chih-tung's "Chinese learning for substance, Western learning for function." Indeed, it was on the basis of them that a group of professors, with the blessing of some leaders of the Kuomintang, in 1933 called for "cultural construction on a Chinese basis." All in all, they would seem to offer ample proof of the traditionalist basis of Sun's thought, were it not for other of his statements that tend to contradict the whole proposition.[89]

The following passage from his lecture of December 1923—in which he professes admiration for Western civilization and calls for China's transformation on the American model—is of special note:

We may ask, why has the United States such good universities and China none? Why is China unable to establish such good universities? It is because European and American civilizations have made tremendous progress during the past two hundred years, especially American civilization in the past few decades. . . . What should then be the ambitions of Chinese youth? They should be determined to reconstruct the Republic of China so that its civilization is equal to that of other countries. . . . If we are determined to improve our country, bent on a single purpose and united in our cooperative efforts, we can still catch up with Europe and America. . . . In order to attain this purpose [of making China prosperous and strong], we must be resolved to save the country by uniting our hearts and combining our efforts, in the same way that the Americans did in their revolution. . . . You must utilize American knowledge to make China become a United States.[90]

Here Sun speaks so highly of American moral strength and so disparagingly of Chinese lethargy that one cannot help questioning the seriousness of his statements on recovering the traditional Chinese virtues.

Our doubts are further increased when we take a second look at the sixth lecture, on the Principle of Nationalism. In regard to the virtue of benevolence, he adds the following: "In the practical expression of the fine qualities of kindness and love, it does seem that China was far behind the other countries, and the reason is that the Chinese have been less active in performance."[91] Again, after calling attention to the wisdom of the ancient political philosophy expressed in the *Great Learning* (*Ta-hsüeh*), Sun observes that it is difficult to tell how inward control, considered so important by the Confucianists, is to be attained. The question seemed to baffle him so much that he wound up counseling that Chinese "young men should certainly learn from the modern culture of the foreigners."[92]

The sixth lecture, on the Principle of Nationalism, is,

in fact, quite confusing. In spite of profuse praise for traditional virtues, Sun stopped short of expounding the virtues themselves. And when it came to practical advice, he turned instead to the West. Apparently he had a firmer grasp of Western culture than of the traditional principles of his own country. His extolling of the traditional virtues has been attributed by some to the pressure of the Kuomintang's right wing, which was highly apprehensive of the Marxist influence brought into its midst by the admission of the Communists.[93] It is significant that Sun's discussion of traditional virtues appeared in his lecture on nationalism. As a revolutionary, he was naturally concerned with strategy, and it is understandable that his praise of traditional virtues was not so much a genuine appreciation as a means for reviving national confidence. Sun once said: "What I am studying is the science of revolution. Whatever learning is helpful to my revolutionary knowledge or capacity will be the material of my study and will be utilized to form my science of revolution."[94]

Sun's attempt to apply classical principles to his revolutionary theory is again seen in his lecture on "The Spiritual Education of the Soldier," the lecture on which Tai Chi-t'ao based his traditionalist interpretation.[95] In it Sun discussed *jen* as the basic spirit of the soldier. It is significant that of all the Confucianist definitions of *jen,* Sun adopted that of Han Yü (768–824), who called it "a love for everyone." A Christian, Sun may have found the definition close to the Christian teaching of "love toward all men."[96] At any rate, in the same lecture, he broadened the concept of *jen* to include the beliefs of the Christians, whose sacrifices for world salvation he cited as examples of practicing *jen.*[97] His illustration of *jen* with Christian rather than Confucian examples seems to reveal a Western orientation. Actually, Sun's purpose in this lecture was to emphasize patriotism, which he termed "the *jen* of the soldier."

Thus, he invoked a traditional concept to buttress his principle of military morale, which he felt to be essential to the success of his revolutionary movement.

An examination of Sun's writings before his lectures on San Min Chu I (The Three Principles of the People) will reveal that his appraisal of traditional thought was in reality largely unfavorable. In 1908 he wrote:

Confucius and Mencius were ancient sages, not scientists of today. In their time science was not yet developed. Some of their sayings are in accord with justice; some are not.[98]

Again, in 1919 he said:

For several thousand years Chinese sages and enlightened philosophers, one following the teachings of the other, all maintained that [absolutism] is natural for men born on this earth. As a result, the relationship between the prince and the minister was conceived to be one of the Three Bonds. That is why Chinese politics failed to make any progress. It is true that they have such ideas as "When the great principle prevails, the world will be common to all"; "Heaven sees as people see, and hears as people hear"; "The people are most important, the prince the least"; and "The people constitute the basis of the state." But all these are no more than a thin thread of light which at any rate fails to arrest the calamitous trends.[99]

This passage is of special significance, for it includes the classical phrase *T'ien-hsia wei kung* (the world is common to all)—a phrase that Sun sometimes wrote in the scrolls and tablets. Such writers as Tai Chi-t'ao pointed to it as evidence of the traditional foundation of Sun's thought. What Sun says in the two passages above should, however, refute the assertion that he was a successor to traditional Chinese thought. At least he did not consider himself such.

Although he frequently quoted from Chinese classics to reinforce his own ideas, Sun seldom expounded concepts of traditional thought at any great length. His writings on the theory of knowledge and action were almost the only place he devoted systematic discussion to any of the ancient principles. But even here, as we have seen, he took a position against the ancient saying "To know is not difficult; to act is really difficult." His criticism of Wang Yang-ming (1472–1529) shows that he was not interested in the essence of Neo-Confucianism. In a lecture at Kweilin in 1921, again discussing his theory of knowledge and action, he made the following statement:

Chinese civilization made great progress in ancient times. European and American civilizations have made great progress in recent times. . . . The reason for the lack of progress in Chinese civilization during the past two thousand years lies in the misconceptions in Chinese thought and learning. Simply speaking, the Chinese have believed that to act is difficult, while to know is very easy. This idea has failed China as it has failed Chinese scholars.[100]

Sun had no intention of reviving the Chinese culture of two thousand years ago. Discussing the progress of mankind in a lecture in 1922, he declared: "A state advances from barbarism to civilization. Similarly, mankind advances from ignorance to knowledge by abandoning old ideas and conceiving new ideas, by abandoning old thought and adopting new thought. Today we should overthrow old ideas and old thought; we should evolve new ideas and new thought."[101]

Sun's education helps explain his views on Chinese culture. In his *Autobiography,* written in 1896, after he was released from the Chinese legation in London, Sun states that he studied Confucian classics until he went to

Hawaii at the age of thirteen (or twelve, according to Western calculation).[102] There is some uncertainty as to when he started his studies. It seems that he went to the village school at the age of ten, although he may have learned from some private teacher to recite some of the elementary Chinese texts when he was only seven.[103] From the age of thirteen to seventeen he stayed in Honolulu, first studying in a British missionary school and later in an American school called Oahu College. He was so enthusiastic about the Western way of life and showed such a deep belief in Christianity that his brother became worried and finally decided to send him home. During 1884–1885 he studied in British schools in Hong Kong where Chinese subjects were least emphasized. He did spend some of his spare time studying Chinese with a senior member of a Christian church, and there is evidence that for a few months during 1885–1886 he concentrated on studying Chinese classics and history.[104] But it is apparent that throughout his school years he had very little time for Chinese studies, and whatever training he received in this field must have been at best fragmentary and superficial. Sun himself admitted that what he learned about Chinese classics while he was a boy he largely forgot later. It was only through his later reading of the English translations of the *Four Books* and the *Five Classics* that he began to understand Chinese learning and history.[105] While in his *Autobiography* he professed to be fond of the writings of the Three Dynasties and the two Han, he was hardly a classical scholar in the Chinese tradition. In fact, he never claimed to be. On questions concerning ancient Chinese institutions he would have to ask experts, while on Western theories and institutions he could express an authoritative opinion.[106] His formal education was practically all on the Western model, with a specialization in medical science. This scientific training shaped his thinking and provided a framework for his writings. Rather than citing the classics as his authorities, as traditional scholars had done, Sun attempted to prove his thesis by referring to facts. If sometimes he was mistaken in his facts, or careless in scrutinizing them, it was still facts that interested him, even in his discussion of such philosophical subjects as knowledge and action. Sun's factual approach was nontraditional and contrasted sharply with the metaphysical disquisitions of the Neo-Confucianists.

Sun attributed the origins of his revolutionary thought to the inspirations he received in Hong Kong, where order, peace, progress, and prosperity constituted a strong contrast to the backwardness he found in his own country. There is no doubt that what he saw in Honolulu in his formative years also contributed to his high regard for Western civilization.[107] He paid special tribute to Christian churches for their part in introducing Western ideas to "open the eyes" of the Chinese. In a lecture in 1912, he said: "Several years ago I advocated revolution and had consistently worked for it. But it is mostly from the church that I learned the truth of revolution. The establishment of the Republic today is due, not to my efforts, but to the service of the church."[108]

The revolution Sun determined to carry out was aimed at more than the overthrow of the existing dynasty. Its major purpose was to change the form of government, and in this it differed from all of the previous rebellions in Chinese history. Sun knew that in order to replace the traditional monarchy with the modern republic, he had to learn the ways and means of the West.[109] Thus, in 1905 he said that to accomplish this fundamental reform, "everything must be learned from others."[110] It was because of this new nondynastic character of the revolution that he opposed the incorporation of the history of the secret societies into the history of the Chinese Republic. In a letter of 1919, Sun pointed out that the secret societies under the Ch'ing dynasty were to be traced to the Ming loyalists, whose chief aim in overthrowing the Manchus had been to revive the Ming dynasty. Although nationalism prevailed in these societies, their internal organization was absolute and hierarchical, and had nothing in common with republican and democratic principles. "Their relationship with the republican revolution was, in fact, superficial."[111]

We may also examine the assertion that Sun's idea of revolution is traceable to the ancient revolutions of China. The basis for the assertion is twofold. First, in his *Autobiography* Sun mentioned that among the historical figures he admired were, in addition to George Washington, King T'ang of Shang and King Wu of Chou. Second, the term *ke-ming* (revolution) that Sun used was a classical Chinese term referring to the T'ang and Wu uprisings in ancient China. But as Sun himself pointed out in his "Spiritual Education of the Soldier," his revolution was different from those of T'ang and Wu. "While the ancient revolutions were revolutions of the kings," he said, "the present revolution is the revolution of the people."[112] As to the term *ke-ming*, it was first used in a Japanese newspaper in 1895, and Sun adopted it when he happened to read the paper in Kobe.[113] It is apparent that Sun's revolutionary thought was not inspired by the ancient uprisings, but that the term was used after his revolutionary movement had come into being.

If there is still any doubt, one should look at a lecture of 1924. "Where did the revolutionary currents come from?" Sun asked. His answer was that they had been "introduced from Europe and America."[114] And earlier, in 1918, he had written: "My revolutionary reconstruction is based on the trends of world evolution and the precedents of other countries."[115] Thus, although Sun made frequent and liberal use of terms and quotations from the Chinese classics, it is obvious that it was only to express his own ideas and to reinforce his own thought, which was largely derived from the West. Said Sun: "One should make use of our ancients, and must not be their slaves."[116]

The Three Principles of the People, the essence of Sun's political doctrine, did not emerge as an integrated system, consisting of three interrelated principles, until after Sun was released from imprisonment in the Chinese legation at London in 1896. During his stay in Europe in 1896–1897,[117] Sun made an intensive study of European social problems and socialist theories:

After escaping from London, I went to Europe to study its politics and customs, and also to make the acquaintance of its governmental leaders and representatives of the Opposition parties. I learned a great deal from what I saw and what I heard during those two years. I realized that although the foremost European countries had achieved power and popular government, they could not accord complete happiness to their peoples. Therefore, the leading European revolutionaries strive for a social revolution, and I conceived the idea of the simultaneous settlement, by means of revolution, of the problems of the people's livelihood, national independence, and people's rights. Hence arose my San Min Chu I.[118]

This account is, in general, accurate and is well borne out by the facts. When the Hsing-chung Hui was organized in Honolulu in 1894, it was stated in the Declaration that the society's purpose was to revive China, and nothing was said about overthrowing the Manchu government.[119] A similar omission was made in the Declaration of the Hong Kong branch the following year.[120] The reason for not openly attacking the Manchu governments in these declarations was, according to the official explanation, to avoid government attention, which might lead to persecution.[121] The explanation seems valid, for in the secret oath taken by members of the Hong Kong Hsing-chung Hui, the following pledge was adopted: "To drive out the Tartars, to revive China, and to establish a popular government."[122] In 1904 Sun wrote into the charter of the Chih-kung T'ang, an overseas Chinese association in the United States, the following objectives, which were in 1905 incorporated into the charter of the T'ung-meng Hui: "To drive out the Tartars, revive China, establish a republic, and equitably distribute land ownership."[123] Thus it is clear that in the early stages, from 1894 to 1904, land reform did not constitute a part of Sun's revolutionary program. The idea of the people's livelihood was conceived after 1896, but incorporated into the program of the revolutionary party only in 1904. If the Three Principles of the People was an integrated system, as Sun and his followers maintained,[124] it was not so until after Sun's exposure to European social problems and socialist theories.

When Sun revisited Europe in 1905, he discussed for the first time his Three Principles and five-power constitution with Chinese students in Belgium, Berlin, and Paris.[125] In October of the same year Sun wrote the Foreword to the *People's Journal,* published in Tokyo, in which he set forth the Three Principles of Nationalism, Democracy, and Livelihood.[126] Henceforth the Three Principles were the slogan of the revolutionary party and the official political doctrine of Sun Yat-sen.[127]

A significant passage in the Foreword to the *People's Journal* reads as follows:

In my opinion, the evolution of Europe and America is based on three great principles, namely, nationalism, democracy and the people's livelihood. After the disintegration of the Roman Empire, nationalism arose and countries in Europe and America became independent. As absolutism developed, and the people could stand it no longer, the principle of democracy was put into action. At the end of the 18th century and the beginning of the 19th, absolutism fell and in its place was established constitutional government. As world civilization advanced, human knowledge grew; what was attained in material development during the past hundred years far surpassed what had been achieved in the preceding one thousand years. The economic problem thus followed the political problem, and the principle of the people's livelihood became active. As a result, the principle of the people's livelihood dominates the twentieth century.[128]

The above passage clearly testifies to Western influence in the formulation of the Three Principles. As the statement was written in 1905, when the Three Principles were first announced, its value as an indicator of their source is greater than that of some later statements. Sun further acknowledged the impact of the West upon the formation of his principles in his *San Min Chu I*, a shorter paper written in 1919. This paper, seized by the Japanese during the Sino-Japanese War of 1937 and retrieved by a Chinese secret agent, was first published after the end of the Second World War,[129] and is generally considered to be a more careful version than that delivered in the lectures of 1924. In this paper Sun wrote: "The three great movements [of nationalism, democracy, and the people's livelihood] forced themselves into our door amid the high tide of world evolution. Unless we abandon our revolution and let ourselves be eliminated by the process of natural selection, we must once and for all attain the three levels of evolution by means of a single revolution."[130]

Sun once said: "The principles that I advocate for the Chinese revolution are partly derived from our traditional thought, partly based on European theories and events, and partly developed from my own ideas."[131] This general utterance should be checked against the more specific statements Sun made regarding particular ideas. In the discussion of Sun's major ideas above, an attempt has been made to trace their individual origins. In summary, we may say that Sun indeed had no intention of copying *in toto* the political institutions of the West, and he displayed his originality on a number of problems. Nevertheless, Western influences were prominent in his major principles. Regarding the overthrow of the Manchus, Sun's idea might well have had precedents in Chinese history, but the nationalism he set forth in *San Min Chu I* was based strictly on Western experience and ideas. Although he criticized Western political institutions, his theory of ability and sovereignty took its inspiration from the works of Swiss and American scholars; and in spite of his observation that China's customs and habits differed from the West's, he discussed China's "right road to government" with reference to Western government.[132] While there were also traditional Chinese elements, these were generally in the form of an illustration or detail. The five-power constitution is an example, for although the powers of control and examination were borrowings from Chinese tradition, underlying the five-power scheme was the Western idea of separation of powers. As to the Principle of Livelihood, its Western inspiration is manifest from its inception to its latest phase. When the *People's Journal* cited in 1905 the ancient "well-field" system, its purpose in doing so was to disarm opposition to the radical idea of land nationalization, which was entirely different from the "feudal" tradition.[133] Nor can it be said that the Principle of Livelihood was based on the Confucian concept of *jen;* Sun himself pointed out that the ancient teaching of universal love was much narrower in scope than modern socialism.[134]

That Sun, a Chinese working in the midst of Chinese society, was subject to the influence of Chinese tradition is not to be denied, but its influence was vague and diffuse in comparison with that of Western ideas. In his eyes, Chinese tradition might have contained some democratic ideas, but it provided no concrete institutions that suited the modern age.[135] His modern education with its scientific basis did not incline him toward traditional Chinese thought, and his long contact with the West convinced him that the imperative need of China was to adapt itself to "the modern trends of the world."[136]

Sun's importance in Chinese history lies in his being the first of his countrymen to know the West well and at the same time bold enough to advocate rebuilding China along Western lines—the most advanced, in his view. He began advocating these ideas as early as the 1890's, when Confucian tradition was still sacred, and modern ideas of nationalism, democracy, and socialism were considered heresy in the extreme. In this respect, he could claim to be a foreseer, or the first Chinese revolutionist.

Notes

CHAPTER V. SUN YAT-SEN

1. Sun Yat-sen, *Kuo-fu ch'üan-shu* (Complete Works of the Founding Father) (Taipei: Kuo-fang yen-chiu yüan, 1960), p. 393.
2. Sun Yat-sen, "Sun-wen Hsüeh-shuo" (The Theory of Sun Yat-sen), in *Tsung-li ch'üan-shu* (Complete Works of the President, hereafter cited as *TLCS*) (12 vols.; Taipei: The Central Committee of the Kuomintang, 1956), II, 100–102.
3. Sun Yat-sen, *Fundamentals of National Reconstruction* (Taipei: China Cultural Service, 1953), pp. 3–4.
4. Sun Yat-sen, *Kuo-fu ch'üan-shu*, pp. 1043–46.
5. Hu Shih, "Wo-men shen-mo shih-hou ts'ai-yu hsien-fa?" (When Will We Have a Constitution?), *Hsin-yüeh* (The Crescent Moon), 2.3: 84 (1919).
6. Chang Chün-mai, "Kuo-min-tang tang-cheng chih hsin ch'i-lu" (The New Dilemma of the Kuomintang Party Rule), *Tsai-sheng* ("The National Renaissance"), 1.2: 2 (1932).
7. Lo Chia-lun, ed., *Ke-ming wen-hsien* (Historical Materials of the Revolution) (Taipei, 1954), V, 572, 579.
8. *TLCS*, X-B, 901.
9. *TLCS*, VII-B, 686.
10. Sun, *Fundamentals of National Reconstruction*, p. 161.
11. *Ibid.*, pp. 112 ff.
12. *Ibid.*, p. 161.
13. *Min-pao* (People's Journal, cited hereafter as *MP*), Nos. 1, 2, 14, 15, 17, 18, 20.
14. *Ke-ming wen-hsien*, V, 57.
15. *TLCS*, VII-A, 138–39.
16. *TLCS*, VIII, 5; II, 35.
17. Sun, *Kuo-fu ch'üan-shu*, p. 888.
18. *TLCS*, VI, 55.
19. *TLCS*, V, 175; VII-A, 141.
20. *TLCS*, VII-B, 677.
21. *TLCS*, VI, 214 ff.
22. Sun Yat-sen, *San Min Chu I*, trans. by Frank W. Price (Shanghai, Commercial Press, 1928), p. 79.
23. *Ibid.*, pp. 36–37.
24. *TLCS*, I, 18.
25. *TLCS*, VII-B, 1221 ff.
26. Sun, *San Min Chu I*, pp. 75–76, 147–48.
27. *Ibid.*, pp. 176 ff.; *TLCS*, VI, 223–24.
28. Sun, *San Min Chu I*, pp. 203 ff.
29. Liang Shih-ch'iu, "Sun Chung-shan hsien-sheng lun yen-lun tzu-yu" (Sun Yat-sen's Discussion of the Freedom of Speech), *Hsin-yüeh*, 2.9 (1918).
30. *TLCS*, V, 160.
31. *TLCS*, IX, 146.
32. Chü Chüeh-sheng, *Hsin-hai cha-chi* (Notes of 1911) (Taipei: China Cultural Service, 1956), p. 128.

33. Sun, *San Min Chu I*, pp. 208 ff.
34. Sun, *Kuo-fu ch'üan-shu*, p. 767.
35. Sun, *San Min Chu I*, p. 35.
36. *TLCS*, I, 244–45.
37. *TLCS*, VI, 197, 232.
38. Sun, *San Min Chu I*, pp. 244–45.
39. Jen Cho-hsüan, *Wu-ch'üan hsien-fa yü Chung-kuo hsien-fa* (The Five-Power Constitution and the Chinese Constitution) (Taipei: P'a-mi-erh, 1957), p. 68.
40. Sun, *San Min Chu I*, pp. 301 ff.
41. *Ibid.*, p. 360.
42. Sun, "Wu-ch'üan hsien-fa" (The Five-Power Constitution), *TLCS*, VII-A, 484–85.
43. *TLCS*, VII-A, 328–29.
44. *TLCS*, VII-A, 491.
45. Sun, *San Min Chu I*, p. 354.
46. Sun, *Fundamentals of National Reconstruction*, pp. 11, 15–16.
47. See Ch'en Chih-mai, *Chung-kuo cheng-fu* (The Government of China) (Shanghai: Commercial Press, 1946), III, 170–71.
48. Ts'ui Shu-ch'in, *Sun Chung-shan yü kung-ch'an chu-i* (Sun Yat-sen and Communism) (Hong Kong: Ya-chou, 1956), pp. 137 ff.
49. *TLCS*, VII-B, 892.
50. *TLCS*, I, 103–4.
51. *TLCS*, VII-A, 54, 66, 443; V, 457.
52. *TLCS*, I, 438; Sun, *San Min Chu I*, p. 416.
53. *TLCS*, I, 458.
54. *TLCS*, VII-A, 202–3.
55. Sun, *San Min Chu I*, p. 441.
56. *TLCS*, V, 409.
57. Maurice William, *The Social Interpretation of History* (New York: Sotery Publishing Co., 1921).
58. *TLCS*, VII-A, 288.
59. *TLCS*, I, 411.
60. *TLCS*, I, 415; Sun, *San Min Chu I*, p. 391.
61. *TLCS*, II, 80–81; VII-A, 123, 201; VII-B, 708.
62. Maurice William, *Sun Yat-sen versus Communism* (Baltimore: Williams and Wilkins, 1932), p. xiv.
63. *Ibid.*, pp. xvii, 4–5.
64. Wang Ch'ang-ku, "Pa Sun Chung-shan shou-shu min-tsu chu-i tzu-hsü" (Concerning Sun Yat-sen's Personally Written Preface to His *Principle of Nationalism*), *Ch'un-ch'iu*, No. 157: 24 (1964); *TLCS*, VII-B, 893.
65. Henry George, *Progress and Poverty* (1879; New York: Robert Schalkenbach Foundation, 1958), pp. 328 ff.
66. The term "equalization of land ownership" first appeared in the charter of the Chih-kung T'ang, 1904.
67. *TLCS*, V, 406; VII-A, 81, 96, 101, 451.
68. *TLCS*, V, 408.
69. *TLCS*, VIII, 136.
70. *TLCS*, V, 404.
71. *MP*, No. 3: 13 (April 1906).
72. *TLCS*, V, 403.
73. Henry George, *Progress and Poverty*, p. 436.

74. Ts'en Hsüeh-lü, *San-sui Liang Yen-sun hsien-sheng nien-p'u* (A Chronological Biography of Liang Shih-i) (Taipei: Wen-shing, 1962), I, 123.
75. Wu Yü-chang, "Sun Chung-shan hsien-sheng wei-ta ti ke-ming ching-shen" (The Great Revolutionary Spirit of Sun Yat-sen), in *Wei-ta ti Sun Chung-shan* (The Great Sun Yat-sen) (Hong Kong: Hsin-ti, 1957), p. 53.
76. Sun, "Keng-che yu ch'i t'ien" (Land to the Tillers), in *TLCS*, VII-B, 1123–25.
77. *TLCS*, VII-A, 260–61.
78. *TLCS*, V, 508 ff.
79. Sun, "Sun-wen hsüeh-shuo," in *TLCS*, II, 90.
80. *TLCS*, II, 94.
81. See David S. Nivison, "The Problem of 'Knowledge' and 'Action' in Chinese Thought since Wang Yang-ming," in Arthur F. Wright, ed., *Studies in Chinese Thought* (Chicago: University of Chicago Press, 1953), pp. 112 ff.
82. Hu Shih, "Chih-nan hsing i pu-i" (To Know Is Difficult, but to Act Is also Not Easy), *Hsin-yüeh*, 2.4: 12 (June 1929).
83. Sun, *San Min Chu I*, p. 417.
84. *TLCS*, VII-A, 538.
85. Feng Yu-lan, "Tsai-lun chih-hsing" (Further Discussion of Knowledge and Action), *Kuan-ch'a* (Observation), 1.6: 1 (Oct. 1946).
86. Tai Chi-t'ao, *Sun-wen chu-i chih che hsüeh ti chi-ch'u* (The Philosophical Foundation of Sun Yat-senism) (Taipei: Chung-yang wen-wu kung-ying she, 1954).
87. Sun Yat-sen, *The Principle of Nationalism*, trans. by Frank W. Price (Taipei: Chinese Cultural Service, 1953), p. 51.
88. *Ibid.*, pp. 51–52.
89. Sun, *Kuo-fu ch'üan-shu*, p. 778.
90. *Ibid.*, pp. 947–50.
91. *TLCS*, I, 135–36.
92. In his Preface to the *Principle of Nationalism* (p. xiv), Sun writes: "In these lectures I do not have the time necessary for careful preparation nor the books necessary for reference. I can only mount the platform and speak extemporaneously (sui-i fa-yen)."
93. Cf. Hu Shih, "Hsin-wen-hua yün-tung yü Kuo-min-tang" (The New Culture Movement and the Kuomintang), *Hsin-yüeh*, 2.6–7: 2–7 (Sept. 1929).
94. *TLCS*, VIII, 117.
95. Tai Chi-t'ao, *op. cit.*, p. 5.
96. *The New Testament*, I Thessalonians 3:12.
97. Sun, "Chün-jen ching-shen chiao-yü" (Spiritual Education of the Soldier), *TLCS*, VII-A, 590–91.
98. *TLCS*, V, 195.
99. *TLCS*, V, 394.
100. *TLCS*, VII-A, 541.
101. *TLCS*, VII-A, 632.
102. *TLCS*, V, 88.
103. Lo Chia-lun, ed., *Kuo-fu nien-p'u* (A Chronological Biography of Sun Yat-sen) (Taipei, 1958), I, 12.
104. *Ibid.*, I, iii, 32.
105. *TLCS*, VII-A, 324.

106. *TLCS*, VIII, 117.
107. *TLCS*, VII-B, 650; Sun, *Kuo-fu ch'üan-shu*, p. 839.
108. *TLCS*, VII-A, 144.
109. *TLCS*, VII-A, 324.
110. *TLCS*, VII-A, 10.
111. Sun, *Kuo-fu ch'üan-shu*, p. 637.
112. *TLCS*, VII-A, 564.
113. Feng Tzu-yu, *Ke-ming i-shih* (Reminiscences of the Revolution) (Taipei: Commercial Press, 1953), I, 1.
114. *TLCS*, VII-B, 1133.
115. Sun, "Sun-wen hsüeh-shuo," *TLCS*, II, 101.
116. *TLCS*, II, 47.
117. According to Lo, *Kuo-fu nien-p'u* (I, 75), Sun stayed in London from October 23, 1896, the day of his release from the Chinese Legation, to July 2, 1897, when he left for Canada. In Wu Chih-hui's *Kuo-fu nien-hsi chi hsing-i* (A Chronological Sketch of Sun Yat-sen and His Activities) (Taipei, 1952), however, it is stated that Sun stayed in London until the end of 1898 or the beginning of 1899 (Wu, p. 11).
118. Sun, "Sun-wen hsüeh-shuo," *TLCS*, II, 164; Sun Yat-sen, *Memoirs of a Revolutionary* (Taipei: China Cultural Service, 1953), pp. 149-50.
119. Sun, *Kuo-fu ch'üan-shu*, p. 351.
120. *Ibid.*
121. See Feng Tzu-yu, *Chung-hua min-kuo k'ai-kuo ch'ien ke-ming shih* (History of the Revolution before the Establishment of the Republic of China) (Taipei: Shih-chieh, 1954), I, 7.
122. Chang Chi, *Chang P'u-ch'üan hsien-sheng ch'üan-chi, pu-pien* (Complete Works of Chang Chi, Supplement) (Taipei, 1952), p. 20. In his "Sun-wen hsüeh-shuo," Sun said that in 1885, the year of China's defeat by the French, he had decided to "overthrow the Manchu regime and establish a popular government" (*TLCS*, II, 156). The decision, however, might not have been a final one in view of his proposals to Li Hung-chang in 1894.
123. Sun, *Kuo-fu ch'üan-shu*, pp. 390, 393.
124. See *TLCS*, VII-A, 24; Hu Han-min, *San-min chu-i ti lien-huan hsing* (The Interrelationships of the Three Principles of the People) (1928); Tai Chi-tao, *Sun-wen chu-i chih che-hsüeh ti chi-ch'u.*
125. Sun, "Sun-wen hsüeh-shuo," *TLCS*, II, 173. It is possible, however, that he discussed the equitable distribution of land ownership without using the term "Principle of the People's Livelihood." See Feng Tzu-yu, *Ke-ming i-shih*, II, 143.
126. *MP*, No. 1 (1905).
127. The term "Min-tsu min-ch'üan min-sheng san ta chu-i" was first abbreviated to "San-min chu-i" by *Chung-kuo jih-pao* (The China Daily) in Hong Kong toward the end of 1905. Feng Tzu-yu, *Ke-ming i-shih*, II, 144.
128. *MP*, No. 1 (1905).
129. Chang Chi, *Chang P'u-ch'üan hsien-sheng ch'üan-chi*, p. 85.
130. *TLCS*, V, 385.
131. *TLCS*, V, 42.
132. Sun, *San Min Chu I*, pp. 290-94.

133. *TLCS,* VII-A, 81.
134. *TLCS,* VII-A, 205.
135. *TLCS,* V, 454.
136. Sun, *Kuo-fu ch'üan-shu,* p. 890.

Chapter VI

THE KUOMINTANG LEADERS

Chiang Kai-shek

AFTER Sun Yat-sen's death in 1925, the struggle for power in the Kuomintang centered around three leaders: Chiang Kai-shek, Hu Han-min, and Wang Ching-wei. Hu and Wang were veteran Kuomintang leaders who had been Sun's lieutenants since 1905 when the Tung-meng Hui revolutionary party was organized. Chiang emerged as an important figure only after the reorganization of the Kuomintang in 1924 when he was made head of the Whampoa Military Academy and entrusted with the organization of the party army. After a series of intrigues and coups, Chiang took over the Kuomintang. Leading the Northern Expedition, he defeated the northern warlords and, after more than a decade of civil wars, more or less unified the country. In 1928 the National Government was established in Nanking, and from then until 1949, except for two very brief periods, Chiang was the "supreme leader" of China. But although he held extensive powers, he was continually beset with serious difficulties. First, there were frequent revolts and civil wars, of which the Communist rebellion was the most serious; and secondly, the Japanese invasion threatened the very existence of the nation. It is therefore not surprising that in his political doctrine Chiang emphasized unity, stability, order, and authority.

As a disciple of Sun Yat-sen, Chiang faithfully accepted the San Min Chu I (The Three Principles of the People) as the guideline for governing China. But in line with his temperament and training he interpreted them conservatively. Adopting the view of Tai Chi-t'ao that in the traditional line of thought reaching back to the ancient sages Sun Yat-sen was the successor to Confucius,[1] he not only maintained, as did Tai Chi-t'ao, that Sun Yat-sen's political doctrine was founded on the traditional concept of *jen,* but also declared that Sun's most advanced knowledge was derived from *The Great Learning* and *The Golden Mean,* the two Confucian classics.[2]

In the midst of recurrent national crises caused by both internal disunity and foreign aggression, Chiang's most urgent task during his two decades of rule was to save the country, and he saw a unified nation with strong governmental power as a prerequisite. Any effective resistance against Japanese aggression would require the mobilization of all national resources under a centralized, powerful leadership. Thus he set the state, to which citizens should pledge loyalty and for which they would sacrifice themselves, ahead of the individual. As cells of the political organism, individuals, he believed, must depend on the state for their existence and growth, their education and welfare. Only when the nation developed and advanced could individuals themselves progress. And only when individuals dedicated themselves to the state could their lives be enhanced and glorified.[3] The state, in short, was the most developed organism, with a capacity for infinite growth and independent ability to achieve its ideals.[4]

Accepting Sun Yat-sen's concept of political tutelage with its corollary of one-party government, Chiang identified the party with the state. Thus he wrote: "So long as the Kuomintang remains in existence, so long will China continue to exist. If China today did not have the Kuomintang, there would be no China."[5] Chiang called the party the lifeblood of the Chinese nation and the members of the San Min Chu I Youth Corps, a Kuomintang organization formed in 1938 to train young people for party work, the new blood corpuscles. As an organic part of the nation, the Kuomintang was open to all, and Chiang considered it the duty of all citizens to join it. "The utmost loyalty to the state, the utmost filial piety toward the nation; to be saints and sages and heroes, to become the lifeblood of the nation and the backbone of the state"—all these were to be attained through working in the Kuomintang and its Youth Corps.[6]

Chiang's organic theory attempted to equate individual freedom and state authority. Since the life of an individual was part of the life of the state, it followed that the will of an individual was part of the state will. Thus "the command of the state should be regarded as the free and voluntary will of the individual, and the demands of the state should become the free and voluntary demands of the individual."[7] Chiang's democracy was not patterned on the nineteenth-century individualistic theories of democracy or the class consciousness of the West. Its spirit was embodied in discipline and the rule of law.[8] There was no place for the theory of natural rights in Chiang's doctrine, since individual rights were created by law and must be confined within the boundaries of law. Echoing Sun Yat-sen, Chiang maintained that freedom was not a Chinese problem, as the Chinese have long had "great freedom"; the problem was rather how to curb licentiousness, which was the enemy of disciplined resistance to foreign aggression.[9]

In his struggles with internal divisive forces, particularly the Chinese Communists, Chiang found it necessary to call for unanimous thought as a requisite of national unification. If faith was strength, the Chinese people must be rallied around a central idea that would inspire their common faith in the nation. War against the enemy, internal or external, required a unified will and a unifying idea. Only when the national policy was backed up by the support of the whole nation could the Communists be stopped and foreign aggression effectively resisted.[10]

The central idea that would unify the will of the people Chiang called the national spirit, or sometimes the national soul. If the state was an organism, it must have a soul that represented the national spirit, national morality, and national character. A soul, Chiang said, was indispensable to the existence of a nation; without it the nation would lose its identity and its *raison d'être*.[11] It was the national spirit that shaped the character of the people: its disappearance would lead to the disorganization of the state and the corruption of the people. Unless the national spirit was revived, the country could not be unified. National salvation, therefore, depended on the revival of the national soul.[12]

The national soul could be found in Sun Yat-sen's Three Principles of the People, which, according to Chiang, was derived from ancient Chinese tradition.[13] Chiang saw Sun's doctrine as a crystallization of Chinese culture, combining traditional virtues as the basis of politics and the theory of "knowledge and action" as the methodology for carrying out revolutionary programs.[14]

This interpretation of Sun reveals the nature of Chiang's conviction. In the traditional virtues Chiang found the nature of China, and in classical philosophy, the essence of the Chinese spirit. Chiang's political doctrine was solidly built on the foundation of Chinese classics, notably *The Great Learning* and *The Golden Mean:* "So long as the traditional philosophy of our nation is soundly established and our traditional virtues developed and glorified, we will easily succeed in our work of national revival."[15]

The quintessence of traditional Chinese philosophy is ethics, Chiang felt. Like the Confucianists, he maintained that ethical principles were more positive, more natural, and reached further into the hearts of the people than laws. But he added something new: while law indicates only whether certain conduct is proper or improper and forbids people to do the improper or to neglect doing the proper, ethics seeks the meaning of life and asks why an action is proper or improper. All Chinese political philosophy, according to Chiang, "can be summed up in one sentence: it aims at raising the character of man, bringing out the value and potential of man and purifying relations between man and man."[16] Broadening the Confucian concept that a good government depends on good administrators, Chiang held that in modern times a good government required good citizens.[17] Nothing was more important for the orderly rule of a country than that each citizen should set his heart right and make his will sincere, and nothing was more logical than to begin the maintenance of world peace with the cultivation of personal life.[18]

Chiang attributed special importance to sincerity, the one principle that should pervade all revolutionary work. If everyone recognized the ultimate good of the San Min Chu I and sincerely adhered to it, the revolution would be a success.[19] Only through sincerity could one become enlightened and avoid a wayward course. And only through sincerity could one influence others and bring them in line with government policies.[20] A veteran in politics, Chiang knew the worthlessness of public declarations. In line with the doctrine of the golden mean, he urged moral men to keep diligent watch over their secret thoughts.[21]

In the Neo-Confucianist tradition, Chiang went beyond moral principles to metaphysical concepts. Mind, he declared, is the master of thought; it must be constantly cleansed of selfish desires; and, in order to conform to heavenly reason, one must fulfill one's own nature. In a vein worthy of Wang Yang-ming, Chiang identified human nature with heavenly reason and set as the highest personal achievement keeping one's nature clean and pure, un-clouded by selfish desires and unchanged by external at-tractions.[22] Here Chiang underlined the basic difference between Chinese philosophy and the Marxist interpreta-tion of history: the Marxists promote class struggles by stressing materialistic conflicts; the Chinese philosophers follow heavenly reason and emphasize the commonality of human nature.[23]

Chiang's call for the revival of the national soul and his interpretation of the national soul as national character are strikingly similar to the disquisitions of K'ang Yu-wei and Liang Ch'i-ch'ao in the early years of the Republic. Chiang, however, went farther than K'ang and Liang in his use of Neo-Confucianism. Where K'ang and Liang indi-cated only the major traditional sources of China's moral-ity, Chiang set forth specific virtues to be cultivated by the Chinese people. His enthusiasm for traditional virtues surpassed that of Liang Ch'i-ch'ao, who maintained a gen-erally critical attitude toward Confucian principles.[24]

By adopting traditional philosophy as the foundation of his political doctrine, Chiang made moral reorganization an important part of his national reconstruction.[25] The traditional virtues he attempted to revive were the Five Universal Obligations (the duties of ruler and subject, father and son, husband and wife, brothers, and friends); the Three Moral Qualities (wisdom, benevolence, and courage); the Four Social Bonds (decorum, righteousness, integrity, and sense of shame); and the Eight Virtues (loyalty, filial piety, benevolence, love, sincerity, right-eousness, harmony, and peace). It is a long list, but some of the qualities are repetitious and some interchangeable in meaning, and for Chiang they were all activated by the principle of sincerity. Thus the object of sincerity is the realization of benevolence, which in turn is the central concept of the Three Moral Qualities, while the Eight

Virtues are but the contents of benevolence applied to various human relationships.[26]

This unitary interpretation of traditional virtues served as the philosophical basis for the New Life Movement, which was in fact an attempt to renovate China's moral life in accordance with traditional principles. The background of the New Life Movement was the war against the Chinese Communists, and it was inaugurated by Chiang in September 1934 in Nanchang, where the headquarters of the Nationalist Army to Exterminate the Communists was located. In the course of his struggle with the Chinese Communists, Chiang had realized that it was not so much military power as the political temper of the people that held the key to the success of his campaigns. He had found laxity in public life and a widespread general apathy. "Officials tend to be dishonest and avaricious; the masses are undisciplined and callous."[27] The New Life Movement was launched to wipe out these unwholesome conditions through the promotion of traditional virtues.

The traditional virtues particularly emphasized were *li* (decorum), *i* (righteousness), *lien* (integrity), and *ch'ih* (sense of shame), which were to be applied to the ordinary life of the common people as well as to the public conduct of government officials. To meet changing times, it was deemed necessary to give the ancient principles a new interpretation. Thus, in line with Neo-Confucianism, Chiang interpreted *li* to mean a regulated attitude (a man's conduct is considered regular if it conforms with law, social norms, and discipline); *i* to mean right conduct; *lien* to mean a clear distinction between right and wrong; and *ch'ih* to mean consciousness of wrongdoing along with a sincere effort to eliminate what one felt to be shameful. By observing these virtues, the people would be able to live "artistically, productively, and lead a military kind of life." They would acquire the habits of orderliness, cleanliness, simplicity, frugality, promptness, and exactness. Suspicion, jealousy, hatred, and strife would be ended, and if everyone led a productive life, beggary and robbery would disappear. As people became military-minded, order and discipline would be preserved; they would be ready to die for the country when necessary.[28]

The New Life Movement was to some extent inspired by the military way of life with which Chiang was familiar, and he himself said that the New Life was in substance a military life.[29] But he was equally emphatic that the army should be built on a moral foundation: the revolutionary motive of a soldier should be based on "benevolence," and his conduct be governed by "sincerity." The four virtues of *li, i, lien, ch'ih* were to constitute the elements of the military spirit, and *li* in particular would become the basis of discipline.[30] Chiang recognized that an army without morals was not only impotent but also dangerous.[31]

Declaring that the scope and glories of Chinese learning could not be equaled by any Western nation, Chiang condemned those who cultivated foreign ways, admired foreign theories, and "blindly" followed them.[32] He made clear, however, that this did not mean that Western methods and technology were not to be adopted in China.[33] In fact, China underwent much modernization under Chiang's rule. But he insisted that whatever was to be absorbed from the West be judged by Chinese standards, that the Chinese not become the slaves of foreign theories. To Chiang, all efforts to achieve Chinese independence would be in vain if the Chinese people lost confidence in their own culture. Furthermore, foreign methods and ideas had no roots in Chinese history; unless they were built on the foundation of Chinese tradition, he maintained, they could never grow and flourish.[34]

To revive confidence in Chinese culture, Chiang went

so far as to credit Chinese thinkers with Western ideas. He traced scientific methods to Confucius because he had advised people to "know the proper sequence or the relative order of things."[35] He read democratic thought into both Confucius and Mencius.[36] He compared Huang Tsung-hsi's *A Plan for the Prince* (*Ming-i Tai-fang Lu*) with Rousseau's *Social Contract* and found Huang's a much greater work.[37] He considered *Writings of Sung and Yüan Philosophers* (*Sung Yüan Hsüeh-an*) and *Writings of Ming Confucianists* (*Ming-ju Hsüeh-an*) "must" reading for young scholars and recommended the works of Wang Yang-ming (1472–1529), Wang Fu-chih (1619–1692), Huang Tsung-hsi (1610–1695), and Ku Yen-wu (1613–1682) to government workers.[38] In contrast to Sun Yat-sen who upheld the Taiping Rebellion (1850–1864), which attempted to overthrow the Manchu rule and institute social reforms, Chiang urged his officials to study the works of Tseng Kuo-fan (1811–1872) and Hu Lin-i (1812–1861), the suppressors of the Taipings, and he frequently quoted from them in discussing administrative methods, military strategies, and political wisdom.[39]

Twenty years of vigorous promotion of traditional virtues and ideas under the Nationalist government did not save China from Communism, but it can always be argued that not enough was done and more efforts should be made. Since his retreat to Taiwan, Chiang has sponsored a movement to revere Confucius and to revive classical studies. In the face of Communist dominance on the Chinese mainland, traditional philosophy and values seem to him the natural weapons to fight the alien ideology that he claims discards ethics and violates all the principles of human nature known to the Chinese for centuries.[40]

As stated earlier, the relative position of Confucianism and legalism has been a perennial subject of debate in Chinese history. The Confucianists favor government by men in which rulers move people by example and teaching; the Legalists advocate government by law in which power and force are instruments of administration. Although Chiang considered Confucian virtues the fundamentals of government, his practical mind realized the necessity for laws and institutions to rule a large country with all the complex problems of modern times. Thus he stressed discipline and the observance of law as indispensable to social stability and administrative efficiency. For administrative methods he borrowed from the experience and ideas of successful administrators in Chinese history who were either Legalists or were Confucianists not afraid of utilizing legalistic ideas. He quoted freely from such Legalists as Kuan Tzu (seventh century B.C.) for economic ideas and Shang Yang (d. 338 B.C.) on military affairs.[41] He paid tribute to the abortive reforms of Wang An-shih (1021–1086) and drew on him for the *pao-chia* local security system. It was from Chang Chü-cheng (1525–1582), however, that he derived much of his administrative method. One of the important administrative renovations under Chiang's rule was the triple-coordination system which aimed at linking up the three phases of administration: planning, execution, and review.[42] While the general scheme of coordination was derived from the West, the idea of review, which involved examination of reports and checking up the results, was taken from Chang Chü-cheng.[43] In personnel administration, especially in the areas of recruitment and training, Chiang was heavily indebted to Tseng Kuo-fan and Hu Lin-i, the Confucian statesmen who did not hesitate to apply legalism in a period of disorder.[44]

Chiang saw no reason why a Confucianist should surrender to the Legalists the practical work of administration and cited with approval the statement of Wang An-shih that "knowledge as set forth in the classics is meant for

the management of practical affairs."[45] He agreed whole-
heartedly with Chang Chü-cheng who denied that his
policy of increasing the country's wealth and military
strength deviated from Confucian morality. "We should
know," observed Chiang, "that benevolence and righteousness are basically related to wealth and strength. To
achieve wealth and strength by acting in conformity with
human nature is the 'way of morality'; to do so by using
measures contrary to human nature is the 'way of might.'
That which is based on 'righteousness' is the 'way of
morality' and that based on 'gains' is the 'way of might.'
The distinction depends on human nature, not on ways and
means."[46]

In the attempt to reconcile Confucianism and legalism,
Chiang maintained that the legal concept of "strictness"
was simply the expression of "sincerity" in Confucianism.
Strictness will not allow any laxity or looseness; it con-
notes a sense of the fullness of perfection. It is closely
related to the moral qualities of wisdom, compassion, and
courage; in social behavior it is essential to the four virtues
of decorum, righteousness, integrity, and sense of shame.
Therefore strictness is a virtue essential to the rule of law,
for only a man of impartiality can faithfully observe the
law.[47]

Chiang Kai-shek did more than anyone else to revive
traditional Chinese philosophy and virtues during the
twenty years the Kuomintang ruled China, and there were
many conditions that made such a revival seem desirable
and necessary. Chiang was involved in a nationalist movement that aimed at unification and independence and that
required the people's loyalty and devotion. Surely the people had to be proud of the nation before they would sacrifice themselves for it. Nothing seemed more logical than for
a nationalist movement to revive the national spirit; and
nothing seemed more natural than for traditional virtues

and philosophy to be the constituent elements of that spirit. It was a necessary psychological reconditioning for a people long subject to the evils of laxity, demoralization, and lethargy. And Chiang was fighting the Chinese Communists on the one hand and the Japanese aggressor on the other. To oppose the foreign ideology of Communism, traditional philosophy seemed a potent weapon; to oppose the Bushido of Japan, the revival of the Chinese national spirit seemed a logical step. That the traditional virtues with their emphasis on loyalty and sincerity could also lead to political stability might well be another reason for their adoption. But all these factors, while they played an important part in Chiang's thought, do not explain the deep conviction with which he preached and glorified the Chinese tradition.

The explanation must be sought in his background and education. Born to a well-to-do salt merchant's family toward the end of the Manchu dynasty, Chiang was educated traditionally. From the age of six until he left China to study in Japan at the age of eighteen, he devoted practically all his time to Chinese classics. Before he was fourteen years old, he had studied *The Four Books, The Book of Odes, The Book of History,* and *The Book of Changes,* and he had begun to compose classical essays. The next three years were spent in reading *The Spring and Autumn Chronicles, The Book of Rites, The Chronological Outline of History, The Dictionary of Characters,* the writings of Tseng Kuo-fan, Sun Tzu's *Art of War,* and the works of ancient philosophers. In 1902 he took the district examination, the first of the civil service examinations, and failed.[48] In later years he recalled that when he was a boy his teacher required him to recite *Great Learning* "two or three hundred times."[49] He was proud of his classical education and thought it useful. Between 1920 and 1924 he wrote his son Ching-kuo a number of letters, urging him to study Chinese classics, especially *The Analects, Mencius, The Dictionary of Characters,* and the *Family Instructions of Tseng Kuo-fan.*[50]

At the age of eighteen, Chiang came across Wang Yang-ming's *Instructions for Practical Living (Ch'uan-hsi Lu)* and after that his interest in Neo-Confucianism never faltered.[51] In his brief biography of his mother, written in 1921, Chiang stated that for several years he had been engaged in the study of Neo-Confucianism, especially the theory of nature and reason.[52] In the years 1918-1919 he was given to meditation and would silently recite the teachings of Mencius, Wang Yang-ming, and Tseng Kuo-fan as a means of self-cultivation. He concentrated on subjects like "the elimination of human desires and the preservation of heavenly reason," on how to cleanse the mind and control unbridled thought. From Confucian teachings he chose four words as his motto—tranquillity, respect, calm, and unity—and asked Sun Yat-sen to write them down for him on a piece of paper, which he mounted and kept on his desk.[53] In 1923 he composed a couplet that shows a strong influence of Neo-Confucianism:

To investigate reason where things begin;
To study the hidden motive when the mind first stirs.[54]

Unlike Sun Yat-sen, Chiang had no direct contact with Western civilization. His study in Japan only reaffirmed his faith in Chinese philosophy. If their adoption of Wang Yang-ming's philosophy had led the Japanese to enthusiasm for action, and the borrowing of Confucianism had contributed to the formulation of Bushido, then it would be an unpardonable folly if China abandoned its own culture.[55]

It has been said that Chiang, who was primarily a soldier, talked about Confucianism without understanding it

and preached it only for ulterior purposes. His educational
background and philosophical orientation, however, refute this. If the traditional movement failed, it was not because Chiang was insincere, but rather because traditional
principles are incompatible with modern times.

When the New Life Movement was launched, objec-
tions were raised that traditional virtues, as formal refine-
ments of behavior, were useless in coping with hunger and
cold. Did not Kuan Tzu, who first talked about the Four
Social Bonds, also say, "Only when one has sufficient food
and clothing can he care for personal honor"? Chiang's
reply was that the four virtues were the basic elements of
man. If one could not be a man, what was the use of having abundant food and clothing? Moreover, as long as
virtue prevailed, even if food and clothing were insufficient,
they could be produced by men. Without these virtues,
men would fight, rob, and steal, so that even if food and
clothing were abundant, they could not be enjoyed.[56] To
Chiang, virtues were of primary importance; methods and
techniques occupied only a secondary position. To solve
the land problem he appealed to the conscience of the
landlords; in the national effort to overcome economic difficulties he asked the people to "spend less and work
harder"—a traditional Chinese response.[57] To be sure, he
also adopted modern methods of economic development,
but his emphasis on the so-called fundamentals may well
have affected the results. The basic question is: Could
traditional virtues, which were evolved in the feudal
period, cope with the complex problems of the modern
age? Had the contact with Western civilization not so
changed the nature of China's problems that they were no
longer susceptible to ancient solutions?

The New Culture Movement dealt Confucianism a severe blow from which it never recovered. The old doctrine
seemed so remote to the young students and progressive

intellectuals that no new interpretation could arouse their interest. After all, even Chiang called himself a revolutionary. When the people were conditioned to hope for change, it was difficult for them to accept again the ancient principles that had failed them for so long—ever since the invasion by the West in the mid-nineteenth century.

Before leaving the subject of Chiang Kai-shek, a word should be said about ghostwriting. Most, if not all, of Chiang's books, articles, and speeches after he became the leader of China were written by his secretaries, among whom Ch'en Pu-lei was the most noted. The question has been raised whether these works really represent Chiang's thought. A recent revelation by T'ao Hsi-sheng, who is reputed to have written *China's Destiny*, sheds light on the question: "It is a fact that in drafting each important piece of work, whether concerning world politics, national policies, or military affairs, Ch'en Pu-lei used the utmost of his brain and energy. Why did he exert himself so much and work so hard? It was because each statement, every paragraph, every sentence, and every word was Generalissimo Chiang's. For each statement, the Generalissimo made at least two or three revisions, sometimes as many as eighteen times."[58] Against this testimony and in view of their consistency of expression, we can safely say Chiang's speeches and writings fairly represent his ideas.

Tai Chi-t'ao

Tai Chi-t'ao's traditionalist interpretation of Sun Yat-sen exerted tremendous influence on the development of the Kuomintang, not only because Chiang Kai-shek adopted it as the official doctrine of the party, but also because it played an important part in the ideological struggle with the Chinese Communists after Sun's death. Tai (1891–1949) had taken part in the organization of the

Chinese Communist party in 1920, but he soon left. Although he was interested in Marxism, he was never a full subscriber to it, nor did he claim that he understood it. He did not begin reading *Capital* until the end of 1919, and then in a Japanese translation which included only Volume I. It is significant that he tried to understand Karl Marx through the writings of Karl Kautsky, whose *Economic Theory of Karl Marx* he translated for *Reconstruction* (*Chien-she*), a magazine published by Sun's group in Shanghai.[59]

During the *Reconstruction* period Tai adopted the economic interpretation of history to explain China's political development and found the causes of the Chinese revolution in the disorganization of economic life that deprived so many people of a living. These unemployed joined the army, which traditionally was for social misfits, or became bandits. Bandits and soldiers were practically the same people; they were soldiers when they were under the protective shield of some sort of state or provincial authority, and they returned to banditry when that shield was taken away. Economic disintegration was therefore the cause of the disturbances, rebellions, and warlordism.[60]

Tai traced the sources of the economic disorganization to the invasion of Chinese markets by foreign manufactured goods, and he attributed foreign powers' intervention in China to their economic interests. But he stopped short of adopting Lenin's theory of financial imperialism. His concept of social classes was founded on property rather than on productive relationships. He divided the people into the propertied and propertyless classes and claimed that the propertyless class was the main force in any rebellion: It consisted of those who were unemployed and who found it so difficult to make a living that they preferred to rebel against the government. The ruling class they intended to overthrow consisted of those who had property and those who were employed but had no property.[61] Tai's concept of social classes was a somewhat muddled one in Marxist terms. However, he could easily claim that the classes in China were anything but well defined.

In 1919–1920 Tai's favorite theme was the revolutionary spirit, which possessed destructive as well as creative power. He held that all revolutionary efforts should be devoted to "rejecting the old organization, the old society, and the old virtues," since old society and politics are necessarily conservative rather than revolutionary, traditionalist rather than creative. "In the eyes of the revolutionaries, all things could have become idols and deserve destruction." At this time Tai recognized the New Culture Movement as a revolutionary process—its true meaning lay in the provision of equal opportunity for knowledge and in the free development of individual intellect.[62] His strong attack on the scholar-gentry as a privileged class hostile to true equality earned him a reputation as a progressive thinker in that period of intellectual turbulence.[63] Despite this, Tai explained some of his revolutionary ideas in traditional terms. He equated the revolutionary spirit of sacrifice with the moral concept of "righteousness," and the spirit of freedom, equality, and fraternity with "benevolence."[64]

In 1923, when Sun Yat-sen decided to cooperate with the Communists, Tai disagreed. He declared that if the Chinese Communists were to be admitted into the Kuomintang, they should be required to give up their Communist membership. He foresaw the conflicts that would inevitably arise between the two centers of power represented by the Kuomintang and the Chinese Communist party. At first he was unwilling to serve if the Communists were to be admitted, but under strong pressure he finally arrived in Canton to accept membership on the Kuomintang Central Executive Committee and an appointment to head the Propaganda Department. He was continually worried, however, about the confrontation of the two parties and the conflicts between the Right and Left wings within the Kuomintang itself. In attempting to solve the problem, he upheld the Three Principles of the People as the highest guiding doctrine with the most progressive elements. He stressed the importance of the masses in a national revolution and ridiculed the traditionalists who traced nationalism to Confucian classics.[65] Seeing the Communists' vigor and the decline of the old Kuomintang members, he tried to invigorate the Kuomintang by agreeing to keep the Communists if they would sever their party affiliations. He hoped to strike a balance between the extreme Right and the extreme Left, but, as often occurs in a compromise, both sides found the idea unsatisfactory.[66]

As the Chinese Communists grew increasingly aggressive, Tai shifted his position to the right. One of the first Kuomintang leaders to recognize the importance of ideology in a modern revolution, he began to advocate the Three Principles of the People as the force to unify the nation and as a powerful weapon to fight Communism. It became necessary to provide a new basis for Sun's doctrine, and Tai found the traditionalist interpretation a useful one. In 1925, at Sun's deathbed, Tai asked him whether the Three Principles were derived from the traditional thought of China. According to Tai's account, Sun gave an affirmative answer.[67] To what extent this account is accurate, and whether Sun understood Tai's request at a time when he was critically ill, are open to question. At any rate, immediately after Sun's death Tai wrote *The Philosophical Foundation of Sun Yat-senism*. In July 1925 he wrote another pamphlet, *The National Revolution and the Kuomintang,* which drew a violent response from the Communists and marked Tai as a formidable enemy of Communism.[68]

In *The National Revolution and the Kuomintang*, Tai argued that the existence of a political party depended on four essential factors: monopolization, exclusiveness, unifying power, and controlling force. Unless the party could monopolize the loyalty of its members, exclude other parties, unite the various factions, and control its organization, it would find it difficult to subsist and impossible to grow. Only when a party had these four characteristics could it claim the faith of its members, and only through the common faith of its members could party solidarity be achieved and party strength be developed. Faith was to be built around the party doctrine, and it was essential that the Three Principles of the People be adhered to by all Kuomintang members. To distinguish the Three Principles from Communism it was necessary to provide the former with a traditional basis. The restoration of national pride and the glorification of tradition could be potent weapons against a foreign ideology.

National revolution was an urgent task for the Chinese at the time. Tai argued with cogency that only after national revival would China be able to participate in the reconstruction of world civilization. Sun's Three Principles included nationalism, which Communism did not. Soviet Russia, said Tai, turned toward nationalism in practice, and in Russia the Three Principles "found their successful implementation."[69] Abandoning his former economic interpretation of history, Tai now pointed to sex as a basic instinct and suggested that racial relationships and national struggles that develop from the instinct of sex were even more dominant than economic problems arising from the instinct for food.

By focusing attention on nationalism Tai not only showed the difference between Sun's principles and Marxism, but also contended that the so-called world revolution was merely a Soviet pretext to serve its national purposes. China could indeed ally with Russia; however, there was no reason for China to sacrifice its independence and freedom for the sake of Russia.[70] Similarly, the Chinese Communists could be admitted into the Kuomintang, but the Chinese Communist party must not be permitted to engage in subversion. The coexistence of two power centers within the Kuomintang was as confusing as it was detrimental to the unity and solidarity of the Nationalist party. Thus on the principle of exclusive loyalty and common belief in one doctrine, Tai laid the groundwork for the ultimate break between the Kuomintang and the Chinese Communists.[71]

If *National Revolution and the Kuomintang* was written for party members, *The Path for the Youth* (1928) appealed to the whole nation to join in the fight against Communism. Condemning Communism as materialistic, unethical, and disruptive of social stability, Tai called for moral restoration, self-reliance, and the conquest of material insufficiency through personal efforts. But the best way to fight Communism was to uphold San Min Chu I, because Communism must be fought with an ideology superior to it. Intellectually, therefore, all efforts must be made to prove San Min Chu I the right doctrine, to develop it to perfection, and to apply it to various areas of social studies. The use of force was not enough; the Chinese must have their own doctrine, founded on traditional virtues and proven to be superior to Marxism in its practicability and moral worth.[72]

Political instability comes from disunity, and disunity is the result of diversified wills and feelings. The question is how to reconcile diversities and bring forth unity. Tai found the solution in knowledge, which should be the force to unify wills and feelings. If the people had a clear recognition of the problems and a firm grasp of the issues involved, they would be able to control their emotions and unite their wills. Tai's stress on knowledge signified the beginning of the reconstruction period during which the Kuomintang was the government party rather than the revolutionary party. In this period stability and unity were essential to good government, just as agitation and campaigns had been necessary to a revolution.

In upholding the political doctrine of Sun Yat-sen, Tai necessarily subscribed to the theory of knowledge and action. In his *Path for the Youth,* however, he urged the Chinese youth to go to the library, stressing the difficulty of knowledge rather than the easiness of action. In Sun's times, when the revolution was in the making, it was necessary to emphasize that "action is easy," to encourage people to join the revolution; in Tai's time, when stability was essential to reconstruction, the emphasis was shifted to "difficult knowledge" so that more effort would be devoted to studies.[73] In line with his concern for social stability, Tai advocated the affirmation of government authority and the establishment of the rule of law. Both were necessary to eliminate the turmoil created by mass organizations, such as student bodies, labor unions, and peasant associations, which, under Communist influence, were practically states by themselves. As a champion of Confucian virtues, it is not surprising that Tai founded his rule of law on social norms: "If we recognize the ethical nature of society, we will see that any discipline or law that has in itself effective sanctions, is derived from the general ethical principle of social norms. Each society has its own norms which bring about a particular kind of law and discipline. To speak of law and discipline without getting into social norms is never to reach their complete meaning; law and discipline which have lost their foundation of social norms are merely scraps of paper that can become void anytime."[74] But Tai did not revive the traditional social bonds at this time; instead he defined social bonds as principles in which people have a common faith. The Three Principles of the People logically fit this definition.

A man of poor health, Tai had a complex, highly emotional personality. Twice he attempted suicide, in 1922 and 1926. The attempt in 1922 may well have been the turning point in his political philosophy—from Marxist interpretation to ethics. According to his own account, he was so upset by the hopeless situation in his native province, Szechuan, to which he was sent by Sun Yat-sen to stop the endless civil wars, that on the way he threw himself into a river to end his life. But he was saved by a fisherman, and before he became unconscious, he saw in the river Buddhist lights that led him down the stream.[75] The incident may have strengthened his belief in Buddhism, but it was not the beginning of his spiritual interest. In 1919, at the time when he was studying and propagating Marxism, he simultaneously introduced the works of Gandhi. Earlier, in 1910, he had translated the works of Tagore. Both men represented the Indian emphasis on spiritualism.[76] But Tai did not officially participate in Buddhist activities until 1931 when Panchan Lama came to Nanking.[77] In Tai's political writings during the 1920's there was no reference to Buddhism, and indeed in his letter to the Kuomintang leaders in Szechuan in January 1924, he launched a violent attack on superstition, idol worship, geomancy, and all kinds of corruptive customs based on mysticism and spirits.[78]

The emotional tensions he experienced in those years might well have reflected the ideological conflicts in his mind. Because of these psychological and ideological complexities, Tai may be said to be a romantic. In spite of his emphasis on knowledge, his writings are marked by emotional appeals to national pride and the traditional sense of justice. But if he was not interested in the minute observance of formal logic, his political writings show a singular poignancy and perception, which are apparently a result of the modern training he received in Japan. He played an important role in the ideological battle with the Chinese Communists in the 1920's. As a close friend of Chiang Kai-shek, his ideas continued to exert an influence on the ideological development of the Kuomintang. But as he became more and more tradition-minded, eventually giving up the modern learning he had studied as a young man, he lost touch with the practical situation of his nation, which refused to return to tradition but went on with all the radical temperaments of a revolutionary age.

Chu Chih-hsin

Chu Chih-hsin (1885–1920), an influential leader of the Kuomintang, combined the heroism of a practical revolutionary with the keen intellect of a party theoretician. Born of a highly literate family, he was steeped in the Chinese classics, while his study in Japan, where he met Sun Yat-sen and joined the T'ung-meng Hui, gave him modern training in politics, law, and economics. With a knowledge of Japanese, English, and Russian, he had direct access to foreign works. He wrote with keen insight and subtle logic. In the depth of his thought and breadth of his knowledge, he was equaled by few leaders in the Kuomintang. As editor of the *People's Journal, The Republic (Min-kuo)*, and *Reconstruction*, he contributed greatly to the exposition of the Kuomintang's principles. His untimely death in 1920, at the age of thirty-five, deprived the Kuomintang of a capable leader whose progressive view might have helped to balance the conservatism of its dominant faction.[79]

Chu turned his attention to the problem of nationalism as early as 1906, when, in the debate with the Constitutional Royalists, he maintained that the feelings of the people should determine their loyalty to a state. In distinguishing the state in terms of law from the state in terms of psychological attachment, Chu was the first Chinese to see the importance of free choice in the determination of nationality. He believed that allegiance to the state should depend not on the accident of birth, but rather on the feelings of the individual who made his choice on the basis of historical relationships. Chu favored nationalism and supported the idea that the nation should form the state. But in line with his theory of free choice, he did not believe that all people of the same nationality should join together to form one state.[80]

In 1919 he gave the state a new interpretation which at once attacked militarism and imperialism. To Chu the state occupied a position between the individual and humanity as a whole. While it was higher than the individual and could set its interests above the individual's, it must yield to the interests of mankind. Since the state was not the ultimate form of human life, it should recognize the rights of other people who live outside of it. Each state should be equal to every other state, claiming no superiority and recognizing the principle of coexistence. For a weak state, which was not secure against outside threats, statism should be advocated. But for strong states, statism was no longer necessary. One had to guard against the development of a state that might be harmful to humanity.[81]

Statism, according to Chu, differed from militarism in that the former was concerned with its own existence and ready to defend it with the strength of all its people, while the latter adopted military force as an instrument of policy and built up its military power at the expense of its cultural and economic development. Militarism was a distortion of statism, although it stopped short of having conquest as its primary purpose. Imperialism aimed at extending one nation's power over other nations. It violated the principle of coexistence and was necessarily involved in aggression. Although the three doctrines were different from one another, it was easy for statism to develop into militarism, especially when a state was threatened by a foreign aggressor and all its national resources were mobilized to build up its military power for resistance. Once militarism was adopted, it was even easier for it to develop into imperialism, since it would seem a great waste if the military power that had been built up were not utilized. Imperialist conquests offered an outlet for military energy and opened up new opportunities for cultural and economic development, which in turn served to sustain the continued growth of military power.[82] Imperialism, therefore, was the ultimate development of militarism rather than, as Lenin maintained, the last phase of capitalism.

Chu saw the fall of imperialism as not so much the result of the struggle between capitalist countries as the outcome of the rise of nationalism inevitably produced by imperialist aggression. Socialism, whose primary purpose was to promote the well-being of humanity, would be a good antidote to imperialism. Under socialism no state would be sacrificed. Nationalism for the purpose of defense would be temporarily permitted, but nationalism for the purpose of conquest would be forbidden. Socialism, according to Chu, would promote national spirit without leading to national conflicts. All nations would contribute to the growth of world civilization, which in turn would enrich the culture of each nation. Further, the existence of the state would not detract from the freedom and happiness of the individual.[83]

Chu believed that nationalism was based on cultural

ties rather than blood relations. People of the same culture and history, who shared the same fortunes and misfortunes, the same rise and decline, would forget their racial origins and base their attachments entirely on historical facts. By saying a nation was formed when a group of people believed they belonged to the same nation, Chu anticipated the later psychological interpretation that views nationalism as a state of mind. In a time of national weakness and difficulties, Chu held, the recollection of historical greatness will help to stimulate the national spirit. But he warned against overemphasizing history, lest all the past be considered glorious and all the present despicable. Historical studies should instead lead to the reaffirmation of faith in the nation, should convince us that what our ancestors could do we can do better. Only when people believe that the potential of the nation lies with them can they confidently exert themselves and avoid abandoning their future to fate. Chu was particularly concerned with the creativity of the present. Any great achievements, even cultural achievements that have only a remote bearing on politics, he believed could raise the spirits of the people and strengthen their confidence. The search for new knowledge, the renovation of thought, and the emphasis on creative work were therefore, for him, the three important factors in stimulating national consciousness.[84]

When Yüan Shih-k'ai revealed his penchant toward dictatorship soon after the establishment of the Republic, the theory of enlightened despotism, advanced by Liang Ch'i-ch'ao near the end of the Manchu regime, was revived. To refute the theory, Chu examined its institutional basis and declared that "enlightened despotism" was a meaningless term; only the underlying intentions of the despot or the results of the regime can determine whether or not a regime is enlightened. All despots claim good intentions, and it is difficult to detect their inner motives,

while the results can be judged only by history. It is therefore meaningless to call an existing regime enlightened.
The essence of despotism is that it is unrestrained by
law: whether the despot is enlightened or not is accidental and therefore irrelevant. Despotism, according to Chu,
is the antithesis of enlightenment. As a means to attain
constitutional government, it will inevitably defeat its
purpose.[85]

Despotism as an unrestrained autocracy does not permit
civil rights and liberty; but without these rights, no real
constitutional government can be established. Historically,
democracy often follows despotism, but historical sequence must not be mistaken for cause and effect. Despotism does not necessarily give rise to constitutional
government, just as it does not necessarily advance the
people's knowledge of democracy. Otherwise, China with
its four thousand years of despotism should have long
ago prepared the Chinese people for democracy.

Anticipating Hu Shih's arguments against dictatorship
in the 1930's,[86] Chu pointed out that knowledge depends
as much upon study as upon experience, and that there is
no reason to believe that despotism will provide democratic education. Only through participation in the government can people gain experience of democracy. To deny
people democracy because they do not have democratic
experience will forever prevent them from gaining this
experience.[87]

Despotism rests on the premise of government interference with individual freedom. Interference restricts the
individual's initiative and hampers the growth of his
strength, destroying his independent and competitive
spirit, which is necessary not only for constitutional government but also for economic development. In short,
despotism leads the people away from enlightenment.[88]

Chu was one of the first of Sun Yat-sen's followers to

show interest in socialism. In 1906 he published the first abridged Chinese translation of the *Communist Manifesto* in the *People's Journal*.[89] In reply to Liang Ch-i'ch'ao's criticism of Sun's program of land nationalization, Chu examined the practicability of socialism in China. He considered the subject of the political revolution to be the common people and its object the government; the subject of the social revolution to be the proletariat and its object the bourgeoisie. He broadened the meaning of "bourgeoisie" to include industrialists and that of "proletariat" to include peasants. On the basis of these definitions Chu argued that if the objects of the political and social revolutions are the same, it is necessary that the two revolutions be carried out simultaneously. Otherwise the bourgeoisie will be left with political power if only a social revolution is consummated, or with economic power if only a political revolution is consummated; in either case the proletariat will be oppressed. On the other hand, if the objects of the two revolutions are different, it follows: (1) If the subject of the political revolution is the same as the object of a social revolution—that is, the bourgeoisie in both cases—then the two revolutions cannot be carried out simultaneously, since it would be impossible to expect the bourgeoisie to overthrow itself. (2) If the subject of the political revolution is not the same as the object of the social revolution, then it is desirable that the two revolutions be carried out simultaneously, since the subject of the political revolution is no obstacle to the consummation of the social revolution. China, Chu felt, fell into the second category. Writing in 1906, he held that the subject of the Chinese political revolution was the common people, who were close to the proletariat, while the bourgeoisie had yet to appear. The line of class struggle was not yet sharply drawn, but it would be if the problem were not solved in time. If the social revolution were begun at a time when capitalism was not highly developed, it would not only have the advantage of least resistance, it would also forestall all the suffering that accompanied the development of capitalism in the West.[90]

In accordance with Sun's program, Chu advocated in 1906 a sort of state socialism with special emphasis on land nationalization. The outlawing of the Kuomintang by President Yüan Shih-k'ai in the early years of the Republic had made it impossible, of course, for Sun to put his socialist program into effect. But Sun had never abandoned his Principle of the People's Livelihood, and in the late 1910's, the Kuomintang came under the radical influence of the New Culture Movement. In 1919 *Reconstruction* and *Weekly Review* (*Hsing-ch'i P'ing-lun*) were founded in Shanghai. Both served as party organs for the discussion of socialism. As editor of *Reconstruction*, Chu published a number of articles in which he showed renewed interest in socialism. He turned somewhat more radical, calling for incorporation of the "middle class" into the proletariat and ridiculing those who stood outside the working class while claiming to be its leaders.[91] He saw in the laborers and peasants an increasing power which would make class struggle inevitable. But although he believed that Communism could be put into effect someday, he could not accept it unconditionally. He reserved the right to study and have a different opinion on it.[92] An iconoclast who refused to accept anything as sacrosanct, Chu believed that nothing is permanent or absolute, but that all principles, institutions, and morality must be evaluated in the light of changing circumstances.[93] With such convictions it is difficult to imagine him a doctrinaire, either Communist or Nationalist.

Hu Han-min

A veteran Kuomintang member, Hu Han-min (1879–1936) was one of Sun Yat-sen's most trusted assistants. After joining the T'ung-meng Hui in Tokyo in 1905, he served in various important posts in the revolutionary party, including editor of the *People's Journal;* governor of Kwangtung province, the revolutionary base of Sun Yat-sen; and secretary-general in the Office of the Provisional President (1912). When Sun left Canton for Peking in 1924, Hu was appointed acting head of the revolutionary regime in Canton. When Sun died there in 1925, Hu was regarded as one of the strongest candidates to succeed him. But in the power struggle that ensued, he lost out initially to Wang Ching-wei, another of Sun's trusted lieutenants, and finally to Chiang Kai-shek, then a young general in command of the new party army that was being trained with the assistance of Soviet Russia.

Hu has been accused by the Chinese Communists of being the leader of the Right wing of the Kuomintang. When he toured the Soviet Union after his loss of power, however, his lectures on politics attracted much attention. A close study of his political ideas shows that it is not quite correct to describe him as a Right-wing thinker, although he was anti-Communist; nor is it surprising that he could talk well before his Russian audience. Among the Kuomintang leaders he was one of the few who had made a serious study of Marxism.

An able student trained in the Confucian tradition, Hu passed the provincial civil service examination and received his *chü-jen* degree at the age of twenty-one. He went to Japan in 1902 and again in 1904 to study first education and later public law and government. He mastered the Japanese language and was able to study

Western theories and institutions in Japanese translation. His training in Japan provided him with a modern, scientific approach to social studies. Thus, in spite of his early dabbling in Neo-Confucianism, his thinking was characterized by acute logic and factual observation, traits not often found in his contemporaries, whose traditional methods often failed to give them a clear grasp of the issues. His familiarity with Chinese classics and history gave him insight into Chinese mentality and political developments, but it never deterred him from studying modern concepts or hindered him from grasping their merits. Unlike Chiang Kai-shek, Hu never seriously attempted to revive China's traditional virtues; in this respect he was much closer to the thinking of Sun Yat-sen. As Sun's close and trusted secretary for twenty years, Hu assisted in the preparation of much of Sun's written work and could well claim to know more of his master's doctrine than other Kuomintang leaders. It was this assumption of the stature of a senior disciple with an unparalleled knowledge of Sun's theories and policies that eventually led to his conflict with Chiang Kai-shek.

Serious, stern, and in poor health, Hu worked hard and expected his revolutionary colleagues to do the same. He rose at four in the morning and worked continuously until nine in the evening. During his tenure as president of the Legislative Yüan from 1928 to 1931 he never once left Nanking on weekends to amuse himself in the foreign settlements of Shanghai as so many Nationalist officials did. Concerned over the laxity, self-seeking, and irresponsibility of the bureaucracy and the Kuomintang leaders, he would lecture them unmercifully and often pointed out their mistakes to their faces. While his sense of responsibility and patriotism evoked admiration, his severity caused resentment. Finally he ran into direct conflict with Chiang Kai-shek. It was said that in one of their stormy meetings he gave the Generalissimo, a strong-willed man himself, such a lecturing that he became infuriated. Had Hu been milder in his manner of opposition, perhaps Chiang would not have had him placed under house arrest in 1931.[94]

The development of Hu's political ideas may be divided into three periods: (1) editor of *Reconstruction*, 1919–1920; (2) official of the Nationalist government, 1928–1931; (3) leader of the Southwestern government at Canton in opposition to Chiang Kai-shek, 1931–1936.

In 1919, the May Fourth Movement, which stressed new culture and radical ideas, began. Sun Yat-sen, squeezed out of the revolutionary government at Canton, retired to Shanghai to write his revolutionary theories. Seeing in the May Fourth Movement a new orientation in Chinese thought, Sun established *Reconstruction* with the dual purpose of shaping the Chinese mind and providing a channel for political studies that needed encouragement. Although Sun had conceived the basic ideas of the Three Principles long before this, it was only now that he found time to put them into writing. In the process of systematization, much had to be studied and clarified. Hu Hanmin and Chu Chih-hsin were therefore appointed editors of the newly established magazine, with the responsibility of studying and discussing theories and institutions pertaining to the construction of a new China.

Hu's interest at this time was socialism, which had been in vogue since the May Fourth Movement. In a series of articles published in *Reconstruction*,[95] he defended Marx's materialistic conception of history against its critics. Recognizing that economics occupies the center of modern social life, he maintained that the First World War was fought for markets and colonies—in short, for reasons of economic interest. He did not discount the possibility that civilization might rise to a spiritual level at higher stages in its evolution, but this represented the hope of the future, not a present reality. He took exception to Edward Bernstein's argument that Marx's materialistic conception of history ignores the important fact that history is made by men. To Hu the concept of class struggle admits the influence of human will, but such influence must follow the natural process of economic development. Thus, social activities are not absolutely free, but neither are they unconsciously mechanical. Dialectical materialism is never fatalistic, and one must not think social changes are automatic at a certain economic level.[96]

Hu made a particularly strenuous effort to clarify the relations between ethics and Marxism. According to him, the materialistic conception of history does not ignore the value of ethics. Dialectical materialism considers morality to be a social attribute that arises from society's demands upon the individual. In primitive society it is necessary to group together in order to fight wild animals and other enemies. It is thus that grouping and mutual assistance, later called "social instincts," begin. As social relations continue, the ways in which man meets his social demands become custom. Man becomes unable to live in society unless he observes social custom. The conception of morality gradually arises, and the individual is moral or immoral depending upon whether or not he satisfies social demands. Therefore, morality is not born of nature, but created by man. It is not innate in an individual, but arises from social relations. Conscience does not exist before society; rather it is the reaction to social demands. If one curbs his selfish instincts and complies with social demands, one will live with a good conscience. But if one lets one's selfish instincts gain the upper hand over one's social instincts, one's conscience will sting one. Arising from social relations, and subject to the regulation of social demands, is morality, which changes as society and social relations change. Citing Marx, that it is "the social being of men that determines their consciousness," Hu asserted that ethical theories were impotent in the formulation of social morals. "Without new social inconsistencies there will be no new problems, and without new problems there will be no new theories."[97] The influence of new theories depends on the degree of social pain arising from the inconsistencies of life.

Following Marx's reasoning, Hu argued that social morals are, in reality, class morals, just as societies since the beginning of history have been class societies. Ethical principles derive their influence from the support of the ruling class. Thus, Hu maintained, Chu Hsi's Neo-Confucianism exerted an influence on China only after it had been adopted by the Ming emperor in the fourteenth century. Anticipating later Marxist criticism of Confucianism, Hu condemned two basic virtues the Confucianists advocated as a means of defense in the class struggle: loyalty on the part of the ruled, to promote obedience and behavior that fits in with the interests of the rulers; and moderation on the part of the rulers, to prevent popular revolts that might topple their regimes. But Hu was never to go so far as some of his contemporaries in his condemnation of Confucianism. While considering Confucian morals incompatible with democratic ethics, he recognized their contribution to the welfare of the weak in ancient times when tyranny had prevailed. It was rather the rigid concepts of "status" and "obligations" introduced by the Neo-Confucianists during the Sung dynasty that had made life unbearable for the Chinese. Still it was futile to blame even the Neo-Confucianists, for they, too, had been unable to picture a time not dominated by despotism. It was not, therefore, ethical doctrine that must be overthrown; but rather the political and social systems.[98]

Becoming increasingly involved in the May Fourth Movement, Hu joined with the New Culture thinkers in condemning Confucianism's unquestioned supremacy, intolerance of other schools, and stereotyped conservatism. Idolism must be overthrown to clear the way for revolutionary thought and action. One must not be numbed by the inertia of habits, nor should one believe that "the ancients are superior to the moderns."[99]

Like all revolutionaries Hu held that there is no such thing as a permanent institution, since the very existence of an institution depends upon its ability to adapt to changing times. To Hu, fragmentary reforms were futile, and the revolution must be aimed at changing the entire political and social system.[100] But in spite of all these radical assertions, Hu showed latent moderation in his claim that socialism is not extremism, and that ideals that do not take social reality into account are nothing more than utopian.[101]

Hu Han-min's most important work as a leader of the Nationalist government at Nanking was *The Interrelationships of the Three Principles of the People,* written in 1928, when the Kuomintang had just seized control of the country and purged the Chinese Communists. The work was devoted to establishing Sun Yat-sen's Three Principles as the supreme doctrine for the reconstruction of China and the best ideology for world revolution. Hu saw as the objects of revolution, whether national or world-wide, militarism, oligarchy (or "class democracy"), and capitalism. Together these constituted imperialism, which must be overthrown before national independence, and ultimately the grand unity of the world, can be attained.

According to Hu, the individual's desire for domination is the basic factor in each of the elements of imperialism. Militarism aims at simultaneously subduing its own people and quelling other nations. While nations' suspicions of one another play a part in international wars, the rulers' search for fame and glory is also important. To Hu, capitalism was the instrument of individual control over industry, commerce, and politics, and capitalist domination was not confined within national boundaries. Bureaucracy, whose sole aim, Hu felt, was to continue its own political power and maintain its special influence, had created a permanent privileged class (oligarchy) in every country. Bureaucrats had no principles other than strategies aimed at promoting their individual interests, and they worshiped authority, money, military strength, and aggression.[102]

Hu saw the three forces of imperialism as natural allies. Bureaucrats—whether government leaders or members of parliament, administrators or politicians—rely upon the capitalists for financial support, which forms the basis of political power in capitalist countries. Capitalism is in turn closely related to militarism, which maintains internal order and expansion overseas. Territorial expansion both benefits the economic interests of the capitalists and gratifies the vainglory of the militarists, who follow close behind them. But before the militarists are engaged in their aggressive activities, the bureaucrats are already busy laying the diplomatic foundations. "Imperialism, like a large river, combines with all the ruling forces as it flows on until it floods and bursts over, submerging the whole world."[103]

The Three Principles, Hu contended, were the best weapon against imperialism, because they took the nation as their basis and hit directly against individualism. According to Hu, modern history proves that whenever the individual is the basis of the state, nationalism degenerates into militarism, democracy into class politics, and the welfare state into capitalism; so long as the society and the economy have the individual as their basic unit, there will always be the oppressors and the oppressed.[104] Emphasizing the necessity for correlation, Hu concluded that each of the Three Principles must be practiced in conjunction with the other two, to prevent this process of degeneration.[105]

Hu compared the Three Principles to other ideologies. Cosmopolitanism, he found, aims at the same thing as Sun's Principle of Nationalism—comradeship among all the people of the world. However, cosmopolitanism attacks state organization to such an extent that it neglects the existence of independent nations as a necessary step toward world organization. The Principle of Nationalism, on the other hand, provides the means for realizing the cosmopolitan goal. In this respect, both anarchism and the Three Principles aim at establishing a society of mutual assistance in which everyone is free to work and serve on a basis of equality and self-government. But, again, anarchism lacks the means of attaining this goal. The Three Principles, in reserving the sovereign rights for the people, establish a direct democracy in which genuine self-government is realized; and under the five-power constitution, the government is an administrative organization for the management of public affairs.[106]

Hu also felt that Communism and the Three Principles share a common ideal—the establishment of a society in which all property belongs to the people and is used by the people for the people. But, he held, Communism defeats its own end. It is based on class struggle and aims at establishing class rule—the dictatorship of the proletariat. The disregard for nationalism was Marx's fatal mistake, and the Communist movement paid highly in the split of the Second International during World War I. Lenin, Hu asserted, realized the mistake and tried to redress the balance by invoking nationalism in the East.[107] But as long as Marxism was shut up behind the iron door of proletarian dictatorship, the state would never wither away, and nationalism as used by the Russians would remain only a means to impose their will upon the world.[108]

For Hu, the means was as important as the end in political and social revolutions. The realization of the end not only depends upon the means, but is directly related to it. While class war might upset capitalism, it could never establish a new world of Communism. Using class struggle as the means was to Hu like riding on the tiger of despotism, which races toward the dead end of bloodshed and destruction.[109]

In maintaining that the Three Principles represented the ideals of cosmopolitanism, anarchism, and Communism, Hu attempted to establish Sun's doctrine as the grand summation of the world's foremost revolutionary theories. By insisting that the Three Principles alone provide the practical procedures for realizing revolutionary goals, he tried to substitute Sun's doctrine for Communism as the guiding principle of world revolution. In both these attempts he built his arguments closely on the teachings of Sun Yat-sen, but with such originality that he can be called a creative as well as faithful interpreter of his master.

It is not completely clear why Hu was placed under house arrest by Chiang Kai-shek in February 1931. The official explanation was that he objected to the proclamation of a provisional constitution. In view of Hu's consistent position that the teachings of Sun as embodied in his major works should be the guiding principles for the nation during the period of political tutelage, it is not surprising that he opposed the proclamation of a new basic law that deviated from Sun's doctrine. But a difference of opinion over some form of law was not important enough for Chiang to take such drastic action. It seems certain that by 1931 Hu had begun to look askance at some of Chiang's policies and modes of government.[110] Considering himself the senior member of the Kuomintang and in a position to know more about Sun's doctrine than anybody else, Hu assumed a mentor's role and proceeded to lecture Chiang. Such presumption the Generalissimo would not tolerate, for besides having a disposition as irritable as Hu's, he, too, had assumed the mantle of Sun and would not recognize a superior authority on party affairs.

Released in October 1931, Hu became the moving spirit of the anti-Chiang movement in Canton, although he stayed for the most part in the nearby British colony of Hong Kong. He was an effective theoretician of the Cantonese faction, and in spite of poor health wrote energetically for the *San Min Chu I Monthly,* which he founded in 1933. He charged Chiang with military dictatorship, which he felt had subverted the program of party rule laid down by Sun Yat-sen for the period of political tutelage.[111] Hu also accused Chiang of abandoning Sun's Principle of Nationalism in his "appeasement" of the Japanese aggressor. In his "National Revival Movement under the Principle of Nationalism," Hu pointed out that traditionally the Chinese did not believe in nationalism, but rather in a cultural universe. The Chinese people's discrimination against "barbarians" had always been of a cultural sort. Foreign tribes would be assimilated as soon as they had adopted Chinese culture. According to Hu, the repeated invasions of China by the frontier tribes was due to this yielding, conciliatory attitude, traditionally regarded by the Chinese not only as a proper policy but even as a virtue. The policy had not resulted in the extinction of the Chinese nation only because of its deep, strong foundations—its vast territory, huge population, and long history—and because of the superiority and immense assimilating power of Chinese culture. But the situation had long since changed, and the foreign nations that now confronted China were of an advanced culture, superior to her own. Thus a tolerant, yielding policy was no longer sufficient, and a national spirit of resistance was the only hope of national salvation.

Hu held that this national grouping and nationalist promotion should be done in the "kingly way," that is, the way of the right, not of might. But while the kingly way does not mean conquest and pillage, neither does it mean appeasement, but rather coexistence on the basis of what is right.[112]

During the 1930's, when the Nanking government under the influence of Tai Chi-t'ao was proceeding to revive Confucianism and Buddhism, Hu hastened to defend the revolutionary nature of Sun's principles. He denounced as completely without foundation Tai's assertion that Sun Yat-sen's thought was the same as the traditional thought of China. Any such attribution, stated Hu, "ignores the greatness and uniqueness of Sun's thought. If Dr. Sun merely desired to succeed Yao and Shun [the ancient sages], and his thought were no other than traditional thought revived, then he would not deserve to be a revolutionary or a statesman." He added: "It is as wicked to compare Sun to Marx as it is putrid to equate him with Confucius and Gautama."[113]

Hu's opposition to the traditionalist interpretation is consistent with the views he held throughout life. Earlier, in 1928, when he was president of the Legislative Yüan of the Nationalist government, Hu had pointed out the difference between government under Sun's Three Principles and the traditional government of China. The Confucian way of government, he stated, centers on *li*, or rules of propriety, and is founded on the belief that government by man is preferable to government by law and that man's virtues are perfectible through self-cultivation.[114] This emphasis on self-cultivation culminated in the teachings of the Neo-Confucianists, who believed in the development of one's nature until all the phenomena of the world suddenly became clear. To Hu this was as mystical as the "sudden enlightenment" of Zen Buddhism and completely divorced from the actuality of the world.[115] Unlike Chiang Kai-shek, Hu considered Wang Yang-ming to be ignorant of the division of labor and therefore guilty of confusing knowledge with action.[116] Feudalism was rot, Hu contended, and Confucianism a product of the feudal age. The revolution sought to sweep away all outworn thought and institutions. He reminded his former colleagues that the Kuomintang was a revolutionary party, which would lose its *raison d'être* if it lost its revolutionary spirit.[117]

If government by *li* was out of date, so were the traditional laws founded on despotism. The new legislation must be based, Hu argued, on the interests of the nation rather than on the interests of families as in old times. It must promote the welfare of the people, foster new enterprises, and direct its attention to industry as well as agriculture. It should also break away from the traditional confusion of public with private law and give the private sector a special status.[118]

Nor, in Hu's view, should China's new legislation follow the old path of the West. Under the Three Principles, individualism with all its natural rights has no place. To Hu, freedom and civil rights are established by society. An individual is granted rights because he is a member of society and his community life requires such rights. By community Hu meant the whole society or the nation. It follows that law should recognize only such rights as are conducive to the welfare of society and the existence of the nation.[119] The protection of private property is in the interest of social rather than individual security.

Individual lives are to be regulated because they are parts of the life of society. Legislation under the Three Principles would prevent individual exploitation as well as social struggle, simply because both were harmful to the common welfare of the nation.[120]

In the early 1930's, the Kuomintang writers, in an attempt to make Sun's doctrine into a complete philosophical system, began to speculate on whether Sun had believed in materialism or idealism. Writing to rectify this trend, Hu pointed out that Sun was not concerned with such metaphysical questions. Sun had devised his own philosophy, postulating subsistence as the central force in history. But although it was Sun's intention to have his theory replace the materialistic interpretation of history, he did not go into details, and the question remained as to how subsistence as the determining factor of history differed from Marx's economic force. It was left to Hu to provide an answer.

"The real force of social evolution," wrote Hu, "is not 'material' or the struggle for material; rather it is the desire to live." Such desire is as apparent in the individual as it is in a society or a nation. It is this desire that serves as the motivating force of all evolution and change. The foundations of the economic structure, or the so-called productive forces as expounded by Marx, are merely the instruments of subsistence. Changes in the economic structure follow changes in the mode of "living" rather than in the mode of production.[121]

The secret of life is the insatiability of human desires. When men cannot live, they want to live; but when they can live, they want a rich, pleasant life; and when they have a rich, pleasant life, they want an enjoyable, luxurious life. From the stage in which one can live to the stage in which one lives a luxurious life, all the changes and developments men effect through their efforts are basically due to the desire to live and live better. It is this desire to have more and more that eventually gives rise to the rich as distinguished from the poor. This is the beginning of social classes; the rise of capitalism is "the inevitable tendency of human nature."[122] Thus, what is called "material" in the Marxian interpretation of history is in fact an external thing which human beings want to attain. "It is the result, not the cause; the branches and leaves, not the roots."[123]

The view that desire uncurbed will lead to evil and misery has been maintained by philosophers since ancient times. In China, Confucius, Lao Tzu and Mo Tzu all taught the control of desire; in the West, philosophers from Plato to Kant have sought to substitute reason for passion and desire. But it was Hu who provided a systematic argument for the theory that desire is the motivation of historical development. If Marx claimed to have turned Hegel upside down in order to set him right side up, Hu could claim to have done the same with Marx's materialistic interpretation of history.

Wang Ching-wei

Wang Ching-wei was born in Canton in 1883. His father, who was sixty-two at his son's birth, was a Chekiang man who had migrated to Canton to serve as a legal secretary to the governor. Ching-wei learned much from his father, who taught him Chinese classics and poetry. When he was fourteen, his father died, leaving practically no estate to his ten sons and daughters. A brilliant and conscientious boy, Ching-wei began to help support his family by winning scholarships and teaching at the age of seventeen. Three years later he went to Japan to study government and law under a government scholarship. There his study of Western theories concerning the nature of the state and the sovereignty of the people emancipated him from the traditional Chinese belief in absolute loyalty to the ruler.[124] In 1905 he met Sun Yat-sen in Tokyo and immediately joined the T'ung-meng Hui. Together with Hu Han-min, Chu Chih-hsin, and others, he edited the *People's Journal.*

In the *People's Journal*, Wang Ching-wei engaged in the steady feud with K'ang Yu-wei and Liang Ch'i-ch'ao, advocating republicanism in opposition to their constitutional monarchy. Wang saw no chance whatever for political reform coming out of the Manchu regime, which, being a minority rule, he felt to be antidemocratic. Revolution would necessarily overthrow the Manchu regime, not because the revolutionaries advocated it, but because of government oppression and the resultant popular discontent and resentment. Wang saw nationalism and democracy as being indispensable to each other. Nationalism without democracy would leave the old oppressive system unchanged; democracy without nationalism was by nature impossible.[125]

Education was Wang's answer to the perennial question of whether the Chinese people, with no democratic tradition behind them, were prepared for a republican form of government. He believed that ideas of freedom and equality, although later they had been suppressed by absolutism, had existed in ancient China, and that national mentality can be changed. Wang predicted that after the republic was established and education widespread, freedom and democracy would be learned by the people in no time. Wang regarded the capacity to learn and adapt to new institutions, especially those congenial to human nature, as man's unique characteristic. What was more congenial to human nature than liberty, equality, and fraternity? Furthermore, if the Chinese people were not prepared for constitutional republicanism, were they prepared for constitutional monarchy? Wang was the first Chinese writer to point out that constitutional monarchy, in order to succeed, requires popular initiative and participation. Republican democracy, achieved through revolution, was, he felt, the best way to accustom people to their role in government.[126]

In late 1909, after repeated uprisings against the Manchus in the south of China had failed, Wang returned to China with plans to assassinate the prince regent of the Manchu government. He thought such an action would draw attention to the revolutionary cause, thereby hastening the end of the Manchu regime. Wang believed two types of people were necessary to a revolutionary party: those with the virtue of perseverance and those with the spirit of sacrifice. In a letter to Hu Han-min, he wrote that Hu had the virtue of perseverance and therefore should stay with the party and continue the difficult task of planning and executing, while he himself, being of an ardent disposition, was more adept in sacrifice.[127] But before Wang could execute his plot it was discovered by the police, and he was arrested and jailed. When he was released after the outbreak of the Revolution of 1911, he was hailed as a national hero and a dedicated revolutionist.

Wang was reputed to be one of the best orators in modern China. His eloquence lay not so much in high-pressure agitation as in gentle persuasion sustained by light emotional appeal and indirect suggestion. His speeches were never too long. He did not talk down to his audience, and unlike Hu Han-min, he seldom hammered at his points with hard logic. In fact, he was more a poet than a logician. In speech as well as in writing it was always his soft sensitivity, abundant imagery, and unassuming modesty that moved his audience and readers. His mind was subtle, ingenious, and refined. In person, he was handsome, courteous, obviously a gentleman in both his modest bearing and his sympathetic attitude. His engaging personality won him friends in various circles, especially among the younger generation who admired his liberal, enlightened outlook.

After Sun Yat-sen's death in March 1925, Wang, in conjunction with Hu Han-min and Chiang Kai-shek, continued the Kuomintang policy of cooperation with the Communists. Hu soon dropped out because of alleged involvement in the assassination of Liao Chung-k'ai, a Left-wing Kuomintang leader. Wang was for some time the leader of the early revolutionary government in Canton, holding the top position both in the government and in the party But Chiang held the military power and before long dominated the political scene. The situation became so unfavorable that Wang left Canton for France in March 1926. He returned the next year to become the leader of the Kuomintang at Hankow, in opposition to the Nanking government led by Chiang Kai-shek. But although he badly needed Communist support in the struggle for power, Wang had no intention of selling out to the Communists. Thus in June 1927, when the Comintern representative M. N. Roy showed him Stalin's telegram ordering that Chinese peasants and workers be armed to help the Chinese Communists seize power, Wang would have no part of it. He split with the Communists but continued to oppose Chiang Kai-shek until 1932, when the Japanese invasion of Manchuria brought him back from France to serve as president of the Executive Yüan. Partly because of his discontent at playing second fiddle to Chiang Kai-shek and partly because of his pessimism over China's prospects in the war with Japan, Wang left Chungking suddenly in December 1938. He urged peace negotiations with Tokyo, and in 1940 set up a government

in Nanking in collaboration with the Japanese. He died
in Japan in 1944.

Paralleling his political career, Wang's political thought
can be divided into three periods: the years 1925–1927
when he was the leader of the revolutionary governments
at Canton and Hankow; the period between 1928 and
1932 when he opposed Chiang Kai-shek and advocated
development of democratic forces; and the period 1932–
1938 when he joined the government led by Chiang. We
are not concerned with his last years, 1938–1944, when as
head of the puppet government under the bayonets of the
Japanese militarists he was no longer his own man. Whatever he said and wrote during those years was outside
the mainstream of Chinese political thought.

During the first period (1925–1927) Wang emerged as
the leader of the Kuomintang Left wing. He cooperated
with the Chinese Communists and hit hard at the Right-
wingers, especially the anti-Communist Western Hills faction. Wang saw revolution as the only means to attain
political progress, which he considered the prerequisite of
economic and social advance. He regarded Buddhism,
Taoism, and all other passive philosophies of life as idle
thinking. Borrowing much from Marxism, Wang saw
world history as evolving from the struggle between the
rulers and the ruled to the struggle between the rich and
the poor. Monarchism was out of date, as were economic
monopolies by trust companies.[128] China should therefore not take Japan's revolution as its model. The Meiji
reform, though it made Japan a powerful state, broadened
the cleavage between the rich and the poor and led to colonial expansion that resulted in international rivalry and
war. Wang looked rather to the Russian Revolution—the
revolution "that shook the world in the twentieth century"[129]—for guidance.

This praise of Bolshevism, coupled with the slogan

"Revolutionaries Turn Left," led to Wang's being dubbed a radical. Actually he never intended to replace the Three Principles with Communism. In his eulogy of the Bolsheviks, he focused on their New Economic Policy, which, in his words, showed "the adaptability of the Soviet leadership—the very reason for their success. . . . The remarkable thing about the Soviet leaders is their determination and courage to carry out socialism gradually."[130] In his emphasis on gradualism Wang was typical of the Kuomintang leaders who cooperated with the Communists but had no intention of adopting Communism.

In 1926, when criticism of the Communists began to grow within the Kuomintang, Wang argued that there should be no conflict between Marxism and Sun's Three Principles. At the same time he took care to point out their differences. If Marxism holds class struggle to be the means of attaining the Communist goal, Wang contended, the Three Principles aim at forestalling class struggle by taking peaceful steps to eliminate the sources of conflict between capitalists and proletarians. He echoed Sun Yat-sen that there was not much capitalism in China to struggle against. A statesman dealing with practical problems, he firmly held that special situations require special treatment. The Principle of the People's Livelihood, with its restriction of capital and equitable distribution of land ownership, was adequate to solve China's problem. It would provide social justice in which the privileged few's desire for domination would be suppressed and the masses' desire for a decent living satisfied.[131]

But as an ardent revolutionist, Wang had no intention of turning reformist, and he counseled that the Three Principles should not be mistaken for social policy. While the latter aimed at reconciling capitalists with laborers and landlords with peasants by means of makeshift compromise, the former was a fundamental solution based on economic and social reorganization. In the heyday of co-operation with the Chinese Communists, Wang had declared that whoever opposed the peasant and labor movements was counterrevolutionary.[132] He had condemned the Right-wingers for forgetting that People's Livelihood was the chief aim of Sun's revolution.[133] However, he saw the Principle of Livelihood as being basically a peaceful solution. Thus in 1927 when the Communists stirred up the countryside by encouraging the seizure of land by the peasants, he declared that the policy of "land to the tillers" should be implemented in a peaceful manner and that, instead of being seized from the landlords, land should be gradually distributed equitably by political and legal means. It was clear that such due process was feasible only when the people had calmed down from their revolutionary fever. Wang therefore suggested that the land problem be deferred until after the revolution when the Kuomintang had attained political power.[134]

Recognizing the importance of the peasants and workers in the revolution, Wang still never lost sight of the role of the other classes. To him the national revolution was to work for the benefit of all classes and be supported by all classes. Its immediate object was the overthrow of the imperialists and the warlords to attain the independence and unification of China. With China in a "sub-colonial status," not only the peasants and laborers but also the intelligentsia and industrialists were subject to imperialist exploitation. This had been the official party line laid down by Sun Yat-sen when the Communists were admitted to the Kuomintang, and it was the line to which both Wang and Chiang Kai-shek, as well as other Kuomintang members, adhered. What often made Wang appear more radical than the others was his ability to turn phrases to tremendous propagandistic effect. When, for instance, he declared that the Soviet Union was the vanguard of anti-imperialism, he was regarded by the conservatives as being extremely pro-Russian. Actually he was recommending that Russia assist China in the fight against imperialism, and not that China be communized. This position was in fact similar to that of Chiang Kai-shek, who at about the same time declared that the Chinese revolution was part of the world revolution. The only difference was that while Chiang was vague about what the world revolution was, Wang defined it as a struggle in which all nations suffering from imperialism should form a united front with Russia.[135]

The only seeming radicalism that might distinguish Wang from other Kuomintang leaders during the early period of the National Revolution was his emphasis upon mass movement. While the conservatives viewed the masses as a riotous element, Wang had a natural faith in them. He had a sincere interest in enlisting their support in the revolution, and he enjoyed speaking to them and receiving their enthusiastic response. But even so, he did not rely entirely upon spontaneous mass movement. In his view, historically it is always a few leaders who first see the needs of the people and risk their lives to advocate revolution. Although in the final stage it is the people who count, they only slowly grasp the revolutionary views of the leaders. "The setback or failure in a revolution is generally not due to the blow dealt by the enemy but to the lack of understanding on the part of the people."[136] This does not mean that a revolution must wait to start until the people understand it. But in the course of the revolution the revolutionists must make every effort to cultivate the people's understanding. In order to succeed, the revolution of the intellectuals and that of the masses must be united.[137]

The awakening of the people and cooperation with the

Communists were basic policies laid down by Sun Yat-sen during the reorganization of the Kuomintang in 1924. That Wang was left of center is not to be denied, but the charge that he was a fellow traveler is unfounded. What singles Wang out during this early period of the revolution is not his adoption of Communist ideas per se, but rather the fact that he cooperated with the Communists longer than other Kuomintang leaders.

From 1928 to 1932 Wang vigorously sought to overthrow Chiang Kai-shek. In Chiang's Nanking government Wang saw a personal dictatorship that flouted the party organization and violated the basic function of political tutelage. As Sun's disciple, Wang wanted the country ruled by the Kuomintang during the transitional period. But the rule of one party, which he termed "democratic centralism" based upon the free wills of party members unified for collective action, was different from the rule of one man. Wang was particularly opposed to Chiang's personal control of the army, which had led to military conflicts and civil wars.[138] The army, Wang contended, must be brought within the control of the party, which in turn should be built on a popular basis. But instead of going to the people, the party under Chiang "is separated from them and stands on their heads." Party members had become a special class, bullying the people and depriving them of civil and private rights.

According to Wang, in order to become a party of the people, the Kuomintang had to organize the people into a democratic force. To achieve this required two steps: self-government had to be established at the local level, and a National Assembly, where the principles and basic policies of the Kuomintang could be presented, had to be convened. Wang was confident Sun's principles would be accepted by the delegates, since "they are the only solution possible for China's problems." In this way the party principles would become the common faith of the people, and the system of one-party rule would be reconciled with the principle of self-determination.[139]

Wang differed from Hu Han-min, who asserted that a provisional constitution was superfluous. He felt that while the provisional constitution should be based on Sun's teaching, this did not provide the necessary legal form. A provisional constitution, he held, should be a mutual limitation which stipulates the rights and duties of the citizens as well as the functions and powers of the government. It must prevent the government from oppressing the people on the one hand, and the people from undermining the government through misuse of their freedom on the other.[140]

Despite his belief in constitutional safeguards of people's rights, Wang did not support the Human Rights Movement of 1929–1930[141] which, according to him, advocated the type of liberalism that had culminated in the French Revolution. Eighteenth-century liberalism had emphasized individual freedom, but had resulted, Wang pointed out, in the rule of the bourgeoisie, who had usurped all privileges. To him, bourgeois democracy was no democracy. Only when the masses of people enjoy equal opportunity in both political and economic spheres can true democracy be attained. In Wang's view, it was a logical development that in the nineteenth century socialism began to take the place of liberalism. But he opposed wholesale importation of any Western socialism, pointing to the Three Principles of the People as the best solution for China. While the details of these principles might be worked out by making use of Western theories and experiences, a working model must be created by the Chinese themselves.[142]

Thus Wang advocated the protection of people's freedom by a provisional constitution while condemning eighteenth-century liberalism. What exactly, then, was his position toward liberty? Wang divided thought into two kinds: political and nonpolitical. In regard to the latter, in which he included academic, religious, scientific, and aesthetic thought, unity is neither necessary nor possible. Any doctrine claiming supremacy in these categories will only be rejected, overthrown, or become stratified. Man's knowledge needs continual expansion: sanctification of a particular idea necessarily discourages further inquiry and exploration and thus brings progress to an end.[143] In regard to political thinking, however, Wang held that whenever it involves action, it can be only relatively free. Since China was badly in need of unification, absolute freedom of political thought would lead to disunity. The counterrevolutionaries, for instance, had to be curbed, if only temporarily, or the revolution would be endangered. In the period of constitutional government the people would be allowed more political freedom than in the period of revolution. The test of a constitutional government is "equal freedom" for all people, while that of a revolutionary government is "adequate exercise of freedom" by those involved in revolution—i.e., the masses of people minus the counterrevolutionaries. Wang's distinction between political and nonpolitical freedom was severely criticized by the human rights advocates, who did not see how freedom could exist without one of its most important components.[144]

When Wang joined the Nationalist government in 1932 as president of the Executive Yüan, he was in name a coleader with Chiang Kai-shek, but it was Chiang who in fact held the supreme power. Still Wang managed to express his opinion on controversial problems. His main concern was how to reconcile liberty and party rule. It was his view that while the people should be allowed freedom of speech and assembly, they should also

have implicit faith in the Three Principles and the Kuomintang. To establish his thesis, however, it was not
enough for Wang to say that political thought is different
from other thought and therefore should have only relative
freedom. He had to go deeper.

Wang started with the recognition that individuals' ideas
are as varied as their interests. Any dogmatic disregard of
these differences will work against individual freedom. On
the other hand, accentuation of these differences leads
only to national disunity, which nobody wants. Discipline
is the cement that unites the people. It supplements rather
than contradicts freedom, so long as it is based on the
free spirit, or spontaneous sentiments, of the people. A
spontaneous basis exists when people, living in the same
environment, have common perception and cognition of
the problems facing them and, developing the same belief, take common action to solve them. But granted that
people have the same perception and cognition of their
problems, must they arrive at the same solution—in this
case, the Three Principles of the People? Here Wang could
only argue that the Three Principles were comprehensive
in nature and basically met China's needs, and that they
were so deeply rooted in China that any attempt to replace them with another doctrine would inevitably result
in political chaos.[145]

The year 1934 saw the launching of the New Life
Movement by Chiang Kai-shek and his decision to com-
memorate Confucius' birthday with great ceremony. Amid
the furor of honoring tradition and ancient sages, Wang
found it necessary to give his views. He was for modernism: a modern state and a modern life. He opposed the
revival of ancient institutions and ideology, especially the
stern moralism of the Neo-Confucianists who, in his
words, "basically do not understand the meaning of
man."[146]

In his *Declining Family and the Upstart,* he compared the laggard China with prosperous Japan. The Chinese, like a declining family, forever harped upon their past glory, refusing to learn from others. The pride they took in their past constituted an insurpassable obstacle to reform. They were unable to admit their weaknesses because they believed that what their ancestors had handed down to them was the best. But the Japanese, who knew they had nothing to be proud of, were ready to recognize the superiority of others, and, undeterred by pride and prejudice, made determined efforts to improve themselves. The result was a foregone conclusion: Japan forged ahead while China lagged behind.[147] Wang was particularly critical of Tseng Kuo-fan, the leading statesman in the nineteenth century, who had made some reforms primarily devoted to military and industrial matters, and who, with his insistence on China's moral superiority, had stopped short of institutional change. The resultant precept, "Chinese learning to constitute the foundation, Western learning to serve functional purposes," had prevented China from undertaking extensive reforms for more than half a century.[148]

Paradoxically, Wang's intensive modernism did not prevent him from paying tribute to Confucius. Although he did not consider Confucianism a religion, he thought it provided a common faith for the Chinese people. In Wang's view Confucius deserved honor because he systematized ancient thought and summed up the essence of Chinese culture so that it could be transmitted to modern generations. To deprecate a man to whom the Chinese owed everything in culture and learning was to Wang a most ungrateful act. Confucianism, of course, was not entirely suitable to modern times, but that was not the fault of Confucius, who had urged "daily renovation of virtues." If Chinese culture lagged behind, it was the duty of those who came after him, in every generation, to bring it up to date. The content of virtues should vary with the times, but the spirit of morality remains unchangeable.[149]

Wang's aim in adjusting Confucian virtues to modern times was progress. He should have recognized the difficulty of modernizing Confucianism, but his romanticism prevented him from making a clean break with the past. The emotionalism that distinguished him as a poet often overlaid the stratum of rationalism in him. It should be noted, however, that in emphasizing the renovation of virtues, Wang showed an unmistakable advance over the eclectic school, which insisted on preserving traditional virtues as the foundation of Chinese culture.

Wang has been criticized for being fickle, unsteady, and inordinately ambitious. He cooperated with his political rivals as often as he fought them. In both domestic and foreign policies he not infrequently reversed himself so completely that criticism would seem justified. In some of these changes he appeared hardly different from politicians who hold one policy while in power and another while out of power. But Wang was a dedicated man. It is neither fair nor correct to compare him to a politician whose sole interest lies in manipulation.

What then is the explanation? It is pertinent to recall that Wang had tried to become a martyr while a young man. Imbued with the spirit of dedication, he became contemptuous of criticism. "I have never been afraid of other people's smearing of me," he said, "for I do not think smearing will have ill effects on my personality."[150] This selfless devotion enabled him to adopt entirely new positions without fear. And it was this same spirit of sacrifice that sometimes prompted him to take fatal actions. "In the new environment of revolution," Wang wrote in 1931 when he was planning a new move to overthrow Chiang

Kai-shek, "even if there arise serious setbacks, they will not affect the course of the revolution in any critical way. . . . The rolling of heads in an endless stream did not stop the progress of the French Revolution."[151] It was not for rhetorical effect that he wrote those words; it was a thought natural to a man who at the age of twenty-seven had written in a Peking prison:[152]

With what pleasure will I meet the executioner's sword,
And give my youthful head to the worthy cause.

Aside from this romantic heroism, Wang's belief in the flexibility of policies as distinguished from principles also accounts for the frequent changes in his political positions. Influenced by evolutionary theory, Wang considered it natural that policies and institutions should adapt to varying environments.[153] Revolution, principles, policies, and methods are all products of the times. Principles, of course, are of longer duration than policies, and they may eventually be effectual in changing the environment. But policies and methods must be formulated on the basis of living facts if they are to be viable.[154]

This conception of adapting to the times, combined with a spirit of martyrdom, was deeply entrenched in Wang's thought and shaped his career, making it possible for him to be at once changeable and determined—a paradox that characterized his whole life and eventually led him to complete disaster.

Notes

CHAPTER VI. THE KUOMINTANG LEADERS

1. Chiang Kai-shek, *Chiang tsung-t'ung yen-lun hui-pien* (Collected Works of President Chiang Kai-shek, hereafter cited as *CHP*), 24 vols. (Taipei: Cheng-chung, 1956), XI, 128.
2. *CHP*, X, 70.
3. *CHP*, XII, 142–43.
4. *CHP*, XII, 239 ff.
5. Chiang, *Chung-kuo chih ming-yün* (China's Destiny), in *CHP*, IV, 133; see also *CHP*, II, 155.
6. *CHP*, IV, 129.
7. *Ibid.*
8. *CHP*, XIX, 377 ff.; XV, 228.
9. *CHP*, IV, 125; XII, 188.
10. *CHP*, XV, 179–80; XII, 394.
11. *CHP*, X, 61.
12. *CHP*, X, 62–63.
13. *CHP*, XI, 230.
14. *CHP*, X, 63.
15. *CHP*, XL, 264.
16. *CHP*, XIV, 82.
17. *CHP*, XIV, 71.
18. *CHP*, XII, 10.
19. *CHP*, X, 67; XIV, 78–79.
20. *CHP*, XI, 76.
21. *CHP*, XII, 3.
22. *CHP*, XII, 4–5.
23. *CHP*, XIV, 84.
24. See above, ch. 2.
25. Chang Ch'i-yün, *San-min chu-i ti li-lun* (The Theory of San-min chu-i) (Taipei, 1952), I, 42–43.
26. *CHP*, II, 53, 17; XIV, 86.
27. *CHP*, XXI, 20.
28. *Ibid.*, p. 18.
29. Chang Ch'i-yün, *op. cit.*, I, 99.
30. *CHP*, X, 306 ff.; XV, 315.
31. *CHP*, X, 233 ff.; XI, 235, 344.
32. Chiang, *Chung-kuo chih ming-yün*, in *CHP*, IV, 47 ff.
33. *CHP*, VI, 14.
34. *Ibid.*
35. *CHP*, XII, 87.
36. *CHP*, XXI, 127.
37. *CHP*, XV, 277.
38. *CHP*, X, 151.
39. *CHP*, XII, 264.
40. *CHP*, XV, 276; XX, 263.
41. *CHP*, V, 11; XII, 248.
42. *CHP*, XV, 130 ff.

43. *CHP*, XII, 308 ff.
44. *CHP*, II, 24.
45. *CHP*, V, 12.
46. *Ibid.*, p. 13.
47. *CHP*, XIII, 14–15.
48. Mao Ssu-ch'eng, ed., *Min-kuo shih-wu-nien ch'ien chih Chang Chieh-shih hsien-sheng* (Mr. Chiang Kai-shek before 1926) (1937), Pts. 1 and 2.
49. *CHP*, XII, 22–23.
50. *CHP*, XXIV, 118, 123, 129.
51. *CHP*, XV, 278.
52. *CHP*, XXIV, 64.
53. *CHP*, XII, 22–23.
54. *CHP*, X, 78–80; XI, 278–90.
55. *CHP*, XXI, 22.
56. *CHP*, XXI, 223.
57. *CHP*, XXIV, 51–52.
58. T'ao Hsi-sheng, "Chi Ch'en Pu-lei hsien-sheng" (Notes on Mr. Ch'en Pu-lei), *Chuan-chi wen-hsüeh* ("Biographical Literature"), 4.6: 10 (June 1964).
59. Tai Chi-t'ao, "Ma-k'e-ssu chu-pen-lun chieh-shuo" (An Explanation of Marx, *Capital*), *Chien-she* ("Reconstruction"), 1.4: 811 ff. (Nov. 1919).
60. Tai Chi-t'ao, "Ts'ung ching-chi shang kuan-ch'a Chung-kuo ti luan-yüan" (Sources of China's Turmoil from the Economic Standpoint), *ibid.*, 1.2: 355 ff. (Aug. 1919).
61. *Ibid.*, pp. 345–55.
62. Tai Chi-t'ao, "Ke-ming! ho ku? wei ho?" (Revolution! Why and for What?), *ibid.*, 1.3: 596 (Oct. 1919).
63. Tai Chi-t'ao, "Lao-tung-che chieh-fang yü nü-tzu chieh-fang yün-tung ti chiao-tien" (The Meeting Point of the Worker-Emancipation and Woman-Emancipation Movements), *ibid.*, 2.2: 269 ff. (March 1920).
64. Tai Chi-t'ao, "Ke-ming! ho ku? wei ho?" *ibid.*, 1.3: 583.
65. Tai Chi-t'ao, *Tai Chi-t'ao hsien-sheng wen-ts'un* (Collected Writings of Tai Chi-t'ao, hereafter cited as *TWT*) (Taipei: Chung-yang wen-wu ch'u-pan she, 1959), III, 946–47.
66. *TWT*, III, 976–86.
67. *TWT*, IV, 1463.
68. Ch'en T'ien-hsi, ed., *Tai Chi-t'ao hsien-sheng pien-nien chuan-chi* (A Chronological Biography of Tai Chi-t'ao) (Taipei, 1958), pp. 40–41.
69. Tai Chi-t'ao, *Kuo-min ke-ming yü Kuo-min-tang* (Shanghai: Ta-tung, 1929), p. 19.
70. *Ibid.*, p. 60.
71. *Ibid.*, Appendix, pp. 87–104.
72. Tai Chi-t'ao, *Ch'ing-nien chih lu* (The Path for Youth) (Shanghai: Min-chih, 1928), pp. 63–65.
73. *Ibid.*, pp. 155, 165–66.
74. *Ibid.*, pp. 95–96.
75. *TWT*, IV, 1462.
76. *TWT*, IV, 1443–44.
77. Ch'en T'ien-hsi, *op. cit.*, pp. 76–77.

78. *TWT*, III, 962–64.
79. For biographical sketches of Chu Chih-hsin, see Hu Han-min, *Ke-ming li-lun yü ke-ming kung-tso* (Revolutionary Theory and Revolutionary Work) (Shanghai: Min-chih, 1932), Collection VII, pp. 1327–40; Tai Chi-t'ao, "Huai Chih-hsin" (I Remember Chu Chih-hsin), *Ch'un-ch'iu* (Spring and Autumn), No. 61 (Jan. 1960); Wang Hsi-wen, "Chu Chih-hsin wai-chuan" (Supplementary Biography of Chu Chih-hsin), *ibid.*, Nos. 51–60 (Aug. 1959–Jan. 1960).
80. Chu Chih-hsin, "Hsin-li ti kuo-chia chu-i" (Psychological Nationalism), *Min-pao* (People's Journal, hereafter cited as *MP*), No. 21: 13–15 (June 1908).
81. Chu Chih-hsin, *Chu Chih-hsin hsüan-chi* (Selected Essays of Chu Chih-hsin) (Taipei: P'a-mi-erh, 1958), pp. 1–27.
82. *Ibid.*, p. 4.
83. *Ibid.*, p. 26.
84. *Ibid.*, p. 7.
85. *Ibid.*, pp. 97–98.
86. See below, ch. 7.
87. Chu, *Chu Chih-hsin hsüan-chi*, pp. 102–3.
88. *Ibid.*, p. 106.
89. Chu Chih-hsin, "Te-i-chih she-hui ke-ming-chia hsiao-chuan" (Brief Sketches of the German Socialist Revolutionaries), *MP*, No. 2 (May 1906).
90. Chu, *Chu Chih-hsin hsüan-chi*, pp. 204 ff.
91. Chu Chih-hsin, in *Chien-she*, 2.3: 584–86 (April 1920); 2.2: 379–80 (March 1920).
92. Chu Chih-hsin, "Ta I-hsin she-yu shu" (Reply to Fellow Member I-hsin), *ibid.*, 1.1: 189–90 (Aug. 1919).
93. Chu Chih-hsin, "Shen-sheng yü ch'in-lüeh" (Sanctity and Aggression), *ibid.*, 1.1: 169–72.
94. *Hu hsien-sheng chi-nien chuan-k'an* (A Special Publication in Memory of Hu Han-min) (Canton: P'ei-ying, 1936), pp. 32 ff.
95. Hu Han-min, *Wei-wu shih-kuan yü lun-li chih yen-chiu* (A Study of the Materialistic Interpretation of History and Ethics) (Shanghai: Min-chih, 1927), p. 14.
96. *Ibid.*, pp. 28, 32.
97. *Ibid.*, p. 224.
98. *Ibid.*, pp. 234–37.
99. *Ibid.*, p. 225.
100. Hu Han-min, "Fu Ma Po-yüan shu" (Reply to Ma Po-yüan), *Chien-she*, 2.4: 824 (May 1920).
101. Hu Han-min, "Chih Yang Chao-i shu" (Letter to Yang Chao-i), *ibid.*, 1.4: 837–38 (Nov. 1919).
102. Hu Han-min, *San-min chu-i ti lien-huan hsing* (The Interrelationships of the Three Principles of the People) (Taipei: P'a-mi-erh, 1951), pp. 2–5.
103. *Ibid.*, p. 17.
104. *Ibid.*, p. 22.
105. Hu Han-min, *Ke-ming li-lun yü ke-ming kung-tso*, Collection 1, p. 34.
106. *Ibid.*, p. 44.

107. Hu Han-min, *Hu Han-min hsien-sheng yen-chiang chi* (Collected Speeches of Hu Han-min) (Shanghai: Min-chih, 1930), Collection 1, p. 32.
108. Hu Han-min, *Ke-ming li-lun yü ke-ming kung-tso*, Collection 1, p. 30.
109. Hu Han-min, *San-min chu-i ti lien-huan hsing*, p. 53.
110. Wu Chih-hui, *Wu Chih-hui hsüan-chi* (Selected Essays of Wu Chih-hui) (Taipei, 1965), II, 321.
111. The Chung-hsing Journal, ed., *Hu-tang lun-wen hsüan-chi* (Selected Essays on the Protection of the Party) (Canton, 1934), Collection 1.
112. Hu Han-min, *Hu Han-min hsüan-chi*, pp. 59–61.
113. *Ibid.*, p. 204.
114. *Ibid.*, p. 90.
115. Hu Han-min, *Ke-ming li-lun yü ke-ming kung-tso*, Collection 1, p. 125.
116. *Ibid.*, p. 128.
117. *Ibid.*, pp. 71 ff.
118. Hu Han-min, *Hu Han-min hsüan-chi*, pp. 91–92.
119. *Ibid.*, p. 94.
120. *Ibid.*, p. 101.
121. *Ibid.*, pp. 214 ff.
122. *Ibid.*, p. 220.
123. *Ibid.*, p. 225.
124. Wang Ching-wei, "Tzu-shu" (Autobiography), *Tung-fang tsa-chih* ("The Eastern Miscellany"), 31.1: 1–3 (Jan. 1934).
125. Wang Ching-wei, "Lun ke-ming chih ch'ü-shih" (On Revolutionary Trends), *MP*, No. 25: 2 (1910).
126. Wang Ching-wei, "Po Hsin-min ts'ung-pao tsui-chin chih fei-ke-ming lun" (Refutation of *Hsin-min ts'ung-pao's* Antirevolutionary Arguments), *MP*, No. 4: 13–31; No. 6: 3–4.
127. Wang Ching-wei, *Wang Ching-wei chi* (Collected Writings of Wang Ching-wei) (Shanghai: Kuang-ming, 1924), IV, 82–84, 86.
128. Wang Ching-wei, *Wang Ching-wei hsien-sheng chiang-yen chi* (Collected Speeches of Wang Ching-wei, hereafter cited as *WCYC*) (Shanghai: Kuang-ming, 1926), pp. 3–4.
129. Wang, *Wang Ching-wei chi*, III, 24.
130. *Ibid.*
131. *Ibid.*, III, 129–31.
132. *WCYC*, p. 129.
133. Wang, *Wang Ching-wei chi*, III, 118.
134. Wang Ching-wei, *Wang Ching-wei hsien-sheng tsui-chin yen-shuo chi* (Recent Speeches of Wang Ching-wei) (1928?), pp. 9–10.
135. *WCYC*, pp. 79, 114–15; Wang, *Wang Ching-wei chi*, III, 66.
136. *WCYC*, p. 11.
137. *WCYC*, p. 18.
138. Wang Ching-wei, *Wang Ching-wei hsien-hsing tsui-chin yen-lun chi* (Recent Speeches and Essays of Wang Ching-wei, hereafter cited as *WYLC*) (Hong Kong: Nan-hua jih-pao, 1930), p. 237.
139. *WYLC*, p. 56.
140. Wang Ching-wei, *Wang Ching-wei hsien-sheng chih ko tang-pu ko t'ung-chih shu* (Letter of Wang Ching-wei to All Party Offices and Comrades) (Hong Kong: Nan-hua jih-pao, 1930), pp. 5–6.

141. See below, ch. 7.
142. *WYLC*, pp. 84, 129, 133.
143. *WYLC*, p. 13.
144. See below, ch. 7.
145. Lin Po-sheng, ed., *Wang Ching-wei hsien-sheng tsui-chin yen-lun chi* (A Collection of Recent Speeches and Essays of Wang Ching-wei) (Shanghai: Chung-hua jih-pao kuan, 1937), Pt. 2, pp. 90–94.
146. *Ibid.*, Pt. 1, p. 165.
147. *Ibid.*, Pt. 1, pp. 171 ff.
148. *Ibid.*, Pt. 1, pp. 173–74.
149. *Ibid.*, Pt. 1, pp. 177 ff.
150. Wang Ching-wei, *Wang Ching-wei hsien-sheng tsui-chin yen-shuo chi*, p. 187.
151. *Fu-hsing Chung-kuo Kuo-min-tang* (Revive the Kuomintang) (Kuomintang chung-yang chih-chien wei-yüan-hui fei-ch'ang hui-i, 1931), p. 16.
152. These lines are part of a famous poem written by Wang Ching-wei when he was imprisoned in consequence of his abortive attempt on the life of the prince regent in 1910. He thought he would be executed, but he was released afterward.
153. *WCYC*, pp. 3 ff.
154. *WCYC*, p. 44.

Chapter VII

HUMAN RIGHTS AND DEMOCRACY

Human Rights and Political Tutelage

IN 1928, after defeating the various warlords, the Nationalist government began the transitional period of political tutelage in preparation for constitutional democracy. Sun Yat-sen's *Fundamentals of National Reconstruction* provided for Kuomintang rule during this period. The Kuomintang directed and supervised the government, which was in turn responsible to it. The Kuomintang was not only above the government but also above the state, which was to be reconstructed under its direction. This one-party dictatorship offered no constitutional safeguard of civil rights, and in the eagerness to consolidate power, individual freedom and security were readily disregarded. Against this situation a group of intellectuals voiced their protest in the years 1929–1930 through the magazine *Crescent Moon* (*Hsin-yüeh*), and out of their efforts the Human Rights Movement was born.

Included in this group were Hu Shih (1891–1962), Lo Lung-chi (1896–1965), and Liang Shih-ch'iu (1902–). All were professors who had studied in the United States. Hu Shih easily became the moving spirit of the crusade. A leader of the New Culture Movement, he had been held in high esteem in China for his intellectual integrity and liberal views. A philosopher in favor of science, he was an admirer of two men whose influence was indelibly impressed on his thinking: Thomas Huxley and John Dewey. From Huxley he took skepticism, which allays belief in dogmatic systems; and from Dewey, pragmatism, which places value on experience derived from coping with one's environment. With these basic precepts it was only natural that Hu Shih shunned ideologies having dogmatic elements and preferred piecemeal solutions to violent revolutions claiming to solve problems once and for all. Communism, with its belief in quickly attaining an ideal state through class struggle and keeping that ideal state unchanged by means of the proletarian dictatorship, was, for Hu Shih, a gross oversimplification that denies evolutionary continuation. It represented the dogmatism typical of the pre-Darwin period—only it was even more dogmatic than the Hegelianism from which it was derived.[1]

Partly because of these convictions and partly because of his scholarly temperament, Hu Shih broke with some of his close associates in the New Culture Movement, notably Ch'en Tu-hsiu and Li Ta-chao, who adopted Communism and chose the revolutionary course.[2] He had stood somewhat aloof from the revolution of 1924-1927, in which the Nationalists and the Communists had joined hands. But, an individualist of the Ibsenian school, he could not long divorce himself from social and political problems.[3]

Thus in 1929, after six years of silence, Hu Shih once again engaged in political discussions. In his "What Path Shall We Take?" he reaffirmed his aversion to grandiose goals preached in zealous doctrines, saying he would rather first study the needs of China and then determine what specific goals were to be attained. He listed five evils that had to be attacked immediately: poverty, disease, ignorance, corruption, and internal disturbances. The crucial question was, Which path should be taken to overcome these evils: revolution or evolution? Hu Shih argued that the difference between the two is relative rather than absolute. Evolution is a gradual process, whereas revolution is evolution accelerated at a certain stage by human effort, which causes changes to appear abruptly, making them seem cut off from historical continuity. Actually, Hu Shih pointed out, revolution has its historical background and basis as well. The difference between revolution and evolution lies, rather, in method and result. Evolution, as an unconscious, natural process, is slow and inefficient, whereas revolution, being conscious, can often attain its objectives in a shorter time. Furthermore, evolution, in spite of the progress it makes, often leaves remnants of old institutions that are no longer useful.

Thus, said Hu Shih, revolution is superior to evolution —but only in general terms; revolutions are of two kinds: peaceful and violent. While he admitted that violent revolution is often necessary in a country where the political system does not protect the new forces from being harshly suppressed by the old, he also stressed its disadvantages. Once begun, an armed struggle has a tendency to expand, resulting in continued disorder and destruction. When revolution becomes the pretext for all kinds of selfish struggle, it can continue endlessly. Revolution in China, as a wanton struggle between the militarists, had completely lost its original meaning of reform. Hu Shih called for a halt to this aimless violence, urging a peaceful revolution in which the intellectual power of the whole nation was concentrated on attacking China's problems. Although a relatively slow process, a peaceful revolution, Hu Shih maintained, would step by step attain its goal.[4] "Revolution" was, in fact, a misnomer, since what Hu Shih advocated was actually reformism aimed at piecemeal solutions rather than at any fundamental social change.

On the question of human rights the *Crescent Moon* writers created a considerable stir. In 1929 it was decreed by the government that "no individual or group shall by unlawful acts violate the person, freedom or property of other individuals." It seems ironic that the human rights protest should have begun with a government decree purporting to protect those rights. But, in fact, basic violations of human rights were being committed by government agencies even after the decree was issued. Censorship, arbitrary arrests, and party interference with judicial procedure were common occurrences. Some of the *Crescent Moon* writers were themselves subject to maltreatment, which could only add to their bitterness.

Hu Shih was the first to voice a protest against the ineffectualness of the decree. Its serious defect, he claimed, lay in its lack of specific protection. Unless the various kinds of freedom and the definite legal procedure for the protection of these were specified, the decree was obviously futile. Furthermore, it was a gross omission to prohibit "individuals and groups" from violating the rights of man without extending this to cover the government, since its agencies were the conspicuous offenders. Finally, the decree declared that punishment of offenders was in accordance with law; yet there was no law that provided for sanctions against the government when it infringed on civil rights.[5]

It was clear to Hu Shih that to safeguard the rights of man the powers of the government had to be limited by a constitution, even during the period of political tutelage. Political tutelage without a constitution was despotism. Moreover, in a nation totally lacking experience in democracy it was necessary that the government as well as the people undergo democratic training. Unless government and party leaders could themselves live under a constitution, and learn restraint as well as how to limit their powers legally, it would be impossible for them to lead the people to democracy.[6]

Of the three human rights advocates, it was Lo Lung-chi who set down the theoretical basis for the campaign. A student of government trained in the United States and Britain, Lo knew more about the technical aspects of human rights than most of his *Crescent Moon* colleagues. One can easily spot the influence of Western philosophers, from Thomas Hobbes to Bertrand Russell, in his writings. More outspoken but less prestigious than Hu Shih, he was the ready target of government reprisal. In 1930 he was arrested for "reactionary utterances," but was immediately released through the intervention of influential friends.[7]

Lo defined human rights as "the right to be man—the conditions necessary for being man." In order to be man, one must live, and in order to maintain a living, one must have the opportunity to provide oneself with food, clothing, and shelter. It follows that security of person is necessary if life is not to be violated by others. But man needs not only to live, but to live happily. He has his individuality and personality, and unless they are fully developed, he will not be at his best and will not live a happy life. But man, Lo realized, is not an isolated egoist. He is a member of a community with which he is inseparably interrelated. His happiness is closely linked to the community's, and he must contribute his best to the community to enable it to attain to the highest common good: the greatest happiness of the greatest number.[8]

In this belief Lo revealed the influence of Bentham. But he differed from Bentham in believing that human rights were founded on "functional" grounds rather than on law. He did not pursue the crucial problem of how individual happiness is reconciled with the happiness of the greatest number. Since the Chinese had traditionally stressed the social responsibility of man, Lo could not think of individual happiness without its social context.

To Lo, freedom of speech was a human right not because it is a natural right or provided by law, but because it is an essential condition for being man. Man thinks and wants to express what he thinks. Freedom of speech is essential not only to the expression of his thought but also to the development of his individuality and personality. It makes it possible for man "to be himself, at his best" and at the same time to contribute his thought to the general well-being. On the other hand, to suppress an individual's freedom of speech is to destroy "not only the life of the individual, but the life of the community as a whole."[9] Life, in this context, must be moral, with a responsibility to one's fellow men and to the community. Thus Lo viewed human rights as an essential condition for the development of man's moral being as well as for his physical existence. Human rights are not to serve an individual's selfish ends or wanton desires; rather, they are to enable mankind to advance to the highest level of achievement.

It is interesting to note that in the voluminous political writings of Sun Yat-sen, the nature of the state is hardly dealt with at all. At a time when the state was considered the supreme authority to which individuals should sacrifice themselves, especially to save it from foreign aggression and internal disorganization, it was natural that the functions of a state were seldom discussed. It was Lo Lung-chi who first brought up the question in his discussion of human rights. "The state exists for its function," wrote Lo. "If the function ends, so ends its *raison d'être*. The function of the state consists in its protection of human rights—the maintenance of conditions essential to being man. Whenever it fails to secure these essential conditions, the state will lose its function, and I will no longer be obliged to obey it."[10] Lo declared that the theory of the state's omnipotence had become bankrupt in the twentieth century, maintaining that the state is only one of the numerous social organizations whose value depends entirely on the effectiveness of its function. The state's authority over the people is limited, not absolute. A people's obedience to the state is conditional upon that state's capability to protect human rights. Here the influence of Harold Laski, especially his views on the dangers of obedience, is apparent.

The rights of man, according to Lo, predate legality: laws are made by men to protect their rights. The making of law is, in fact, one of the rights of man, and the people are obliged to obey only laws made by themselves. Lo took pains to deny a charge made by Wang Ching-wei that the human rights protagonists followed an eighteenth-century mode of liberalism.[11] Nevertheless, he cited with approval Rousseau's postulate that law is the expression of the general will, calling attention to man's right to resist oppression as set forth in the 1789 French Declaration of the Rights of Man. To Lo, Locke's right of revolution was man's ultimate right to protect his other rights. "All human rights can be violated and trampled upon, but not the right of revolution, which will forever be held by the people—as the ultimate weapon for their survival."[12]

The ultimate weapon, Lo implied, should not be used lightheartedly. Like Hu Shih, he believed that violent revolution was limited as an instrument of reconstruction. Terror may have temporary effects on social psychology, but without basic material improvements, psychological outbursts will not lead anywhere. The human rights advocates all had in common the belief in a peaceful transition to constitutionalism as the final safeguard of the rights of man.

As intellectuals and college professors, the human rights advocates were particularly concerned with freedom of thought and speech. They opposed the policy of "unification of thought" favored by the Kuomintang in its attempt to uphold the supremacy of Sun Yat-sen's doctrine. Liang Shih-ch'iu, the third of the human rights advocates and a professor of literature, pointed out that unification of the country must not be confused with unification of thought. While the former was necessary, the latter was neither desirable nor feasible. Because of differences in heritage, environment, and education, men think differently. A thoughtful man is one with rational power and judgment. He derives his ideas from his own knowledge and experience. Thought is by nature independent. It is answerable only to one's conscience, and it cannot be corrupted by money or suppressed by force. A despot, Liang held, could kill a person for his idea, but the idea itself would not thereby be extinguished. It would spread the more quickly because of the obstacles placed in its way.[13]

Liang rejected the concept of absolute truth. No one doctrine in the world could be held supreme. Noting the modern trend toward specialization, Liang saw no generalization comprehensive enough to regulate ideas in all fields. After all, progress depends on experiment and open discussion. If thought were ever to be effectively controlled, the result would be unthinkable stratification. Therefore, to Liang, political unity did not depend upon unification of thought. Rather than relying on coercion, which can secure at most temporary submission, political unity must be based on general consent promoted by tolerance. Coercion of thought could, at best, produce blind followers or opportunists and, at worst, cause violent reactions that would disrupt the political and social order.[14]

The human rights protagonists rejected Wang Ching-wei's contention that political thought as distinguished from religious, scientific, and other academic thought should enjoy only relative freedom—that is, more in the period of constitutional government, less in the period of political tutelage, and none during the period of revolution. In Lo Lung-chi's conception, political thought was closely related to religious and academic thought, and it was impossible to tamper with one without involving the others. He challenged the power of the government to determine whether the people should have more political freedom in one period and less in another. "If such regulation is permitted, popular sovereignty will come to an end."[15]

Lo Lung-chi held that freedom of speech is an inalienable right of the people, admitting no interference, even by law. The phrase "no freedom beyond law" as provided in some constitutions was, in his words, "a deception, for the very meaning of freedom of speech is that law shall not interfere with free expression." The lack in China of a legislature truly representative of the people made it particularly incumbent upon the Chinese to press for freedom of speech, to prevent parliament from suppressing it by means of law. Lo conceded that freedom of speech did not give one the right to libel and slander, but beyond this it was absolute. "Unless freedom is absolute, there will absolutely be no freedom."[16]

The human rights protagonists denounced the Kuomintang's belief in political tutelage as basically unsound. Seeing democracy as a process of education, Hu Shih argued that people can learn about democracy only in a democracy. The Kuomintang's exercise of dictatorial powers could never train people in the ways of a democratic government.[17] In Lo Lung-chi's view, the whole idea of political tutelage was contrary to the conception of the modern state. The Kuomintang, ignorant of the nature and purpose of the state, regarded the state as an end, maintaining that the people existed for the state rather than the other way around. To Lo the state was the instrument of the people for the attainment of certain common goals through restraint and cooperation. Three of the state's functions were of primary importance in this connection: protection of the rights of the people; development of the people; and the promotion of happiness for all. Lo saw no chance of attaining these common aims if the people were not permitted to take part in government. A dictatorship, whether of one person or of one party, could hardly be expected to safeguard the liberties of the citizen, to develop his personality and individuality, or to provide an environment of peace, tranquillity, order, and justice —the conditions essential to happiness. One-party rule by the Kuomintang would never achieve the purposes of the state. For when the party is supreme, the state and its aims are submerged in the party.[18]

Although the Human Rights Movement made a great stir in China, its practical effects were few. Two forces worked against it: nationalism and socialism. At a time when the Chinese nation was confronted with serious difficulties, both external and internal, the theory that the individual was more important than the state seemed remote from immediate needs. The socialist attack on the entire socioeconomic system made the assertion of individual rights appear insignificant. The struggle for social justice dwarfed the movement for individual freedom. The human rights thinkers were not insensitive to the demands for social change; but the stress upon the rights of the individual as a special issue, separate from the social and economic demands of the times, could only diminish their influence.

The Human Rights Movement arose out of the shortcomings of the Chinese political system. If the movement failed to achieve immediate results in the political field, its educational significance should not be minimized, for it called attention to the basic constitutional principles that must be learned and practiced by any who aim toward democracy. Its succinct exposition of the liberal conception of the state reminded the political leaders of their duties and functions as agents of the state and reaffirmed the civil rights of the people, so often disregarded. The human rights protagonists lived to see much of what they had advocated incorporated into the Constitution of the Chinese Republic seventeen years later, although the advent of the Chinese Communists in 1949 prevented its application on the Chinese mainland.

Democracy or Dictatorship

Around 1930 the Blue Shirts were organized in China by young military officers, mostly former cadets of the Whampoa Military Academy, who were extremely loyal to Chiang Kai-shek. The Blue Shirts, apparently named after the fashion of the Fascist Black Shirts, were later reorganized into the Fu Hsing (Revival) Society. Because its activities were more or less secret, there is only scattered documentation regarding the society's aim and organization. There is no doubt that it upheld the Three Principles of the People, but of the three, it emphasized nationalism. Members of the Fu Hsing focused on national interest and on developing the economy through regimentation and state control. Viewing the utopia of a world commonwealth as a remote dream, they advocated national self-sufficiency during international conflicts and economic wars. Thus they rejected civil liberties, considering it reactionary to uphold the freedom of the individual at the expense of the nation. To attain its objectives, the Fu Hsing felt not only that the Kuomintang should maintain its one-party rule over China, but that authority should be centralized in the dictatorship of the supreme leader. Action was the Society's keynote. "Necessity is truth; action creates theory," wrote one leader. He went on to advocate suppression of the intellectuals to make sure that disagreement and criticism would not detract from unified action.[19]

It is obvious that the Fu Hsing owed its origins to Italian Fascism, whose influence on China in the early 1930's can be traced. The continued strife among the various factions in the Kuomintang, the armed revolt of the Communists, the aggression of Japan—all these had put the country in a turmoil. The young, impatient military men were not the only ones susceptible to totalitarianism. Even the intellectuals found themselves examining the question of dictatorship with keen interest.

The debate on democracy versus dictatorship was carried in the *Independent Review* (*Tu-li P'ing-lun*), of which Hu Shih was editor. True to his scholarly impartiality, Hu offered space to both sides. Those involved, mostly college professors, had studied in the West and were generally regarded as independent thinkers. Although those on the side of dictatorship might have been influenced by the same social forces that affected the Revival Society, they had no connection with its militancy and tended to express their views more as scholars than as active participants in politics.

The debate began on the question of China's unification. The armed strife rampant among the various groups both within and outside of the Kuomintang had become an acute problem to those who considered unification a prerequisite of national reconstruction. Speaking from the standpoint of history, Tsiang T'ing-fu (1895–1965), then professor of history at Tsing Hua University,[20] attributed China's failure during the twenty years after the establishment of the Republic to its lack of unification. The various administrations spent so much energy dealing with their political enemies that there was little left for anything else. While engaging in a civil war, they had had to give up reconstruction to maintain a large army and, in the attempt to overcome their enemies, they had resorted to dubious tactics.

Tsiang viewed absolutism as an indispensable stage in the formation of a national state. Pointing to the example of England, Tsiang held that the War of Roses had raged throughout the fifteenth century with no tangible results. It was toward the end of the century, when Henry VII unified England and began a century of absolutism, that the English people were provided with the opportunity for rehabilitation. It was thus that the English national state came into existence, culminating in the seventeenth-century revolution, which brought political conflict to an end, thereby making way for constructive developments. Had there not been any Tudor autocracy in the sixteenth century, there could not have been any genuine revolution in the seventeenth century. The same was true of Bourbon absolutism before the French Revolution, and of Romanov absolutism before the Russian Revolution.

The situation in China in the 1930's, Tsiang argued, was the same as that of England before the Tudor autocracy. The Chinese had had internal disturbances, but not a true revolution. It was true that China had had several thousand years of absolute government, but the Chinese monarchs, because of peculiar circumstances, had not fulfilled their historic mission. As a result, China was still a dynastic state, not a national one, and although the Chinese were generally remarkable for their loyalty to individuals, families, or localities, they were vague in their conception of the state. In addition, out of centuries of monarchical rule no class had emerged to serve as the nucleus of a new political force. The traditional practice of Chinese monarchism had been to destroy all classes that could possibly become a center of political power to challenge the royal family. As a result, when the Manchu dynasty was overthrown, the state had become a heap of loose sand. And that was the situation in which China now found itself.

To Tsiang, political history in all countries is divided into two phases: the building of a state and the promotion of national welfare through the state. Since China had not completed the first phase, it was futile to talk of the second. The urgent task before China was to build a unified state; only absolutism could do this.[21]

The issue, then, was whether absolutism represented a necessary stage in national reconstruction. Hu Shih, democracy's exponent, hastened to refute the whole notion. Pointing out that the scope of national reconstruction was very broad, and the factors involved were highly complex, he found it impossible to single out "absolutism" as the only cause or condition. Although a state had resulted under the Tudors of England, the Bourbons of France, and the Romanovs of Russia, it was hardly correct to assert that the formation of the state was in each case due to absolutism. Hu Shih listed a number of other factors that had figured in the formation of the English state, including the birth and propagation of the new English language and literature, the influence of Oxford and Cambridge universities, the impact of London as England's political, economic, and cultural center, the rapid development of the textile industry, and the rise of the middle class. Most of these factors, moreover, had appeared in England before the Tudor dynasty, although their development was accelerated in the ensuing century of unity and peace. Hu Shih recognized that unified political control is indispensable to the building of a national state, but he rejected the use of the term "absolutism" to describe that goal, and he reminded his opponents that the reign of Henry VIII, although noted for its unified political power, had also marked the period in which parliamentary power began to rise.

Carrying his argument further, Hu Shih held that China had long been a nation-state. In national consciousness, in unity of language, history, and culture, in continuity of political institutions, China "in the past 2000 years was qualified to be a nation-state." It was true that the political solidarity and unity of the Chinese state had proved inadequate in modern times. But these defects were due to the poor social and political order rather than to the absence of a nation-state, the existence of which could not be questioned.[22] Hu Shih's view that China had long been a nation-state might indeed be challenged, for its validity depended on one's definition of nation-state.

Granted that absolute rule was not indispensable to the building of a national state, would it not then be necessary to use force to unify the country? If the answer was positive, did it not follow that a dictatorship in which all authority is centralized would be better equipped to do the job? The sociologist Wu Ching-ch'ao (1901–), after surveying political divisions and reunifications throughout Chinese history, concluded that military force had invariably been used in unifying the country.[23] The historical finding was irrefutable, but, Hu Shih argued, times had changed and what was applicable in the past might not be applicable to the present. Two factors, he felt, had to be taken into consideration in tackling the problem of unification: the attitude of the Chinese people and the physical conditions of the country. Hu Shih had no difficulty in showing that in the history of Republican China, military force had not always been successful in achieving unity, and that what military force failed to accomplish was sometimes attained by a change in popular opinion. While old China had not had democratic thought, Hu Shih emphasized, modern China did. And this anti-despotic attitude could become a powerful obstacle in any attempt to unify the country by means of a military dictatorship.[24]

Hu Shih's treatment of physical conditions was, however, limited. While he mentioned the size of the country and the difficulties of transportation, a deeper approach would necessarily have touched upon the economic system that shapes the physical conditions. It was Ch'en Chih-mai (1908–), then a professor of political science, who pointed out that economic development is the basic centripetal force in bringing distant places together. When a country is economically underdeveloped, it can be a conglomeration of isolated districts, each maintaining a self-sufficient economy and even a political independence, resulting in a highly provincial outlook. This is a formidable force against which unification efforts, even if backed up by a powerful military force and directed by an absolute ruler, may break down. A modern economy founded on division of labor would, on the other hand, require close correlations of various constituent parts, and would cut through geographical areas and surpass political divisions. Such an economy could wipe out historical provincialism and weld the country into an integrated whole.[25]

The importance of economic development having been recognized, the next question was, What political system would be most conducive to modern economic development? This problem formed a major part of the controversy, for the participants were concerned more with the practicability than the moral value of political systems. The value of democracy, for instance, was generally not challenged by its critics, but its feasibility for China was.

Among those who favored dictatorship was Ch'ien Tuan-sheng (1900–), who became known to the West as a liberal through his book *The Government and Politics of China* (1950), in which he criticized the Kuomintang leaders for invoking the successes of Fascist Italy and Nazi Germany to "hypnotize themselves into believing in totalitarian party leadership."[26] But in the 1930's he was emphatic in the view that totalitarianism would best meet China's needs. Thus in his "Democracy or Totalitarian State," published in 1934, Ch'ien considered democracy no longer suitable to the changing world. The achievements of the Soviet Union and Italy, and the abandonment of democracy in Germany, Ch'ien stated, "dealt fatal blows to democracy whose weaknesses were starkly exposed."[27] The decline of democracy he attributed to the growing class consciousness of the proletariat and the increasing number of economic functions assumed by the state. Ch'ien saw economic nationalism as the dominating force in international relations, under whose impetus rivalry between nations is intensified to an extreme degree. Under these circumstances it is essential that the state be capable of taking quick action. But state powers are limited in a democracy, and parliament has no real organizational link with the business world. Noncooperation between political parties makes speedy decisions further impossible, and labor unrest both reflects and aggravates the low rate of production and the imbalance between production and consumption. These factors make for confusion and inefficiency in democracy. Ch'ien predicted democracy's eventual replacement by dictatorship. Only the latter, he felt, could force people to accept a controlled economy in the interest of the whole nation.

An underdeveloped country like China must have a strong government capable of achieving industrialization within a short time. Ch'ien granted that the Nationalist government of the time was a dictatorship, but it was too weak to be useful. It was in need of modernization, strengthening, and a sense of high purpose. Ch'ien admitted that individual freedom would be curtailed under a dictatorship, but argued that the standards and values set up by individuals are often overemphasized. "Individual evaluation is meaningless outside of social evaluation. . . . In a totalitarian state, social value becomes the standard of all evaluation. But that does not mean cultural retrogression."[28]

Ch'ien was obviously mistaken in his belief that democracy had declined in the West. Neither in the United States nor England nor Switzerland could democracy be said to have proved incapable of coping with economic problems. Nor was there labor unrest serious enough in these countries to be counted a threat to democracy. There had indeed occurred augmentation of executive power in times of crisis, but a centralized democracy was not to be mistaken for a dictatorship. It should be noted that Russia, Italy, Turkey, and Germany, the countries cited by Ch'ien as having undergone democratic decline, had never had a democratic tradition in the first place. The adoption of dictatorship in them, therefore, was no index of democracy's decline.[29]

Hu Shih rose to democracy's defense, presenting it as a viable political alternative to dictatorship. Dictatorship, he said, was impracticable in China for three reasons: China did not have any one man capable of being dictator; it did not have a problem great enough to rally the people's emotions and intellects in support of one; and its people were uneducated in the highly technical operations of a dictatorship.[30] In making the first two points Hu Shih apparently had in mind the Kuomintang, composed of such rival factions that a claim by any leader to be the dictator would lead to a split and civil war.[31] The best solution to this rivalry he believed was a democracy, which would protect the civil rights of the people and open the door of the government to all political parties.[32] Of more importance to the basic issue of practicability, however, was the third point, which Hu Shih explicated as follows:

After observing government and politics in the various countries during the past several decades, I find constitutional democracy an elemetary system suitable for a nation that lacks political experience. . . . The advantage of democracy lies in the fact that it does not require outstanding talents; that it has the flexibility of gradually extending political rights; that it can deliberate collectively and pool the common sense of numerous ordinary citizens in governing the state; and that it provides the great majority of the people with the opportunity of participating in politics, thus training them to value and protect their own rights. In short, democracy is a government of common sense, while enlightened despotism is a government by able heroes. It is difficult to have able heroes, but it is relatively easy to train for common-sense politics. In a country such as ours, where able persons are few, the best political training is by way of a constitutional democracy, with political rights gradually extended to the people.[33]

To stress the contrast between what he believed to be the difficulty and complexity of dictatorship and the ease and simplicity of democracy, Hu Shih termed the former "graduate school politics" and the latter "kindergarten politics." Britain he held up as a typical example of common-sense democracy, by means of which the British had successfully "muddled through" for centuries. Expert administration had not been extensively applied in Britain until the latter part of World War I. American democracy, in Hu Shih's view, had been "kindergarten politics" until the appearance of the brain trust in the 1930's. Both Great Britain and the United States had had a long history of democracy, and yet expert administrations had come into existence in them only in recent times. Thus, modern dictatorship was a fairly complex form of government, requiring not only the high wisdom of the supreme leader, but numerous experts and millions of technicians to augment it—a requirement that China was in no position to meet.[34]

Hu Shih's use of the term "kindergarten politics" to describe democracy raised much objection. Ting Wen-chiang (V. K. Ting, 1887–1936), a noted scientist whose independent views were well respected by the intellectuals, pointed out that democracy was not as elementary as Hu Shih represented it, especially in modern states. The successful operation of a democracy was even more difficult than that of a dictatorship. It was impossible to expect that of 400 million ignorant citizens, each one could lead himself and build a new state without direction from centralized authority. True democracy had not really been attained even in the West, where political apathy had caused power to slip into the hands of a few.[35] To Ting, government by the Kuomintang was already a sort of dictatorship. To establish a democracy in China would require a revolution and a long educational process to train the people in democratic practices. These were not possible now when China was confronted with foreign aggression on an unprecedented scale and unusual economic difficulties. The only alternative was to turn the presently ineffectual Chinese despotism into an efficient modern dictatorship. This action alone, Ting felt, could save China from utter disaster.[36]

Ting's sense of China's critical situation impelled him toward authoritarianism, which seemed to promise quick results. But short cuts are not always the best way of reaching a goal. A pragmatic reformer, Hu Shih was more interested in taking small steps in the right direction than in risking the future of the nation by precipitate measures. His claim that democracy was kindergarten politics, in which a citizen need only cast his ballot at election time,[37] referred to the minimum work required of a citizen in an elementary democracy. His critics missed the point, charging that he did not understand the complexity of governmental process in a democratic country like the United States, with its checks and balances, public criticism and control, and so forth.[38] Actually, Hu Shih's purpose was to start in China with the most simple democracy, in which both citizens and government leaders would learn by experiment. The earlier a democracy was adopted, and therefore the earlier the Chinese people were given an opportunity to learn, the sooner they would advance to a more complicated democracy.

In identifying dictatorship with expert politics, Hu Shih apparently confused politics with administration. Dictatorship is the assumption of totalitarian power by a supreme leader. It does not necessarily entail expert knowledge or even a technical advisory staff. And although a modern dictatorship needs experts, so does a modern democracy. Hu Shih, however, was not far from the truth if by experts he meant those millions of fanatic, well-trained cadres ready to obey their leader without the shadow of a question, who are indeed unique to the paraphernalia of a dictatorship.

The advocates of democracy in the *Independent Review* debate were not doctrinaires. As we have seen, in his experimental approach Hu Shih did not aim at a high-level democracy for China at the outset. Although preferring a parliamentary government, he did not insist on China's exactly duplicating the Western model; a modified legislative body, so long as it represented the people and possessed the power to change the government peacefully, was acceptable.[39]

A more eclectic point of view was that of Ch'en Chih-mai. Although he preferred democracy, Ch'en warned against attempts at setting up an ideal democracy at once.

The essence of democracy is to solve political problems by peaceful means rather than by force. In so far as the Kuomintang was willing to follow this path, it should be given a chance to carry out Sun Yat-sen's principles and to proceed gradually toward constitutionalism. It was not necessary to insist on universal suffrage since, in effect, no country in the world had yet adopted complete universal suffrage. Nor was it necessary to demand that a legislature should truly represent the people, for all parliaments inevitably reflect some special interest of society.[40]

In a joint statement of October 27, 1934, Wang Ching-wei and Chiang Kai-shek declared that "in the present environment and time, there is for China neither the necessity nor the possibility of adopting the governmental form of Italy or Russia." In December 1934, a draft constitution was submitted to the Central Executive Committee of the Kuomintang for approval. These developments discouraged the advocates of dictatorship and made it rather superfluous to argue for democracy. As a result, the debates subsided. But as constitutional rule was deferred again and again, the struggle for democracy assumed a new form. Splinter parties rose to take the place of independent thinkers as academic discussion gave way to political struggle.

The Influence of Hu Shih

In the content of his thought, Hu Shih represented the spirit of liberalism. He championed modernization and fought the ingrained traditions of prejudice and folly. He advocated liberty and democracy and insisted that men be liberated from inhuman social conventions. While he attacked without reservation the evils of traditional institutions, he had faith in the ordinary man—in his capacity for self-government and his potential as a moral being. He upheld science and maintained that practical results must be the criteria of action. In the reshaping of China's intellectual outlook, his importance cannot be exaggerated.

It is true that Hu Shih was not a great architect of philosophical systems. A pragmatist, he was, in fact, adverse to system-making. What interested him, rather, was the achievement of piecemeal improvements. But what he lacked in transcendent originality, he gained in intellectual sobriety. Tolerant and fair-minded, he reasoned carefully and wrote clearly. It was his cogent arguments and lucid style that appealed most to his young readers.

With an immense reputation as the nation's leading thinker, Hu Shih was able to criticize the government without fear. Though severe, his criticism was constructive. And while he disagreed with the Nationalist government on numerous subjects, he supported it on two important issues: resistance against Japanese aggression and war against Chinese Communism. It was for the former purpose that he agreed to serve as Chinese ambassador to the United States between 1938 and 1942, and for the latter that he fled the Chinese mainland in 1948 and returned to Taiwan in 1958 to become president of Academia Sinica, China's leading research institute.

Hu Shih's anti-Communist position caused Peking great discomfort, for though the man had fled, his influence remained. "The thought of Hu Shih," wrote a Chinese Communist historian, "ran rampant in China for more than thirty years, capturing numerous persons. Even after the Liberation, his influence remains unextinguished." It was to wipe out this influence that in 1955 the Chinese Communists staged a nationwide campaign to "liquidate the thought of Hu Shih." Numerous articles were written in response; those collected in *Criticisms of the Thought of Hu Shih* take up fully seven volumes. Much of the material is repetitious, and some of the condemnations are almost entirely concocted out of misrepresentations.

The Communist attack centered on Hu Shih's pragmatism, condemned as "subjective idealism under the name of experience." Hu Shih was accused of placing nature and society within the experience of man's perception and thereby rendering the existence of the world dependent on man's consciousness.[41] In so doing, he was committing the serious error of "denying the objectivity of truth." The pragmatic test of truth should be its effectiveness in the solution of problems in one's life; but this, according to the Communists, was "a subjective proposition with no regard to objective facts," and was in direct violation of Marxist principles—that consciousness depends on material and that the objective world exists before man's experience.[42]

Another target of the Communists' attack was Hu Shih's advocacy of evolution over revolution. This step-by-step reformism, they declared, recognized changes only in quantity and not in nature. It refused to recognize abrupt changes in history such as the establishment of the People's Republic. The Communists further accused Hu Shih of rejecting the law of inevitable historical development, of exaggerating accidental connections in his explanation of events, and of substituting subjective causes for real causes.[43]

What irked the Communists most was Hu Shih's theory of five evils which maintained that the nation's troubles were caused not by feudalism or imperialism but by the vices of the Chinese people. Hu Shih's belittling of Chinese culture also provoked violent reaction. In an intensively nationalistic vein, Communist writers charged that Hu Shih's underestimation of Chinese culture had destroyed national pride and had provided the imperialist powers with a pretext for aggression.[44]

Many of those who wrote critically of Hu Shih confessed that they had been under his influence before the Chinese Communists seized control of the mainland. But in a disavowal of their former views, they joined in the chorus of "liquidating the reactionary, bourgeois thought of Hu Shih." One cannot help wondering whether they would retract their present views if the Chinese Communist regime should topple.

Notes

CHAPTER VII. HUMAN RIGHTS AND DEMOCRACY

1. Hu Shih, "Chieh-shao wo-tzu-chi ti ssu-hsiang" (Introducing My Own Thought), in *Hu Shih wen-ts'un* (Collected Writings of Hu Shih) (Taipei: Yüan-tung, 1953), 4.4: 609.
2. See above, ch. 4.
3. In a paper read in Cornell University in 1914 when he was a student, Hu Shih thought that Henrik Ibsen, the Norwegian dramatist, represented the great spirit of individualism in the nineteenth century, with its characteristic attack on hypocrisy and oppressive conventions.
4. Hu Shih, "Wo-men tsou na-t'iao lu" (Which Road Shall We Take?), *Hsin-yüeh* (Crescent Moon), 2.10: 14 ff. (Dec. 1929).
5. Hu Shih, "Jen-ch'üan yü yüeh-fa" (Human Rights and the Provisional Constitution), *ibid.*, 2.2: 2 (April 1929).
6. Hu Shih, "Wo-men shen-mo shih-hou ts'ai k'o-yu hsien-fa" (When Will We Have a Constitution?), *ibid.*, 2,4: 7 (June 1929).
7. Lo Lung-chi, "Wo-ti pi-pu ching-kuo yü fan-kan" (My Arrest and My Reaction), *ibid.*, 3.3: 7 ff. (1930).
8. Lo Lung-chi, "Lun jen-ch'üan" (On Human Rights), in Hu Shih and others, *Jen-ch'üan lun-chih* (Collected Essays on Human Rights) (Shanghai: Hsin-yüeh, 1930), pp. 39–40.
9. *Ibid.*, p. 43.
10. *Ibid.*, p. 44.
11. See above, p. 213.
12. Lo Lung-chi, "Lun kung-ch'an chu-i" (On Communism), *Hsin-yüeh*, 3.1: 15 (March 1930).
13. Liang Shih-ch'iu, "Lun ssu-hsiang t'ung-i" (On Unity of Thought), *ibid.*, 2.3: 2 (May 1929).
14. *Ibid.*, p. 6.
15. Lo Lung-chi, "Wang Ching-wei lun ssu-hsiang t'ung-i" (Wang Ching-wei's Discussion about Unity of Thought), *ibid.*, 1.12: 4 (Feb. 1930).
16. Lo Lung-chi, "Kao ya-pi yen-lun tzu-yu che" (To Those Who Suppress Freedom of Thought), *ibid.*, 2.6–7: 9 (Sept. 1929).
17. Hu Shih, "Wo-men shen mo shih-hou ts'ai k'o-yu hsien-fa," p. 4.
18. Lo Lung-chi, "Wo-men yao shen-mo-yang ti cheng-chih chih-tu" (What Kind of Political System Do We Want?), *Hsin-yüeh*, 2.12: 1–18 (Feb. 1930).
19. Liu Chien-ch'ün, "Fu-hsing Chung-kuo chih lu" (Road to China's Rejuvenation), in *Chung-kuo ke-ming* (The Chinese Revolution), 3.4 (Feb. 1934). For an interesting, though not always reliable, account of the leadership of the Fu Hsing Society, see *Ch'un-ch'iu* (Spring and Autumn), Nos. 95–97, 100, 114 (1961).
20. Tsiang T'ing-fu later joined the Nationalist government to become, at various times, ambassador to the Soviet Union, chief Chinese delegate to the United Nations, and ambassador to the United States.

21. Tsiang T'ing-fu, "Ke-ming yü chuan-chih" (Revolution and Absolutism), *Tu-li p'ing-lun* (The Independent Review), No. 80: 2–5 (Dec. 1933).
22. Hu Shih, "Chien-kuo yü chuan-chih" (National Reconstruction and Absolutism), *ibid.*, No. 81: 3–5 (Dec. 1933).
23. Wu Ching-ch'ao, "Ke-ming yü chien-kuo" (Revolution and National Reconstruction), *ibid.*, No. 84 (Jan. 1934).
24. Hu Shih, "Chung-kuo wu tu-ts'ai ti pi-yao yü k'o-neng" (Dictatorship Is neither Necessary nor Possible in China), *ibid.*, No. 130: 3 (Dec. 1934).
25. Ch'en Chih-mai, "T'ung-i ti chi-ch'u" (The Foundations of National Unity), *ibid.*, No. 134: 25 (Jan. 1935).
26. Ch'ien Tuan-sheng, *The Government and Politics of China* (Cambridge: Harvard University Press, 1950), p. 138.
27. Ch'ien Tuan-sheng, "Min-chu cheng-chih hu? Chi-ch'üan kuo-chia hu?" (Democracy or Totalitarian State?), *Tung-fang tsa-chi* ("The Eastern Miscellany"), 31.1: 18 (Jan. 1934).
28. *Ibid.*, p. 24.
29. Cf. Chu I-sung, "Kuan-yü min-chu yü tu-ts'ai ti i-ko ta lun-chan" (The Grand Debate on Democracy and Dictatorship), *Tsai-sheng* ("The National Renaissance"), 3.4–5: 28–47 (July 1935).
30. Hu Shih, "Chung-kuo wu tu-ts'ai ti pi-yao yü k'o-neng," p. 4.
31. Hu Shih, "Ts'ung min-chu yü tu-ts'ai ti t'ao-lun li ch'iu-te i-ko kungt'ung cheng-chih hsin-yang" (To Seek a Common Political Belief from the Discussions concerning Democracy and Dictatorship), *Tu-li p'ing-lun*, No. 141: 18 (March 1935).
32. Hu Shih, "Cheng-chih kai-ke ti ta-tao" (The Great Path of Political Reform), *ibid.*, No. 163: 4–5 (Aug. 1935).
33. Hu Shih, "Chung-kuo wu tu-ts'ai ti pi-yao yü k'o-neng," p. 4.
34. *Ibid.*, pp. 4–5.
35. Ting Wen-chiang, "Min-chu cheng-chih yü tu-ts'ai cheng-chih" (Democracy and Dictatorship), *Tu-li p'ing-lun*, No. 133 (Dec. 1934).
36. Ting Wen-chiang, "Tsai-lun min-chu yü tu-ts'ai" (Further Discussion of Democracy and Dictatorship), *ibid.*, No. 137: 21–22 (Jan. 1935).
37. Hu Shih, "Ta Ting Tsai-chün lun min-chu yü tu-ts'ai" (Reply to Ting Wen-chiang on Democracy and Dictatorship), *ibid.*, No. 133 (Dec. 1934).
38. See Chu I-sung, *op cit.*, p. 12.
39. Hu Shih, "Ts'ung min-chu yü tu-ts'ai ti t'ao-lun li. . . ."
40. Ch'en Chih-mai, "Min-chu yü tu-ts'ai ti t'ao-lun" (The Discussion of Democracy and Dictatorship), *Tu-li p'ing-lun*, No. 136 (Jan. 1935).
41. *Hu Shih ssu-hsiang p'i-p'an* (Criticisms of the Thought of Hu Shih) (Peking: San-lien shu-tien, 1955), I, 55.
42. *Ibid.*, VII, 5.
43. *Ibid.*, VI, 51–59.
44. *Ibid.*, I, 109; II, 172, 180.

Chapter VIII

THE THIRD FORCE

ALONG with the Kuomintang and the Chinese Communist party, the Democratic League formed the third major political force in China in the 1940's. Organized in 1941, it was first called the Democratic Political Organizations League and consisted of five political and social organizations: the State Socialist party (later the Democratic Socialist party), the China Youth party, the Rural Reconstruction group, the Third party (later the Peasant-Labor Democratic party), and the Vocational Education Society. In 1941 the renewed armed conflict between government troops and the Chinese Communists had become a serious threat to the united front against Japan. The League called for national solidarity and rapprochement between the Kuomintang and the Chinese Communists, favoring the formation of a coalition government with all parties participating. Opposing unification by force, the League stressed democracy as the only way to unify the wills of the people. Since it was a combination of political and social groups ranging from left to right, the League during its early years refrained from taking a stand on social and economic problems, confining itself to demanding the end of one-party rule. In September 1944, the League was reorganized into the Democratic League, with individuals rather than organizations as its constituency. Many individuals without affiliation to any particular group could now join. Some of these were members of the National Salvation Association, a radical group sympathetic to the Chinese Communists.[1]

The new League reaffirmed its stand on democracy, advocating a parliamentary form of government. More significant was its declaration on economic problems, which showed unmistakable socialist influence. To appease the more conservative elements, the Democratic League upheld private property in principle, but at the same time it declared that the purpose of economic democracy was equalization of wealth and the closing of the gap between the rich and the poor. The state should safeguard the peasants' right of land utilization and limit the size of private property as a preliminary measure toward nationalization. Natural resources that could be used in the public interest should be nationalized, and enterprises of a monopolistic nature should be operated by the state. The League favored workers' participation in the management of public enterprises and of large private industries.

In 1946 the State Socialists and the China Youth party withdrew from the Democratic League to join the reorganized Nationalist government. The League, under the influence of the radical elements, sided with the Chinese Communists and boycotted the newly reorganized government as well as the Constituent Assembly, which had been summoned to adopt the constitution. Thereafter, the League turned more and more to the left until it joined entirely with the Communists in the last phase of its struggle against the Nationalists.

Among the political and social organizations of the League, the State Socialist party, the Rural Reconstructionists, and the China Youth party occupied the most important place in terms of political and ideological influences. The remaining pages of this chapter will be devoted to an examination of the ideas of these groups' leaders.

State Socialism: Carsun Chang

The State Socialist party was organized in 1932 after the Japanese invasion of Manchuria. It became the Democratic Socialist party in 1946 when it combined with the Democratic Constitutional party, a political group supported by Chinese overseas. In political origin, the State Socialist party is traceable to the Study Clique and the Progressive party, who were opposed to the Kuomintang in the early years of the Republic.[2] In doctrinal beliefs, however, it differed greatly from its early prototypes, reflecting the vast changes in the twenty years between the establishment of the Republic and the Japanese invasion of Manchuria. As declared in the platform of 1935, the party's objective was "to awaken the common consciousness of the nation, to fulfill the harmonizing function of society, and to achieve the free development of the individual—all through the strength of the state."[3]

The founder and head of the party until his resignation in 1950 was Carsun Chang (Chang Chün-mai, 1887–1969). Born at the end of the Manchu dynasty, Chang belonged to the transitional period between old and new. He was in time to enter such new institutions as the Language School in Shanghai and Kiangnan College in Nanking and was at the same time tutored in the classics, still emphasized in this period. At the age of twenty he was sent to study in Japan on a government scholarship. He was admitted to Waseda University, majoring in political science and economics. After completing his studies in Japan, he returned to China to take the national civil service examination in Peking. He passed with distinction and was appointed to the Hanlin Academy by the imperial government just before it was overthrown by the Revolution of 1911.[4]

In Japan Chang associated himself with Liang Ch'i-ch'ao, then engaged in his fierce debate with the T'ung-meng Hui over the issue of constitutional monarchy or republican democracy. During the early years of the Republic, he served as a close adviser to Liang and took part in the latter's important decisions on political strategy. As a result, Chang is generally classed as a member of Liang's clique and an opponent of the Kuomintang.

In 1918, Chang accompanied Liang on a tour of Europe. There he came under the influence of the ideas of Rudolf Eucken and Henri Bergson and decided to study philosophy. Chang, while he admired Eucken's and Bergson's life views, particularly their emphasis on spiritual strife and intuition, stopped short of subscribing to their anti-intellectualism. He attempted to redress the balance with neo-Kantism. "I like the philosophy of free will, action and change taught by Eucken and Bergson. But to know change without knowing permanence, to know movement without retirement, to know action without knowing the wisdom that differentiates between right and wrong, is like painting scenery of lofty, striking peaks without broad, level roads within the range of vision."[5] Thus Kant became Chang's favorite among Western philosophers, particularly since idealism remained the major basis of his philosophy. "If mind could be abandoned," Chang wrote, "man would have no thought and no conceptions. What then can we say about science and philosophy?"[6]

This lingering between idealism and vitalism, reason and intuition, was to a considerable extent traceable to Chang's early contact with classic Chinese philosophy. The principle of reason and the function of intuition as expounded by the Neo-Confucianists had dominated Chinese thought for centuries. The theories of Kant, Eucken, and Bergson appealed to him not so much be-

cause they were new as because they provided a logical
equivalent to his early training. In Kant he found a philosophy similar to that of Chu Hsi; in Eucken and Bergson
one that supplemented the teachings of Wang Yang-ming.
What he did not find, either in these Chinese philosophers or in their Western counterparts, was a synthesis
that reconciled the two doctrines, that combined reason
and intuition, principle and life. It was this synthesis that
Chang provided, applying it to the realm of political and
social philosophy, to the whole content of individual and
collective life, from ethics to politics to culture. Chang's
hope was to construct a unified system of political, economic, and educational thought.

In the realm of political philosophy Chang's first concern was the state. In traditional China the criterion for
determining aliens was a cultural one: a foreign race accepting Chinese culture would be considered Chinese.
As pointed out before, because of this concept the Chinese, though possessing a common language and common
customs, had not developed the concept of a nation-
state.[7] Although Chang felt the idea of a world commonwealth to be laudable, he regarded it as utopian and not
to be attained in the foreseeable future. In an age of foreign aggression and international communism, the only
means of survival was the building of a nation-state that
would become the rallying point of the people's moral
efforts and the basis for social reconstruction.[8]

To Chang the state was primarily a spiritual entity in
which everyone works for the common good. It is the
embodiment of man's sentiment, reason, and will. It is in
the state that true sentiment finds its expression in love of
country, reason in creative thought and cultural achievements, and good will in intentions toward others. But
Chang did not entirely exclude the material from his conception of the state, an eclecticism that enabled him to

reconcile authority and freedom. The material is found in the authority that constitutes the motivating power of the governmental machine, while freedom is the motivating power of human progress and as such is the operation of the mind. But, Chang argued, man's will is expressed in all social phenomena and social organizations. Juxtaposed against individual freedom, the governmental machine seems mechanical and materialized, but in reality it is built by human will to meet the needs of the objective environment. Thus each system of authority in society is permeated with human will and does not stand outside of mankind as the material world does. Since the political machine embodies human ideas, it is the product of the mind. The same is true of the economic structure, which, in so far as it is subject to political control, is never entirely material in nature. Here Chang found fault with Marxism, which views economic systems as material elements existing outside of mankind, restricting human thought and regulating politics, law, and morality. Isolating and abstracting, Marx had made politics and law the superstructures, without realizing that in actuality economic structure cannot exist apart from them. Marx's basic error, Chang concluded, was his failure to recognize the spiritual element in social phenomena.[9]

Chang devised his functional theory in an attempt to resolve the controversy over authority and freedom. By function he meant the variable relation caused when human will enters the objective environment. Man's application of reason to the objective environment results in the expression of the human spirit and the formation of social phenomena. Economic, political, and legal phenomena are all developments of the functional relation; therefore, he reasoned, there should be no distinction between the superstructure and the basic structure. The three phenomena are simply the three dimensions of the basic functional relation, although they appear to be three machines after they have become formalized. Each institutional machine is the rule or path through which mankind advances, providing orderliness and regularity. Although it appears in a material form and possesses objective authority, it is in fact formulated by the human will, and although from the standpoint of authority human society appears to be a machine of determinism, from the standpoint of human spirit it is free in operation. In claiming historical inevitability, Chang wrote, the Marxists "recognize the materialized machine which they isolate but fail to recognize the human will."[10]

Chang's functional theory viewed the universe from two perspectives: from its inner nature or substance and from its outside activity or function. From the standpoint of function, the world shows change; from the standpoint of substance, it signifies permanence. Change and permanence are the two ultimate principles that explain any phenomenon of the universe. The two supplement each other; it is only with permanence that change can be shown, and only with change that permanence can be established.

Thus to Chang the state is founded on both reason and experience. As a public institution, it has universality and permanence, underlaid by reason. In addition to its *raison d'être,* the state possesses also "ether" (*ch'i*) or "corporeal matter" (*chih*)—both terms taken from the Neo-Confucianists. While "ether" changes and displays variety, "reason" remains constant and preserves unity. Reason, with its quality of harmonizing, has its own nature which is more than the sum total of things. Similarly, the state is not the sum total of individuals. It transcends its individual members and achieves its own harmony; it permeates the individuals that make it up and represents their generality. The generality or public nature of man-

kind thus becomes the rational basis of the state. And the
state in turn comes to possess the qualities of universality and permanence that constitute its own nature.[11]

But, according to Chang, the state also has its practicality, that is to say, its empirical basis. Its performance
is bound to vary with actual social conditions. Various
social groups and elements, and even the level of civilization, are all important factors in determining the phenomena of the state. Thus the performance of a state under
absolutism is different from that under capitalism. But
though a state's performance and functions—that is, its
practicality—vary, its nature as a public instrument remains
unchanged for all eras. Ignorance of this principle, Chang
argued, led Marx to the erroneous conclusion that the
state will wither away when there is no longer a confrontation between classes:

From the permanence of the state we can explain its authority
and sovereignty; from its changeability we can understand its
adaptability to facts, its permission of freedom, and its practicality which makes it possible constantly to reconstruct itself.
From the viewpoint of permanence, the state is rational; from
the viewpoint of changeability, the state is practical.[12]

Although he attempted to establish a permanent basis
for the state, Chang had no intention of declaring its
perfectibility. He aimed rather at reconciling the contradictions inherent in the concept of state, that is, authority
and freedom, permanence and changeability, will and environment. His sources of inspiration, as we have seen,
were varied. Chang utilized not only Kant's idealism, Euck-
en's inward unity, and Bergson's dynamic process, but
Whitehead's functionalism, and, last but not least important, the philosophy of reason of the Neo-Confucianists.
His system can truly claim to be a synthesis of old and
new, of East and West.

Viewing both authority and freedom as indispensable to the state, Chang saw them as operating in separate spheres of activity: in administrative affairs, the state should have enough authority to ensure efficiency and speedy action; in social and cultural affairs, the people should have the freedom to develop in different directions. The question is whether administrative matters can always be separated from social and cultural affairs. Chang gave no detailed answer but did specify that individual freedom should not be interfered with in the realm of thought and creative work. Recognizing the importance of authority to a modern government, he insisted that authority implied responsibility and must be exercised in accordance with law. But freedom, like authority, must also be exercised in the interest of the state and of the people as a whole. In Chang's view, authority and freedom are not mutually opposed but supplement each other. Only through freedom can people develop their potential, and it is in their moral and intellectual development that the source of the state's strength lies.[13]

Chang proposed a new form of government that would merge the advantages of both dictatorship and democracy, that would combine power and effectiveness with freedom, without which culture is impossible. While a political system based on force might achieve glorious results within a short time, it could hardly be expected to continue peacefully for a hundred years. For stability and duration a democracy was far preferable.[14] The question was how to modify democracy so as to incorporate the advantages of a dictatorship.

The modified democracy proposed by Chang was a "national government" in which all political parties would participate. A National Assembly, elected by the people, would select a number of executive councilors who would constitute the national government, and it would pass a

five-year administrative program, which the Executive
Council would carry out but could not change. The National Assembly would determine the budget and enact
law, but would have no power to force the resignation of
the Executive Council by a vote of no confidence. Thus
the government would enjoy a greater measure of stability than the cabinet. But it would not be entirely beyond
the control of the National Assembly, since the administrative program would be examined every year—or at a
certain stage of the program—by the National Assembly or
some citizen organization to see whether it was being satis-
factorily implemented. If the work of a ministry fell short
of the goal of a program, the executive councilor in charge
of the ministry would resign, that is, if the National Assembly so resolved.[15]

Chang's scheme was inspired by the coalition governments in Britain and France during World War I, and it
assumed complete cooperation between various political
parties. While unanimity is possible in time of war or
grave crisis, political parties inevitably resume their rivalry once a crisis has passed. The five-year plan was
also based on the assumption that parties would agree to
the basic policies embodied in it. Although such agreement may exist at the outset, it is unlikely that it can last
for five years. The rise of an unforeseen situation or of a
controversial issue can easily split the coalition. Chang's
syncretic scheme, it would seem, is more ideal than practical.

In economics, Chang's syncretism sought to combine
the advantages of socialism with those of capitalism. Unlike Sun Yat-sen, Chang was rather late in showing interest in socialism. It was not until after World War I
that he began to discuss socialism in the magazine *Emancipation and Reconstruction* (*Chieh-fang Yü Kai-tsao*).[16]
He was apparently impressed by the "mixed economy"

advocated by such German Social Democrats as Philipp
Scheidemann, whom he met in Berlin in 1919.[17] Chang
rejected Marxism for its violence and class struggle as
well as for its dialectical materialism and dictatorship, and
he voiced opposition to Sun's cooperation with the Soviet
Union in 1923.[18] But he recognized the importance of
the problem of social justice and deplored capitalistic
laissez faire. The problem was how to attain social justice
for the poor without sacrificing individual freedom. Chang
felt the solution lay in democratic socialism.[19]

Another major objective in Chang's socioeconomic
program was the attainment of self-sufficiency. In a study
of Chinese customhouse statistics, Chang found that
China imported not only machines and weapons, but also
such necessities as food and clothing. In the interest of
national independence, self-sufficiency had to be immediately achieved in these latter areas and in basic industries
such as steel, electric power, and chemicals. Since private
enterprise in China, in the areas of both capital and technology, was weak, Chang proposed that the state be called
in to direct China's economic development.[20]

Chang recommended a planned economy in which the
state would play an important role. His scheme, while it al-
lotted a wide scope to public enterprise, also permitted
the existence of private ownership. The distinction he
made was as follows: if an industry could be managed
privately without detriment to the national interest, it
would be so operated; otherwise, it would be operated by
the state. Small businesses, from art shops to grocery
stores, could be privately owned or operated as cooperatives. Public utilities, such as electric power and local
transportation, should be run by public corporations in the
various localities. Light industries, such as textile mills,
could be privately owned, provided they were maintained
under state supervision. All national communications,

such as railroads and telegraphs; national resources, such
as mining and water resources; and heavy industries, such
as steel plants, should be state-operated.[21]

The state would, through its experts, draw up a national
economic plan determining the proportion of public to
private enterprises, allocating capital and technical personnel to the industrial and agricultural sectors, and assigning to individual industries priorities in regard to their
establishment and expansion. Private property would not
be confiscated. But while individuals would be permitted
to retain ownership of their enterprises, their earnings
would be limited to a maximum of 8–10 percent. Any
surplus would be returned to the state. Chang believed that
in this manner social justice could be achieved without the
sweeping Marxist nationalization of productive instruments. The nation's economic development would be
planned and directed without totalitarian regimentation.[22]

Like many of his contemporaries Chang saw a close relation between Chinese politics and culture. Political and
economic reconstruction depended on the transformation
of the people's philosophy of life, which would in turn
give rise to the new culture. "With the new culture there
necessarily will be political and economic reconstruction;
without it political and economic reconstruction will be
like trees without roots, waters without sources."[23] Here,
of course, Chang disagreed with Marxism, which maintains that productive forces are the determining factors in
political and economic changes. For Chang culture consisted of spiritual and material elements, but it is the mind
that shapes the material.

Chang recognized serious defects in China's old culture. In politics he saw the tradition of absolute monarchy,
unopposed by an aristocracy, as having led to subservience, ignorance, and lack of public spirit. From the
extended-family unit had arisen such undesirable traits as

dependence, jealousy, and insincerity. In learning, the complexities of the written language and the lack of logical development had inclined scholars toward philological investigation and textual comparison, which had restricted free thinking and obstructed the building up of great philosophical systems. And their concern with human relations had led Chinese thinkers to neglect the study of nature. "They emphasize good, but not truth."[24]

Chang recognized the weaknesses in the intellectual and moral tradition of Chinese civilization. Civilization "is a product of time—whatever fits the time is superior; whatever does not is inferior."[25] Chang considered the classical learning of the Han dynasty (206 B.C.–A.D. 219) and the Neo-Confucianism of the Sung dynasty (960–1276), both of which persisted in China until modern times, to be an unsuitable spiritual basis for modern political, social, and intellectual development.[26] It is true that in his *Third Force in China* he asserted that the roots of democracy are found in Chinese history, that socialist ideas are not lacking in traditional Chinese political thought, and that "the revival of philosophical and scientific thought in Europe, as expressed in terms of Rationalism, Natural Rights, and Natural Law, was inspired to a great extent by the study of Chinese Classics,"[27] but this was written for Americans at a time when, in order to win their support in the struggle against Chinese Communism, it was necessary to convince them that democracy was not impossible in China. Earlier, in a more scholarly mood, he was much less positive in his evaluation. In a 1935 address to the Chinese people, Chang said: "From Confucius and Mencius to the Neo-Confucianists of the Sung and Ming dynasties, emphasis has been upon moral principles. The spirit of modern government is democracy, which cannot be found in Chinese classics. As to learning, the modern methods of deduction and induction are also not found in

Chinese classics. Rather than lingering on the graves of the ancients, we might as well frankly recognize that our future culture must be created anew."[28]

To create anew, for Chang, was to absorb the best of Western culture to make up what was wanting in China. Although imitation might be necessary at the first stage, creation—a synthesis of old and new, of West and East— was the ultimate aim. China had not only to borrow but to digest what was borrowed from others. She must not copy the superficial, but absorb the essence, the spirit, of Western culture. On the other hand, it was essential that she not forget herself. In borrowing from the West, she must select what she most needed, what was best suited to her national traits, reformed as they might be. She should not abandon her ancients indiscriminately, but should grasp the essence of their teachings and select what was applicable to the modern age. In short, she must find herself and have her own point of view. Only then would she have a standard of selection and a basis for synthetic creation.[29]

Chang was confident that China was capable of the great synthesis. Had not China, after adopting Buddhism from India, created new sects of its own? And was it not the philosophers of the Sung dynasty who, stimulated and awakened by Buddhism, developed Neo-Confucianism? These were reconstructions on a large scale. If the Chinese had done it in the past, there was no reason why they could not do it again with regard to Western culture. China lacked only confidence. Chang ransacked Chinese history for heroes who would serve as sources of inspiration, which led him sometimes to an extreme glorification of Chinese culture that stood in sharp contrast to his criticism of its inadequacy.[30]

Chang saw cultural reconstruction as a job for the intellectuals. He established a number of institutes, notably the Hsüeh Hai Institute in Canton in 1935 and the National Culture Institute in Yunnan in 1939, for the training of leaders. These were small schools with carefully selected students. Chang hoped that through close teacher-student contact, with special emphasis upon self-cultivation and living experience, a leadership could be formed and trained to assume responsibility in cultural, political, and social reconstruction.[31]

The masses Chang did not think capable of wise government. They were too preoccupied with making a living to participate in national politics, naturally viewing political issues from the standpoint of special interest, and it was impossible to expect them to understand the highly complicated relationships between various interests.[32] Government by the elite was therefore unavoidable, although its duty was to work in the people's best interest.

Chang deplored any mass movement that served merely as a political instrument for the advantage of certain parties or groups. People should help one another to attain adequate knowledge and moral living through love, education, and care. It was only once they had gained personal independence and were capable of sound judgment that their participation in politics would be useful.[33] Still, successful government is governed by able leaders. "A great task requires a great man." According to Chang, the great leader must be good in health, superior in intellect, and rigorous in morality. He must be able to synthesize old and new, to shape the course of action, and to lead all parties and groups toward the common goal. This idea is reminiscent of Confucius' government by superior men, but is also traceable to Plato's ideal that the philosophers are to rule the state. In actuality, it is a synthesis of both, with new specifications that were Chang's own.

The grand synthesis Chang developed was a remarkable achievement, the more so since it was the most comprehensive system ever attempted by contemporary Chinese thinkers. But in spite of his party's vigorous attempts at propagation, its influence was quite limited. A philosophical interpretation based on reason was too metaphysical for an age of war and revolution in which science and practical results were valued. Its spiritual emphasis was hardly appealing to a nation badly lacking in material development. His attempts at syncretism, though they emphasized conscious creation, were often mistaken for a conservatism unworthy of the revolutionary age. And his theory of leadership, with its condescending attitude toward the masses, could hardly contribute to its popularity. Of greater import was the political situation of the time in which the small parties could hardly compete with the major ones. "The distinctive importance of culture," wrote Chang, "lies not in its immediate success, but in its permanent contributions to mankind."[34] Chang's comprehensive system was no doubt intended by him to be a permanent contribution to Chinese culture.

Chang Tung-sun: Reason and Society

A coleader of the Democratic Socialist party, Chang Tung-sun (1886–) shared much in common with Carsun Chang. Both were interested in pure philosophy and both were involved in politics without relinquishing speculative pursuits. After a period of study in Japan, Tung-sun returned to China about the time that the Chinese Republic was established. He served as a secretary in the Nanking provisional government in 1911–1912, and in 1916 became secretary-general of the Chinese Senate. Though closely associated with Liang Ch'i-ch'ao and the Progressive party, he maintained his independent thinking. He did not hesitate to oppose Liang's enlightened despotism or his pessimistic view that it was futile to discuss government systems. In the early years of the Republic, Tung-sun advocated a democratic government that was self-limiting and would promote the people's liberty and moral development.[35] In view of China's despotic tradition and bureaucratic tendencies, he proposed that public opinion and opposition parties be strengthened as agencies capable of checking government power.[36]

During the period of the May Fourth Movement, Tung-sun, like many other Chinese thinkers, became actively interested in socialism. He edited the journal *Emancipation and Reconstruction* in Shanghai and had constant contact with Ch'en Tu-hsiu. But when the Comintern representative Voitinsky proposed the organization of the Chinese Communist party, he was opposed to the idea. He desisted from attending meetings at Ch'en's house and did not join the party when it was finally formed.[37]

At that time, Tung-sun considered socialism the most progressive *Weltanschauung* for the social reconstruction of China. But though he acknowledged Marxism's scientific basis, he refused to regard Marxism as socialism's ultimate principle. To him, socialism represented not a rigid program of material reconstruction, but a "general direction" of social development which stressed spiritual and moral reformation as prerequisites of material and economic progress. Since socialism aimed toward spiritual liberation and world reformation, it was not the exclusive property of any class, not even the proletariat; rather it had to be achieved by all classes working together.[38]

This idealistic view of socialism as a new civilization whose classes all worked together was the major reason Tung-sun opposed the formation of the Chinese Communist party, which, under the guidance of the Russian Communists, naturally followed the class struggle orientation. The view that China was not industrially developed and therefore unsuitable for class struggle persisted in Tung-sun up to his debates with Ch'en Tu-hsiu in 1921. Tung-sun agreed with Ch'en that socialism was inevitable, but he insisted that its advent must wait until the rise of the proletariat. The China of the 1920's, economically under-developed, had no proletariat to speak of. It would take a long time to attain socialism. And when it came, it would not necessarily take the form of Communism. He felt, there-fore, that the Chinese should join with other nations in developing a more perfect socialism for the future world.[39]

After a period of active journalism, Tung-sun turned to education. In 1929 he joined Yenching University, where he taught philosophy until 1941 when the university was closed by the Japanese. At Yenching he led a serene academic life, but his concern with national problems led him to politics before long. In 1931 he formed with Carsun Chang the State Socialist party because, as an advocate of democracy, he could not let the Kuomintang's one-party rule go unchallenged. The two men agreed that as soon as the Kuomintang ended its dictatorship, their party would be dissolved.[40]

Tung-sun criticized the Chinese Communists' rigid ap-plication of the Marxist formula to China in a number of articles published in the 1930's. Maintaining that the Chi-nese had failed to develop a class consciousness, he con-tinued to question the practicability of basing a political movement on any single class.[41] He was equally critical of the Kuomintang's concept of "political tutelage," which he denounced as self-contradictory.[42]

When the Sino-Japanese War broke out in 1937, Pei-ping fell into the hands of the Japanese. The Nationalist forces were driven out of North China, but Chinese Com-munist guerrillas managed to infiltrate the occupied area. Tung-sun was in contact with the Communist guerrillas at this time. Perhaps this episode was the beginning of his sympathy with the Chinese Communists, although he did not for a moment give up his faith in democracy. In 1941, immediately after the outbreak of the Pacific war, he was arrested by the Japanese for his anti-Japanese activities. Imprisoned for six months, he three times attempted suicide. A man of delicate health but quick temper, he preferred dying to suffering a lingering existence and endless humiliation at the hands of the Japanese. A philosopher, he felt, should have no fear of death, and, like Socrates, should be willing to find out what it is. But Tung-sun found that while it was not easy to live, it was even more difficult to die, and though his mind wanted to die, his body, with its built-in mechanism of self-preservation, refused to obey. The experience convinced him that dualism, of which he had formerly disapproved, was not, after all, without foundation.[43]

It was not until after World War II, between 1946 and 1948, that Tung-sun published his four books summing up his views on politics and culture. *Knowledge and Culture*, published in 1946, was written in 1940. Largely devoted to the discussion of the elements of knowledge, the work also deals with the relationship between philosophy and culture. The other three works deal with the interaction of thought and society, the rational basis of democracy, and the significance of democracy and socialism.[44] In social organization Tung-sun saw the simultaneous existence of two tendencies: social antagonism arising from the division of classes and interests, and social integrity based on the interdependence of the various classes and groups. When social conflicts greatly increase and the centrifugal tendencies become too strong, moralists, or idealistic enthusiasts, arise to teach new principles of social integrity in their attempt to raise society to a higher level. While their ideas may be called utopian—for social change is necessarily shaped by actual conditions—that is not to say that utopian ideas are not important in social change.[45]

For Tung-sun, then, utopia and ideology differ only in degree. He disagreed with the Marxist belief that ideology represents the interests of a certain social class. As a basis of a political movement, ideology is utopian thought taken over by "cunning" leaders to promote the interests of a certain class or group. Marxists confuse idealists, who create utopian thought, with cunning leaders, who use it for practical purposes. In their confusion, Marxists accuse original thinkers and cunning politicians alike of deceiving the people.

Tung-sun believed that one's thought is determined by one's situation. But situation, he pointed out, is different from social class. One's situation is one's sociocultural environment, which consists not only of class interest but also of such elements as institutions, customs, language, and the spirit of the age. Situation is not an isolated, permanent fact, but rather a developing condition, embracing not only the past but also the future. For this reason the Chinese proletariat would not necessarily think in the same way that the Indian workers do. While class interest is often reflected in man's thought, such reflection, according to Tung-sun, is not inevitable, for the reason that the influence of social structure on thought is more pronounced than that of class interest; men think in certain categories, or frames of thought, which are shaped by different social patterns.[46]

Taking such a broad view of social situation, it was natural that Tung-sun considered Marx's historicism inadequate. Against the Marxian materialistic interpretation of history he offered a "technical interpretation," in which implements are the determining factors in historical development. One's mode of social life changes with the appearance of new implements invented to meet practical needs. Essential implements are of two kinds: those used in production and those used for defense purposes. Thus Tung-sun recognized the importance of the economic factor, but not to the exclusion of other factors; his emphasis upon the contributions of inventors is significant, as it introduced the human factor in social change, and pointed up intelligence and knowledge as fundamental forces in historical development.

For Tung-sun, reason is the basic determinant of social development; the conquest of nature, the breaking up of customs, the overthrowing of cultural inhibitions—all depend on it. His technical interpretation is, indeed, an intellectual interpretation. Historical development he divided into three stages. The first stage is characterized by the powerful dominance of natural forces under whose influence primitive men, confronted by the constant threat of death, seek salvation by invoking the aid of the supernatural. Their intelligence in this phase is devoted to the creation of superstitions, magic, and religions. The second stage is characterized by severe clashes between man and man as each struggles to make a living. Intelligence in this phase is directed toward the sole objective of getting ahead, and cunning, deceit, and cruelty arise, with the result that the powerful oppress the weak, the wealthy exploit the poor, and the clever deceive the ignorant. But all is not darkness in this pathetic society, for in this period intelligence, spurred on by living needs, also breaks away from superstition and magic and applies its power to science and technology. The resultant invention of machinery represents a great leap forward in augmenting material supplies and raising the standard of living. But if industrialism is essential to the well-being of the people, capitalism is exploitation of the many by the few. It is in the third stage of historical development that reason will reign, as intelligence is devoted to the building of a rational and just society.[47]

Tung-sun's intellectual interpretation was not, however, wholly idealistic in nature; though intended to replace Marx's materialistic historicism, it did not discount material factors. Tung-sun realized that human intelligence develops in a material environment. His theory gave full recognition to the importance of the instruments of production and defense in historical development. But though he considered intelligence to be the basic element in human progress, and reason its very spirit, his was an attempt to reconcile mind with material, and reason with environment.

To Tung-sun, a rational society is a social democracy established within a nation-state. Democracy he conceived as a civilization, not merely a system of government; democracy is an attitude toward life and a mode of thinking. As the spirit of the people, it grows only in nation-states, since only among people having national consciousness can a general will be formed.

Tung-sun took his concept of general will from Rousseau. Admitting that the theory of people's consent is inaccurate in actual historical fact, he insisted that it is still the only possible rational explanation of government. In an attempt to reconcile Rousseau and Bentham, Tung-sun equated common good with general happiness and saw in its pursuit the realization of the general will. Democracy's ultimate goal is the attainment of general happiness, i.e., happiness for everyone, an ideal that should never be forgotten, even though it may not be attained in the immediate future. Bentham's "happiness of the greatest number" is a practical formula good for a certain stage of democratic development; it must not be construed to mean that the happiness of the minority should be sacrificed.[48]

For Tung-sun, then, democracy is the only rational system; it accords with human nature and makes social progress possible. It stands for liberty and equality which, founded on reason, contribute to the fulfillment of one's own personality and that of others. Democracy is a new civilization sustained by moral forces, and, conversely, it raises the moral level of the individual by liberating his efforts for the common good.[49]

One may ask how Tung-sun's concept of democracy fit in with Chinese culture. Tung-sun saw his ideas as being rooted in Chinese tradition, which roots he felt could be strengthened to promote democracy. He admitted that his concept of personality as one of democracy's cornerstones was a Western one; in Chinese society the ethical emphasis fell upon human relations. In the West the concept of personality had arisen out of self-consciousness, which in China was submerged in the concept of unity—"man and nature are one"—and in the hierarchy of the family. Nevertheless Chinese tradition did recognize the value of the individual and had due regard for personal dignity, and it was this tradition, Tung-sun maintained, that could be developed and brought close to the Western concept of personality.[50]

Freedom was another basic tenet of Tung-sun's democracy that had no basis in Chinese tradition. But Tung-sun sought its equivalent in the Chinese concept of *tzu-te,* or self-fulfillment, which is attained when one follows one's nature and lives in harmony with reason. According to this notion, the supreme state of contentment and freedom is reached when one is in complete possession of oneself, or as Mencius says, "when all things are complete in us." *Tzu-te* is, of course, a precept of self-cultivation rather than a civil right safeguarded by law. But it was Tung-sun's belief that on the basis of this spiritual freedom it would not be difficult to establish institutional freedom. A close understanding of the spirit of Western democracy and the development of basic related Chinese concepts were for him the keys to institutional modernization.

Democracy as a rational society, according to Tung-sun, is a moral order. Although morals change with the times, the basic principles of morality remain the same. With Kant, he held that morality is self-limitation practiced by rational beings, but denied that this conception was based on subjective idealism, maintaining that morality arises from the objective necessity of group living. Morality, Tung-sun argued, plays a major role in shaping man and society, as witnessed by the fact that historical disasters are often traceable to the moral perversions of political leaders. Individual habits, moreover, will not be corrected automatically by a change in economic conditions but must be reformed by individual efforts.[51] In this respect Tung-sun held to the Chinese belief in moral cultivation, particularly in the tradition of the Neo-Confucianists of the Sung and Ming dynasties.

For Tung-sun, true democracy was necessarily socialistic, just as true socialism was necessarily democratic; the two were intermingled. Unless social justice is realized in the distribution of wealth, liberty and equality, on which democracy is based, are mirages. But at the same time democracy is needed to remedy such evils of socialism as bureaucratic despotism. Tung-sun believed that socialism, like democracy, was a moralistic rather than a materialistic order. Only in socialism, he argued, could a high level of morality be attained; the elevation of one's personality proceeds from treating others as equals.[52]

Reason required that socialist democracy be established by peaceful means, and it was Tung-sun's belief that violent revolution only upsets the harmony and balance of a rational society, exacerbating reaction and destruction, which actually set back progress. Although not absolutely opposed to revolution, he felt that true progress lay in construction. Revolution may be justified by practical necessities, but it is by no means an indispensable process. At a time when the Communists were proclaiming revolution to be universal, Tung-sun warned that it was not an end in itself, and that all efforts should be made to avoid permanent revolution. Class struggle only worked against freedom and democracy. "So far as struggle continues, there will be no peace; without peace there will be no construction; without construction there will be no freedom and democracy."[53]

Among modern Chinese political thinkers Chang Tung-sun stands foremost as a speculative philosopher. Although frequently called upon to suggest practical solutions in the course of his participation in politics, he always cleaved to the abstract. It was his profound conviction that reason guides human conduct and constitutes the only foundation of a rational society. He recognized, however, the weaknesses of idealism and ingeniously attempted to bolster his abstractions with statements on the importance of material environment to social development. Tung-sun's originality lies in his attempt to build a philosophical system in which reason and environment each had its appropriate place.

The sources of Tung-sun's philosophy are various and complex. The emphasis upon reason is traceable to the Neo-Confucianists, as well as to the theories of Spinoza and Kant, with which he was thoroughly conversant. He owed much to Marxist theory in his recognition of economic factors, but his broad view of environment was derived from a critical study of modern sociological works ranging from Gumplowicz to Mannheim. His attempt to bring utopia down to earth has historical as well as sociological precedents.

Tung-sun's profound understanding of Chinese and Western philosophies placed him in a unique position to make comparisons and seek a synthesis. His original contribution lay in his approach to the problem of synthesis not through a superficial examination of social traits and institutions, but through analyzing the basic concepts of the two civilizations. He was thereby in a position to point up the truly significant similarities and differences between them. Whether or not one agrees with him that Chinese concepts could be developed to meet the demands of democracy and socialism, his particular approach opened a new avenue to the understanding of Chinese and Western cultures.

Like his long-time friend Carsun Chang, Chang Tung-sun began his public career in close association with Liang Ch'i-ch'ao. A younger man than Liang, he received more exposure to the radical developments of the twentieth century, and his avid reading enabled him to keep up with the times. Still, he belonged as much to the older generation as to the new, and thus the influence of syncretic reformism upon his thought is unmistakable. While realizing the full impact of China's invasion by Western civilization, Tung-sun still felt Chinese tradition and culture to be far from extinct. His was an emphasis upon the development of the Confucian spirit to bring it close to Western concepts.

Both Carsun Chang and Chang Tung-sun were fundamentally philosophers of reason. But while Carsun Chang emphasized will and intuition, Tung-sun placed importance on environment and society. In their political thought, the former tended toward nationalism and the latter toward socialism, albeit a socialism merged with democracy and purged of violence and extremism—a rational restraint that reminds one of the moderation found in Confucianism.

Liang Sou-ming: Chinese Culture and
Rural Reconstruction

Liang Sou-ming was born in Peking in 1893, of a scholarly family which had migrated from Kweilin, Kwangsi. His grandfather and father had served as government officials under the Ch'ing dynasty. But the family was never very rich, and in Liang's father's time, they lived rather modestly. Liang learned to read at the age of six. His father, a believer in K'ang Yu-wei's civil service reform, decided to educate his son in the new way. Thus Liang was not required, as other boys, to recite Confucian classics, but rather read such new books as *Geography In Rhyme*.[51] Later, when he read the classics at a more mature age and with a fresh mind, he was better able to reflect on their significance.

Probably because of ill health Liang did not do well in elementary school, but he made good progress in high school, where he is known to have read progressive magazines and showed independent thinking in his compositions. After graduating from high school (1911), he served as an editor of the *Minkuo Pao,* a republican journal. He was one of the few eminent writers in contemporary China who did not receive a college education. He never studied abroad, and because of his deficiency in English he usually relied on Chinese translations of foreign works. This inability made it difficult for him to have any thorough knowledge of the West, though it did contribute to his faith in Chinese teachings.

Like many young men of his time, Liang took part in the Chinese Revolution of 1911, and was thus associated with the T'ung-meng Hui. But he was also an admirer of Liang Ch'i-ch'ao and often visited the office of the Democratic party. He soon became disillusioned with party politics, however, and a brief dabbling in socialism got him no-where. Frustrated by politics and distressed at the sufferings of the people living in conditions of poverty and brutality, Liang Sou-ming sought salvation in Buddhism, the teachings of which, especially those of the Wei-shih (or Idealist) school, he studied assiduously from 1913 to 1921. This grounding was to prove useful when he came to expound Confucianism shortly afterward.

Liang took up an extensive reading of the Confucian classics in 1916–1917, but not until four years later did he actually adopt its doctrine. Religion in China was not an exclusive affair, and it was not unusual for a Confucian scholar to be deeply involved in Buddhism. But in Liang's case the break was a sharp one. He adhered firmly to Confucianism from that time on. But he also offered a new interpretation of it that was to give it fresh life.

The reasons Liang finally adopted Confucianism are not clear. We do know that in 1918 his father committed suicide as a protest against the new trend toward Westernization. A scholar of the Confucian school, the old man had recognized the wisdom of the reforms proposed by K'ang Yu-wei in 1898, but he could not bear the complete abandonment of Confucian virtues now advocated by the new thinkers,[55] and he had opposed constitutional government in 1912. Liang's belief in Buddhism had grieved his father greatly. Inheriting his father's courage and serious purpose, Liang felt deeply repentant that his unorthodoxy had made the old man so unhappy, and it was probably this remorse that led him to Confucianism.[56]

The first fruit of this return to Confucianism was the publication in 1922 of *Eastern and Western Civilizations and Their Philosophies*. Liang's intention in this work was to counteract the effect of the New Culture Movement. The book deals with the basic factors that shape the world's major cultures. Defining culture as a nation's mode of living, and life as the continuous exertion of the will, Liang contended that the differences between the East and West sprang from their diverse attitudes toward life. He recognized three different tendencies in the history of the world's cultural development: (1) to go forward, that is, to strive after the things one wants, to satisfy one's desires by attacking the problem and changing the situation; (2) to look inward, that is, to achieve harmony and equilibrium in the self by moderating one's desires and making the best of the situation in which one finds oneself; (3) to go backward, that is, to get away from life, or to solve all problems by abolishing life itself. Occidentals had taken the first path, especially since the Renaissance, and their lives had assumed the form of strife. They had conquered nature and fought for their rights. They had greatly advanced materially and had laid the foundations of liberty and equality; but in so doing they had accentuated the confrontation between man and man. If Westerners had reaped the fruit of intellectual development, they suffered from spiritual discord and social unrest.

The Chinese had taken the second path. They valued inward satisfaction and de-emphasized material enjoyment. They lived in harmony with nature rather than trying to conquer it. They had therefore lagged behind in technology and industry, and because they did not care about struggle and liberation, they had also failed to develop democracy.

The Indians had taken the third path, with the result that religion flourished at the expense of material and social developments. Liang, formerly Buddhism's votary, now considered the predominance of religion in India a spiritual abnormality.[57]

In the Confucian conception of life Liang saw Chinese culture's most precious heritage. Confucius had glorified life and viewed it as altogether a good thing. The notion that life grows in accordance with the principle of nature appealed to Liang. With Mencius, he held that human nature is good. All men are born with "intuitive ability," or the innate capacity for good, and with "intuitive knowledge," the innate sense of right and wrong. Intellectualization he distrusted, because it led to calculation and the violation of human feelings. To respond according to intuition was, on the other hand, a natural fulfillment, resulting in a good life, or "a life that is just right." A life that is just right is not to be attained by the application of law and force, for these hamper the inward spring of life and upset the natural equilibrium.[58]

Liang saw the Confucian way of life as being far from passive. The Confucian virtue *jen,* or humanity, denoted a state of strength and liveliness. The ideal Confucian life was therefore active, and at the same time inwardly peaceful. Its vigor could not be exhausted by worries about loss and gain, or vitiated by selfish desires.

The West, Liang believed, had reached the stage in which the Confucian way of life could benefit it. In its forward-looking attitude the West had directed itself only toward the search for material progress, completely abandoning the pursuit of inward perfection. It should now veer away from the narrow, oppressive world view that intellectualization had imposed upon it. Although Liang wanted China to learn from the West how to develop her economy and strengthen her national defenses, and in particular to expand her scientific and democratic knowledge, he warned against intellectualization. Since a large part of the world was fast approaching a stage that necessitated a more humane conduct, Liang felt it incumbent upon the Chinese to renew the Confucian attitude toward life.[59]

Liang's buoyant confidence in the future of Confucianism was encouraged by the views of contemporary Western thinkers, particularly Bertand Russell and John Dewey who, visiting China in the early 1920's, had expressed admiration for Chinese culture and suggested a synthesis between East and West. Like Carsun Chang he was influenced by Rudolf Eucken, who stressed a spiritual life in which man lives in harmony with nature, and by Henri Bergson, who offered a theory of life emphasizing the role of intuition. Russell, too, had pointed out that the development of the intellect at the expense of both instinct and spirit may produce a curious inhumanity and cynicism. Basically, however, Liang was a Confucianist of the school of Mencius and Wang Yang-ming. His three-path cultural development was too neat a division to encompass the vast complexities of world culture. It can, for example, easily be argued that Western civilization is not wholly materialistic and that the Chinese did not entirely disregard their objective environment. Religion and morality, moreover, are to some extent shared by all mankind. But Liang was looking for the unique characteristics of each major type of culture. The singling out of certain major features of a civilization may be considered inadequate by a careful scholar, but it is necessary for a philosopher who must build his system on trends and essentials. A philosopher, Liang once said, is by nature an extremist, for it is only by grasping a central point and developing it to the utmost that he can hope to evolve a system.[60]

The central emphasis in Liang's cultural theory was a people's attitude toward life, which he considered to be the foundation of its culture. The weakness of this theory is apparent: it fails to give adequate recognition to the objective environment and material forces that undoubtedly play their role in cultural development. On the other hand, by focusing on the mentality of the people, Liang called attention to a factor often ignored by his contemporaries.

His interpretation gave Confucianism a new vigor badly needed at the time. Under the attacks of the New Culture Movement, Confucianism had been in retreat, and attempts to defend it had been ineffectual. Liang's exposition turned a fresh stream of thought on stock notions, reviving Confucianism not as a prop for dead institutions but as an outlook that promised a vigorous, cheerful life to the Chinese people.

In 1949, Liang completed his book *The Essentials of Chinese Culture.* In it he adhered to the thesis of his earlier work, that China differed from the West in having taken a divergent road in her cultural development. But the focus of his study now shifted. Where his earlier volume is devoted to an explanation of the Confucian view of life, the later one deals with the nature of Chinese society. China, in its truly traditional form, declared Liang, is an ethical society. It emerges from the clan but is founded on ethical relations.[61]

Ethical relations develop from feelings and affections, Liang stated; they stress moral obligations assumed by each person toward people on all sides. This web of relations, connecting and binding one individual to another, constitutes group life. But the bonds forming this sort of group life differ from the boundaries and confrontations that characterize Western organizational life. Liang attributed China's lack of large organizations to her indifference to structured religion, a major institution in the West. Conceding that China, too, had its organizations, Liang thought that for the most part Chinese life centered around the family, while Western life revolved around organizations.

Liang ascribed the credit for transforming China from a clan-based society to an ethical-based society to Duke Chou and Confucius. Duke Chou, Liang declared, inaugurated rites and decorum in ancient times as the instruments of the ethical society, while Confucius offered "reason" as its ideological foundation. Reason was, for Liang, the principle that defines Chinese attitudes and shapes Chinese society.

Liang in his earlier work adopted the terms "intuition" and "social instinct" to explain the Chinese attitude toward life, but in *The Essentials of Chinese Culture* he substituted the term "reason" (*li-hsing*). Perhaps Liang deemed the shift necessary to explain the institutional aspect of Chinese civilization, a more static subject than life. "Reason," with its stress on the quiet side of the mind, might have seemed to him a more appropriate term in this context than "intuition," which better describes the active disposition toward life. He might also have been influenced by Chang Tung-sun, whose *Reason and Democracy* appeared in 1946. (The two writers admired each other and held similar views on a number of philosophical problems.) Whatever the reasons, the shift was not really significant, for in Liang's vocabulary "reason" and "intuition" were synonymous. Indeed, Wang Yang-ming, to whom Liang owed much of his philosophy, used "reason," "intuitive knowledge," and "mind" interchangeably. They all denote the same "principle of nature" which is common to the minds of all people. Reason, therefore, is none other than human nature, which innately distinguishes good from evil, values sentiment over calculation, and calls for self-abnegation and mutual respect. It follows that in an ethical society ruled by reason, harmonious understanding prevails. There is no confrontation of powers or opposition of classes.

Class confrontation was for Liang irrational, since it is based on force and self-interest and is an outgrowth of organizational life. China as an ethical society was not faced with this problem. Liang admitted that some economic exploitation did exist in China, "now advancing and now receding," but Chinese citizens, irrespective of their social status, were free to buy land. Land ownership had never been concentrated in the hands of an economically dominant class.

Nor was China governed politically by any particular class. Since 221 B.C., the end of the feudal age, Liang said, China had been governed by officials appointed and dismissed by the ruler. Coming as they did from the people, and serving as administrative agents for only a certain length of time, they could not really be said to constitute a class opposed to the ruled. Furthermore, political opportunities in the form of civil service examinations were open to everyone. With governors and governed exchanging positions frequently, class differentiation on a political level could hardly exist.

Even the emperor had not been supported by any powerful class. He had been, as it were, a lonely fellow reigning at the top but requiring the support of the people as a whole. Some members of the imperial clan were close to him and in a way took part in policy-making, but in general they had shared his fate rather than his power. The imperial clan was, further, a small one; it had neither land nor people that could serve as the base of political power. China was not, therefore, a class society, but one of diverse occupations in which scholars, peasants, artisans, and merchants mingled on a common basis.[62]

It is obvious that Liang in his analysis of Chinese society idealized the Confucian state and ignored practical developments that had departed from the Confucian ideal. He frankly disregarded material forces, which for him played a significant role only in Western civilization. In claiming that Chinese culture was largely the creation of great geniuses like Duke Chou and Confucius, Liang consciously and directly challenged historical materialism, for it was his belief that historical development is never unilateral in the Marxian sense. There are, Liang held, diverse paths of development, blazed by men of genius, and China was a notable example.

Liang realized that Chinese society had shown its weaknesses in recent times, but he believed them to be weaknesses only in the context of the modern world. Due to its deficiencies in organization and its lack of a class structure, China was not quite a state in the modern sense of the word. China could be described as a nonmilitary culture, not because it lacked soldiers, for it had many, but because its military forces had not been institutionalized into a military class per se. The Chinese state had been absorbed into society, in which government functions had been reduced to a minimum. China's laissez-faire tradition, in Liang's view, was due less to the ideological influence of Taoism than to the nature of the ethical society. The lack of organization and of class struggle, the replacement of law by rites and decorum as the guides to conduct, and the tradition of solving problems through self-control and inward perfection made it difficult in China to develop such concepts as democracy, civil rights, or separation of powers.[63]

Unfortunately China's ethical society, with its inward-looking mentality and lack of organizational life, had proved deplorably inadequate to meet the Western challenge, Liang realized. The Chinese had begun to lose confidence in their own culture, but their discontent and aversion had only added to their confusion. The Chinese cultural crisis caused by Western invasion, he declared, could be solved only by self-revitalization. Against his earlier opinion that China should follow the West's example, with certain basic revisions, he now, in the late 1940's, viewed Westernization as a blind alley for China. Western civilization, pathetic and devoted to strife and power, was unworthy of China. Liang also now saw that it was im-

possible in China, where the social conditions necessary
for the development of democracy and capitalism were
lacking. Nor would Communism have a better chance,
since there was no proletariat to speak of and Chinese
peasants were at the same time too ignorant and too conservative to take the initiative in violent social revolution.[64]

The solution to China's cultural crisis, Liang maintained,
lay in upholding her traditional spirit and reconstructing a
new society on the basis of the old. Predominantly agricultural, made up of largely rural elements, China must
attempt rural reconstruction. Although unrest and disorder
had swept the rural areas as a result of plunder by the
warlords on the one hand and the negligence of the government on the other, the rural population, in Liang's
opinion, formed a potential social force that, if galvanized,
could serve as the foundation of a new social order.

Liang first expounded his program for rural reconstruction in 1923 when he lectured in Shantung province. He
apparently derived inspiration from Chang Shih-chao, who
had also called for the establishment of an agricultural
state.[65] In 1927–1928 Liang presented his plan for rural
development to General Li Chi-shen, then governor of
Kwangtung, who approved the idea. But the plan was
never put into practice, as conditions in Canton were not
ripe for the experiment. Liang went on to Honan province
in 1929 and there helped to organize the Institute of Village Government. His rural movement came to a head in
1931 when, under the sponsorship of Governor Han Fu-
ch'ü, he succeeded in establishing the Shantung Rural Reconstruction Institute, which supervised the Tsoup'ing
and Hotse experimental districts.[66]

While he was the outstanding figure in the movement,
Liang was not its only exponent. In the 1920's and thir-
ties a number of rural experimental districts and stations

were established in various provinces: among the better-
known were the Tinghsien district in Hopeh province,
ably led by James Yen of the National Association of the
Mass Education Movement; the Hsiaochuang Rural
Teachers Institute near Nanking; and the rural stations of
the Chinese Vocational Education Society in K'unshan
near Shanghai. The Nationalist government, in connection
with its local government program, also set up experimental districts: in Chiangning, Kiangsu, and in Lanhuo,
Chekiang.[67] And in Shansi province Governor Yen Hsi-
shan had launched his own program of rural reconstruction.[68] The private institutions were primarily concerned
with rural education; the government experiments, with
local government. While programs were sometimes extended to include other areas of local life, their major
objective was to solve local problems. Liang's originality
was his belief that in rural reconstruction alone lay the
solution to the entire Chinese problem.

The objectives of Liang's program were threefold. First,
though in agreement that economic development was a
prerequisite to China's social program, Liang felt strongly
that China was an agricultural country whose self-
sufficient, consumption-oriented economy differed fundamentally from Western industrialism. He did not entirely
discount industrialization, but he firmly believed that industry should be developed by way of agriculture. The
hegemony of agriculture would protect China's economy
from all the evils of industrial capitalism. While land ownership should not be abolished, peasants should have their
own land to till. Cooperative association, he maintained,
was the best way to establish equitable economy.[69]
This insistence on an agrarian economy was consistent
with Liang's view that China must develop what she already had. Agricultural development was the natural way
to avoid urbanism, one of the worst outgrowths of West-

ern civilization. A rural society, with its emphasis upon peace and moderation, was the only hope for the revival of Confucian values.

Second, education was to be reorganized so as to vitalize the rural populace and mobilize it as a huge social force behind the new order. Intellectuals were urged to return to the countryside to serve as teachers and leaders in the fight against looseness and confusion. Liang stressed the importance of personal contact, not only in the student-teacher relationship, but also between leaders and the masses. Schools would replace administrative organizations in a realization of the classical ideal of uniting politics and education. While knowledge, especially that of the techniques of agricultural production, was a great part of this process, particular stress was to be laid on the formation of character. It was Liang's hope to turn the local communities into havens of Confucian virtue. To this end, he would revive the Rural Compact of the Sung dynasty, particularly the moral injunctions calling for mutual encouragement in the cultivation of virtues, mutual aid in the event of emergencies, and reconciliation and rapport in place of lawsuits and struggles.[70] Sustained by compatible rites and customs, these moral teachings would form the basis of a renewed ethical society.

Third, Liang believed that political transformation depended upon the success of social reconstruction. Political disunity, he pointed out, arises from social disorder. It is only when social disintegration is checked and stability re-established that political progress is possible. Social unity, he thought, should be restored from below—through rural reconstruction. If the loose, disorganized life in the vast rural area were tightened up, and isolated members of local communities brought together, a social force based on common attitudes and beliefs would arise.

The resulting unity would not, then, be a product of coercion, but an outgrowth of voluntary understanding.[71]

In Liang's conception, the rural reconstruction movement was not to be involved in any political power struggles. He conceived of the national office of the movement, when organized, as a brain trust whose ideas would constitute the guidelines for government action. The movement would not, therefore, be a political party with the right to formulate policies. It would be, rather, a social force capable of influencing the government through reason and public opinion.[72]

This relationship between the movement and the government presented the greatest stumbling block to the success of Liang's program. How could the movement attain its aims without the government's support? Where was the assurance that the ideas of the movement, which itself wielded no political power, would become government policies? To Liang the Nationalist government was short-sighted and incapable of recognizing the nature of China's social problem. And yet he expected it to adopt his ideas. In point of fact, the Nationalist government had its own policies, and although willing to let him talk, it had no intention of accepting Liang's rural reconstruction program as the only solution to China's problems. Liang had hoped that his movement could develop into a huge social force, but he soon became disappointed with its slow progress. The conservative villagers did not stir easily, and it was difficult to bridge the mental gap between peasants and intellectuals. Nor did the intellectual leaders of the various rural reconstruction groups agree with each other concerning basic policies. As a result, the great social force so eagerly expected by Liang did not develop.

When the Japanese invaded China in 1937, the rural movement was for all practical purposes brought to an end. Rural reconstruction as a solution to local problems had had its place in time of peace. In time of war and revolution, the call for an ethical society seemed remote and idealistic. Liang sensed this, and in 1941 when the Nationalists and Communists renewed their struggle, he helped to organize the Democratic Political Organizations League in an attempt to solve problems politically. The political approach failed too, however, and in 1949 the Communists seized the country by force. Liang went to Peking and became a member of the Communist-sponsored Political Consultative Council. In 1953, at a high-level Communist meeting, he spoke out against the poverty of the peasants under Communist rule. This infuriated Mao Tse-tung, and a "purge of Liang Sou-ming's thought" ensued. In an extensive Communist-organized campaign, he was roundly denounced as the reckless exponent of idealistic, feudalistic, and antirevolutionary ideas.[73] Thus the outspoken philosopher, noted for his courage and high principles, was brought to silence.

The China Youth Party: Tseng Ch'i and Others

The China Youth party (Chungkuo Ch'ingnien Tang) was organized in Paris on December 2, 1923, by a group of Chinese students who saw China gravely endangered by internal chaos and external aggression. In adopting the name China Youth for their party, the founders were inspired by the work of the Young Italy and Young Turkey organizations, which had spearheaded the nationalist movements in their respective countries. As a revolutionary group, the China Youth party kept its organization secret and used front agencies to carry out its activities. The party was brought into the open in 1929, but since the Nationalist government permitted no other political parties during the period of political tutelage, it still remained in essence an underground organization.

After the Japanese invasion of Manchuria in 1931, the Chungkuo Ch'ingnien Tang offered its support in a united front against Japanese aggression. It finally received official recognition in 1932, when its leaders were invited to the government Conference on National Emergency. It was also represented in the People's Political Council organized by the government in 1938 to receive suggestions on national affairs from different parties and groups. In 1946 it took part in the Constituent Assembly, which passed the Chinese constitution on December 25. Its members were elected to the First National Assembly, and several of its leaders served in the constitutional government under the Kuomintang. In the ensuing civil war, in which the Communists defeated the Nationalists, the China Youth party, unlike some groups of the Democratic League, continued to support the Nationalist government. The party moved its headquarters to Taiwan after the Communist takeover; but with some of its senior leaders remaining in Hong Kong, it was no longer a united, vigorous organization.[74]

The China Youth party stood for nationalism, even more rigidly than the Kuomintang. It was fervently anti-Communist in the 1920's when it denounced Sun Yat-sen's cooperation with the Russians and the Chinese Communists. It called for the building of a modern state by the Chinese themselves through a strengthening of defense establishments and the molding of character according to nationalist principles. China, it asserted, must be able to uphold its sovereignty and independence. It rejected the slogan "anti-imperialism," because it did not believe in world revolution or interference with other nations' social systems. In education, it denounced schools under the control of foreign missionaries and advocated that students be inculcated with loyalty to the state.

The China Youth party had no intention of using militaristic or imperialistic tactics, however. It favored China's cooperation with other nations on an equal basis and had no objection to the ideal of a world commonwealth (ta-t'ung chu-i), so long as it was recognized that the building of China into a strong state must be the starting point for any such scheme.

In its passionate advocacy of devout attachment to the state, the Chungkuo Ch'ingnien Tang did not lose sight of democracy's importance. It consistently opposed the one-party rule of the Kuomintang and demanded people's sovereignty. Like many of its contemporaries and fore-runners, the China Youth party believed that the government, to be freely elected by the people, should work for the greatest happiness of the greatest number. Civil rights, local self-government, and judicial independence received top priority in the party's political program.

In the area of economics the China Youth party opposed the concept of class struggle but favored industrialization through state assistance. While it had no interest in a radical socialist transformation, it supported a social policy that would promote the well-being of the workers and peasants and ensure a decent living to all. It favored protection of private property, but with moderate regulation to prevent the development of bureaucratic capitalism. It agreed that peasants should have their own land to till, but did not think it necessary that all landowners should be tillers. Made up largely of middle-class intellectuals, the Chungkuo Ch'ingnien Tang was interested in enlarging the middle classes, not only as a sustaining force of democracy but also as a social coalition capable of bridging the gap between rich and poor.[75]

The leader of the party was Tseng Ch'i (1892–1951),

a native of Szechuan province, who founded the party with eight other Chinese students. He showed his literary talents in middle school, where he is known to have delighted in classical thought and poetry. Before reaching the age of twenty, he had served as editor of a number of newspapers in Szechuan. He went to Japan in 1916 to study, but returned to China in 1918 with a large number of Chinese students in protest against Japan's aggressive policy in China. He set off for Paris in 1919 and stayed there for five years. While studying abroad, however, he continued to apply himself to the study of Chinese books. One finds in his diary covering the years in Japan and France an account of his continuous reading of the classical works, with practically no discussion of Western authors.[76] This, of course, does not mean that he was not exposed to foreign ideas, but it does indicate that Chinese learning constituted the foundation of his thought and contributed to the formation of his character.

Tseng, however, was no blind believer in Confucianism. Priding himself on being a man of action, he was eager to learn, whether from classical studies or from the actual life of the West, what would be most conducive to building China into a strong, modern state. It was clear to him that moral cultivation, while important in itself, would not necessarily lead to action. Ability to act was essential if the warlords were to be overthrown and foreign aggression resisted. Tseng therefore felt that Confucianism must be supplemented by legalism, that the moral principles of the former must be reinforced by the forcible tools of the latter. Believing that human nature is both good and evil, he held that only through a combination of sincerity and power could a leader coordinate his followers and control his enemies. While he had a great esteem for Wang Yang-ming's moral teaching, especially his theory of the unity of knowledge and action, he took

as guides to actual political action the works of Wang An-
shih (1021–1086), Fang Chung-yen (989–1052), Chang
Chü-cheng (d. 1582), and Tseng Kuo-fan (1811–1872)
—all notable in Chinese history for their "practical"
statesmanship.[77]

Unlike some of his contemporaries, Tseng did not attempt to trace nationalism to the Ming dynasty or earlier,
holding that the concept of state in the modern sense of
the word did not exist in traditional China, where universalism had prevailed. Only through contact with the West
had China become gradually conscious of state relations.
The patriotic demonstrations after the Japanese Twenty-
one Demands in 1915 were great landmarks in the development of Chinese nationalism. Tseng had been exposed to these agitations, and when he visited Japan and
France later, what he saw and learned only reinforced his
faith in nationalism. He saw in the clamors for interna-
tionalism merely isolated voices from a few intellectuals
who had grown weary of war; as state power grew strong
and active, nationalism remained the main motivating
force in Europe.[78]

Tseng believed the origins of the state to be utilitarian;
states arise because of men's recognition of their usefulness. Under the organization provided by the state,
people are protected by law and assisted by the government, peace and order are maintained, and conflicts and
disputes between individuals and communities are resolved. To reconcile state authority with individual liberty,
Tseng offered the opinion that so long as men live in society, individual freedom cannot be absolute. A member
of the state can enjoy only relative freedom, to the degree that regulation necessary to the well-being of the entire community permits.[79]

Tseng was neither a profound thinker nor a precise
one. His moderate views and open mind, however, fitted

well with his conception of a democratic party unhampered
by a dictator and a rigid ideology. Though the moving
spirit of the China Youth party, he was not always its
official leader. Li Huang was its chairman in the years
1931–1932, Yü Fu-hsien from 1932 to 1935, and Tso
Shun-sheng from 1935 to 1938.[80] Very little is known
about Yü Fu-hsien except that he represented the faction
desiring a strong leadership with centralized powers. The
Yü group attained control of the party in 1932 upon the
resignation of Tseng Ch'i and the entire Central Committee, but its three-year interim rule represented a side
stream rather than the main current of China Youth leadership. However, Tso and Li, close associates of Tseng
Ch'i, played an important role in the formulation of the
party's policies, and their ideas shed light on the diversity
of the China Youth party's principles.

Tso Shun-sheng (1893–1969), writer and lecturer, was
noted for his lively sense of the practical world. Having a
keen historical perception, Tso wrote essays distinguished
for both their literary skill and their sobriety of judgment.[81] A man of letters rather than a political theoretician, he offered advice firmly grounded on common sense.
While he recognized that Confucianism had its virtues—
tolerance and broad-mindedness, respect for reason and
a simple and honest life—Tso realized that old teachings may not be suited to new situations. China's modernization particularly required gains in scientific
knowledge.[82]

Tso's writings on party politics reveal his practical sense
of democracy. It is exceedingly important, he wrote, for
a good leader to avoid the inclination toward self-
righteousness. It is only human for a leader to be pleased
with popular praise and support, but he must also heed
criticism and tolerate opposition. Nor should a good citizen blindly believe in a political leader and be irrevocably

bound to a single party. Political doctrines, all claiming infallibility and demanding rigid application, are sometimes more dangerous than lethal weapons and capable of leading to large-scale bloodshed. Nationalism as advocated by the China Youth party, Tso declared, while it held that national interests should be the major premise in all political considerations, could be flexibly construed according to individual beliefs. National policies should be adjusted to political realities rather than rigidly adhere to a single doctrine.[83]

More Western-oriented in his theories, Li Huang (1895–) was one of the cofounders of the China Youth party while a student in Paris. A professor of history upon his return to China, he incorporated modern sociological research into his political thinking. Li inveighed against anarchists such as Peter Kropotkin and Elisée Reclus, who had discredited the state as a product of early manipulation by the privileged class, i.e., the magicians and priests. In refuting this theory, Li resorted to anthropology. With Émile Durkheim, he maintained that primitive totem society was founded on common religious beliefs which had determined not only its political organization but also its economic life. In the totem clans there had been no special class of magicians and priests, since the supernatural power of the totem was shared by all members of the community. Political organization, therefore, originally came out of spiritual needs; it had arisen to meet the common needs of the people rather than as an instrument serving the interests of the privileged few.[84] Li's exposition, based on the experience of a certain primitive society, was of course not a complete explanation of the origins of the state. But it pointed up the deficiencies of the anarchist theory and proved useful to those who believed political organization could arise in a variety of ways.

For Li, nationalism was a general consciousness arising from the correspondence, or interaction, between the sentiments and wills of the individuals within a group. The nationality, or personality, of the nation rested on the unique ideal and life style adopted by a people and embodied its common memories and experiences of the past. These experiences did not belong to any particular class as asserted by the Marxists, but to the people as a whole. Thus Li viewed the living forces of history and the common bonds of spiritual cohesion as the essential elements of nationalism. Love for one's fatherland was, he felt, as much an innate ability as love for one's parents. An individual owed his education, moral cultivation, and material enjoyment as much to the state as to his parents. Patriotism is therefore a natural sentiment growing out of one's gratitude to the nation. It is each citizen's moral obligation to contribute to his nation's protection and glorification, to sacrifice self-interest for the common good.[85]

Though based on Mencius' theory of intuitive ability and knowledge, Li's moral conception of nationalism by no means exalted Chinese learning. Recognizing in nationalism a modern concept, Li knew that traditional teachings would not be of much use in its acceptance. Traditional attachments, particularly to the family, had to be abandoned if nationalism were to develop in China.[86] On the other hand, he was opposed to the transplantation of Western civilization to China and to any synthesis between East and West. "The contact of cultures is not like pouring milk into coffee when white mixed with black will turn gray."[87]

For Li, culture changes without ceasing—in the form of invention, creation, and continuous replacement of the old by the new. He felt that while the Chinese should adopt Western forms and methods, they should at the same time employ their own talents to create a new culture.[88] From Bergson he derived his concept that a culture, like life itself, is an endless stream of becoming. In stressing this creative side of cultural development, Li helped call attention to a point that had largely been ignored by the cultural disputants in China.

Notes

CHAPTER VIII. THE THIRD FORCE

1. I-sheng, "Chung-kuo min-chu t'ung-meng" (The China Democratic League), *Tsai-sheng* ("The National Renaissance"), No. 5: 14 (Jan. 1946).
2. Chün-sheng, "Chung-kuo kuo-chia she-hui-tang" (The State Socialist Party of China), *Tsai-sheng*, No. 5: 23 (Jan. 1946).
3. *Tsai-sheng*, 3.1: 2 (March 1935).
4. Hou-sheng, "Chang Chün-mai hsien-sheng ti che-hsüeh ssu-hsiang" (The Philosophical Thought of Carsun Chang), *ibid.*, 4.16 (June 1953).
5. Chang Chün-mai (Carsun Chang), "Wo chih che-hsüeh ssu-hsiang" (My Philosophical Thought), *ibid.*, 4.17: 12 (July 1953).
6. *Ibid.*, p. 18.
7. Chang Chün-mai, *Li-kuo chih tao* (How to Establish the Foundations of the State) (1938), p. 14.
8. *Tsai-sheng*, 3.1: 2 (March 1935).
9. Chang Chün-mai, *Li-kuo chih tao*, p. 382.
10. *Ibid.*, pp. 385–86.
11. *Ibid.*, p. 388.
12. *Ibid.*, p. 390.
13. *Ibid.*, pp. 99, 101, 106, 153–54.
14. *Ibid.*, p. 141.
15. *Tsai-sheng*, 3.1: 4–6 (March 1935).
16. *Ibid.*, No. 108: 4 (April 1946).
17. Chang Chün-mai, *Li-kuo chih tao*, p. 197.
18. Hou-sheng: "Chang Chün-mai hsien-sheng ti she-hui chu-i ssu-hsiang" (The Socialist Thought of Carsun Chang), *Tsai-sheng*, 4.17: 34 (July 1953).
19. *Tsai-sheng*, 3.1: 23 (March 1935); Chang Chün-mai, *Chung-hua min-kuo hsien-fa shih-chiang* (Ten Lectures on the Constitution of the Republic of China) (Shanghai: Commercial Press, 1947), p. 130.
20. Chang Chün-mai, "Kuo-chia min-chu cheng-chih yü kuo-chia she-hui chu-i" (National Democracy and State Socialism), *Tsai-sheng*, 3.1: 23 (March 1935).
21. Chang Chün-mai, *Li-kuo chih tao*, pp. 243–44.
22. *Ibid.*, pp. 247–50.
23. *Ibid.*, p. 278.
24. Chang Chün-mai, *Ming-jih chih Chung-kuo wen-hua* (The Chinese Culture of Tomorrow) (Shanghai: Commercial Press, 1936), pp. 106, 114.
25. Chang Chün-mai, *Li-kuo chih tao*, p. 277.
26. Chang Chün-mai, *Ming-jih chih Chung-kuo wen-hua*, p. 132.
27. Carsun Chang, *The Third Force in China* (New York: Bookman Associates, 1952), pp. 329, 331, 333.
28. Chang Chün-mai, *Ming-jih chih Chung-kuo wen-hua*, p. 132.
29. *Ibid.*, pp. 159–60.

30. See *Tsai-sheng*, 1.4: 31 (Aug. 1932).
31. *Ibid.*, 4.22: 13 ff. (Dec. 1953); 4.23: 13 (Jan. 1954).
32. Chang Chün-mai, *Li-kuo chih tao*, pp. 360–62.
33. *Ibid.*, pp. 360, 370.
34. *Ibid.*, p. 279.
35. Chang Tung-sun, "Chih-chih ken-pen lun" (Fundamentals of Government), *Chia-yen* ("The Tiger"), 1.4: 1–18 (May 1915).
36. Chang Tung-sun, "Tui-k'ang lun chih chia-chih" (The Value of the Theory of Opposition), *Yung-yen* ("The Justice"), 1.24: 1–12 (Nov. 1913).
37. Chou Fu-hai, "Fu-sang chi-ying su tang-nien" (Reminiscences of School Years in Japan), *Ch'un-ch'iu* (Spring and Autumn), No. 208 (March 1966).
38. Chang Tung-sun, "Wo-men wei shen-mo chiang she-hui chu-i" (Why Do We Talk Socialism?), *Chieh-fang yü kai-tsao* (Emancipation and Reconstruction), 1.7: 7 (Dec. 1919).
39. Chang Tung-sun, "T'ao-lun she-hui chu-i ti i-ko shen-shuo" (An Explanation concerning the Discussion of Socialism), *Kai-tsao* (Reconstruction), 3.6 (Feb. 1921).
40. Chang Tung-sun, *Li-hsing yü min-chu* (Reason and Democracy) (Shanghai: Commercial Press, 1946), pp. 4–5.
41. Chang Tung-sun, "Chieh-chi wen-t'i" (The Question of Classes), *Tsai-sheng*, 1.4: 21 (Aug. 1932).
42. Chang Tung-sun, "Min-chu yü chuan-cheng shih-pu-shih hsiang-jung ti mo?" ("Is Democracy Incompatible with a Strong Government?"), *ibid.*, 1.7: 4 (Nov. 1932).
43. Chang Tung-sun, *Min-chu chu-i yü she-hui chu-i* (Democracy and Socialism) (Shanghai: Kuan-ch'a she, 1948), pp. 77–97.
44. The other three books are *Ssu-hsiang yü she-hui* (Thought and Society), *Li-hsing yü min-chu* (Reason and Democracy), and *Min-chu chu-i yü she-hui chu-i.*
45. Chang Tung-sun, *Chih-shih yü wen-hua* (Knowledge and Culture) (Shanghai: Commercial Press, 1947), p. 81.
46. *Ibid.*, p. 84.
47. Chang Tung-sun, *Li-hsing yü min-chu* (Reason and Democracy) (Shanghai: Commercial Press, 1946), pp. 23, 41–46.
48. Chang Tung-sun, *Ssu-hsiang yü she-hui* (Thought and Society) (Shanghai: Commercial Press, 1946), p. 167.
49. *Ibid.*, p. 179.
50. Chang Tung-sun, *Li-hsing yü min-chu*, p. 66.
51. *Ibid.*, p. 178.
52. Chang Tung-sun, *Ssu-hsiang yü she-hui*, p. 79.
53. Chang Tung-sun, *Li-hsing yü min-chu*, pp. 143, 146.
54. *Ti-ch'iu yün-yen.*
55. Ch'en Tu-hsiu, *Tu-hsiu wen-ts'un* (Collected Writings of Ch'en Tu-hsiu) (Shanghai: Ya-tung, 1927), Vol. II, Bk. 1, p. 368.
56. For biographical material on Liang Sou-ming, see Liang Sou-ming, *Wo-ti tzu-hsüeh hsiao-shih* (A Short Account of My Self-Education) (Shanghai: Hua-hua, 1947); *Chiao-yü lun-wen chi* (Collected Essays on Education) (Chungking: K'ai-ming, 1954), pp. i–viii, 84–87; *Chung-kuo min-tsu tzu-chiu yün-tung chih tsui-hou chüeh-wu* (The Final Wakening of the Chinese National Self-

Salvation Movement, hereafter cited as *CKMT*) (Shanghai: Chung-hua, 1938), pp. 1–29.

57. Liang Sou-ming, *Tung hsi wen-hua chi ch'i che-hsüeh* (Eastern and Western Civilizations and Their Philosophies) (Shanghai: Commercial Press, 1930), pp. 63, 65–66.

58. *Ibid.*, p. 118.

59. *Ibid.*, p. 200.

60. Liang Sou-ming, *Chao-hua* (Morning Talks) (Shanghai: Commercial Press, 1941), p. 146.

61. Liang Sou-ming, *Chung-kuo wen-hua yao-i* (The Essentials of Chinese Culture) (Hong Kong: Chi-ch'eng, 1963), p. 81.

62. *Ibid.*, pp. 150, 158–59.

63. *Ibid.*, pp. 165, 189.

64. *CKMT*, pp. 177, 179.

65. See above, pp. 44–45.

66. *CKMT*, pp. 7 ff.

67. See Chang Yüan-shan and Hsü Shih-lien, eds., *Hsiang-ts'un chien-she shih-yen* (Experiments in Rural Reconstruction) (Canton: Chung-hua, 1938), Vol. II.

68. *CKMT*, pp. 301 ff.

69. Liang Sou-ming, "Chung-kuo chih ching-chi chien-she" (Economic Reconstruction in China), *Hsiang-ts'un chien-she* (Rural Reconstruction), 6.16: 12 ff. (May 1937).

70. For these medieval compacts, see Ch'ien Mu and others, *Chung-kuo hsüeh-shu-shih lun chi* (Essays on Chinese Intellectual History) (Taipei, 1956), I, pp. 1–27.

71. *Hsiang-ts'un chien-she*, 6.11–12: 5, 7 (March 1937); Liang Sou-ming, "Chung-kuo cheng-chih wen-t'i chih chieh-chüeh" (The Solution of the Chinese Political Problem), *Hsiang-ts'un chien-she*, 6.11–12: 5, 7 (March 1937).

72. *Ibid.*, p. 6.

73. Chou Ch'ing-wen, *Feng-pao shih-nien* (Ten Stormy Years) (Hong Kong: Shih-tai p'i-p'ing she, 1959), pp. 434–37. For articles denouncing Liang Sou-ming, see *Liang Sou-ming ssu-hsiang p'i-p'an* (Criticisms of the Thought of Liang Sou-ming), 3 vols. (Peking: San-lien shu-tien, 1955–57).

74. For the history of the China Youth party, see *Chung-kuo Ch'ing-nien-tang tang-shih tzu-liao* (Materials on the History of the China Youth Party) (Taipei: Min-chu-ch'ao she, 1955); Liu-hsia, *Shih-pa-nien lai chih Chung-kuo Ch'ing-nien-tang* (The China Youth Party in the Past 18 Years) (Chengtu: Kuo-hun, 1941).

75. For the basic objectives and policies of the party, see *Chung-kuo Ch'ing-nien-tang tang-shih tzu-liao*, Collection 1, and Yü Chia-chü's economic articles in *Min-hsien* (People's Constitution), 1.5–6 (1944).

76. Tseng Ch'i, *Tseng Mu-han hsien-sheng i-chi* (Collected Works of Tseng Ch'i) (Taipei: Chung-kuo Ch'ing-nien-tang, 1954), pp. 371–475.

77. *Ibid.*, pp. 313, 374, 406, 459.

78. *Ibid.*, p. 132.

79. *Ibid.*, pp. 142, 148.

80. *Ibid.*, pp. 537–38.

81. See his *Chung-kuo hsien-tai ming-jen i-shih* ("Interesting Stories

of the Contemporary Prominent Chinese") (Hong Kong: Freedom Press, 1951); *Wan-chu-lou sui-pi* ("Sketches Written in the Wanchu Chamber") (Hong Kong: Freedom Press, 1954).

82. Tso Shun-sheng, "Nu-li yü ssu-so" (Assertion and Thinking), *Min-hsien*, 1.1: 3 (May 1944).

83. Tso Shun-sheng, *Fan-Kung, cheng-chih chi* (Anti-Communist Political Essays) (Hong Kong: Freedom Press, 1952), pp. 70–71.

84. Li Huang, "Kuo-chia chu-i ta k'e-nan" (Answers to Questions on Nationalism), in *Kuo-chia chu-i lun-wen chi* (Essays on Nationalism) (Shanghai: Chung-hua, 1926), pp. 51–57.

85. Li Huang, "Shih kuo-chia chu-i" (An Explanation of Nationalism), *ibid.*, pp. 8, 14–15.

86. Li Huang, "Tsai-t'an kuo-chia chu-i ti chiao-yü" (Further Discussion of Nationalist Education), *ibid.*, p. 151.

87. Li Huang, "Kuo-chia chu-i chi ch'i yün-tung" (Nationalism and Its Movement), in *Chung-kuo wen-t'i ko-p'ai ssu-ch'ao* (Various Schools of Thought on the Chinese Question) (Shanghai, 1936), p. 339.

88. *Ibid.*, pp. 337–41.

Chapter IX

CHINESE COMMUNISM I—FROM CH'EN TU-HSIU TO CH'EN SHAO-YÜ

Ch'en Tu-hsiu

FOR Lenin the Bolshevik Revolution of 1917 was merely part of the world revolution to overthrow capitalism everywhere. The East occupied an important part in this global strategy, not only because its huge population was rapidly drawn into the revolutionary struggle, but also because a Communist victory there would help prevent capitalist states from crushing Soviet Russia.[1] Lenin outlined his strategy for the colonial and semicolonial countries at the Second Congress of the Communist International in 1920. In the colonial and semicolonial countries, he said, a purely proletarian movement was out of the question since there was practically no industrial proletariat. The Communists should enter into a temporary alliance with the bourgeois democrats, but should not merge with them and should under no circumstances lose their independence. Support was to be given to the bourgeois democratic movement only on the condition that proletarian elements would later group together and fight the bourgeoisie. Concerning the role of the peasants, Lenin considered it necessary to render special assistance to their struggle against the landlords and against all manifestations or survivals of feudalism. Efforts should be made to give the peasant movement the most revolutionary character possible, and the proletariat was to establish the closest possible alliance with it.[2]

Early in 1920 the Comintern representative Grigorii

Voitinsky was sent to China to promote Communist activities. In Peking he saw Li Ta-chao, who recommended that he go to Shanghai to discuss the matter with Ch'en Tu-hsiu. After the 1919 May Fourth Movement Ch'en had become interested in socialism. As late as December of that year, however, in the "Declaration of the [*New Youth*] Journal," he had shown himself to be still more a scholar interested in social justice and mutual assistance than a firm believer in Marxism-Leninism. Although sympathetic to Bolshevism, he did not accept it without reservations.[3] It was through the efforts of Voitinsky that he was finally converted to Communism.

Ch'en's leap, from democracy and liberalism to the authoritarian doctrine of Communism, appears great. But Ch'en was at heart a rebel and an iconoclast. Like other radicals-turned-Communist, he was deeply frustrated by continued foreign aggression and exploitation and the recurrent civil wars waged by unprincipled Chinese warlords. The Comintern's belief in fighting imperialism and feudalism and its proposed solution of complete political and social transformation appealed to his rebellious soul. What most attracted Chinese radicals to Bolshevism was the seemingly short time in which it had succeeded in sweeping away the old and bringing in the new. To the frustrated and impatient, Communist methods were highly effective.[4]

The Chinese Communist party was established in July 1921, and Ch'en became its head. For some time he was popular among his followers, but as the party began to experience difficulty, especially after Chiang Kai-shek took steps to curb Communist activities in March 1926, opinion became divided. The factionalism arose partly as a result of interference by Comintern representatives in party affairs; the Russians concentrated on gathering support for certain policies and upon criticizing others.

When both the Left and Right wings of the Kuomintang were purged of Communists in 1927, Ch'en was blamed for the failure. A concerted attack on him was inspired by the Comintern, which wanted a scapegoat. Ch'en was charged with Menshevism, Rightist opportunism, and capitulationism, and later, after his expulsion from the Chinese Communist party, of Trotskyism. Since our concern is primarily with the main currents of Chinese political thought, Ch'en's advocacy after his expulsion falls outside the scope of this study, and I shall examine here only the charges against him as head of the Chinese Communist party.

The attribution of Menshevism to Ch'en was based largely on two articles he had written in 1923.[5] A lack of faith in the working class was charged to him for having written that "though the proletariat is an important element in the national revolution, it is not an independent revolutionary force." The criticism of overestimating the power of the bourgeoisie was leveled against him for his statement that "in the colonial and semicolonial countries the force of the bourgeoisie is after all more concentrated than that of the peasantry and more powerful than that of the proletariat." He was also charged with belittling the role of the peasantry for his assertion that peasants were geographically spread out and therefore diffused as a social force, low in culture and therefore simple in desire and conservative in attitude, content with the little they had and therefore opposed to hazardous ventures.[6] He was further accused of viewing the revolution as primarily one of the bourgeois and proletarian classes. It was said that the concepts of agrarian revolution and of democratic dictatorship of the workers and peasants did not exist for him.[7]

These charges, based on Ch'en's writings, are not without foundation. It is worthy of note, however, that these statements were made at an early stage in the so-called national democratic revolution, when the role of the bourgeoisie was explicitly recognized by both Lenin and the Comintern. To be fair to Ch'en, while he asserted that the proletariat and peasantry were too weak to go it alone, he realized that the bourgeoisie was also in its infantile stage and therefore incapable of carrying out the revolution independently. While acknowledging the peasantry's weaknesses, he recognized the necessity of its sympathy and support. But since he viewed the existing struggle as a national democratic revolution, he held that the peasant movement in China had to wait till the national revolution was realized. With the subsequent capitalization of agriculture, and the growth and concentration of the rural proletariat, there would arise the need for and possibility of a Communist revolution in the rural areas.[8] In thus designating a waiting period for the agrarian revolution, Ch'en showed his affinity with the theory of two-stage revolution.

Ch'en had originally opposed the Comintern policy of Chinese Communist membership in the Kuomintang. It was only after the Comintern representative Maring raised the question of discipline that he gave in.[9] Once the policy was adopted, Ch'en deemed it his duty, as head of the Chinese Communist party, to convince his followers of the necessity of the national bourgeois revolution. He wrote: "If it is admitted that the social conditions in semicolonial China require a bourgeois democratic revolution, it follows that without the assistance of the bourgeoisie, the revolution would lose its class significance and social basis."[10] Caught in the middle, he found it necessary to condemn on the one hand the "romantic Leftism" of some Chinese Communists who rejected cooperation with the bourgeoisie, and on the other the Rightist tendencies of some Kuomintang members who stood for conciliation with the reactionary bourgeois elements. Admitting that the victory of the democratic revolution would be the victory of the bourgeoisie, he reasoned that only through such victory could the proletariat obtain the opportunity of developing its own potential.[11] To those who objected that cooperation with the bourgeoisie would confuse class issues, Ch'en replied that the class consciousness of the proletariat would grow with industrialization and its consequent class differentiation.[12]

The question is whether Ch'en's views violated the directives of the Comintern. An examination of the theses and resolutions of the Comintern shows, first, its belief that the Kuomintang, based partly on the liberal democratic bourgeoisie and petty bourgeoisie and partly on the intelligentsia and workers, constituted the only serious national revolutionary group in China. Since the independent workers' movement in China was still weak, and since the nation's central task was still revolution against the imperialists and their feudal agents within the country, the Comintern considered it essential that the actions of the Kuomintang and the Chinese Communist party be coordinated. But at the same time it insisted that membership in the Kuomintang need not lead to obliterating the specific character of the Chinese Communist party, which should maintain its independence.[13] Second, the Fifth Comintern Congress believed that in united-front tactics a dual method should be used, that is, unity from below as well as from above. A united front solely from above must be categorically rejected,[14] since the most important task was to establish a basis for a powerful mass party through organization and education of the working masses. The Chinese Communist party should appear under its own banner, but at the same time must avoid any conflict with the national revolutionary movement.[15]

Third, concerning the role of the peasantry in the national revolution, the Comintern declared as early as 1923 that the Chinese national revolution against feudalism must coincide with the peasant agrarian revolution. Only then could revolution succeed. It was up to the Chinese Communist party to establish a union of workers and peasants, but leadership must be assumed by the proletariat. It was the Chinese Communists' role to "steadily push the [Kuomintang] on to the side of agrarian revolution."[16]

It is clear that Ch'en's views on the Kuomintang very nearly approximated those of the Comintern. Though eager to cooperate with the Nationalist party, it can hardly be said of him that he "hauled down the flag" of the Chinese Communist party, which, in fact, was very aggressive under his leadership during the early years of the united front. Nor can it be charged that he neglected the role of the masses, since under him the party did make strenuous efforts to organize the people. Ch'en's belief that the peasant movement in China must wait until the realization of the national revolution was thus the only area in which he did not fully agree with the Comintern.

In regard to the charge of Rightist opportunism, Ch'en was accused of continued capitulation to the Kuomintang in the period of 1925–1927, and of not being able determinedly to oppose its Rightist tendencies, to resist the coup of Chiang Kai-shek in March 1926, or to exploit the general strikes of the Shanghai workers in the interest of the Chinese Communist party. These appeasements, claimed his accusers, led to the April 1927 purge of the Chinese Communists by the Kuomintang at Nanking.[17] The unfavorable events in Hankow, the critics charged, developed as a result of the same weak policy, which had aimed only at winning the support of the Kuomintang Left. To this Kuomintang faction the Chinese Communist lead-

ership had been willing to turn over the control of the
trade unions and peasant associations, and it was to appease it that the so-called excesses in the peasant movement had been curbed.[18]

How do these charges stand up in the light of Comintern directives? As late as March 13, 1926, the Sixth
Executive Committee of the Comintern still declared that
the Kuomintang at Canton, which personified "the vanguard of the Chinese people in its struggle for independence," was "a model for the future revolutionary-
democratic structure of the country."[19] Only seven days
later, Chiang Kai-shek took measures to restrict the power
of the Communists, at the same time offering to continue
cooperation with the Russians. Moscow accepted. It was
not until December 1926, when the Nationalists occupied
Wuhan and the conflicts between the Kuomintang Right
and Left had intensified that the Comintern began to realize the significance of the new class regrouping. It gave
official recognition to the Left wing at Wuhan as the bloc
of "more revolutionary character"—the bloc of the proletariat, peasantry, and urban petty bourgeoisie, excluding
the greater part of the big capitalist bourgeoisie. The big
capitalist bourgeoisie, warned the Comintern, was trying to
regain a leading role with the object of crushing the revolution, and it directed the Chinese Communist party to
"tactically exploit all contradictions among the bourgeois
strata withdrawing from the revolution." It then made the
following significant observation:

The structure of the revolutionary State will be determined by
its class basis. It will not be merely a bourgeois-democratic
State. It will represent the democratic dictatorship of the
proletariat, the peasantry, and other exploited classes. It will
be a revolutionary anti-imperialist government in the period of
transition to non-capitalist (socialist) development.[20]

Thus the Comintern somewhat belatedly shifted its view of the composition of the Kuomintang and subtly changed its conception of the two-stage revolution. Still, its leaders insisted that the Chinese Communists not abandon the Kuomintang: "The entire process of development of the Chinese revolution, its character, and its prospects demand that the Communists stay in the Kuomintang and reinforce their work in it."[21] Even after the Left under Wang Ching-wei decided to oust the Communists in July 1927, the Comintern directed the Chinese Communists, while they should leave the national government at Wuhan, not to withdraw from the Kuomintang.[22] Herein lies the most basic issue in the controversy concerning the revolution. For Ch'en Tu-hsiu, who had repeatedly advocated Communist withdrawal, it was this policy of continued attachment that was responsible for the failure of the Communist movement. He wrote:

The general cause of the failure of the Chinese revolution during 1925–27 was the basic mistake made by the Comintern in the evaluation of the revolutionary character of the bourgeoisie and in the analysis of the class composition of the Kuomintang. From this basic mistake there emerged the wrong policies. The major one of these was support for the bourgeoisie, thus depriving the proletariat of a true, independent party that could lead the revolution with thoroughness.[23]

There is some truth in this contention. The failure to recognize the Kuomintang as a bourgeois party with a basic anti-Communist bent contributed to the easing of proletariat vigilance and the strengthening of the bourgeois position. On the other hand, under the conditions then prevailing in China, it is doubtful that an independent Communist movement could have done any better.

Ch'en's critics held that, even working within the Kuomintang, the Chinese Communist party could maintain its independence and defeat the reactionary elements through mobilization of the masses. Ch'en disagreed. The masses, he felt, could not be won over so long as the party "concealed its political physiognomy and mingled organizationally with the bourgeois class."[24] The obstacles to achieving Communist hegemony under the banner of the Kuomintang are not to be denied. Ch'en's critics, however, argued that these difficulties could have been overcome if Ch'en had not been ignorant of the methods of revolutionary struggle.[25] While this optimism may be questioned, it is still true that Ch'en was far from skillful in the application of dialectic tactics. One could hardly expect that a scholar and a university dean of principle or a gentleman with his reputation would be terribly at home with tactics of struggle, with conspiracies, or with treachery. His rigid logic and stern integrity made it difficult for him to engage in a subtle yet bold exploitation of his adversaries' inconsistencies.

One further question may be examined before leaving this topic. Ch'en was denounced for failing to understand the revolutionary transition from one stage to another. The charge is not without foundation, but it should be pointed out that the idea of transition from bourgeois to noncapitalist (socialist) development was mentioned for the first time in a Comintern resolution of December 16, 1926. The way in which it was stated carried with it no sense of urgency: "The CCP should concentrate all its efforts on making a reality, in the long run, of this revolutionary perspective of transition into noncapitalist channels of development."[26] Within only a few months the revolution had met with failure and Ch'en had been ousted. The rapid changes in China's political climate seem to have caught both the Comintern and Ch'en off guard, so that it was too late really to effect any transition. The Comintern's mechanical concept of two-stage revolution hamstrung Ch'en with a rigid interpretation of the revolution that made it difficult for him to understand the need for a subtle transition at a critical time. One may even doubt that the Comintern had itself understood the implications of its statement. As late as July 14, 1927, the Executive Committee of the Comintern, in the Resolution on the Present Stage of the Chinese Revolution, still directed the Chinese Communist party to "complete the bourgeois-democratic revolution."[27]

It is the irony of fate that Ch'en should have joined the Communist movement only to have his life end in dismal failure. Had he remained an independent thinker, he might have contributed a great deal more to Chinese thought. As head of the Chinese Communist party, however, he chose to follow the Comintern's directives. Unfortunately for him, even a faithful interpretation of the Comintern line was futile; Stalin's ignorance of the Chinese situation was further complicated by his struggle with Trotsky, whose criticism only made him cling more tenaciously to his unrealistic policies. Ch'en fell a victim not only to the relentless development of Chinese history but also to the personal feud between two Russian giants.

Ch'ü Ch'iu-pai

Succeeding Ch'en Tu-hsiu as head of the Chinese Communist party in 1927 was Ch'ü Ch'iu-pai (1899–1935), a native of Kiangsu province. Both his granduncle and uncle had served as provincial officials under the Manchu dynasty, but with the overthrow of the regime in 1911, the family rapidly became poor. His father knew something about books and painting, but not much else to make a living. Faced with financial difficulties, he left his family and wandered to another province. The care of Ch'iu-pai and his four brothers and sisters fell then to his mother, a capable woman who was fond of poetry and taught him to recite it when he was a child. But the financial burden proved too much for her, and in despair she committed suicide, when Ch'iu-pai was sixteen. The event had indelible effects on his mind: he found gross injustice in society, but he continued to feel both a profound affection for his mother and a kindness toward his father.[28]

Too poor to study at Peking University, Ch'ü Ch'iu-pai entered the Russian Language School, where he distinguished himself as a brilliant, hard-working student. He received a good grounding in Chinese classics and developed a strong interest in Buddhism. One of his wishes at this time was that he, like the Bodhisattvas, could benefit mankind by good deeds. It was the student movement of May 4 that broke the shell of his lonely life, and he participated in it with great enthusiasm. With some close friends he founded and published the *New Society Weekly,* where ideas on socialism were aired. But the group's conception of socialism was a vague one, somewhat, as Ch'ü put it, like "viewing the morning mist through a screen." The many different kinds of socialism tended to confuse their youthful minds. The *New Society* was later suppressed by police and the young editors set up another magazine, *Humanity.* They continued their broad discussion of socialism, including the idealistic notion that it solved all social problems.[29]

In 1920 Ch'ü was offered the position as Moscow correspondent for the *Peking Morning Post*—a hazardous job, not only because Russia had become Communist, but because the new country had yet to emerge from revolutionary chaos. Some of Ch'ü's relatives strongly advised against the trip. But there was little hope for him where he was, with his broken home and insurmountable financial difficulties, and he saw in Russia a gleam of light that might dispel the darkness of China.[30]

He left for Russia in the fall of 1920 with high hopes. What he had learned about dialectical materialism he wished to verify from actual experience. In order to contribute to the regeneration of China, he had to sort out the confusion in his own mind. Not yet a Marxist, he still believed in some kind of dualism—the interaction between mind and practical life.

The culture of a society is the crystallization of the social spirit. Social progress is but the movement of the social mind. While my rational studies should stress scientific socialism, my mental development will find nourishment in mystical Russia.[31]

Thus idealism and in some sense Buddhist idealism occupied an important place in Ch'ü's thought. The process of life was for him a reflection of myriad changes in the mirror of mind. He did not discount economic life, which he believed to be the foundation of civilization. But while he felt an economic basis was the soil that nourished the plant, it was the plant itself—the social mind—that produced the flower.[32]

Ch'ü's individualistic romanticism often gave rise to an inner conflict, causing him much pain. He loved nature and valued love and sentiment. But inclinations like these were not exactly compatible with revolutionary society and class struggle. He experienced many moments of distress in Moscow. The poverty, hunger, and chaos that prevailed became more and more unbearable, particularly since he was afflicted with tuberculosis. He often expressed a longing to go home. In September 1921, he actually decided to leave Russia, but a return trip through Siberia was difficult to arrange, and he found it necessary to wait until a more opportune time.[33] Had he returned then, before becoming a Communist, the history of Chinese Communism might have been different.

In January 1922 the Congress of the Toilers of the Far East was convened in Moscow. Ch'ü was made interpreter. He was delighted, for although his feelings were not always harmonious with Communism's hard struggle, he believed Russia to be the hope of the world. If the bleak Russian cold and poverty sometimes dampened his spirit, the Russian people's massive response to Communism fired his enthusiasm. Therefore, in February 1922, through the persuasion of a former schoolmate, Chang T'ai-lei, whose friendship he valued in this wilderness, Ch'ü joined the Communist party.

The question was whether, with his delicate soul and poetic feelings, Ch'ü would be capable of leading a revolution that stressed violence and struggle. For a time he was. In 1923 he returned to China and was soon elected a member of the Central Committee of the Chinese Communist party. He was one of the few Chinese Communist leaders who had a firsthand knowledge of Russia and the Soviet leaders. He knew the Russian language well and had a gift for writing. He immediately took upon himself the responsibility of expounding Communism to the Chinese people. As a Communist theoretician, he had few equals among his comrades who, at this early stage, had received most of their ideas about Marxism and Leninism through translations.

In 1923, while Ch'en Tu-hsiu was wrestling with the problem of cooperation with the Kuomintang, Ch'ü undertook to praise the "proletarian civilization." It was his contention that mere technological development does not liberate mankind from the cruelty of nature. On the contrary, material progress weakens man by increasing his material desires and worries, binding him tighter to mate-

rial needs. A good life can be attained only in the proletarian civilization, or "artistic civilization," as he called it.
Under capitalism, Ch'ü held, science is restricted to the
conquest of nature, whereas under socialism it can be applied to the rectification of human relations. Only if the
scientific law of cause and effect is used to liberate mankind from the "natural traits" of society can harmony and
the artistic life be realized. The ideas of Tolstoy, which
Ch'ü had up to now held in high regard, were abandoned,
and he criticized the idea of a return to primitive nature
as unrealistic. Similarly, he condemned Neo-Confucianism
as a static view contrary to historical development.[34] Thus
Ch'ü made a declaration against his former thoughts, although behind his conception of artistic life the old strain
of idealism lurked.

Compared with Ch'en Tu-hsiu, Ch'ü's writings in the
early 1920's indicate a greater confidence in the proletariat
and a lesser degree of trust in the bourgeoisie. While Ch'en
regarded the victory of the national revolution as belonging
to the bourgeoisie, Ch'ü declared it to be a victory of the
proletariat. The proletariat, he asserted, had arisen to assume the role of the revolutionary vanguard after the 1919
May Fourth Movement. Its power of class struggle had
increased with its revolutionary experience. On the other
hand, capitalism by its very nature would not submit voluntarily.[35] It was necessary, therefore, for the proletariat
to continue the task of revolution with the goal of eventually establishing its dictatorship.

Ch'ü in his early writings stressed the importance of
the peasantry as a revolutionary force. As early as 1923,
he pointed out that the proletariat and the peasantry occupied the "vanguard" position in social reconstruction,
although it was necessary that the proletariat should lead
the peasants, just as the Communist party should lead the
proletariat.[36] In 1925, a year before Mao Tse-tung wrote

his famous Report on the Hunan Peasants emphasizing the agrarian revolution, Ch'ü maintained that the Chinese peasants could be organized into a "great revolutionary force."[37] He disagreed with Ch'en Tu-hsiu that the peasants tended toward conservatism. They were, he argued, conservative only when they had property. Since most of the peasants in China were landless, they were necessarily revolution-oriented. In May 1926, on the eve of the Northern Expedition, Ch'ü called for the arming of the workers and peasants in preparation for "direct revolution."[38]

At the beginning of 1926 with the appearance of the anti-Communistic Kuomintang Right, Ch'ü called on the proletariat through an extension of the principle of class struggle to assume the leadership of the national revolution. The main thrust of the struggle, he said, should be directed against both foreign imperialists and Chinese capitalists. Ch'ü felt that class struggle should be placed above national liberation, for only through it could the Chinese proletariat understand the meaning of the overthrow of imperialism. He expressed this opinion before Chiang Kai-shek's anti-Communist coup of March 1926. One concludes that Ch'ü had already recognized the futility of cooperating with the bourgeoisie and was ready to rely largely on the working class for the consummation of national revolution.[39]

Ch'ü became the leader of the opposition Communists in April 1927, when he published *The Issues of the Chinese Revolution*. The book served as a forcible indictment of the existing Communist leadership. He chose as the object of his attack P'eng Shu-chih, a top leader and Ch'en Tu-hsiu's closest lieutenant, severely condemning his theory of "two-stage revolution."[40] For Ch'ü, a victory in the national revolution should mark also the beginning of socialism. He admitted that the Chinese revolution was essentially bourgeois democratic, that its impetus was agrarian, and that it aimed chiefly at achieving democracy through overthrow of the landlord class. But he insisted that an agrarian revolution also had a socialist objective, namely, the overthrow of the comprador bourgeoisie—i.e., the landlord-warlord-bureaucratic class which served the interests of the imperialists. Its victory necessarily transcended the narrow confines of bourgeois revolution and in thus passing on to noncapitalist development would lead directly to socialist revolution. There was, therefore, only one revolution, not two stages of the same revolution.[41]

Similarly, the proletariat should from the beginning direct its efforts at achieving hegemony. It would be a grave mistake for it to surrender its leadership at the first stage and resume it at the second. Addressing himself to the new Kuomintang Right, which had just emerged under Tai Chi-t'ao and Chiang Kai-shek, Ch'ü attacked the Communist leadership for its underestimation of the national bourgeoisie as a reactionary force. The national bourgeoisie, Ch'ü argued, was not a purely industrial class, but an industrial-commercial class. Because of its close economic ties with the commercial class and the petty bourgeoisie, it was a political force of considerable influence, especially if it succeeded in winning the support of the small traders and the petty bourgeoisie.[42]

According to Ch'ü, the national bourgeoisie suffered from imperialist oppression and was therefore anti-imperialist. As it moved gradually from commerce to big industry, it tended toward political compromise. Thus, while opposed to imperialism, it did not want to overthrow it. It supported moderate reforms, but shrank from revolutionary measures. Fearful of proletarian class struggle, it was eager to enter the revolutionary camp and capture its leadership. The danger of the national bourgeoisie thus lay in its reformism, which made it appear less reactionary than the bureaucratic comprador bourgeoisie and enabled it more successfully to win the support of the petty bourgeoisie. Since the upper sector of the petty bourgeoisie, the small traders in particular, was basically an unstable force, it would cooperate readily with the national bourgeoisie when the revolutionary struggle became intense. A military dictatorship by the national bourgeoisie could even win over small peasants attracted to the peace and order it offered.[43]

But, to Ch'ü, the fact that the national bourgeoisie was capable of gaining hegemony in the revolution did not mean that it would necessarily succeed. It all depended upon whether the proletariat was ready to break away from the national bourgeoisie. The proletariat, he felt, had to make every effort to win the support of the peasants, the petty bourgeoisie, and the urban poor, as well as the soldiers; it had unceasingly to fight off, isolate, and paralyze the compromising influence of the national bourgeoisie.[44] In his trenchant analysis of the national bourgeoisie, Ch'ü put his finger on the very issues that divided Ch'en Tu-hsiu and his critics.

With such a record, Ch'ü was the natural choice of the opposition as the man to succeed Ch'en Tu-hsiu. Ch'ü had represented the Chinese Communist party in the Comintern on several occasions and was well liked by the Russian leaders. In the Emergency Conference held on August 7, 1927, to depose Ch'en, Ch'ü had followed the Comintern line, denouncing him for his failure to seize the Kuomintang leadership and to win over the peasants through vigorous agrarian revolution.[45] As successor to Ch'en, Ch'ü established a new party line. A new upsurge of the revolutionary tide was at hand, he asserted, and the workers and peasants must make bold attempts to achieve hegemony and establish dictatorship in the form of soviets. Anticipating the thought of Li Li-san, his successor, Ch'ü held that the success of a general uprising would depend on a large city being able to serve as a directing center for nearby peasant uprisings.[46]

Thus the theoretical stage was set for a series of uprisings in the latter part of 1927. It has been generally believed that these uprisings were designed by the Kremlin to show the Trotskyite opposition that the Comintern line was capable of achieving important results. Since Communist representatives Besso Lominadze and Heinz Neumann took part in the Nanchang and Canton uprisings, in all probability the Comintern had approved the policy in principle. There is evidence, however, that in regard to the Nanchang uprising at least, the Comintern had its reservations. A letter to the Chinese Communists on the eve of the uprising directed that if they were assured of its success, they could proceed; otherwise they should not launch it.[47] It may be noted that the Nanchang uprising in August and the autumn uprising in Hunan and Hupeh were decided upon before the August 7 Conference; the Canton uprising of December alone was planned and staged under the leadership of Ch'ü.[48]

All the uprisings were crushed, the one in Canton being the greatest disaster. The Chinese Communists occupied Canton for three days, setting fire to buildings and killing thousands of people. But it ended in terrible defeat. Not only was a significant portion of party personnel annihilated, but the Communist-controlled labor and peasant organizations in the Canton area were entirely wiped out.

The February 1928 Comintern meetings raised the question of *putschism* in connection with the uprisings, admonishing the Chinese Communist party that it must "struggle against *putschism* in certain strata of the working class, against unprepared and unorganized actions in town and country, against playing with insurrection."[49] Ch'ü and his group for their part vigorously defended themselves against this charge. The resolution of the Sixth Congress of the Chinese Communist party, which was held in Moscow in July 1928, asserted that neither the autumn uprisings nor the Nanchang and Canton uprisings had been acts of *putschism,* and that the Canton uprising in particular was of great historical significance, having launched the new era of Chinese soviets. It attributed the failure, rather, to insufficient preparation, charging that "after the uprising, the change of tactics had not been effected in time and combat against *putschism* not carried out thoroughly."[50] The Sixth Congress dismissed Ch'ü as party chief, ending his leadership of less than a year.

Ch'ü, however, had not entirely lost favor with the Comintern. He remained in Moscow as the Chinese Communist delegate to the Comintern, and he was sent to take part in the International Day against Imperial War in August 1930 in Paris. Subsequently, after Li Li-san failed in his general attack on the urban centers, which will be described at greater length in the next section, Ch'ü returned to China to help liquidate the Li Li-san line. He saw in Li Li-san's strategy, however, a similarity to his own in the Canton uprising, and instead of attacking him, as he had intended, Ch'ü adopted a compromising attitude and even expressed empathy. "Had I remained in China after the Sixth Congress and continued to be the leader instead of Li Li-san, I would for all practical purposes have taken the same mistaken path as Li, though I might not have been so careless and haphazard or, if you like, so bold as he."[51]

Ch'ü's vacillating attitude antagonized Ch'en Shao-yü, who succeeded Li Li-san as head of the Chinese Communist party and who considered the latter's political strategy to be a violation of that of the Comintern. Dismissed from the Chinese Communist Politburo in 1931,

Ch'ü went to Shanghai and, together with Lu Hsün, took a leading part in the League of Left-Wing Writers. He published a large number of essays in which he criticized the traditional culture of China and attacked the "romanticism" and "idealistic morality" of the liberal, humanistic writers. His writings conveyed the Marxist spirit of class struggle with poignancy, depth, and freshness. In 1934 he was recalled to Juichin, capital of the Chinese Soviet regime, to serve as commissioner of education. But he no longer had any power, and, suffering badly from tuberculosis, he did little but teach dramatic arts to a group of students. When the Communist forces retreated from Kiangsi in the famous Long March, he was left behind. While trying to go to Shanghai by way of Swatow, he was captured in Fukien by the Nationalist forces. After four months of imprisonment, he was executed on June 18, 1935.

It was in prison that Ch'ü wrote *Superfluous Words,* a personal testament and revelation. It is a tragic story, written with elegance, pathos, and wisdom. The distress and despondency expressed in it are perhaps natural to a person whose life is coming to a close. But what particularly strikes one is the candid confession of weakness and inner conflict. Ch'ü admitted that he was basically an old-fashioned man of letters with Confucian sentiments, incapable of abandoning a program of tolerance and conciliation—"the morality of a weakling," as he put it. He was, he said, forever lacking in firmness and resolution, and in contrast to the Communist spirit of struggle, had permitted the intrusions of generosity and honesty.

My basic nature, I believe, does not make for a Bolshevik fighter, or even a revolutionary novitiate. But because of pride, I did not have the courage, after joining the group, to recognize my own self and ask them to wash me out.[52]

It was a "historical misunderstanding," he wrote, that he should have been involved with the Chinese Communist movement and become the leader of the party. In some ways it was. But tragedies are created as much by men as by circumstances. Personal ambition and political misconception undoubtedly also played their part in his tortuous career.

Li Li-san

Li Li-san, the leader of the Chinese Communist party from 1928 to 1930, was born in 1897 or, as others think, about 1900, in Liling, Hunan. He went to France in 1919 on a work-study program. There he organized with Chou En-lai and others a socialist study group among Chinese students. In 1921, when the Chinese Communist party was formed in China, he took part in establishing the Paris branch. Returning to China the following year, he organized strikes among miners in Anyüan, Kiangsi, and among the Canton-Hankow railroad workers. He went to Shanghai in 1923 to lead the labor movement there. His work among the Shanghai workers in the May Thirtieth Incident of 1925* attracted much attention, and he was sent to Moscow to attend the fourth session of the Communist International Federation of Trade Unions. He was elected to the Politburo of the Chinese Communist party in 1927.

Li is described by one of his contemporaries as "coarse and loud-speaking."[53] A man of supreme confidence, he would not hesitate to express and insist on his own opinion. He advocated bold action and thought little of those who shrank from violence. In the Nanchang uprising of 1927, he had vigorously opposed those who counseled

---

* The Shanghai municipal police under a British officer fired on a Chinese crowd demonstrating against foreign exploitation. The incident resulted in a nationwide movement of anti-imperialist demonstrations and strikes.

caution. He regarded a reign of terror against the "reactionaries" and the wealthy gentry as a revolutionary necessity, and he regretted that this had never come about. A severe critic of Ch'en Tu-hsiu's Rightist opportunism, he had been a defender of Ch'ü Ch'iu-pai.[54]

When Li took over the leadership of the Chinese Communist party, the Comintern policy toward the Chinese revolution was a cautious one. In a letter to the party on February 8, 1929, the Executive Committee of the Comintern (ECCI) warned that the disarray and depression left in the revolution's wake would wear off only very slowly. It pointed out that partial economic revival could open the road to peaceful political and economic development that would render any new rise of revolutionary tide impossible.[55] A more optimistic note was sounded in an ECCI letter of June 7, in which the Chinese Communists were told that the worsening economic and political situation of the peasant masses would unquestionably intensify the class struggle in the rural areas and "create the conditions for a new and powerful surge of the peasant movement." Still, cautioned the ECCI, this fact should not be construed to mean that there was already a powerful rise of the revolutionary tide.[56] The Comintern's view was echoed in the June 1929 resolution of the Central Committee of the Chinese Communist party, which stated that while indications of a new upsurge were in evidence, the revolution was not imminent.[57] Internal and external developments in the following months, however, caused Li to believe that the revolutionary tide was rising even faster than the Comintern thought. The extensive civil wars between Chiang Kai-shek and his opponents, among whom were Generals Feng Yü-hsiang, Yen Hsi-shan, Li Tsung-jen, and Chang Fa-k'uei, had deepened the political and economic crisis. International developments also appeared favorable. The economic depression in the United States, the sharpening of imperialist conflicts in China, and the clashes between the Soviet and Chinese forces on the Manchurian border led Li to the conclusion that an uprising staged at this time would not only revolutionize China but lead to a general collapse of all the capitalist countries.

Li first expressed this view in his article "The Various Questions Prior to the Rising Tide of the Revolution," published in May 1930. He saw in the Chinese revolution a decisive struggle against world imperialism, a struggle that would necessarily break out first in China, where imperialism's basic inconsistencies were most concentrated and severe. Such an outbreak would inevitably lead to the world revolution, since working classes throughout the world would stand on China's side.[58] The relationship of China's anti-imperialist struggle to world revolution had been much discussed in the early stages of Chinese revolutionary theory, but it had met with diminishing emphasis since the Wuhan crisis. The revival of the theme with its broadened implications was Li's own. There is no evidence that the Comintern had influenced him in this thesis.

The second question Li's article raised was how to meet the revolutionary situation. An analysis of the deepening political and economic crisis led him to the conclusion that a new revolutionary surge was indeed coming. He admitted that there was as yet no signs of it on a nationwide scale. But under the daily maturing objective conditions "any problem can break out into a revolutionary upsurge." Believing that the solidarity of "reactionary rule" was not the same for various areas of the country, Li upheld the possibility of achieving initial victory in one or several of the important provinces. Success in establishing revolutionary political power in these provinces would intensify the struggle elsewhere and would lead immediately to the victory of Soviet power on a national scale.[59]

Li viewed the proletariat as being the decisive force in this struggle. Without a massive number of strikes in the urban and industrial centers, especially among railway workers, seamen, and armament workers, one could not hope to hold the provinces, he said. It was "an absolutely wrong idea" to attempt "encircling the city with the country or seizing the urban centers by means of the Red Army alone." The organization of political strikes, to be developed into general strikes, and the arming of the workers must be the basis of any armed uprising. Li did not minimize the importance of peasant uprisings, army mutinies, or attacks by the Red Army. But he thought they should be closely tied to class struggle involving the workers, who must assume leadership. Any focal point for revolutionary struggle must therefore be the large cities.[60]

As to the revolution's orientation, Li maintained that it was still democratic. Since the bourgeoisie had now joined with the reactionaries, its overthrow was necessary to complete revolutionary success. After the proletarian leadership had been consolidated and Soviet power established, the victory of the democratic revolution would transform itself into the victory of socialism. "The beginning of revolutionary victory, the beginning of the establishment of a revolutionary regime, is the beginning of a revolutionary transformation. There will not be any interim stage."[61]

Such were Li Li-san's principal ideas on the Chinese revolution. They were incorporated into the resolution of the Chinese Communist Politburo of June 11, 1930, which constituted the official declaration of the Li Li-san line.[62] The resolution, adopted about a month after the publication of his article, called for national armed uprisings. These uprisings were staged in the summer of 1930, with Wuhan as their major objective; forces that attacked Changsha, Nanchang, and other cities in the lower and middle Yangtze valley were to converge on Wuhan. But although the Chinese Communists succeeded in taking Changsha and other cities, they were unable to hold them. The Nationalist counterattacks rapidly swept the Communists away: their forces were routed, their labor organizations destroyed, and numerous of their cadres captured. By September it was clear that Li Li-san's program had failed.

The Third Plenum of the Central Committee of the Chinese Communist party, held in September 1930, subjected Li Li-san's policy to review. Dominated by Chou En-lai and Ch'ü Ch'iu-pai, the meeting decided to pass only mild criticism. The Chinese Communist leadership, Chou declared, had "made exaggerated and incorrect evaluations of the speed and degree of development of the revolution and sporadic practical mistakes occurred." But there was "no difference in line" between the Chinese Communist leadership and the Comintern. Ch'ü concurred, and this consensus was adopted by the Third Plenum.[63]

The controversy as to whether the Li Li-san line differed from the Comintern's centers around the latter's directive of July 23, 1930.[64] A close comparison of this document with the Chinese Communist Politburo resolution of June 11, reveals some disagreement. The Chinese Politburo held that the basic political and economic crisis was growing equally acute for all parts of the country, with no fundamental difference from one area to another; once a gigantic struggle had broken out in the urban centers, there would be revolutionary fervor throughout the nation. The Comintern, on the other hand, held that no direct revolutionary situation as yet existed in China as a whole, even though events were moving in that direction. The Chinese Politburo viewed the unevenness of revolutionary development in the cities and the countryside as being superficial, whereas the Comintern held that the labor and peasant movements had not in fact merged into one and did not ensure forces required for an effective offensive against imperialism and the Kuomintang. Finally, it was Li Li-san's belief that a successful democratic revolution would develop immediately into a socialist revolution, while the Comintern anticipated a gradual and steady transition, by a series of intermediate stages.[65] These, then, were fundamental differences between the Comintern and Li Li-san, although in some cases the statements on both sides were far from sharply drawn.

The ECCI found the Third Plenum's criticism of Li Li-san inadequate, and in a letter to the Chinese Central Committee on November 16, 1930, declared that very serious differences had arisen between them. Li Li-san's strategy had "made not only particular mistakes, but created an entire system of erroneous views." His ignorance of concrete reality had led him to take an "anti-Marxist, anti-Leninist position," which was bound to lead to *putschist,* adventurist tactics. From this opportunist position, the ECCI continued, he had derived the theory that a revolutionary situation had already matured on a national scale and was developing on a world scale. And like Trotsky, he mistakenly believed that once the revolution achieved some success, it would pass immediately from a bourgeois democratic to a proletarian revolution.[66]

The Comintern's condemnation of Li Li-san as anti-Marxist, anti-Leninist, and Trotskyite was hardly justified. Much of the difference between the two was in the nature of tactical error rather than ideological. The only point of Li's bearing any resemblance to Trotsky was his statement that once the revolution achieved success, it would immediately become socialist. But then the Comintern had talked of the transition to socialism ever since its attack on Ch'en Tu-hsiu. The difference was again a matter of degree and timing. Li, in his interpretation, gave greater speed to the event than the Comintern wished. Li's misfortune lay not so much in his impetuous theoretical formulation as in the failure of his uprisings. Moscow had applauded the early success of the August uprising.[67] It was the later failures that the Kremlin, as ever searching for a scapegoat, disapproved of. But what disturbed the Comintern most was "some dangerous notes" sounded in Li's speeches. In defense of his policy he had gone so far as to say that the Comintern was ill-informed, that China had a special position, and that the Comintern did not understand the trend of the Chinese revolution. "He was bold enough," the Comintern complained, "to oppose loyalty to the Comintern to loyalty to the Chinese revolution . . . saying that after the capture of Hankow it would be possible to take a different tone with the Comintern."[68]

In response to the Comintern's call for a fresh struggle against Li Li-san's ideology, the Enlarged Fourth Plenum of the Chinese Communist Central Committee was convened on January 13, 1931. The Li Li-san line was soundly denounced in accordance with the Comintern's letter of November. The Chinese Communist party declared that henceforth it would carry out all instructions of the Comintern, and to signify the complete purge of the Li Li-san line, it dismissed Li from the Central Committee.[69]

Before the arrival of the November 16 letter, Li had been sent to Moscow to report to the Comintern. He was severely interrogated first by the Eastern Department of the Comintern and then by the Presidium of the ECCI, a procedure that in fact amounted to a Communist trial. Under the Comintern's powerful pressure he finally broke down, repenting all the errors attributed to him and pledging himself to carry out the Comintern line when he returned to China. But he was kept in Russia for fifteen years. In 1945 he was sent to Manchuria with the Russian occupation army. Though appointed to various government positions in Communist China, he was no longer an important figure. Reports have it that he committed suicide in August 1967, during the turmoil of the Cultural Revolution.

Ch'en Shao-yü

Ch'en Shao-yü, also known as Wang Ming, became general secretary of the Chinese Communist party in 1931. He was born in 1907 to a comfortable family in Liuan, Anhwei. While a middle school student at Wuhan, he joined the Communist Youth Corps. In 1925, after he became a member of the Chinese Communist party, he was sent to study at Sun Yat-sen University in Moscow. He returned to China for a short time in 1927 to serve as interpreter for Pavel Mif, head of the University, at Wuhan. In Moscow the following year, he was called to interpret for the Chinese Communists who attended the Sixth National Congress of the Chinese Communist party in the Russian capital. This provided him a further opportunity to get acquainted with the Chinese Communist leaders and the burning issues following the disaster of the Canton uprising. During all this time he was closely associated with Mif, who, as head of Sun Yat-sen University, was keen on training his students for leading roles in the Chinese Communist movement. A group of students, later known as the Twenty-eight Bolsheviks, or Russian Returned Students, gained Mif's special confidence and support. Ch'en was the group's leader.

When Mif was sent to Shanghai as Comintern representative in the summer of 1930, his favorite students accompanied him. Ch'en Shao-yü, regarded by Mif as one of the most important and gifted leaders of the Chi-

nese Communist movement,[70] quickly involved himself in
the intraparty struggle. Ch'en worked closely with his
mentor, faithfully upholding the Comintern line and skillfully giving it Chinese expression. He had earlier distinguished himself as a Communist theoretician by the
publication of his *Armed Uprising* in 1928. Writing immediately after the Canton uprising, Ch'en maintained in
this work that general strikes are essential to an armed
uprising. Military operations are important, but he warned
against overemphasizing them, especially at the expense
of the masses, who are the true social foundation of uprisings.[71]

Ch'en was more optimistic about guerrilla warfare than
Li Li-san. While admitting that there were undesirable or
dangerous elements in it, he, like Lenin, considered it
a necessary device. The important thing was to eliminate
its disorganized, spontaneous aspects and to link it to
the armed uprising of the proletariat, thus making it into
the highest form of class struggle.[72]

Like Li Li-san, Ch'en Shao-yü laid great stress on the
role of the urban industrial proletariat. Proletarian armed
uprisings, he said, could not be regarded as merely a
reflection of or supplement to rural guerrilla warfare. Industrial cities alone could provide the organized center of
revolution, and the proletariat its sole directing force.
Still, Ch'en realized that the countryside was important.
"A peasant movement without the workers' movement,
just as a workers' movement without a peasant movement,
can never be successful."[73] According to Ch'en, it was
the party's imperative duty to unite the diffuse, uncon-
nected peasant struggles with the new urban revolutionary
upsurge. Herein lay the difference between Li Li-san and
Ch'en Shao-yü. The former concentrated all his attention
on the taking of the key cities. The latter emphasized
an all-round coordination of proletarian uprisings, guer-

rilla warfare, and military operations, with the proletariat assuming leadership over all.

When Li had first announced his political line in his articles in 1928, Ch'en, together with the other Russian Returned Students, had opposed it.[74] He had renewed his opposition after the June 11 Resolution, embodying the Li Li-san line, was passed; consequently he was suspended from his post as director of propaganda. At the Third Plenum of the Chinese Communist party in September 1930, he attacked not only the Li Li-san line but also the compromising attitude of Ch'ü Ch'iu-pai. As a result, he was dismissed from all responsibilities in the party.

Following the Third Plenum Ch'en wrote *The Two Lines,* in which he simultaneously attacked the Li Li-san line and expounded his own strategy. Here he viewed China not as a predominantly feudal state, but as a semi-colonial economy with precapitalist features. Because of imperialist invasion, he contended, capitalism in China had developed in a distorted form, giving rise to a most complex economy, which included imperialist capitalism, national capitalism, commercial capitalism, simple commercial economy, and even natural economy. Because of the complex nature of China's economic relationships, the essential content of the Chinese revolution had to be agrarian. Ch'en placed little faith in the petty bourgeoisie, which, according to his analysis, was composed of various elements ranging from exploiters to exploited. The upper stratum of the petty bourgeoisie, as well as the big and middle bourgeoisie, all belonged to the reactionary camp. In his view, there was no intermediate group or third force among these social strata that could be won over to the revolution.

Since the content of the Chinese revolution had to be agrarian, Ch'en saw the important task of the party as being the establishment of soviets, and the creation of a Red Army that could sustain a soviet regime. Soviet power, an essential stage in the development of the revolution, therefore was to play the double role of completing the bourgeois democratic revolution and preparing for gradual transition to the proletarian revolution. In Ch'en's opinion, Li Li-san's unpardonable mistake was to skip over this transitional stage. The correct strategy was to strengthen the soviet bases and prepare them, "in accordance with the future military and political environments," to seize one or more industrial and administrative centers.[75] Ch'en, unlike Li, did not anticipate that the seizure of one or more key cities would be decisive in the revolutionary struggle. Earlier, in *Armed Uprising,* he had pointed out that uprisings, in order to be successful, should not be confined to one or several cities. They must be organized in one or several provinces, since in an agricultural country like China, the armed peasant units would play an especially significant role.[76]

Ch'en modified his views on the peasant movement, however, when in 1932, he published in Moscow the second edition of *The Two Lines.* In a postscript to the book he denounced the theory that Chinese peasants had a greater revolutionary character than the workers. He called erroneous those who assigned an unusual revolutionary character to the peasantry while reducing the status of the proletariat merely to that of its accomplice. These people, he charged, overemphasized the peasantry's independent political role while failing to realize the essential character of proletarian leadership.[77] When the book was first published in 1931, Ch'en had intended it primarily as a denunciation of Li Li-san's "Left" deviation. Now, in the postscript, he was leveling criticism against the Right deviation represented by Mao Tse-tung, who then headed the Chinese Soviet government and, naturally, placed particular emphasis on the peasantry's revolutionary role. Little wonder that in 1945, when Mao Tse-tung was in power, the Ch'en Shao-yü line was chosen for condemnation.

With the powerful support of Pavel Mif, Ch'en Shao-yü was, in January 1931, elected to lead the Chinese Communist party. He remained in office for a year and a half until he left for Moscow in the fall of 1932. Although relinquishing his leadership to Ch'in Pang-hsien, another member of the Russian Returned Students group, he remained active in Comintern conferences as spokesman for the Chinese Communist party. When the Seventh Comintern Congress was held in 1935, the general theme of discussion stressed the working class's united front against fascism. The new general secretary of the Comintern and major speaker at the congress meetings, Georgi Dimitrov, was most concerned with the capitalist countries, particularly with joint action by supporters of the two Internationals—the Communist and the Second International. Because the objective of any united front in China would have to be imperialism rather than fascism, the task of dealing with united-front tactics in China fell upon Ch'en Shao-yü.

Speaking at several meetings of the Congress between August 7 and 11, Ch'en proposed an appeal to all the Chinese people—to all parties, groups, troops, mass organizations and to all prominent political and social leaders —to unite with the Chinese Communists into an All-China United People's Government of National Defense. He stressed particularly the participation of the younger members of the Kuomintang and the Blue Shirt League. An organization on this scale was necessary, Ch'en declared, to avert the unprecedented national crisis caused by the Japanese invasion. In Ch'en's view, there was no means of saving the country now except general mobilization of the entire nation for a decisive and relentless struggle against imperialism. And for this the Communist party had no other means at its disposal than the tactics of the anti-imperialist united front.[78]

In a sense the Chinese Communists had been applying the tactics of the united front for years. After the Japanese invasion of Manchuria in 1931, they had stepped up their united-front activities, through open appeals to the people and through actual cooperation with the anti-Japanese forces. Their support of the 19th Route Army during the defense of Shanghai in 1932, their agreement with the same army during the Fukien rebellion, and their cooperation with General Feng Yü-hsiang in organizing the Popular Anti-Japanese Allied Armies in Kalgan the same year were all notable attempts to put their united-front slogan into practice. More extensive in scope was the Chinese People's Basic Program for Fighting Japan, initiated by the Chinese Communist party and published under the signatures of Madame Sun Yat-sen and others in May 1934. This program proposed the creation of an all-China committee for armed defense, to be elected by workers, peasants, soldiers, students, and businessmen.[79] All these tactics, however, were designed to form a united front from below, that is, an alliance with non-Communist mass organizations. The Chinese Communists had up to now remained hostile to the Kuomintang government, which they denounced for having adopted a "traitorous" appeasement policy toward the Japanese. Ch'en Shao-yü's proposal at the Seventh Comintern Congress, calling as it did for an alliance with all parties, including the Kuomintang, therefore signified a new departure in their thinking.

To carry out his program, Ch'en proposed a revision of China's soviet economic policy. Abandoning his former opposition to lenient treatment of rich peasants, he now assumed a conciliatory posture, even toward small landlords, who, because of their economic and social condition, could "by no means be considered landed gentry." Policy in the area of taxation, finance, and trade should also be reconsidered, with a view to giving it a more "popular and clearly national character" in order to facilitate the mobilization of broad masses of people.[80]

Ch'en felt, however, that participation of the Chinese Communist party in the united front must not interfere with its struggle for proletarian hegemony. Mindful of the mistakes committed by Ch'en Tu-hsiu during 1924–1927, Ch'en Shao-yü warned that his new policy must not in any way conflict with the task of class struggle. The Communists must still make every effort to capture the trade unions and the youth organizations, fight systematically for the leadership of the proletariat, regardless of sacrifice, and not abandon their independence in relation to their temporary allies.[81]

On August 1, 1935, a declaration by the Chinese Communist party in Moscow called for a united front with the Kuomintang and all other parties, regardless of hostilities they might have had in the past. Some writers suggest that the declaration was made solely by Ch'en in the name of the Chinese Communist party.[82] While this sounds unusual, it is not impossible. But whoever was responsible for the August 1 declaration, it was Ch'en who first provided the ideological basis in China for an anti-Japanese united front from above. Not until December 1935 did Mao Tse-tung speak on the subject, and his discussion did not go beyond the basic principle as laid down by Ch'en Shao-yü.[83]

Ch'en's report at the Seventh Comintern Congress proved to be his last major discourse. Mao Tse-tung soon consolidated his control over the Chinese Communist party, replacing the Russian Returned Students as formulator of party policy. As a theoretician, Ch'en was a faithful exponent of the Comintern line; his main objective in office had been to check both the "Left" and Right deviations. He was less urban-minded than Li Li-san, but he did not place as much emphasis on the countryside as Mao Tse-tung. In the organization of his anti-Japanese united front, he had had to soften his position on intense guerrilla warfare in the rural areas and to recognize the intermediate group of rich peasants and smaller landlords as a national revolutionary force. When continued emphasis was placed on the peasantry under Mao's leadership, however, he began to feel that the urban workers were being neglected. He found it necessary to point out to the Chinese Communist cadres that many of them completely lacked experience with the masses beyond the soviet areas, and that some of them had no idea whatever of the workers' movement in the large cities.[84]

As a result of his disagreement with Mao, the Chinese Communist Committee rebuked Ch'en in 1938. The rectification movement Mao launched in 1942 further criticized him. He and other Russian Returned Students were accused of lacking practical revolutionary experience as well as being theoretically incapable of coping with the Chinese conditions. The Ch'en group, the Maoists charged, were "erroneously afraid" to accept the Red Army movement as a peasant movement led by the proletariat, and were opposed to "the so-called peculiar revolutionary character of the peasants." Ch'en's ideas, they charged, were rooted in subjectivism and formalism and had developed into doctrinairism.[85] The criticism was not entirely unfounded, for of all the Communist leaders Ch'en suffered most from rigid adherence to doctrine. His writings were more a careful exposition of Communist strategy than a bold advancement of revolutionary ideas, smacking of a Russian-oriented discipline that was somewhat divorced from the realities of China. Stylistically, Ch'en Shao-yü lacked the flair of Li Li-san, the subtle elegance of Ch'ü Ch'iu-pai, and the ingenuity of Mao Tse-tung.

Notes

CHAPTER IX. CHINESE COMMUNISM I

1. V. I. Lenin, "Better Fewer, But Better," *Selected Works*, 2-volume edition (Moscow, 1947), II, 854.
2. V. I. Lenin, *Selected Works*, 12-volume edition (Moscow, 1937), X, 236–37.
3. *Hsin Ch'ing-nien* (*HCN*), 7.1: 1–4 (Dec. 1919).
4. Chang Kuo-t'ao [*Autobiography*] (manuscript, 1958), pp. 238–39.
5. Ch'en Tu-hsiu, "Chung-kuo kuo-min ke-ming yü she-hui ko chieh-chi" (The Chinese National Revolution and the Various Social Classes); "Tzu-ch'an chieh-chi ti ke-ming yü ke-ming ti tzu-ch'an chieh-chi" (The Bourgeois Revolution and the Revolutionary Bourgeoisie). Both articles are printed in *Chung-kuo ke-ming wen-t'i lun-wen chi* (A Collection of Articles on Problems of the Chinese Revolution, hereafter cited as *CKK*) (Shanghai, 1930).
6. "Chung-kuo kuo-min ke-ming yü she-hui ko chieh-chi," *CKK*, pp. 39, 42, 44.
7. Ts'ai Ho-shen, "Lun Ch'en Tu-hsiu chu-i" (On Ch'en Tu-hsiu-ism), in *Ch'en Tu-hsiu p'ing-lun* (Discussions concerning Ch'en Tu-hsiu) (Peiping: Tung-ya, 1933), p. 18.
8. "Chung-kuo kuo-min ke-ming yü she-hui ko chieh-chi," *CKK*, pp. 39, 43.
9. Ch'en Tu-hsiu, "Kao ch'üan-tang t'ung-chih shu" (A Letter to All Comrades of the Party), in *Kung-fei huo-kuo shih-liao hui-pien* (A Collection of Historical Materials concerning the National Subversion of the Communist Bandits, hereafter cited as *KFHK*) (Taipei, 1964), I, 429.
10. "Tzu-ch'an chieh-chi ti ke-ming yü ke-ming ti tzu-ch'an chieh-chi," *CKK*, p. 56.
11. *Ibid.*, pp. 58, 60–61.
12. *Ibid.*, pp. 47.
13. ECCI Resolution on the Relations between CCP and KMT, Jan. 12, 1923, in Jane Degras, ed., *The Communist International* (London: Oxford University Press, 1960), II, 6.
14. Thesis on Tactics adopted by the 5th Comintern Congress, July 1924.
15. ECCI Resolution, Jan. 12, 1923, Degras, *op. cit.*, II, 60.
16. ECCI Instructions to the 3rd Congress of the CCP, May 1923, *ibid.*, II, 25–26.
17. Ts'ai Ho-shen, *op. cit.*
18. Ch'en was also denounced for failing to organize uprisings in the Hunan-Hupeh area. According to Ts'ai Ho-shen, the Russian adviser Mikhail Borodin was no less responsible than Ch'en for the hesitancy of the Chinese Communist party during the Hunan crisis in 1927. Even M. N. Roy, reputed to be a radical, was as eager as Ch'en and Borodin to win the support of the Left Kuomintang led by Wang Ching-wei. And though Roy was once in favor of a militant line against the Kuomintang government at Hankow, his sub-

sequent vacillation helped to kill the aggressive plan. Ts'ai Ho-shen, "Chi-hui chu-i shih" (History of Opportunism), in *KFHK*, I, 584. For the reliability of Ts'ai's article, see Wang Chien-min, *Chung-kuo kung-ch'an-tang shih-kao* (Draft History of the Chinese Communist Party) (Taipei, 1965), III, 723–26.

19. Degras, *op. cit.*, II, 277.
20. *Ibid.*, II, 342.
21. *Ibid.*, II, 345.
22. Ch'en Tu-hsiu, "Kao ch'üan-tang t'ung-chih shu," *KFHK*, I, 32.
23. Ch'en Tu-hsiu, *Wo-men ti cheng-chih i-chien shu* (A Statement of Our Political Views) (Shanghai, 1929), p. 13.
24. *Ibid.*, p. 7.
25. Chinese Communist party, *Pa-ch'i hui-i kao ch'üan-tang tang-yüan shu* (Letter from the August 7 Conference to All Members of the Party), *KFHK*, I, 449.
26. Degras, *op. cit.*, II, 342.
27. *Ibid.*, II, 395. See also *Chung-kuo Kung-ch'an-tang ti-liu-tz'u ch'-üan-kuo ta hui i-chüeh-an* (Resolutions of the 6th National Congress of the Chinese Communist Party; 1928), pp. 2, 18.
28. For biographical sketches of Ch'ü Ch'iu-pai, see Li Ch'ang-ke, "Ch'ü Ch'iu-pai fang-wen chi" (An Interview with Ch'ü Ch'iu-pai), *KFHK*, II, 535–43; Ssu-ma Lu (Smarlo Ma), *Ch'ü Ch'iu-pai chuan* ("The Ch'ü Ch'iu-pai Story") (Hong Kong: Tzu-lien, 1962).
29. Ch'ü Ch'iu-pai, *O-hsiang chi-ch'eng* (Journey to the Hungry Land), in *Ch'ü Ch'iu-pai wen-chi* (Collected Works of Ch'ü Ch'iu-pai) (Peking: Jen-min wen-hsüeh ch'u-pan she, 1953), I, 24.
30. *Ibid.*, I, 3–5.
31. *Ibid.*, I, 88.
32. Ch'ü Ch'iu-pai, *Ch'ih-tu hsin-shih* (The Inner Story of the Red Capital), *ibid.*, I, 98.
33. *Ibid.*, I, 138–40.
34. Ch'ü Ch'iu-pai, "Hsien-tai wen-ming ti wen-t'i yü she-hui chu-i" (Problems of Modern Civilization and Socialism), in Ch'en Pen-wen, ed., *Hsin chu-i p'ing-lun* (Criticisms of the New Doctrines) (Shanghai: Min-chih, 1928), I, 202 ff.
35. Ch'ü Ch'iu-pai, "Shih-chieh ti she-hui kai-tsao yü Kung-ch'an-kuo-chi" (World Social Reconstruction and the Communist International), *Hsin Ch'ing-nien* (quarterly), No. 1: 19 (June 1923); "Sun Chung-shan yü Chung-kuo kuo-min ke-ming" (Sun Yat-sen and the Chinese National Revolution), *ibid.*, No. 2: 176 (June 1925).
36. Ch'ü Ch'iu-pai, "Hsien-tai lao-tzu chan-cheng yü ke-ming" (Modern Labor-Capitalist War and Revolution), *ibid.*, No. 1: 58 (June 1923).
37. Ch'ü Ch'iu-pai, *"Pei-ching t'u-sha yü kuo-min ke-ming chih ch'ien-t'u"* (The Peking Massacre and the Future of the National Revolution), *ibid.*, No. 4: 419 (May 1926).
38. Ch'ü Ch'iu-pai, "Shih-chieh ke-ming ti nung-min cheng-tang chi nung-min hsieh-hui" (The Peasant Party and the Peasant Association in the World Revolution), *ibid.*, No. 5: 621 (July 1926).
39. Ch'ü Ch'iu-pai, "Kuo-min ke-ming yün-tung chung chih chieh-chi fen-hua" (Class Division in the National Revolution), *ibid.*, No. 3: 311 (March 1925).
40. P'eng Shu-chih, "Shui shih Chung-kuo kuo-min ke-ming chih ling-

tao che?" (Who Are the Leaders of the Chinese National Revolution?), *ibid.*, No. 4: 468 (Dec. 1924).

41. Ch'ü Ch'iu-pai, *Chung-kuo ke-ming chung chih cheng-lun wen-t'i* (The Issues of the Chinese Revolution) (Chinese Communist party, 1927), p. 84.
42. *Ibid.*, pp. 49, 57.
43. *Ibid.*, pp. 51, 53, 58.
44. *Ibid.*, pp. 79–80, 106, 110–13.
45. *Pa-ch'i hui-i kao ch'üan-tang tang-yüan shu, KFHK*, I, 453 ff.; Ch'ü Ch'iu-pai, *Chung-kuo ke-ming yü Kung-ch'an-tang* (The Chinese Revolution and the Chinese Communist Party; 1928), pp. 74–84.
46. Ch'ü Ch'iu-pai, *Chung-kuo ke-ming yü Kung-ch'an-tang*, pp. 136–40.
47. Li Li-san, "Pa-i ke-ming chih ching-kuo yü chiao-hsün" (The Events and Lessons of the August 1 Revolution), *KFHK*, I, 489.
48. Ch'ü Ch'iu-pai, *Chung-kuo ke-ming yü Kung-ch'an-tang*, p. 122.
49. Resolution of the 9th ECCI Plenum on the Chinese Question, Feb. 25, 1928, Degras, *op. cit.*, II, 439.
50. *Chung-kuo Kung-ch'an-tang ti-liu-tz'u ch'üan-kuo ta-hui i-chüeh-an*, pp. 9, 24.
51. Ch'ü Ch'iu-pai, *To-yü ti hua* (Superfluous Words), in Ssu-ma Lu, *op. cit.*, Appendix, p. 146.
52. *Ibid.*, p. 152.
53. Siao-yu, *Mao Tse-tung and I Were Beggars* (London: Hutchinson, 1961), p. 185.
54. See Po-shan (Li Li-san), *Kung-ch'an-kuo-chi tui Chung-kuo ke-ming chüeh-i-an—tai-hsü* (Preface, Resolutions of the Communist International on the Chinese Revolution) (Shanghai, 1930), pp. 17, 56–58.
55. Degras, *op. cit.*, III, 3.
56. *Ibid.*, III, 32–33.
57. Wang Chien-min, *op. cit.*, II, 38; Conrad Brandt and associates, *A Documentary History of Chinese Communism* (London: George Allen, 1952), pp. 170–71.
58. *Pu-erh-se-wei-ke* (The Bolsheviks), 3.4–5: 19–21 (May 1930).
59. *Ibid.*, pp. 24–25, 29–32.
60. *Ibid.*, pp. 33, 35.
61. *Ibid.*, p. 39.
62. For text, see Wang Chien-min, *op. cit.*, II, 42–52; Brandt and associates, *op. cit.*, pp. 184–200.
63. Brandt and associates, *op. cit.*, p. 202; Tso-liang Hsiao, *Power Relations within the Chinese Communist Movement, 1930–1934* (Seattle: University of Washington Press, 1961), pp. 66–67.
64. The document is dated June 1930, probably by mistake, in Degras, *op. cit.*, III, 114 ff.
65. Wang Chien-min, *op. cit.*, II, 45; Degras, *op. cit.*, III, 115, 119. Cf. Hsiao, *op. cit.*, pp. 25 ff.
66. Degras, *op. cit.*, III, 137.
67. *Ibid.*, III, 135.
68. *Ibid.*, III, 141.
69. For text of the Resolution of the Enlarged 4th Plenum, see Wang Chien-min, *op. cit.*, II, 74–79; Brandt and associates, *op. cit.*, pp. 209–16.

70. P. Miff (Mif), *China's Struggle for Freedom* (London: Modern Books Ltd., 1936?), p. 71.
71. Ch'en Shao-yü, *Wu-chuang pao-tung* (Armed Uprisings) (Shanghai, 1929), pp. 5, 11–12, 83.
72. *Ibid.*, p. 16.
73. *Ibid.*, p. 108.
74. Wang Chien-min, *op. cit.*, II, 96; Hsiao, *op. cit.*, p. 134.
75. Wang Ming (Ch'en Shao-yü), *Liang-t'iao chan-hsien* (The Two Lines) (Chinese Communist party, 1931), p. 35.
76. Ch'en Shao-yü, *Wu-chuang pao-tung*, p. 160.
77. Hsiao, *op. cit.*, p. 205.
78. *7th Congress of the Communist International* (Moscow, 1939), p. 286.
79. Wang Chien-min, *op. cit.*, p. 34.
80. *7th Congress of the Communist International*, p. 303.
81. Wang Ming, *Lun fan-ti t'ung-i chan-hsien wen-t'i* (Problems of the Anti-imperialist United Front) (Paris, 1935), pp. 94, 98–99.
82. See Wang Chien-min, *op. cit.*, III, 34, 39; Robert C. North, *Moscow and Chinese Communists* (Stanford: Stanford University Press, 1965), pp. 176–77; Charles B. McLane, *Soviet Policy and the Chinese Communists, 1931–1946* (New York: Columbia University Press, 1958), p. 67.
83. See Mao Tse-tung, *Selected Works* (London: Lawrence and Wishart, 1956), I, 153; Ch'en Shao-yü, *Hsin hsing-shih yü hsin cheng-ts'e* (The New Situation and the New Policy) (Paris, 1936).
84. Ch'en Shao-yü, "Chung-kuo Kung-ch'an-tang tsai hsien-shih huan-ching chung ti jen-wu" (The Tasks of the Chinese Communist Party in the Present Situation), in *T'ung-i chan-hsien ti Chung-kuo Kung-ch'an-tang* (The Chinese Communist Party in the United Front) (Hong Kong, 1938).
85. Mao Tse-tung, *Selected Works*, IV, 192, 208.

Chapter X

CHINESE COMMUNISM II—
MAO TSE-TUNG

MAO TSE-TUNG was born in 1893 to a peasant family in Hsiangt'an, Hunan. His father, a harsh and extremely frugal man, engaged in small trading and owned a few acres of land. Mao was sent to a village teacher at the age of eight, to learn how to read and write. He was, however, required to do farming work in the early morning and at night. He liked reading, especially popular novels such as *The Water Margin, The Tale of the Three Kingdoms,* and *The Monkey.* The fighting, rebelliousness, and heroism in these stories fascinated him. He usually sneaked out to the hills and there, behind the tombs, concentrated on his books.

Mao and his father frequently quarreled. The former had no interest in farming, the latter considered studying futile. But if their views of life were different, they were equally stubborn and violent in temperament. While Mao's hatred for his father is exaggerated by some writers, there is little doubt that his father's repressiveness contributed greatly to Mao's rebelliousness.

Mao showed extraordinary independence in his early school life. No sooner had he entered the First Provincial Middle School than he found its curriculum and regulations unbearable. He left it after half a year and devised a plan of study for himself. Every day he went to the public library, where he devoured translations of Adam Smith, Charles Darwin, John Stuart Mill, J. J. Rousseau, and others. His thirst for "new" knowledge was motivated by a strong desire to reform China, which had steadily declined under foreign aggression.

When Mao entered the First Normal School in Changsha in 1913 a new phase in his academic life began. Here he encountered more mature students and more scholarly teachers. The teacher who influenced him most was Professor Yang Ch'ang-chi, whose daughter he later married. Yang had studied in England and Japan, concentrating on ethics and logic. Under his influence Mao read and wrote extensive comments upon a Chinese translation of Friedrich Paulsen's *A System of Ethics*. Mao's iconoclastic and rebellious spirit showed clearly in his premise that tradition could stifle what was new and that a complete destruction of tradition was needed to bring about a new society.[1] Becoming a devoted reader of *New Youth*, he accepted the new thinkers' theory that China must be modernized. Earlier he had admired K'ang Yu-wei and Liang Ch'i-ch'ao, but now his admiration shifted to Ch'en Tu-hsiu and Hu Shih. He became more and more radical in his attitude toward the problem of reform. But his mind at this time, in his own words, was still "a curious mixture of ideas of liberalism, democratic reformism, and Utopian Socialism."[2] He was antimilitarist and anti-imperialist, but he had yet to become a Marxist.

At the Normal School Mao excelled in essay-writing. In addition to novels and poetry, he studied the classical essays of Han Yü and the classical history books. He paid no attention to English and other foreign languages —a negligence he later turned to his advantage. Because of this deficiency, he had to rely entirely on Chinese translations of foreign works, particularly of Marx and Lenin, and what he lost in indirect contact with their ideas, he gained in flexibility of interpretation. He was never doctrinaire as some of the Russian Returned Students, but was able to view Chinese problems more from the standpoint of a Chinese. Thanks to his interest in Chinese novels, his writings are marked by clarity, vividness, and humor. He once admonished his comrades: "The foreign type of stereotyped essays must be banned, empty and abstract talk must be stopped, and doctrinairism must be laid to rest to make room for the fresh and lively things of Chinese style and Chinese flavor which the common folk of China love to see and hear."[3]

In the fall of 1918, after graduating from the Normal School, Mao went to Peking. He obtained a job as assistant in the library of Peking University, where he read for the first time the *Communist Manifesto,* Kautsky's *Class Struggle,* and Kirkup's *History of Socialism.* Mao converted to Communism more out of practical than ideological motives. Although he might not have known much about Marxism at the time, he deeply believed that to bring about extensive reforms in China a revolution was necessary. Greatly impressed by the success of the Bolshevik Revolution, he came to the conclusion that the best, the simplest way to start a revolution was to follow the Russian example.[4] By the summer of 1920, Mao had become a Marxist "in theory and to some extent in action." He attended the First Congress of the Chinese Communists in 1921.

In January 1935, after years of struggle, Mao gained control of the party at the Tsunyi Conference held in the course of the Long March that finally brought the Chinese Communists to Yenan. His rise was due partly to the ineffectual leadership of the Russian Returned Students, but more to the actual power he wielded in his capacity as chairman of the Central Soviet government, which had ruled a vast area during the period 1931–1934. The Communist victory over the Nationalists in 1949 established him as the supreme ruler of the Chinese mainland.

In the area of ideology, Mao's reputation is formidable.

The Chinese Communists claim that he has creatively developed Marxism-Leninism and greatly enriched the Communist heritage. What are his contributions? How valid are the Chinese Communist claims? We will discuss these questions in the following pages.

The Role of the Peasantry

Mao rose to power by way of the peasant movement. Because of this unique aspect of his career, he has been viewed by some writers as heretical regarding one of the vital presuppositions of Marxism-Leninism, namely, the leadership of the proletariat.[5] On the other hand, there are writers who maintain that Mao's view of the peasantry was very close to that of Lenin's.[6] The controversy centers around Mao's March 1927 article "Report of an Investigation into the Peasant Movement in Hunan." A significant passage from the article, appearing under the subtitle "Vanguard of the Revolution," reads as follows:

This enormous mass of poor peasants, altogether comprising 70 percent of the rural population, are the backbone of the peasant association, the vanguard in overthrowing the feudal forces, and the foremost heroes who have accomplished the great revolutionary undertaking left unaccomplished for many years. . . . Being the most revolutionary, the poor peasants have won the leadership in the peasant association. . . . This leadership of the poor peasants is absolutely necessary. Without the poor peasants there can be no revolution. To reject them is to reject the revolution. To attack them is to attack the revolution.[7]

Since the designation "vanguard" had usually been reserved for the proletariat in Marxist literature, Mao's use of the word "vanguard" to describe the peasantry was regarded as further evidence of heresy. The criticism is without basis, since in 1926 the Comintern itself described the Kuomintang government as "the vanguard of the Chinese people" in the national revolution.[8] Ch'ü Ch'iu-pai had also used the term to describe the peasantry and the proletariat together.[9] If the Kuomintang, a national bourgeois party, could be termed by the Comintern the vanguard of the people, it could hardly be heresy to describe the peasantry as such. One must also remember that Mao was discussing the role of the peasantry in the context of the bourgeois national revolution, and that the article was written as a report specifically on this subject. He was not discussing the general political line of the party, nor speaking in the capacity of party leader. His stress on the peasantry and omission of any mention of the proletariat are not unnatural in view of the limited purpose and scope of the article.

Of course, the idea for a peasant movement did not originate with Mao. In 1920, Lenin assigned a special position to the peasantry in the noncapitalist countries, where, he said, peasants' soviets were possible.[10] Enjoining his comrades to give the peasant movement the most revolutionary character possible, he had urged the close alliance of the West European proletariat with the Eastern revolutionary peasant movement.[11] Following Lenin's line of thought, the Comintern maintained in 1922 that "to succeed, the revolutionary movement in the backward countries of the East must be based on the action of the peasant masses."[12] In March 1926, a year before Mao wrote his Hunan peasant report, the Comintern stressed the peasant question as "the most important question of the Chinese national liberation movement. . . . The victory of the revolutionary democratic tendency . . . depends on the degree to which the 400 million Chinese peasants take part in the decisive revolutionary struggle."[13] While it is true that in all its resolutions on

the peasant question, the Comintern called for leadership
of the proletariat, so also did Mao in his various discussions of Chinese class struggle.[14] If in later years the
rural base areas were cut off from the urban proletariat,
the Chinese Communist party would always be there to
provide the "proletarian ideological leadership."[15] The
fact that there were not many workers in the party should
not affect its overall representation of the proletariat. A
proletarian party, Lenin stressed, is led by professional
revolutionaries and it does not matter whether its members are students or workers.[16]

Nor was Mao the first actually to foster the peasant
movement in China. P'eng Pai, a Chinese Communist,
had organized peasant unions in eastern Kwangtung as
early as 1922. Mao did not interest himself in the peasant
movement until 1925, sometime after the May Thirtieth
Incident. His first assignment in this field occurred in 1926
when he was placed in charge of the Peasant Movement
Training Institute in Canton. But if he was not the first
one to recognize the important role of the peasantry in
the Chinese revolution, it was he who unswervingly stood
for it and who finally made it successful. No Communist
leader preceding him had worked so persistently nor with
such unfailing faith in the peasant movement. Ch'en Tu-
hsiu, sensitive to Kuomintang reaction, was opposed to
aggressive action on the peasant front. Ch'ü Ch'iu-pai,
while recognizing the importance of the peasant movement, was preoccupied with urban uprisings. Li Li-san,
focused upon attacking urban centers, did not care much
about the countryside. And Ch'en Shao-yü, in spite of
his two-pronged attack on the Right and "Left" opportunists, was neither by temperament nor by experience qualified to play an important role in the development of the
peasant struggle. It fell to Mao Tse-tung to devise the
strategy of peasant revolution that would sustain the Chi-

nese Communist party in difficult days. Much of his inspiration he drew from Chinese history. "The gigantic scale of peasant uprisings and peasant wars in Chinese history is without parallel in the world. These struggles of the peasants—the peasant uprisings and wars—alone formed the real motive force of historical development in China's feudal society."[17] Since China remained a semifeudal society, Mao saw the peasantry as the major force in the Chinese revolution. His insight was vindicated by events, and by skillfully using the peasants, Mao strengthened his party and led it to final victory.

Revolutionary Bases in Rural Areas

While Mao did not originate the peasant movement, he was the first to recognize the importance of revolutionary bases in the rural areas. In October 1927, after the failure of the Autumn Uprisings, Mao led the remnants of his armed force to the Chingkang mountains in the border area of Hunan and Kiangsi, where he established his first rural base for the revolution. The Sixth Congress of the Chinese Communist party, held in Moscow under the direct supervision of the Comintern in July 1928, began to take note of the revolutionary bases of the Soviet regime.[18] Still, as late as July 1930, the Comintern was more concerned with the building of the Red Army than with the development of rural areas.[19] Mao, however, believed the establishment of these bases to be important not merely to the strengthening of the army, but to the consolidation and development of Red political power for the purpose of expediting the nationwide revolutionary upsurge. This last process was admittedly a protracted, difficult one, but Mao saw no hope of attaining political power through armed uprisings without at first establishing strong rural bases.[20] Heralding a new departure that caught his urban-minded comrades by surprise, Mao asserted that the correct strategy was to surround the cities from the countryside.[21]

For Mao there were decisive reasons for the establishment of revolutionary bases in the rural areas. Since the imperialist and reactionary forces were strongly entrenched in the urban centers, the only way to continue the struggle was to avoid decisive battles with the enemy in the cities at a time when the revolutionary forces were still weak. It was necessary therefore to "build the backward villages into advanced, consolidated base areas, into great military, political, economic and cultural revolutionary bastions, so that they can fight the fierce enemy who utilizes the cities to attack the rural districts."[22] Mao believed that conditions existed in China that would make it possible for the revolutionary base areas gradually to win an overall victory for the revolution. The unevenness of China's economic development (a localized agrarian rather than a unified capitalist economy); the immensity of China's territory, which gave the revolutionary forces sufficient room to maneuver in; the disunity inside China's ruling group—all these conditions enabled the Chinese revolution first to triumph in the rural areas and then to complete the protracted, arduous task of winning a national victory.

While Mao drew his concept of the rural revolutionary bases largely from practical conditions then prevailing in China, a consideration of historical conditions contributed its part to the formulation of his strategy. Historically, there were in China many examples of peasant wars of the roving insurgent type, notably the revolts of Huang Ch'ao in the ninth century and Li Tzu-ch'eng in the seventeenth. They had all failed because the rebels attacked and retreated, in one direction or another, but always without strong bases to fall back upon. Mao learned much from these failures, and it was to guard against them that he advanced the concept of revolutionary bases, calling resolutely for the elimination of the idea of roving insurgency.[23]

Principles of War

No Chinese Communist leader has so strongly and so categorically stressed military power as Mao Tse-tung. "Political power grows out of the barrel of a gun"; "whoever wants to seize the political power of the state and to maintain it must have a strong army"; and "the world can be remolded only with the gun" are some of his famous aphorisms.[24] This military power, he thinks, will grow out of the rural base areas. To protect and expand these, he considers it necessary to make extensive use of guerrilla warfare, at least in the initial stage. The precepts of guerrilla warfare are summed up in his famous sixteen-word formula: "Enemy advances, we retreat; enemy camps, we harass; enemy tires, we attack; enemy retreats, we pursue."[25] It is apparent that guerrilla warfare is devised primarily to cope with an enemy who is superior both in number and in equipment. Swiftness is therefore of the essence. Part of the enemy force—the weakest part—is selected for attack at the time and place best suited to the Communists. It is then induced to advance in such a way that it can be separated from the main force. The guerrillas then attack it, and quickly retire, before the enemy's reinforcements arrive. The guerrilla forces must hold the initiative at all times, whether in attack or in retreat. In the face of a stronger enemy, the guerrilla forces will retreat more often than they attack, but all retreats prepare for the final blow, which, executed by a concentrated force, aims not merely at defeating but at annihilating the enemy force. In thus annihilating the enemy forces bit by bit, the guerrilla forces wear down his superiority.[26]

Guerrilla warfare, so widely identified with Mao's military strategy, is, however, only one part of the picture. Though essential to the growth of the Communist military power, it is, after all, limited in purpose. In a protracted war the strategic task is to develop guerrilla warfare into mobile warfare. The former should in no case be abandoned, but its role becomes that only of supporting regular warfare.[27]

The principles of mobile warfare are basically those of guerrilla warfare: concentration of force, surprise attack, and quick withdrawal. In mobile war there are no fixed battle lines, as its main objective is to wipe out the enemy's effective strength, not to hold or seize a certain city or locale. Positional warfare is deferred until such a time as the Communist force is strong and no longer handicapped by the enemy's superiority and entrenched position.[28] The essential feature of Mao's strategical scheme is the continuous development from the lower (guerrilla) form to the higher (mobile) form of warfare until the enemy's superiority has been destroyed. The Communist force is then ready to engage in positional warfare.

The sources of Mao's principles of war are varied. Strategies and stratagems described in such novels as *The Tale of Three Kingdoms* and *The Water Margin,* which Mao read and reread while a youth, must have inspired him greatly. The influence of Sun Tzu, China's classical military writer, who teaches "attack where the enemy is unprepared; sally out when he does not expect you," is not to be denied.[29] It is also known that he studied the famous battles in Chinese history very carefully.[30] But it was actual experience, drawn from years of defeats and victories, that formed the basis of his military doctrine. Mao early recognized that in military matters the experience of the Russian Bolsheviks was irrelevant, and he said so.[31] "The laws of war, like the laws governing all other things, are reflections in our mind of objective realities."[32] Mao's military laws are laws learned from war.

The New Democracy

On New Democracy (1940) is Mao's first systematic approach to the questions of the form the Chinese state would take. The work gains significance not only because it laid the foundation for the Chinese political structure of 1949, but because the form of state it proposed differed from Soviet Russia's pattern. Mao's proposed form was not that of a proletarian dictatorship, nor of a democratic dictatorship of the workers and peasants as suggested by Stalin in 1926 and adopted by the Chinese Communists in the rural areas in 1930–1934. It was, as Mao described it, a "democratic republic under the joint dictatorship of all anti-imperialist and anti-feudal people led by the proletariat."[33] Specifically, it was a joint dictatorship of several "revolutionary" classes, those, namely, of the proletariat, the peasantry, the intelligentsia and other sections of the petty bourgeoisie. In 1949, on the eve of the total Communist victory, Mao added yet another class, the national bourgeoisie.[34] The inclusion of the national bourgeoisie in the government after the victory of the proletarian revolution constituted a clear departure from orthodox Communism. Mao himself emphasized that his new-democratic republic was different from the socialist republic of the Soviet Union. The Soviet type, good for industrially advanced countries, Mao believed unsuitable to the revolutions in colonial and semicolonial countries. His New Democracy was especially designed as a transitional form for these countries.

Since it was a semicolonial and semifeudal country, China's revolution, according to Mao, had necessarily to be divided into two stages. The first stage was to change the semicolonial and semifeudal society into an independent, democratic society. The second was to develop the revolution further by building up a socialist society.[35] Any attempt to skip the first stage and to build a socialist society on the ruins of a semicolonial and semifeudal society was unrealistic.[36] On the other hand, Mao emphasized, the two stages must be consecutive without any intervening period of bourgeois dictatorship.[37] This stipulation was not the same as Li Li-san's theory of direct transition to the socialist revolution; for Mao envisaged a long duration of the New Democracy, which would in turn provide the conditions for the socialist revolution.

To Mao, there were practical considerations for the new-democratic republic's consisting of classes other than the proletariat and the peasantry. The participation of the intelligentsia, an important part of the urban petty bourgeoisie, was desirable, since it would play a central role in cultural reconstruction. The eradication of foreign and feudal influences and the building up of a new-democratic China further demanded the efforts of a large number of educators, teachers, scientists, engineers, writers, artists, and ordinary cultural workers. "All intellectuals who have performed meritorious service to the people should be esteemed as valuable assets of the nation and society."[38]

But the national bourgeoisie's inclusion in the New Democracy requires more explanation, inasmuch as victory of the proletarian revolution, according to orthodox Marxist reasoning, presupposes the overthrow of the bourgeoisie. Mao justified his deviation as follows:

The national bourgeoisie at the present stage is of great importance. Imperialism, a most ferocious enemy, is still standing alongside us. China's modern industry still forms a very small proportion of the national economy. . . . To counter imperialist oppression and to raise her backward economy to a higher level, China must utilize all the factors of urban and rural capitalism that are beneficial and not harmful to the national economy and the people's livelihood; and we must unite with the national bourgeoisie in common struggle.[39]

He makes it clear, however, that while the national bourgeoisie should be brought in, it must not have the chief role in state power.

The concept of New Democracy, while unusual in the sphere of Communist ideology, is a natural outgrowth of the united-front strategy advocated by the Communists after 1935. It may be recalled that at the Seventh Congress of the Comintern in 1935 Ch'en Shao-yü, who reported on the Chinese situation, called for participation in the United People's Government of National Defense of all parties, groups, or organizations wanting to join in the war of resistance against the Japanese. Mao endorsed Ch'en's report and immediately took steps to effect a united front. The agreement with the Kuomintang to resist the Japanese aggression in 1937, the cooperation with all those in Japanese-occupied areas engaged in the fight against the foreign aggressors, the rallying of the third parties to the support of the Communists during the war—all these kept the slogan of the united front alive and made necessary the continuation of a concept that included several classes in the state system.

The system of New Democracy, or the people's democratic state, was carried over in the 1954 Constitution, because it was believed to be the best state form for the transformation of Chinese society. It would give scope to the initiative for building socialism while providng adequate strength in the fight against all antisocialist forces.[40]

People's democracy was, furthermore, different from the Soviet system. And given Mao's keen interest in the national form of Communist institutions, it was understandable that he should want it retained beyond the period of absolute necessity.

This emphasis on a national form of Communism underlies all of Mao's thought on revolutionary strategies and social reconstruction. The national standpoint is particularly notable in his discussion of China's new culture. "New-democratic culture," he writes, "is national. It opposes imperialist oppression and upholds the dignity and independence of the Chinese nation. It belongs to our nation, and bears our national characteristics." Mao is of the opinion that China should absorb the progressive cultures of foreign countries as ingredients of her own culture; but she must digest what is absorbed, and should never take in anything uncritically. He is opposed to wholesale Westernization, which he denounces as a formalist absorption of foreign things. On the other hand, he is opposed to feudal and superstitious ideas, particularly a feudal system of education based on the worship of Confucius. But he also believes something good can be learned from China's ancient culture. One must, he says, respect one's history and its dialectical development, although not to the extent of uncritically eulogizing the ancient and disparaging the modern. Chinese Communism, the framework of Chinese culture, must have its own form—the national form. "In applying Marxism to China, Chinese Communists must fully and properly unite the universal truth of Marxism with the specific practice of the Chinese revolution; that is to say, the truth of Marxism must be integrated with the characteristics of the nation and given a definite national form before it can be useful."[41]

Socialist Transformation

The new-democratic economy outlined in Mao's *On New Democracy* and *On Coalition Government* (1945) is a moderate socialism. Recognizing that the revolution was still in the bourgeois democratic stage, Mao considered it necessary to regulate rather than abolish capitalism. He advocated nationalization of enterprises that were monopolistic in character or too large for private management. But the new-democratic republic would not forbid the development of capitalistic production that did not dominate the livelihood of the people. The reason Mao gave for this mild position was China's backward economy and its lack of native capitalism. To replace foreign exploitation and native feudalism with capitalism "developed to a certain degree" was regarded as an unavoidable process. In the agricultural sector Mao supported Sun Yat-sen's slogan "Land to the tillers." But unlike Sun, he advocated confiscation of land from the landlords and its transferral to the peasants. Under the New Democracy, China's national economy would be composed of three sectors: state, private-capitalist, and cooperative.[42] While not strictly a socialist economy, this system contains elements of socialism.

After the Communists took control of the Chinese mainland in 1949, the economic program adopted was similar to that outlined by Mao in the above-mentioned works. Following a period of preparation in which inflation was curbed, transportation restored, and land reform, with its violent struggles, completed, Peking proclaimed in 1953 the first five-year plan. Under it the Chinese Communists pushed forward industrialization and socialist transformation simultaneously. Through high rates of taxation, fines and penalties, and exercise of the government's power of monopoly over raw materials and services, the private sector of the economy was rapidly absorbed into state enterprises. In the agricultural sector the establishment of the new collectivist system, which began in 1952 with the lower-stage cooperatives, was practically completed in 1958 when more than 95 percent of peasant households throughout the country were organized into higher-stage agricultural producers' cooperatives, or collective farms.

Although they acknowledge a debt of learning to the Soviet Union in economic development, the Chinese Communists claim that Mao discovered a peaceful method of socialist transformation. The national bourgeoisie in China were allowed to remain in business, and its enterprises were only gradually taken over by the state, without violent struggle or bloodshed.[43] But while in practice the pattern of socialist transformation in China does differ from that of the Soviet Union, in theory Mao's claim to originality on this score is questionable. We know that Stalin was opposed to Bukharin's formula concerning capitalist elements peacefully growing into socialism,[44] but he insisted that the slogan of exterminating the kulaks should not be extended to the new, urban bourgeoisie which arose after the New Economic Policy. The reason for this difference was that the nepmen, or private capitalists, who had in the main been deprived of their production base, did not play a substantial part in Russia's economic life.[45] The Chinese national bourgeoisie being similarly weak, it was not difficult for Mao to see that what was applicable to the nepmen in Russia could be equally applicable to the national bourgeoisie in China.

The institution of the Chinese communes, rather, is what constitutes the real departure from the Soviet structure. In 1957 the Weihsing commune, an experimental model consisting of 9300 families, was organized in the wheat-growing province of Honan. A year later, Peking ordered that the agricultural producers' cooperatives be merged into communes. The underlying motives for this extraordinary step are complex. To increase agricultural production and to step up industrial construction in support of the Great Leap Forward, the economic drive then developing, are undoubtedly among the causes of the establishment of the communes. The crisis over Quemoy in the fall of 1958, with the possible military intervention of the United States, could well have been another factor in the expansion of the commune program, since economic self-sufficiency and independent military strength, in the form of extensive organization of local militia, would help meet the contingency of an atomic war. But a more basic cause seems to lie in the belief that the commune was a short path to the stage of pure Communism, and if successful, would result in China's surpassing Russia in reaching the ultimate stage of Communism.

Soviet Russia had tried the commune but had found it necessary to abandon it. Writing in 1930, Stalin argued that the conditions in Russia were not yet ripe for agricultural communes. He insisted that the agricultural *artel* (cooperative) must be the main link in the collective-farm movement. He condemned as reckless haste the attempt to transfer the individual peasants straight to the organization of the commune.[46] Intoxicated by the initial successes of the collective movement in China, Mao apparently forgot Lenin's warning about not exceeding the development of the masses. In setting up communal life in the form of common dining halls and public living quarters, he also forgot the traditional force and the innate conservatism of the peasantry. He misread the mentality of the peasants when he believed that they would support a program depriving them of the material incentive to work. Impatient to reach the final stage of Communism and eager to provide Chinese Communism a national form that should not only be different from but also superior to the Russian pattern, Mao let his subjective thinking interfere with his recognition of the objective conditions. The result was a dismal failure.

Contradiction and Rectification

Mao's essay *On Contradiction,* originally delivered as a series of lectures in Yenan in 1937, was revised in 1952, when he included it in his *Selected Works.* In it he followed the theory of dialectical materialism expounded by Marx, Engels, and Lenin and therefore offered nothing original in the way of basic concepts. But delving into some particular aspects of the theory and relating theoretical concepts to actual conditions, he did clarify and develop some significant points.

First, he called attention to the particularity of contradiction and to its great importance in dealing with revolutionary problems. There are two processes of cognition: from the particular to the general, and from the general to the particular. It is through the interconnection of these two processes that man's knowledge advances. One should not regard general truths as something emerging out of a void, but should undertake a painstaking study of concrete things. "We who are engaged in the Chinese revolution," Mao says, "should not only understand the particularity of each of the contradictions in the light of their totality, that is, from the interconnection of those contradictions, but should also study the aspects of each contradiction as the only means of understanding the totality."[47]

Mao elucidated what he regarded as the principal contradiction and the principal aspects of a contradiction. Inherent in the developmental process of a complex thing are many contradictions. One of them is the principal contradiction whose existence and development determine or influence the existence and development of other contradictions.[48] It plays the leading role in the process of development. In studying any process, it is of utmost importance to discover this principal contradiction. Once it is grasped, all problems can readily be solved. The same is true of the two aspects—or opposites—of a contradiction. In any contradiction, whether principal or secondary, the development of the contradictory aspects is uneven. Of the two contradictory aspects one becomes the principal, and the other secondary. The former plays the leading role and determines the nature of a contradiction.

But the relative position of the two contradictory aspects is not a fixed one, according to Mao. The contradiction between the principal and secondary aspects gives rise to a series of intricate struggles, as a result of which the two contradictory aspects can change roles. When they transform themselves into each other, the nature of the thing will change accordingly. Mao used this theory to explain the contradiction between the productive forces and the relations of production, between theory and practice, and between the economic foundation and the superstructure. While acknowledging that the productive forces, practice, and the economic foundation generally play the principal and decisive role, he asserted that under certain conditions, such aspects as the relations of production, theory, and the superstructure can in turn play the principal and decisive role. "While we recognize that in the development of history as a whole it is the material that determines spiritual things and social existence that determines social consciousness, at the same time we also recognize and must recognize the reaction of spiritual things and social consciousness on social existence, and the reaction of the superstructure on the economic foundation."[49] Engels had tried to qualify Marx's precept that production is the decisive factor in historical development by recognizing the impact of state power and ideology upon economic developments;[50] but Mao provided a logical answer to the question through his theory of contradiction.

Another significant point Mao discussed in his *On Contradiction* is the role of antagonism. Mao holds that antagonism is a form of contradiction, but not the universal form. "Some contradictions are characterized by open antagonism, others are not. Based on the concrete development of things, some contradictions, originally non-antagonistic, develop and become antagonistic, while others, originally antagonistic, develop and become non-antagonistic."[51] He gives as an example the contradiction between correct ideology and erroneous ideologies within the Communist party, a contradiction which does not manifest itself in an antagonistic form, although it can become so if handled improperly. He recommended that comrades who had committed mistakes be given an opportunity to correct them and that struggles in these cases not be pushed to excess.[52]

In 1957 Mao developed this theme and applied it to the contradictions existing among the Chinese people. Two international events—the Hungarian uprising in 1956 and Khrushchev's attack the same year on Stalin's brutal treatment of his opponents—gave him further cause to reflect on the problem of contradictions within a Communist country. In February 1957, at the Eleventh Session of the Supreme State Conference, Mao delivered a speech which was revised and published in June of the same year under the title of *On the Correct Handling of Contradictions among the People,* in which he distinguishes two types of social contradictions—those between the enemy and ourselves, and those among the people.

The former is antagonistic in nature, the latter is not.[53] There would appear to be a striking resemblance between this distinction and Stalin's of 1930, when the latter differentiated between contradictions within the bond, that is, those between the proletariat and the main mass of the working people, and contradictions outside the bond, that is, those between the proletarian dictatorship and the capitalist elements of the country.[54] But Mao's theory differs from Stalin's in two respects. First, to Mao's mind, the contradiction between the working class and the national bourgeoisie belongs to the category of nonantagonistic contradictions, i.e., those among the people; and second, although the Communist government genuinely represents the people, there are still certain contradictions between the two.[55]

To Mao, different contradictions should be resolved by different methods. While coercive measures may be taken to suppress the reactionary classes and elements, "democratic methods" should be used to deal with the contradictions among the people. The proper way to settle controversial issues or questions of an ideological nature was by discussion, criticism, persuasion, and education. To provide a guideline for handling nonantagonistic contradictions, Mao revived the formula "unity, criticism, unity," which he had successfully used in resolving contradictions inside the Chinese Communist party in 1942. The Chinese Communists, Mao held, must start from the desire for unity in handling contradictions among the people. Those contradictions must be resolved through criticism or struggle, and a new unity arrived at on a new basis.[56]

In 1957 it was unity with the intellectuals that Mao was particularly concerned with. The several million intellectuals, traditionally occupying an influential place in Chinese society, continued to be an important factor in

Communist China. Their knowledge and services were badly needed for the task of socialist construction, but because of their bourgeois background and non-Communist education, many of them retained their independent thinking. Believing the vast majority of intellectuals to be patriotic and willing to serve their socialist motherland, Mao declared a new political line under the classical slogan: "Let a hundred flowers blossom, let a hundred schools of thought contend." Different forms and styles in art, he stated, should develop freely, and different schools in science be allowed to contend with one another. Questions of right and wrong in the arts and sciences would be settled by free discussion and patient reasoning. Even Marxism was open to criticism, he alleged, since Marxism was scientific truth and had no need to fear criticism.[57]

The response to Mao's call was, however, as unexpected as it was violent. After an initial hesitation, the intellectuals launched an extensive attack on the Chinese Communist party, expressing resentment and hatred. What upset Peking most was the widespread student riots in university cities. The students denounced Communist oppression and called for a struggle for freedom and human rights. The Communist government finally suppressed the riots by force, arresting numerous participants in the process.

This violent reaction put an end to Mao's liberalization policy, and rectification campaigns were launched in 1958. Instead of treating the intellectuals in a general sense, as part of the people, Peking now divided them into three categories: left, middle, and right. The leftists supported socialism and the Communist leadership, and therefore were viewed as causing no trouble. The majority of intellectuals Peking regarded as elements willing to advance with the proletariat. For these people the moderate policy would be continued and efforts should be made to "unite with them, win them over, and educate them." It was, of course, the rightist intellectuals who became the target of the rectification campaign, and Peking called for a resolute struggle against them. Patient persuasion was no longer appropriate; instead, methods of exposure, isolation, and separation, and in certain cases punishment and suppression, were used.[58] It became apparent that in a Communist country ruled by force, free discussion could be permitted only to those who supported the regime. It was not the social status of a person that determined the nature of a contradiction; rather it was the nature of the contradiction, antagonistic or nonantagonistic, that determined the social status—that is, whether he was to be considered within or outside the people.

Ideological Disputes

Peking's ideological relations with Moscow have deteriorated to such an extent that neither the downfall of Khrushchev nor the Vietnam war have succeeded in reconciling the split between the two countries. The conflict began in 1956 at the 20th Congress of the Soviet Communist party, when Khrushchev proposed the negation of Stalin and a peaceful transition to socialism by the "parliamentary road." Attempts to bring China and Russia together were made at the 1957 and the 1960 meetings of the representatives of Communist parties, but the compromise agreements on Communist ideology reached at these meetings failed to improve relations between the two countries. The Soviet party, determined to carry out its policy of peaceful coexistence, refused to be hampered by the qualifications and restrictions contained in the 1957 and 1960 agreements. Instead, it applied a succession of political, economic, and military pressures against

Peking in an attempt to bring the Chinese into line. The Soviet Union recalled its technicians from China, refused to provide her with a sample of the atomic bomb, gave India military aid during the Sino-Indian border war, and supported subversive elements in the Ili region of the Sino-Soviet border. The Sino-Soviet dispute was thus not only brought into the open, but was extended to diplomatic relations. That Khrushchev's actions and dicta gave impetus to the ideological conflicts is not to be denied, but the worsening state relations were also an expression of basic ideological differences between the two major Communist parties.

Khrushchev's complete negation of Stalin irked the Chinese Communists not only because it undermined Mao's authority, but also because the Chinese Communist movement had been closely associated with Stalin's leadership. The victory of the Chinese revolution was, of course, due to the brilliant strategy of Mao Tse-tung, but its fundamental principles had been laid down by Lenin and upheld by Stalin. For the Chinese Communists Stalin represented the realization of the principle of dictatorship of the proletariat, which put an end to the system of exploitation in Russia, built up a strong socialist economy, and provided the international Communist movement with a powerful leadership.[59]

The Chinese Communist party concedes that Stalin made mistakes, but insists that his merits outweigh his faults. Stalin, Peking declares, defended and developed Marxism-Leninism against opportunism. He provided great assistance to the revolutionary struggles and was an irreconcilable enemy of the imperialists and reactionaries.[60] In Peking's eyes, Khrushchev's violent attack on Stalin was an attempt to pave the way for revisionism.

In the ideological sphere the Chinese Communists argue that Khrushchev's "combating of the personality cult" stood in violation to Lenin's teachings on the interrelationships of leaders, party, class, and masses, and contravened the Communist principle of democratic centralism. They remind their Soviet comrades that an effective Communist party must have a fairly stable nucleus of leadership, consisting of a group of long-tested leaders who are good at integrating the universal truths of Marxism-Leninism with the concrete practice of revolution.[61] Peking is against dishonest and excessive eulogy of individuals, but it opposes as well the belittling of the role of former Communist leaders.

It is on the question of war and peace that the ideological dispute between the two countries centers. Impressed with the destructive power of nuclear weapons, Khrushchev advocated a general international line under three slogans: "peaceful coexistence," "peaceful competition," and "peaceful transition." The development of nuclear weapons, declared the Soviet Communist party, perforce had changed the old notions about war and class struggle. It would be futile to establish a Communist civilization on the ruins of centers of world culture, on ground laid waste and contaminated by nuclear fallout. An "all-round cooperation" with the capitalist countries was, thus, necessary.[62]

The Chinese Communists denounced the Khrushchev line as revisionism. China, they declared, would fight for the maintenance of world peace, but not as those who "beg the imperialists" for it. World peace could be defended effectively only by relying on the development of socialist forces, on the revolutionary struggles of the proletariat and working people of all countries, and on the struggles for liberation by the oppressed nations. A single spark from a war of national liberation or from a revolutionary people's war to their mind cannot lead to a world conflagration. On the contrary, the victory of these revolutionary wars will directly weaken the forces of imperialism and greatly strengthen the forces that prevent the imperialists from launching a world war.[63]

The Chinese Communists do not believe that the contradictions between the proletariat and the bourgeoisie, and those between the oppressed nations and imperialism, can be resolved without revolutionary struggle. Nor will the contradiction between the two world systems of socialism and capitalism disappear in the course of "peaceful competition." Peking denounces as subjective and fallacious the Russian reasoning that a world without wars and without weapons can come into being while imperialism and capitalism exist.[64] It firmly believes that imperialism is the source of wars in modern times: "As long as the imperialist system still exists, war, the most acute form of violence, will not disappear from the world."[65] Peking has no objection to peaceful coexistence with countries having a different social system, but, it argues, the principle of coexistence cannot apply to relations between oppressor and oppressed nations, or to relations between oppressed and oppressing classes. Asking oppressed nations to coexist peacefully with colonial nations is like asking them to "tolerate colonial rule rather than to resist or wage struggles for independence."[66]

The pro-Soviet Communists have addressed their attack to Mao's thesis that imperialism and all reactionaries are paper tigers. They assert that his underestimation of American military strength can easily lead Communist China into a dangerous confrontation with the United States. What Mao actually means to say is that looking at the problem as a whole, from a long-term point of view, it is the people and not the imperialists or reactionaries who really hold power. Mao explained his idea in a speech at the Moscow meeting of the Communist and Workers' parties in 1957:

All the reputedly powerful reactionaries were merely paper tigers. . . . For struggle against the enemy, we formed over a long period the concept that strategically we should despise all our enemies, but that tactically we should take them all seriously. This also means that in regard to the whole we should despise the enemy but that in regard to each and every concrete question we must take them seriously. If with regard to the whole we do not despise the enemy we shall be committing the error of opportunism. Marx and Engels were only two persons. Yet in those early days they declared that capitalism would be overthrown all over the world. But in dealing with concrete problems and particular enemies we shall be committing the error of adventurism if we do not take them seriously.[67]

That Communist China does not take nuclear weaponry lightly is demonstrated by the great effort it has made to develop the atom bomb. Still it is Mao's conviction that although nuclear weapons have tremendous destructive power, the "outcome of a war is decided by the people, not by one or two types of weapon."[68] It is not nuclear weapons that determine man's fate, but the masses of the people who are the "decisive force in history."[69]

The Chinese Communists believe that the struggle against imperialism can be won without using nuclear weapons. On the contrary, by achieving and maintaining nuclear superiority, the socialist countries can prevent the imperialists from launching an all-out nuclear war and thus help bring about the complete prohibition of nuclear weapons. In their view, it is through a strengthening of socialist unity, a broadening of the national liberation movement, and an intensification of the proletarian struggle that the imperialist powers will be weakened and de-

feated.[70] Peking's global strategy rests on the premise that
the U.S. and the imperialist countries of Europe will be
besieged and destroyed by liberation movements in Asia,
Africa, and Latin America. Lin Piao, the exponent of
Mao's military principles, writes:

Taking the entire globe, if North America and Western
Europe can be called "the cities of the world," then Asia,
Africa and Latin America constitute "the rural areas of the
world." . . . In a sense, the contemporary world revolution
also presents a picture of the encirclement of cities by the
rural areas. In the final analysis, the whole cause of world
revolution hinges on the revolutionary struggles of the Asian,
African and Latin American peoples who make up the overwhelming majority of the world's population. The socialist
countries should regard it as their internationalist duty to support the people's revolutionary struggles in Asia, Africa and
Latin America.[71]

Lin Piao sees the revolutionary struggles in various areas
as merging into "a torrential world-tide of opposition to
U.S. imperialism," destroying it "piece by piece, some
striking at its head and others at its feet."

In their ideological debate with the Russians, the Chinese Communists have adhered closely to Lenin's teachings, which is not surprising when one considers that
many of the Chinese leaders, such as Mao Tse-tung,
joined the Chinese revolution at the call of Lenin. For
forty years they had fought on his revolutionary principles. From their broad, protracted revolution against the
massive strength of their internal and external enemies
they had finally emerged victorious. Having won their victory in this way, they naturally believed that their experience should serve as the guideline for revolutionary movements in the underdeveloped countries. Khrushchev's
general international line was to them not only a betrayal

of Lenin's revolutionary teachings, but contrary to all
that they had learned from experience.

The Great Proletarian Cultural Revolution

The Great Proletarian Cultural Revolution, which was
launched in 1966 with the organization of Chinese youth
into the paramilitary Red Guards, and which has plunged
China into fierce turmoil, was a gigantic struggle against
those who had faltered in following Mao's general line.
Though Mao's image had been built up to the extent of
idolization, the failure of the Great Leap Forward in 1958,
the peasants' discontent with the people's commune, the
ideological dispute with the Soviet Union, and the increasing isolation of Peking in world politics gave rise to opposition to his strategies. Alarmed by the powerful influence his opposition was gaining, and anxious to ensure
the continuation of his branch of Communism after his
death, Mao deemed it necessary to carry through a thorough political purge and extensive cultural transformation.
The tasks of the Cultural Revolution, as declared by the
Central Committee of the Chinese Communist party, were:
first, to struggle against and overthrow those persons in
authority who were taking the capitalist road; second, to
criticize and repudiate the reactionary bourgeois "academic authorities" and the ideology of the bourgeoisie
and all other exploiting classes; and third, to transform
education, literature, and art and all other parts of the
superstructure that did not harmonize well with the socialist economic base.[72]

In the early stages of the Cultural Revolution much
stress was laid on changing certain cultural predispositions.
The Maoists maintained that the bourgeoisie, though deprived of political and economic power, still wielded
cultural power in the areas of ideas, customs, and habits,

which they used to capture the minds of the masses. The Maoists viewed bourgeois influence in these areas as an impediment to the development of socialism and even as an active preparation for the restoration of capitalism. "Every counter-revolutionary restoration," we are told, "starts in the realm of the mind—including ideology, the superstructure, theoretical and academic work, literature and art—so as to mould public opinion."[73] The Chinese must, therefore, create a literature and an art that serves and protects the interests of a communistic order.

The main target of the Cultural Revolution was the "handful of party persons in authority who are taking the capitalist road." The contradiction between these persons on the one hand, and the masses of workers, peasants and soldiers, and revolutionary cadres and intellectuals on the other, belonged, according to the Maoists, to the category of principal contradictions and was an antagonistic one. These representatives of the "bourgeoisie" had to be completely refuted, discredited and overthrown, and their power seized by the Red Guards.[74] By insisting that only a handful of bourgeois elements had wormed their way into the party apparatus, the Maoists attempted to maintain the distinction between "contradictions between the enemy and ourselves" and "contradictions among the people." They asserted that the great majority of people were not antagonistic to the general line of Mao Tse-tung, and that on those who had been hoodwinked by the reactionaries, only a moderate method of debate and reasoning should be used. But the demarcation between antagonistic and nonantagonistic contradictions was a delicate one: it broke down easily amid turmoil and tension. This was especially true of places where the struggle was acute and violent, and where the overenthusiastic Red Guards got out of hand.

The organization of young students into Red Guards to

carry out the Cultural Revolution represents a forceful application of Mao's favorite strategy—the mass line. His confidence in the masses is well summed up in his oft-quoted sayings that "the people, and the people alone, are the motivating force in the making of world history" and that "the masses have a potentially inexhaustible enthusiasm for socialism."[75] These are not rhetorical phrases, but rather deep convictions derived from long and extensive revolutionary experience. Mao rose with the masses of the peasantry, and it was their support that carried him to victory. In the early part of his career as a Communist, he warred frequently against the party machine, and now, late in life, he again fights it. Although he never forgets the importance of the party organization, it is with the masses that he feels most comfortable.

Mao did not during this period use peasants and workers to carry out his struggle,[76] apparently because they were settled in their vocations, and any active participation on their part would have disrupted the economy of the nation directly. He must have thought, too, that students, being less settled down and more inclined to agitations, would enthusiastically participate in a stormy movement. Mao, of course, had not forgotten that power grows out of the barrel of a gun. He therefore made Lin Piao, minister of national defense, his heir apparent, so as to gain the support of the military. But the opposition, which had controlled the party machine for so long, was well entrenched in the various provinces. It responded by organizing masses of its own, stirring up the peasants and workers, and infiltrating into the military commands in various regions. The result was violent clashes and social turmoil throughout the nation.

In a way the violent struggle of the Cultural Revolution is in keeping with Mao's revolutionary views and temperament. Mao has taught that struggle is life and that contradictions continue to exist in a socialist society. "The class struggle," he wrote in 1957, "between the proletariat and the bourgeoisie, the class struggle between the different political forces, and the class struggle in the ideological field between the proletariat and the bourgoisie will continue to be long and tortuous and at times will even become very acute."[77] In launching the Cultural Revolution in the evening of his life, he is in fact reaffirming his belief that a person's life may end, but that class struggle must go on.

Notes

CHAPTER X. CHINESE COMMUNISM II

1. Li Jui, *Mao Tse-tung t'ung-chih ti ch'u-ch'i ke-ming huo-tung* (The Early Revolutionary Activities of Comrade Mao Tse-tung) (Peking, 1957); see also Jerome Ch'en, *Mao and the Chinese Revolution* (London: Oxford University Press, 1965), pp. 44–45.
2. Edgar Snow, *Red Star over China* (New York: Modern Library, 1944), p. 147.
3. Mao Tse-tung, *Hsüan-chi* (Selected Works, hereafter cited as *HC*), III (Peking, 1953), 845; *Selected Works* (hereafter cited as *SW*), 4 vols. (London: Lawrence and Wishart, 1954–56), IV, 62.
4. Siao-yu, *Mao Tse-tung and I Were Beggars* (London: Hutchinson, 1961), p. 190.
5. Benjamin I. Schwartz, *Chinese Communism and the Rise of Mao* (Cambridge: Harvard University Press, 1964), p. 199.
6. Karl A. Wittfogel, "Peking's Independence," *The New Leader*, July 20–27, 1959, p. 14.
7. *HC*, I (Peking, 1951), 22–23; *SW*, I, 32.
8. Resolution of the 6th ECCI Plenum, March 13, 1926, Jane Degras, ed., *Communist International* (3 vols., London: Oxford University Press, 1956–65), II, 277.
9. See above, p. 316.
10. V. I. Lenin, *Selected Works*, 12-volume edition (Moscow, 1937), X, 198.
11. *Ibid.*, X, 236.
12. Theses of the 4th Congress, Nov.–Dec. 1922, in Xenia J. Euden and Robert C. North, *Soviet Russia and the East* (Stanford: Stanford University Press, 1957), p. 233.
13. Degras, *op. cit.*, II, 279.
14. "Analysis of the Classes in Chinese Society," March 1926, *SW*, I, 20.
15. *SW*, I, 98.
16. See "What Is to Be Done," Lenin, *Selected Works*, II, 136.
17. *HC*, II (Peking, 1952), 595; *SW*, III, 76.
18. *Chung-kuo Kung-ch'an-tang ti-liu-tz'u ch'üan-kuo ta-hui i-chüeh-an* (Resolutions of the 6th National Congress of the Chinese Communist Party) (1928), p. 39.
19. Degras, *op. cit.*, III, 116.
20. "A Single Spark Can Start a Prairie Fire," *SW*, I, 116; *HC*, I, 103.
21. "Resolutions on Some Questions in the History of Our Party," *SW*, 178; *HC*, III, 962.
22. *HC*, II, 605–6; *SW*, III, 85.
23. "On the Rectifications of Incorrect Ideas in the Party," *SW*, I, 115; *HC*, I, 99.
24. "Problems of War and Strategy," *SW*, II, 272–73; *HC*, II, 510–11.
25. "Strategic Problems of China's Revolutionary War," *SW*, I, 212; *HC*, I, 204.
26. *SW*, I, 175 ff.; *HC*, I, 167 ff.

27. "On Protracted War," *HC*, II, 461.
28. *SW*, I, 197, 248; "The Present Situation and Our Tasks," *HC*, IV (Peking, 1960), 1247.
29. Sun Tzu's work is translated by Samuel B. Griffith under the title *The Art of War* (London: Oxford University Press, 1964).
30. "Strategic Problems of China's Revolutionary War," *HC*, I, 201–2, 241.
31. *Ibid.*, I, 170.
32. *Ibid.*, I, 179; *SW*, I, 187.
33. *SW*, III, 118.
34. "On the People's Democratic Dictatorship," *HC*, IV, 1477.
35. "On New Democracy," *HC*, II, 656.
36. "On Coalition Government," *HC*, III, 1061; *SW*, IV, 275.
37. *HC*, II, 656; *SW*, III, 130.
38. *SW*, IV, 299–300.
39. "On the People's Democratic Dictatorship," *Selected Works of Mao Tse-tung* (Peking: Foreign Languages Press, 1961), IV, 421; *HC*, IV, 1484.
40. See *The Historical Experience of the Dictatorship of the Proletariat* (Peking: Foreign Languages Press, 1964), p. 49.
41. *SW*, III, 154.
42. *SW*, IV, 274, 276.
43. See Arthur A. Cohen, *The Communism of Mao Tse-tung* (Chicago: University of Chicago Press, 1964), pp. 108 ff.
44. J. V. Stalin, *Works* (Moscow, 1955), XII, 314.
45. *Ibid.*, XII, 192.
46. *Ibid.*, XII, 216.
47. "On Contradiction," *HC*, II, 778; *SW*, II, 26.
48. *HC*, II, 786; *SW*, II, 35.
49. *HC*, II, 792; *SW*, II, 41.
50. Engels to J. Black, Sept. 21–22, 1890; Engels to Schmidt, Oct. 27, 1890; Engels to F. Mehring, July 14, 1893; in Karl Marx and Frederick Engels, *Selected Works* (Moscow, 1955), II, 488–501.
51. *HC*, II, 801; *SW*, II, 50.
52. *HC*, II, 802; *SW*, II, 51.
53. Mao Tse-tung, *Four Essays on Philosophy* (Peking: Foreign Languages Press, 1966), p. 80.
54. J. V. Stalin, *Works*, XIII, 21–23.
55. Mao Tse-tung, *Four Essays on Philosophy*, pp. 81–82.
56. *Ibid.*, p. 87.
57. *Ibid.*, pp. 116–17.
58. Teng Hsiao-p'ing, "Report on the Rectification Campaign," Sept. 23, 1957, in *Communist China, 1955–1959* (Cambridge: Harvard University Press, 1962), p. 344.
59. *The Historical Experience of the Dictatorship of the Proletariat*, pp. 7, 26, 32, 39.
60. *The Polemic on the General Line of the International Communist Movement* (Peking: Foreign Languages Press, 1965), pp. 120–21.
61. *Ibid.*, p. 131.
62. See *Two Different Lines on the Question of War and Peace* (Peking: Foreign Languages Press, 1963), pp. 22–24.
63. *The Polemic on the General Line of the International Movement*, pp. 28–29.

64. *More on the Differences between Comrade Togliatti and Us* (Peking: Foreign Languages Press, 1963), pp. 54–55.
65. *Long Live Leninism* (Peking: Foreign Languages Press, 1960), p. 30.
66. *The Differences between Comrade Togliatti and Us* (Peking: Foreign Languages Press, 1963), p. 26.
67. *Ibid.*, p. 18.
68. *Selected Works of Mao Tse-tung* (Peking, 1961), IV, 100.
69. *Workers of All Countries Unite, Oppose Our Common Enemy!* (Peking: Foreign Languages Press, 1962), p. 7.
70. *Two Different Lines on the Question of War and Peace*, p. 26.
71. Lin Piao, *Long Live the Victory of People's War!* (Peking: Foreign Languages Press, 1966), p. 49.
72. *Decision of the Central Committee of the Chinese Communist Party concerning the Great Proletarian Cultural Revolution,* adopted Aug. 8, 1966 (Peking: Foreign Languages Press, 1966), p. 1.
73. *The Great Socialist Cultural Revolution in China* (Peking: Foreign Languages Press, 1966–67), I, 25.
74. "A Great Historic Document"—Editorial of the *Red Flag* and of the *Jen-min jih-pao*, May 18, 1967, in *Survey of China Mainland Press*, No. 3943, p. 3.
75. *Quotations from Chairman Mao Tse-tung* (Peking: Foreign Languages Press, 1966), pp. 118, 121.
76. In the latter part of 1968, because of widespread chaos caused by the unruly Red Guards, Mao Tse-tung began to rely on the workers, organized as "propaganda teams," to stabilize the situation.
77. Mao Tse-tung, *Four Essays on Philosophy*, p. 115.

INDEX

M